FOUNDATIONS and PRINCIPLES of GUIDANCE

FOUNDATIONS and

PRINCIPLES of

Allyn and Bacon, Inc.

Boston

GUIDANCE

EDWARD C. GLANZ

Provost, Southampton College
of Long Island University

formerly Professor and Chairman, Division of Psychology and Guidance, College of Basic Studies, Boston University

By the same author:

Groups in Guidance, Second Edition

Library of Congress Catalog Card Number: 64-13411

Printed in the United States of America.

Fifth Printing . . . November, 1968

Contents

Part One: Foundations of Guidance

Part Two: The Tools of Guidance

Part Three: Guidance in Operation

If a man does not keep pace with his companions,
perhaps it is because he hears a different drummer.
Let him step to the music which he hears,
however measured or far away.

Henry David Thoreau

The Free and

THE FREE and responsible person strives to solve problems of life as they are encountered; also, he can reflect upon himself and his life. He uses his total capacity to know and to understand himself as he seeks to integrate his learnings with his concept of self to create a life.

He chooses among available alternatives. He recognizes that his freedom is limited by his nature as a person and the culture that gives meaning to his life. He learns to be free and responsible, progressively building upon past experience to face the present and future.

He recognizes that he is cumulatively a product of his physical, emotional, and psychological nature as he learns from experiences. The values he learns and accredits are determining forces in the establishment of his life objectives and his life purposes.

He understands that freedom is the opportunity to use his total capacity to solve problems. He views his freedom to create his own life as his most precious possession. He knows he is constantly in the process of becoming.

He defends and attempts to extend the freedom of others to live their lives with a dignity and integrity that are extensions of his respect for his own dignity and integrity as a person. He respects and is re-

Responsible Person

sponsible to his own free, open society and culture as a surrounding and supporting force that permits him to be free to choose and to value.

The free person accepts the responsibility for his decisions. He seeks aid and counsel from others in resolving any issue, but accepts the implications and consequences of his actions.

He accepts youthful dependence while striving for mature independence. He attempts to understand the irrational and the rational forces within himself. He seeks security, acceptance, and self-esteem in psychologically healthy ways. He is capable of loving and being loved.

He values education as an opportunity to learn creatively about life while preparing himself to live a fuller life. Educational decisions become related to step-by-step formulations of career concepts. He views work and career development as expressions of his own relations to the world.

The free and responsible person views life as an opportunity to realize his own potential as an individual while demonstrating by each act of life that he knows self-realization is at the same time social self-realization.

Edward C. Glanz

FOUNDATIONS and PRINCIPLES of GUIDANCE

FOUNDATIONS OF GUIDANCE

THE FREE and responsible person, capable of reflective thinking and appropriate problem-solving, creates values to guide the personal process of determinating life objectives and purposes. Guidance, through and with education, focuses upon the individual in this process. The unique American concept of education for all concentrates upon the development of the total capacity of each person, and also recognizes that education must serve that society of which each person is a part. The individual and society thus become better able to fulfill their own destinies through education.

The worth of the individual is one of the most basic values within a free society, and the individual is the raw material of guidance. The infinite variability of students within a democracy dictates that each person be aided through guidance to have equal access to all available

PART ONE

opportunities for self-recognition, self-assessment, and personal development.

Guidance touches the beginning learner and extends throughout a life-long educational process. The roots of guidance can be traced to the basic concepts of education and philosophy developed in Europe and America for the last few centuries. However, modern guidance has become a potent force only very recently. The emergence of guidance has provided for the individualization of education while aiding education to serve and reconstruct the society in which it exists.

Part One examines some of the problems guidance faces as it attempts to achieve its purposes. The chapters of Part One present four basic approaches to assessing the foundations of guidance within American education: (1) The Nature of Guidance, (2) Roots and Dreams, (3) The Interdisciplinary Foundation of Guidance, (4) The Purposes of Guidance.

THE NATURE OF GUIDANCE

THE ISSUE. "Our time is difficult and dangerous because ours is a time of change in the relation of men to the universe: a time in which men must at last accept the individual responsibilities for choice and for decision which they have concealed from themselves in the past by the acceptance of institutional authority, and which the new institutional authorities of the totalitarian State would deprive them of forever. The future must be won now, for if it is not won now it will be foreclosed by dogma. And the future can be won now only by winning now the revolution of the individual.

"What is at stake, not only for us but for the world, is what we in the United States have called the American Proposition. The American Proposition is the proposition that if men are free to think for themselves and to believe as they think and to say as they believe—the world in which they live and which together they compose will be a better world: juster, stronger, wiser, more various. It is the most courageous, the most high-hearted of all propositions: The most daring, the most revolutionary of earthly acts of faith. It is, indeed, the one new and wholly revolutionary idea the world we call the modern world has produced, for it affirms the maturity of man as mind and spirit and rests its hopes for the future upon man's will.

"Our reliance in this country is on the inquiring, individual human mind. Our strength is founded there: our resilience, our ability to face an ever-changing future and to master it. We are not frozen into the backward-facing impotence of those societies, fixed in the rigidness of an official dogma, to which the future is the mirror of the past. We are free to make the future for ourselves. And we are free because it is the man who counts in this country: always and at every moment and in any situation, the man. Not the Truth but the man: not the truth as the state sees the truth or as the church sees the truth or as the majority sees

CHAPTER ONE

the truth or as the mob sees the truth, but the truth as the man sees it, as the man finds it, for himself as man. Our faith is in the infinite variety of human beings and in the God who made them various and of many minds; in their singularity, their uniqueness, the creativeness of the differences between them. Our faith, in simple, sober truth, is in the human being, the human spirit, the hungers and the longings that lead it toward its images of truth, its perceptions of the beauty of the world." (Archibald MacLeish: *Freedom Is the Right to Choose*)[1]

Guidance is a relative newcomer to the educational scene. The issues of what guidance is, what guidance can or cannot do, who does guidance, and the relationship between guidance and education are very real issues in schools and colleges. An understanding of the relationship of education and guidance can help to establish a background against which guidance as a process may be viewed. An examination of the nature of guidance, its philosophical premises, its relationship to the sponsoring educational institution and to the surrounding culture can help to illuminate how guidance relates to the individual.

EDUCATION AND GUIDANCE

Education and guidance are related processes designed to provide developmental experiences for the individual within a free, democratic

[1] Reprinted courtesy of the author.

society. Education as an institution within our society and as an instrument of that society is charged with the creation of informed, thinking citizens. Furthermore, it must be recognized that educated citizens are theoretically capable of meaningful existence as free and responsible members of a sponsoring society and culture.

The total process of education is concerned with populations, groups, and classroom units in order to provide the end result of developmental experiences for individuals. Guidance as a process centers upon individuals first and then becomes concerned with small groups, large groups, and larger populations as they contribute to individual growth. Education focuses upon groups or large numbers of persons; guidance focuses upon the single person. Guidance bridges the gap between education as a societal process and the inherent promise which a free society makes to the individual—developmental freedom through education.

The potential present within a society and its educational resources needs to be translated into usable patterns and forms for its members. Education utilizes administrators, teachers, and curriculums to create meaningful patterns of learning experiences for an entire society. Guidance attempts to aid the single person to integrate all of these data and resources and to incorporate them into a personally determined framework of thinking, problem-solving, and value-patterning for life as a citizen. Guidance is the primary instrument for the individualization of the entire process of education.

Education preserves the cultural heritage of a society through the transmittal of learnings that have been accumulated in the past. At the same time education is concerned with the creation of dynamic persons through open learnings—learnings evolved out of an individual's problem-solving interaction with an ever-changing present and an unknown future. Guidance concentrates upon such uncertain, open learnings in education and upon helping persons to apply and to use the closed or accumulated type of learnings. Education assesses the dimensions of the past and present so that individuals may profit from such knowledge as life is faced. Guidance centers upon the future function of the person as a thinking, problem-solving organism that is a product of education. Education and guidance are interdependent and are designed to serve the individual in different but related fashions. Guidance can create closure for the educational process as individuals are served and assisted in their development.

Guidance cannot exist without an educational foundation that permits persons to learn how to think, to learn facts, to acquire knowledge, and to create concepts; education is incomplete without guidance to focus its potential for individuals within a society.

CONCEPTS OF GUIDANCE

The development of the capacity to think critically, to learn from the past and present in order to solve future problems, is the basic process with which guidance is concerned. Problem-solving underlies all content learning in education and permits the formulation of the qualitative beliefs and values that determine the development of a person's life. Values and purposes in life are developed out of the interaction of a broad base of content learning with thinking and learning processes. Guidance focuses upon the functions of decision-making and problem-solving which create the personal value structures and life objectives for each individual.

Thinking or problem-solving not only involves the intellect, but it also takes place within a total organism subject to emotional distortion, emotional satisfaction, beliefs and values, and variable environmental forces. As decisions are made, as problems are solved, as characteristic patterns of behavior are acquired, the individual creates patterns of problem-solving that build personal values and life objectives as well as permit the person to face and to solve succeeding problems.

The problem-solving capacity of the individual is the most basic element in learning and living. As values—the directing forces of life—are accepted, the problem-solving process becomes interdependent with values in the patterning of later individual development and personality. The problem-solving process and the development of personal values and life purposes out of a surrounding culture are the essential factors that mold an individual. Guidance is concerned with the development of the individual—his problem-solving, life values, and life objectives.

The open-ended, developing nature of a person creates an orientation toward the future as he is aided through guidance. An individual is always a product of his past, operating in a present, but potentially different in the future. As a human being, a person is able to recognize that he is determined by his own experience; however, a person can always become something else through the freedom to choose. Guidance is concerned with the commanding sense of future time within the life of each person. Each individual is open-ended; each person is always becoming.

Guidance may therefore be defined as the process of helping individuals to solve problems and to be free and responsible members of a world community within which they live. Guidance seeks to help each person to be free to create a meaningful life. The limits to this freedom must be the limits of one's own potential for living. Freedom to create a life of purpose presupposes and builds upon the other freedoms of an open, democratic society—(1) freedom *from* economic wants, artificial restrains, and constraints to act contrary to one's own decisions and judgments, and (2) freedom *of* thought, speech, religion, and the other traditional freedoms. Guidance specializes in the development and nurture of an individual's freedom *to* live as a person of dignity and worth.

Guidance is therefore longitudinal in perspective and developmental in design. Guidance is in the business of helping persons to learn how to be free and responsible. Guidance workers are those who seek to help individuals to accomplish these tasks. Most guidance workers are full-time specialists who use various tools and work for these results in differing service-type environments. Teachers, administrators, and other school personnel may all become involved in guidance work as they concentrate, with students, upon the examination and accreditation of personal values and the selection of life objectives through decision-making and problem-solving.

The world of the person is the whole of his environment, but it is also the inner world of feelings, emotions, and values. The human organism is constantly involved and participating in a process of thinking, problem-solving, decision-making, and plan-developing. Through these processes each person adopts personal values and life objectives which guide and direct his efforts. Every person is a product of his own experience and, while existing as a person, is creating patterns of values and objectives that determine the dimensions of the future. Guidance, as a part of education, focuses upon the individual and his use of the facts, knowledge, and concepts that are obtained through education. The goal of guidance is the mature self-directed person with the skills of critical thinking that permit him to become free and responsible.

THE NATURE OF GUIDANCE

The growth process that is separated into various areas in the school is unitary in the home; the parents fulfill multiple educational roles. Many significant experiences precede the entrance of the child into the ordered learning experience we know as formal schooling.

The school must begin with the child as he exists at entrance, and, through learning and educational experiences, help to create the most effective individual possible.

Education as a formal process is conducted by persons readily recognized by pupils and public alike. The duty of the teacher is to assist students in learning and ordering facts and knowledge in all subject-matter areas. Supervisors and curriculum-makers are charged with the creation of the curriculum or the experience content of the learning process. Administrators must integrate the over-all educational process in an institutional form. Guidance workers are the fourth major group involved in the total educational process. Guidance identifies and characterizes the individual learner. It is responsible for aiding the person in the acquisition of effective problem-solving and decision-making patterns that, through formal and informal learnings, establish values and life objectives.

Philosophical Premises

The unique characteristic of guidance within education is its concern for the effective development of the individual. Guidance views the individual as an organism that makes decisions, solves problems, accredits values, selects life objectives, and constructs a self that interacts with the world.

Man as an organism cannot live through his instincts or conditioned responses to his environment. Man as a thinking being lives through his capacity to make decisions and to solve problems. Man can collect and order data, but he must then integrate the related and unrelated facts into concepts that are meaningful and useful both in the immediate and distant future.

Problem-solving as a process takes place within a total personality. Reason cannot exist or operate exclusive of feelings, emotion, and an awareness of the previous experience of the self. What we know as personality consists of the concept of self that is created as life is lived and the characteristic patterns of decision-making and problem-solving that are developed. Problem-solving cannot be viewed as exclusively intellectual, emotional, or similarly one-dimensional regardless of the aspect of the personality that is isolated.

The individual must constantly face and solve problems, for the term *problem* is not confined to the common concept of something which is wrong. The quality of problem-solving depends upon the integrated functioning of the person. Reason, emotion, physical factors, spiritual consciousness, and other dimensions of personality must be maintained in effective balance, in an integrated state, if life is to progress efficiently. The distortion of any single element or the inadequate integration of the multiple elements of personality can lead to a lowered level of decision-making capacity, and a poorer quality of problem-solving. In short, the quality of man as a human being arises out of his ability to solve problems in an effective fashion, to operate as an integrated personality, to adjust to the world.

Guidance workers need to be specialists in understanding persons as problem-solving organisms. Such a specialty demands a most broadly based factual and conceptual knowledge of the forces affecting a person and the world within which the person lives. Such knowledge must encompass the forces that arise from within the person, those in the environment that affect him, and the relationship of all these forces with which the person must deal.

The young child in the first grade who is having difficulty in learning to read may be struggling to maintain himself as a person of worth in his own eyes. The failure to learn symbols and the interrelationships of the symbols that is reading may be a weapon the child is using in his struggle with his parents. The child cannot view reading as a tool to be learned and used in future study. Reading becomes an area where failure can be a potent retaliatory concept that is used against the dominating, suffocating overprotection of parents. The child is solving a problem and effectively meeting the crucial issue of the moment. Until this overwhelming issue can be partially resolved and he can be free to attend to reading as a learning exercise, rather than as a problem-solving tool in an area where it is inappropriate, the child will refuse to learn to read.

The total person learns to read; an organism can solve problems that are present within life and solve them in a fashion and with a quality that is determined by his capacity for problem-solving. The demonstration of these facts by children is frequently overlooked, for the function of school failures within the life of the person is not understood.

The college freshman with singleness of purpose drives himself beyond physical endurance to achieve honor grades. The fear of failure, the specter of personal inadequacy are emotional distortions that ultimately preclude performance as a healthy human being, much less as an intelligent student in freshman English or Biology. The high school student values the affection of the new transfer girl beyond the previously honored values of academic achievement and intellectual progress. The causal factors may not be emotional distortion, spiritual depravity, or physical illness. The boy may simply be behaving in a confused, immature fashion. He may not be able to appreciate the implications of his actions. He may need help in ordering the facts and concepts into a more integrated pattern within which both sets of values may be incorporated.

A student at any age level or a person out of school may come to believe that life is useless, not worth the effort and time that it takes. Such a person refuses to solve problems of any type, refuses to become concerned about himself or life. Such lack of action is a denial of one's responsibility to live as a human being. If the problems that create such behavior are not solved, the person can seek ultimately to destroy himself, or can live as a vegetable, simply enduring life.

Individual behavior is extraordinarily complex. A person must face problems that arise out of the self, out of the environmental surroundings, or any combination of these forces. Intellectual ability, aptitude potentials, fear, hate, love, egotism, or even physical handicaps are but simple examples of internal elements that can complicate the functioning of a human being. External forces such as the changing sociological currents that can exist in a neighborhood, the cultural forces present within the subgroup into which one is born, sexual values that have been learned, and even vocational choice patterns that conflict with cultural expectations are again only beginning items within a long list that could be compiled. Internal elements that affect thinking, such as intelligence, aptitude, or even emotional temperament, may be primarily personal in origin, but they affect relationships with the surrounding world. External forces such as legal dicta, moral principles, and even group customs and mores may be perceived as environmental or may be internalized and constructed as values that operate as if they were inborn. There is of course no outside and inside for a person or for a personality. The person exists and operates within a concept of "life space," the consciousness of being a person within a world, within bounds of time.

The individual must constantly work through problems and achieve solutions in order to live in the world. The confusion, pernicious influences, and even the deterioration of personality that can occur in the process of problem-solving can create additional barriers to living. Facts, forces, feelings, attitudes, emotions, concepts, and an awareness of the self must be weighed, assessed, and ultimately incorporated into problem-solving processes. Decisions, action, or inaction can result. Problems must be solved if the person is to exist as a person, for if the self is viewed as a pawn life becomes a process in which forces are not understood and life is endured rather than lived.

The guidance worker who would help persons to solve problems must understand the processes that enter into problem-solving. That effective decision-making and problem-solving can accredit specific values as guides to the creation of a life is a basic assumption of guidance.

Freedom and Responsibility

The positive concept of individual freedom is the opportunity to solve problems with the total capacity of the self. The free person is conscious of himself as a creative, problem-solving organism living in a supporting world of people and things. Individual responsibility is the recognition by the self of the obligation to face life as a problem-solving process and to accept the consequences of one's own actions. Freedom permits a person to think, to act, to solve problems; responsibility demands that thinking and problem-solving, to the level of one's own capacity, is necessary for meaningful existence, and that such an existence is a constant obligation with consequences. Individual freedom and individual responsibility are interrelated concepts. Man's freedom grows out of his personality structure and his opportunity to choose his own actions. As man learns to be free and responsible, he can create his life.

The degree of success in problem-solving achieved by the person is not a function of freedom but rather of the potential or capacity of the personality as a problem-solving organism. Circumstances can limit the nature of the solution developed when a problem is faced. Yet such circumstances are always a part of the problem. Individual freedom is positive in nature. It is freedom to think, to solve problems; freedom *from* or *of* is not the same as freedom *to*. Individual freedom to create a life is not a passive or negative concept. It exists within and is the central concept of the total freedoms that do exist in an open democratic society.

Responsibility exists when a person recognizes that freedom requires that his potential must be utilized to solve problems, and that he must accept the consequences of his own actions. The person who is free and not responsible is the person who has the opportunity to make decisions, to solve problems, but who denies that such an opportunity demands that he must do so. Irresponsibility exists when problems are purposely ignored, when a person believes that others will assume the responsibility for his life or when he refuses to accept the consequences of his own actions.

The concept of individual freedom demands that an identical opportunity be available for all other persons. Freedom thus contains the concept of responsibility for the self and for the extension of freedom to others. The freedom of another cannot be abridged or destroyed in the name of freedom, or the nature of freedom itself is destroyed. The nature of individual freedom therefore governs a person in his own actions and controls the relationships of man to man.

When men are free they can be creative problem-solvers, creative human beings who can voluntarily act in concert with others to build a responsible society. A responsible society guarantees individual freedom and the opportunity for persons to live as creative human beings. This intimate relationship of the free individual and the free society reveals that the destruction of one inevitably leads to the destruction of the other.

Man's obligation to other men and to a society is to protect and to extend the right of each person to be free and responsible. Each person can only relate to other persons as he can recognize and respect their essential integrity and dignity. One cannot live for another, one cannot solve problems for another; one cannot abridge the humanity that is inherent in all individuals. As one can protect, respect, and honor the freedom of another, one can help another to live, to solve problems, and to create a life that has meaning.

Free and responsible men are the foundation for the initiation and maintenance of the free and responsible society. Individual freedom—freedom to live as a person—becomes the standard of personal life and the means for the continued support of a free and responsible society.

Freedom and responsibility have been seen to be outcomes of man as a problem-solving being. That guidance, concerned with man as a problem-solving organism, is equally concerned with freedom and responsibility is readily apparent. To help man fulfill his potential and to be a decision-making, problem-solving, and value-accrediting organism is to help man to become free and responsible. To help individuals to recognize the nature of individual freedom as well as personal and societal responsibility is to work for the fruition of man as man, and to work for the construction and maintenance of free and responsible society.

Values and Guidance

Persons torn by conflict, acting out emotional distortions of personality, creating personal success through a sadistic exploitation of others, or immobilized by guilt or anxiety are handicapped in their ability to solve problems, to live as effective human beings. Handicaps of this and other types may be clearly seen as outcomes of personality development and an inability to live in accord with one's concept of life. Personality development and growth depend upon the standards of life that are accepted by the person and the values that are learned and used as guides to fulfill personal growth and the formation of personality.

Values are learned principles by which a person lives. Values are at the core of the concept the person creates of himself as a self. As such, values not only help to create the person, but also to control and direct him in the life that surrounds and follows his construction of values.

The interaction of the person as a problem-solving organism with a surrounding environment is the raw material out of which values are selected. Values are acquired through contact with others, out of meaningful experiences, and always out of the texture of the culture that circumscribes and supports the growth of a person into a personality. The learning process is the means by which the person selects and integrates his experience into patterns, abstractions, and ultimately into values. Future interactions, learnings—future thinking and development—are in turn products of past values and present experience.

To assume that values should be acquired haphazardly, with no regard for their operational effectiveness, consistency, or relatedness denies the known importance of values in directing and controlling life. Man can create values that are inconsistent, contradictory, and ultimately destructive even of man as man. To assume that values should be delivered in appropriate wrappings is both undesirable and unrealistic. Values must be learned freely but they must also be measured and judged against the standard of man as an organism dedicated to a creative existence as a free and responsible person.

Values are the means by which man directs his efforts to live and to experience satisfaction from the life that is created. Values are the most basic expressions of man's concept of life. Man creates his world, lives in his world, and recognizes his relatedness to other men through his value system. An inability to live up to a personally constructed value system or the pursuit of contradictory or conflicting values characterizes persons with personality problems. The adoption of values predates such conflicts, although the value conflict may be obscured by operational or personality issues.

To help man explore his processes of decision-making and problem-solving and to help him be free and responsible is also to help him understand how he selects his own value structure and measures it against the experience of life. To create a life, to build a life as a free, thinking person is to be able to fulfill one's nature as a human being. The life that one lives, the life that one creates as an individual is one's most precious possession. The person who is free and responsible can create the dimensions of life to fulfill the potentialities inherent in and consistent with the self. The meaningfulness of life, judged by the person himself, is the ultimate standard by which values must be assessed.

Students have no choice but to be concerned with values. Problem-solving and learning accredit values which define the dimensions of life. If guidance is concerned with decision-making and problem-solving, it must be involved with values and the assessment of the nature of the life that an individual creates. Guidance can assume no control over persons, the direction of life, or the nature of life. Guidance workers can neither judge nor condemn. The individual must understand the processes that underlie the development of his life and must explore the implications of any problem-solving action. Guidance must help the person to see himself and the process of solving problems more clearly and more fully. The illumination of the processes through which man becomes a person can help the individual to understand how the potentialities that are inherent in himself can be developed. Men grow, develop, interact with a surrounding culture, build values and create personalities which in turn build their lives. Guidance is dedicated to assisting in the effective completion of all of these events within the life of the individual. The guidance worker assumes the responsibility of helping another to develop his full potential, and to build a life which is both free and responsible.

Values, freedom, responsibility, and problem-solving are all intimately related. If guidance workers are to aid persons to decide issues, to solve problems, and to live, guidance workers must understand the nature of freedom, responsibility, and values, as well as the problem-solving process.

The Total Person

The complexities of human life often defy comprehension. Yet the components of all lives are much the same. All men have physical structure, intellectual capacity, emotional potentials, and a concept of themselves as persons. All men must live in a world of varying but similar dimensions. The varying natures of men arise from the quantitative difference of the qualities within each man, the unique patternings of even identical qualities, and the variations of the environment that support life and interact with each man as a unique organism.

Man is neither wholly rational nor entirely emotional, wholly mind or body, completely conscious, or totally driven by unperceived forces. These are false dichotomies. Man is a complex organism consisting of all these elements and many more. When man acts, the whole man is involved. More than simply responding to stimuli, man is capable of directing his own life and patterning it in accord with his own concepts of the meaning of life and the values he has acquired to help him to achieve that meaning. Man as a free and responsible person is open-ended and must face the responsibility of determining his own destiny.

Man as a problem-solving organism can take into account many of the forces that can affect the quality of the solution to any problem. Skill in problem-solving is thus a reflection of individual capacity and acquired skill in applying appropriate techniques. Reason in man provides the integrating and conceptualizing element in behavior. Man receives information about himself and his world through his senses. His intelligence allows him to perceive patterns, to construct abstractions and to use concepts in problem-solving. Man's intelligence can be the governing element in determining behavior. He may not always act intelligently and what is intelligent behavior may be debated. Yet man's behavior arises out of his capacity to perceive, to construct concepts, to use ideas, and to solve problems.

Emotions are created out of man's reaction to perceived experience. The total organism can experience joy, sorrow, pain, satisfaction, or even fear. Emotions are the psychological accompaniment to problem-solving behavior. Man establishes his life directions through the adoption of values. Emotional reactions accompany man's progress or lack of progress, achievement, or failure in fulfilling his values which are his directions or guides to behavior. The healthy person cannot seek pure emotional experiences. Emotional experiences arise out of living and reflect a person's value structure.

Emotions alone cannot solve problems, make decisions, or guide thinking; however, emotions must be involved in effective problem-solving. Emotions give the organism the potential for evaluating experience. As such, emotions can help a person in living and solving problems. Emotions are reflections of values and can aid the person to assess progress, failure, or even a static state. Fear warns against the potential danger of values to the self. Satisfactions and feelings of happiness confirm the achievement of value concepts. Emotions cannot reason, emotions cannot solve problems or logically develop subsequent steps in behavior. Emotions can reveal values, can provide an individual with an assessment of his status in seeking whatever values are held.

The most deeply held value pattern is the concept of the self as a person—the self-concept: "This is me; this I believe!" The emotional intensity of experiences that threaten or enhance the self are revealments of the importance of such values to the person as a unique being. This concept of self, developed gradually, in halting and even contradictory fashion as the person grows and matures, is created by the person in the same way as a single value or pattern of values may be created.

The self-concept value is a directing value within personality, clothing the self with meaning. It is the directing value structure for the person. Problem-solving, thinking, emotional experiences, and all of life are outgrowths and expressions of the self-concept.

Distortions of the self-concept can lead to distortions in problem-solving, in valuing objects, in accrediting persons or experiences, and in the emotional or assessment experiences of the entire organism. Again the nature of the individual's reality contact—contact with the world as it is—through his total organism is the key to the effective functioning of the person in an environment.

Life Purposes

The objectives that an individual creates for himself are outgrowths of problem-solving behavior as his total personality within a world. The construction of patterns of behavior, the capacity to live as a free and responsible person, the values created to make life meaningful, the integrated nature of the person's concept of himself, and the quality of the reality contact are all predeterminers of life objectives. Whether vocational goals or personal creativity is at issue, the evaluation of the purposes a person establishes is an outgrowth of his essential nature.

Unrealistic, distorted, or even inconsistent and contradictory purposes in life are possible. Man is not always capable of totally integrated thought or behavior. Man's purposes reveal the processes that underlie them. Man's concept of himself is exposed as purposes, goals, and objectives are established.

The purposes that man establishes for himself are outgrowths of his capacity to solve problems, to live, to adopt or create values, and to live as a free and responsible person within a free and responsible society.

THE BECOMING PERSON

Each individual exists with a sense of time, and is uniquely conscious of his past, present, and future. Guidance is concerned with all three time concepts, but it must be acutely aware of the future which an individual can create. Others have commented upon this characteristic in men as "time-binding." The physician is interested in preventive health measures, but most frequently focuses his efforts to cure a present disease or the consequences of past illness. The guidance worker must be aware of and work with pasts and presents, but he must focus primarily upon futures.

The potentialities of each person are seldom fully visible at any period of the present or past. Man possesses inherent growth and creativity potentials that belong to him because he is man. The flow of time blends unevenly within persons so that individuals must be understood as dynamic organisms always in the process of becoming, but at varying rates. The future is a product of the past, present, and potential of each person.

The nature of man arises out of his biological structure, out of his culturally based learning, and out of the creative potential resulting from these factors. Gardner Murphy (1958) has identified such a view of the nature of man by referring to "animal man," "cultural man," and "creative man." Creative man is an organism concerned with a future sense of time; creative man is a developing person. Guidance, as a process involved with man, is thus directly related to the person as a creative, developing creature. The implications for guidance as a process are significant.

Physical Man

Even though clear genealogies are not available, man's physical ties to the animal world are real. The ways in which man is different from animals have been only partially explored. Yet there are many physical facts about man which are important. His body, his physiological functioning, even his mortality are constant reminders of his link with all of animal life. Man, however, is unique as an organism capable of symbolic, problem-solving communication and thought that can create a culture to surround and support himself.

An understanding of the growth or development stages of man is vital for guidance workers. The psychological stages of infancy, early childhood, prepuberty, puberty, adolescence, adulthood, middle age, and old age are rooted in physiological growth patterns (Erikson, 1956). Characteristic problems of life must be faced and solved as each life stage occurs. Psychological growth may be halted, regression may even take place, but physical growth and aging is unalterable. Although variations in physical growth or aging are expected, time is a constant physiological factor within man as a mortal creature.

Man's physical structure permits living and learning. His senses permit perceptions that through abstraction can be organized into concepts. Emotions are psychological responses, but are more the total reaction of the organism—man's responses to his own behavior. Illness can be a malfunctioning of the physical or of the psychological nature of man. Psychosomatic medicine has taught us that physiological and psychological problems may be intimately related. Physical, emotional, or psychological illness can overtake man when he is unable to use his total structure as a human being.

The essential importance of the physical nature of man is in the recognition of it as a part of man. Although it is only a part, the physical or even the structural nature of man is too frequently overlooked. Imagine that Johnny, who fell asleep in his eighth-grade geography class, is sent to the office. He may have been bored, incapable of understanding the work, physically ill, or tired from too little rest. His problem could be any of these or other possibilities. The physical organism is involved in any and every conceivable problem.

Problem-solving processes are centered in a physical structure that is man's most distinctive possession, his brain. Thought processes function outside of a purely physical realm through man's symbolic concepts; yet man is physical in every act or thought, for it is the total organism that behaves and lives.

Cultural Man

Although man is a product of his structure, his characteristic complexity must develop within a favorable environment. Man's complexity is created out of the most helpless, dependent beginnings. Apes, deer, and even chickens are more capable at birth than man. Man more than any other animal cannot grow and develop alone, automatically.

The environment that is man-made is culture. Culture provides the raw material with which the organism can interact in order to create life, in order to become a person. Physical man is a product of his heredity. Cultural man arises out of the supporting environment which is created by other men and which is learned.

Man creates a culture, maintains it, and passes it on to succeeding members of that culture. As man grows and develops, he can also contribute to his culture and help pass it on to others. Culture is not only music, literature, and opera. The father who drinks beer in the kitchen in his undershirt is also a part of the culture that surrounds and supports a growing child.

The institutions of a culture are varied and dynamic. The family, the church, the school, the home, the fabric of a culture as revealed in the customs and mores of a subgroup and in its codes and laws—all are creations and instruments of a society. As instruments, they provide values, behavior guides, and standards for new and growing members of the culture. Whether it be proper ways to kill a saber-toothed tiger or the best way to launch a rocket, culture approves and regulates man's values. A closed society leaves little if any choice in value structure for its members; an open society prides itself on the freedom of values and demands few value absolutes. All cultures have established value absolutes, and the assumption that one mode of life is inherently superior to another has led to much chaos and many wars. Our society believes that citizens should live in a free and responsible manner. The values of life, liberty, and happiness are guaranteed in our own free society. As these cultural and societal values are deeply held, so we become interested in their application to others in surrounding societies and cultures. These freely offered values are our most valuable contribution or export to a world of individuals.

Each individual is the product of the interaction of a physical nature and a surrounding culture. The developments of early life and the basic value patterns of a culture are the guiding elements that influence the learning, developing person.

Creative Man

School debates have long been held on "Nature vs. Nurture." That each man is composed of varying amounts of both is the answer offered in the "back of the book." Yet is not this view of man essentially narrow, restrictive, and an outcome of man as a "physical-cultural" entity?

The limitations of man as a physical animal are many. His speed of running is slower than a deer's, his visual acuity less than the hawk's. The limitations that culture place upon man are less clearly understood. An ancient Chinese practice was to bind women's feet to make them tiny and culturally beautiful. Other civilizations bind skulls for similar reasons. Our culture does not promote the binding of feet or head, but sometimes our own culture as well as others can bind men's minds. When a culture, either purposely or incidentally, encourages or allows artificial limitations to be placed on man's problem-solving processes, a type of "mind-binding" occurs.

When one "right" way or cultural value precludes questioning or discussion, cultural "mind-binding" occurs. When values are served to citizens as mandatory items on the thought menu, "mind-binding" takes place. Yet an even more insidious disease can cripple persons and societies. When men's minds are not viewed as creative instruments, when men's thought processes are limited by what is known of man's physical and cultural nature, the most limiting type of "mind-binding" exists.

Man's distinctive possession is his ability to think and exist within a "life space" [Kurt Lewin's term used by Gardner Murphy (1958)]. Each person's life space is partly physical, partly cultural. Yet it is more. Man's creative existence can break through the barriers of physical or cultural limitations. Man cannot run as fast as a deer, yet man can fly in space at speeds well beyond any deer. Such achievements are gradually developed out of growing accumulated knowledge. Yet at times man can break through physical and cultural limitations, building upon what appears to be no previously accumulated background. Yet the background is there, it is in man's creative use of his capacity to think, to live, to exist within his own "life space" and still to extend beyond it. Technological or scientific inventions occur and leap over an accumulated knowledge, through spaces of knowledge that are later filled in.

Ideas of individualism, brotherhood, liberty, freedom are often compounded out of a gradual or carefully patterned foundation, but are also creations of men, often through a break in the growing, developing pattern of man's contribution to man.

The potential for man and men is unknowable. Man's instrument for his own and the world's future is his power to exist, to create within a life space. The complex growing organism we know as man is a thinking animal living within his own created world of culture, yet always extending and leaping beyond the seemingly surrounding and limiting barriers.

Guidance and Individuals

Guidance can solve neither all the problems of the world nor all the problems of individuals. Guidance cannot promise mental health to all nor the achievement of happiness or success. Guidance can only offer aid to man as tasks are undertaken. Guidance is a process that offers aid to persons as they attempt to live meaningfully. Guidance is concerned with individuals as problem-solving organisms. Guidance aids man at the heart of the creative process of living and problem-solving, and specializes in help to becoming man in decision-making, problem-solving, life-building.

SUMMARY

Guidance is a part of education but a separate process designed to help individuals to focus life objectives. The definition of guidance has been offered and the elements of guidance were examined. The nature of guidance reveals a philosophical base, a clear relationship to the development of freedom and responsibility in persons, and an involvement in value construction.

The concern for the total person relates guidance to the physical, cultural, and creative nature of man. Creative man has been presented as a developing organism related to his present and past.

REFERENCES AND SUGGESTED READINGS

Anderson, Harold H., "Creativity and Education," *A.H.E. College and University Bulletin,* XIII (Special Issue), 1961.

Anderson, Harold H., *Creativity and Its Cultivation,* New York: Harper, 1959.

Arbuckle, Dugald S., "Counselor Education—Philosophy and Objectives," *A Progress Report on Standards,* Washington, D.C.: American Personnel and Guidance Association, 1962.

Benezet, Louis T., "Guidance in Moral and Spiritual Values," in M. D. Hardee (ed.), *Counseling and Guidance in General Education,* New York: World Book, 1955.

Berger, M., *et al., Freedom and Control in Modern Society,* New York: Van Nostrand, 1954.

Blumberg, A., "Some Thoughts on the Teaching of Values," *Journal of College Student Personnel,* II, 1961.

Brameld, Theodore, *Philosophies of Education in Cultural Perspective,* New York: Dryden, 1955.

Brameld, Theodore, "What Is the Central Purpose of American Education?" *Phi Delta Kappan,* XLIII (1961), 9–14.

Bryson, Lyman, *Science and Freedom,* New York: Columbia University Press, 1947.

Collins, Anthony, *A Philosophical Inquiry Concerning Human Liberty,* 1735 (3rd ed., corrected), London: Printed for R. Robinson at the Golden Lion in Saint Paul's Churchyard.

Combs, A. W., and D. Snygg, *Individual Behavior* (rev. ed.), New York: Harper, 1959.

Compton, Arthur H., *The Freedom of Man,* New Haven: Yale University Press, 1935.

Dahlke, H. O., *Values in Culture and Classroom,* New York: Harper, 1958.

Dewey, John, *Democracy and Education,* New York: Macmillan, 1915.

Dresser, H. O., *Voices of Freedom,* New York: Putnam, 1899.

Erikson, E. H., "The Problem of Ego Identification," *Journal of the American Psychoanalysis Association,* IV (1956), 56–112.

Hahn, Milton E., "Forgotten People: The Normal Individual, and in, Professional Psychology," *American Psychologist,* XVII (1962), 700–705.

Hook, Sidney, *Political Power and Personal Freedom,* New York: Collier Books, 1962.

Huxley, Aldous, "Human Potentialities," in S. M. Farber and R. H. L. Wilson (eds.), *Control of the Mind,* New York: McGraw-Hill, 1961, pp. 60–76.

Jacob, Philip E., *Changing Values in College,* New York: Harper, 1957.
Jersild, Arthur T., *In Search of Self,* New York: Bureau of Publications, Teachers College, Columbia University, 1952.
Keesing, Felix M., *Anthropological Contributions to Value Theory* (rev. restricted ed.), Stanford: Stanford University Department of Sociology and Anthropology, 1955.
Kendler, H. H., "Problems in Problem-Solving Research," *Current Trends in Psychological Theory,* Pittsburgh: University of Pittsburgh Press, 1961.
Lowe, C. Marshall, "Value Orientations–An Ethical Dilemma," *American Psychologist,* XIV (1959), 687–693.
McMurrin, Sterling M., "Education for Freedom in a Free Society," *Higher Education,* XIX (1962), 3–6.
MacLeish, Archibald, *Freedom Is the Right to Choose,* Boston: Beacon, 1951.
Malinowski, Bronislaw, *Freedom and Civilization,* New York: Roy, 1944.
Mathewson, R. H., *Guidance Policy and Practice* (3rd ed.), New York: Harper, 1962.
May, Rollo (ed.), *Existential Psychology,* New York: Random, 1961.
May, Rollo, "Freedom and Responsibility," speech to American Personnel and Guidance Association Convention, April, 1962.
Mooney, R. L., *Creation and Counseling,* Columbus, Ohio: Bureau of Educational Research and Science, 1960.
Morgenbesser, S., and J. Walsh, *Free Will,* Englewood Cliffs, N.J.: Prentice-Hall, 1962.
Morris, Charles, *Varieties of Human Value,* Chicago: University of Chicago Press, 1956.
Murphy, Gardner, *Human Potentialities,* New York: Basic Books, 1958.
Palmer, George H., *The Problem of Freedom,* Boston: Houghton Mifflin, 1911.
Patterson, C. H., "The Place of Values in Counseling and Psychology," *Journal of Counseling Psychology,* V (1958), 216–233.
Plutchik, Robert, *The Emotions: Facts, Theories, and a New Model,* New York: Random, 1962.
Rand, Ayn, *The Objectivist Ethics,* New York: Nathaniel Branden Institute, 1961.
Rogers, Carl, "Learning to Be Free," speech to Conference on Evolutionary Theory and Human Progress: Conference C, The Individual and the Design of Culture, sec. 2–4, 1960.
Rogers, Carl, *On Becoming a Person,* Boston: Houghton Mifflin, 1962.
Rogers, Carl, "The Place of the Person in the New World of the Behavioral Sciences," *Personnel and Guidance Journal,* XXXIX (1961), 442–451.
Rogers, Carl, and B. F. Skinner, "Some Issues Concerning the Control of Behavior," *Science,* XXX (1956), 1057–1066.
Shoben, E. J., Jr., "A Rationale for Modern Student Personnel Work," *Personnel-O-Gram,* XII, No. 3 (1958), 9–11.
Skinner, B. F., "Freedom and the Control of Men," *The American Scholar,* XXV (1955), 47–65.
Thoreau, Henry David, *Walden,* Boston: Houghton Mifflin, 1957.
Trager, Helen G., and M. Radke-Yarrow, *They Learn What They Live,* New York: Harper, 1952.
Trump, Lloyd, *New Directions to Quality Education–the Secondary School Tomorrow,* Washington, D.C.: National Association of Secondary School Principals, NEA, 1960.

Universal Opportunity for Higher Education, Educational Policies Commission, NEA, Washington, D.C., 1963.
Weill, Blanche C., *Through Children's Eyes,* New York: Island Workshop Press, 1940.
Williamson, E. G., "Value Orientation in Counseling," *Personnel and Guidance Journal,* XXXVI (1958), 520–528.
Wrenn, C. Gilbert, "Philosophical and Psychological Bases of Personnel Services in Education," in *Personnel Services in Education,* 58th Yearbook of National Society for the Study of Education, Part II, Chicago: University of Chicago Press, 1959, 41–81.
Wrenn, C. Gilbert, "Psychology, Religion, and Values for the Counselor," *Personnel and Guidance Journal,* XXXVI (1958), 331–334.

ROOTS AND DREAMS

THE ISSUE. Present-day guidance has not sprung full blown from any drawing board; guidance has arisen out of the environment of American history and education. Guidance is a peculiarly American concept with implications for free men all over the world.

All movements must begin; all movements must be nurtured by philosophical and cultural determinants that make it possible for them to prosper. Guidance has prospered and stands on the edge of a major breakthrough into educational, philosophical, and political frontiers that are still unexplored.

What is there about guidance that has supported its virile growth within the half century that pedagogues claim "must pass before half of the schools accept a new idea"? Guidance has not only been accepted by virtually all schools; guidance is recognized as the focus of the effort that can help to fulfill the purpose of American education.

What are the roots and the dreams that have permitted the budding of this sensitive dimension of free education?

Men have created a responsible society to serve individuals and are struggling to provide for the maintenance of that society. Guidance is intimately involved in the preservation of free education and a free society. How, why, and when has this involvement taken place? What are the frontiers beyond the threshold upon which guidance now stands?

CHAPTER TWO

HISTORICAL BACKGROUNDS

The origins of the word *guidance* must be left to the explorations of word specialists. Certainly the concept of helping another to find his way is as old as man's language and man's existence. Guidance as a principle dedicated to the creation of free and responsible men to extend the fruits of a free society to other men is much more recent. Some might say that such a development has not yet occurred. However, guidance has become central to education. The individual is the most precious product of a free society and the task of education is to serve the individual and the society. To help each individual learn how to create a life of meaning and purpose for himself and for his society is the task guidance undertakes.

Some would trace American history back to the Magna Charta of the thirteenth century. Others would, and could perhaps, follow the threads of freedom back to the first recorded history of man. Man has dreamed many dreams, but he has not been able to realize a dream of the scope and stature of that of individual freedom. Necessarily the establishment of such a concept ne[illegible]ds to be explored to its depths. Guidance has come lately upon the [illegible]ne and builds upon the efforts of all who have gone before. Guid[illegible] helps to express and realize man's hopes for assistance in the [illegible]nal task of creating a free and responsible individual. [illegible]lom and guidance are intertwined, even though guid[illegible] history.

The industrial revolution br[illegible]nd productivity within the grasp of the little [illegible]put power to work for him, the little man had [illegible]hers. The world of machines brought unknown complexity into jobs, society, and interpersonal relations. Guidance was one of the results of such forces. It was needed to help bring order out of complexity. At first guidance could be only technical; essentially a sorting process for economic forces not yet clearly seen. However, guidance could never have become more than a technical service and sorting process if all men were not seen to be the primary gainers. The industrial revolution helped to establish the foundation for guidance, but more importantly it made it possible for man to come closer to his dreams of self-determination and freedom.

Urbanization and immigration were two patterns of history that accompanied the full-blown industrialization of America. The factory, demanding cheap labor, became the center of the community. Railroads were needed to haul raw materials and products. Houses were needed to protect the worker. Immigration, urbanization, and the industrial revolution—one would have been impossible without the others. The stage was being set and the forces were developing. There was no single pattern, no master plan. Circumstances permitted that which had not before been possible.

A rich fertile land, with a heritage of protest against the status quo and the past and with an obsession for independence and freedom of action, was offered the tools to create a society. The raw materials were present and the tools were available. The ends were only dimly seen by those who worked and occasionally dreamed.

The idea of humanitarianism grew only as men were able to produce so much that there seemed to be enough for all. Why could not others be helped to profit when there was so much? The traditions of a Judaic-Christian people provided the altruistic foundation for the utilizations of industrial success. The cause of free public education was advanced as a practical necessity to fill the needs of a growing industrial America while also serving as the fulfillment of a dream never before translated into action on a national scale.

The giants of American history who guided a rebellious people to the creation of a new country did not foresee free public education for all through secondary school. Schooling for all through elementary periods, to provide "reading, 'riting, and 'rithmetic" was even then the dream of only a few. Nineteenth-century America began to believe that more was possible. Education could be the twofold servant of a better society and of a more productive world of industry. The rigid societies of the old world not [illegible]y could not dream thus, but also lacked the power of the "fr[illegible]" and the factory. The old world had neither the philoso[illegible]ortunity; America possessed both and more —the desir[illegible]ossessions.

The dream of educating a total population was translated into action. The nation bound its new immigrant masses into what Max Lerner (1957) has called "The American Civilization." Many who are still alive can recall a time when the vision was unreal. Many may not even recall the time when it became a practical hope. It was the hope, the belief, the dream of a free society that was determined to make the future more than the past had been. Some who were to work to make it possible did not even know for what they were working. Their children have profited and now assert that the time their parents sought is here. All are entitled to an education commensurate with their talents and abilities; they want to build a life of their own. They are not working merely for the future. The time is now for them and their offspring to have that for which their forebears dreamed and worked.

Today's children turn to education and to guidance for fulfillment of their own destinies. The power, the raw materials, the opportunities, the returns are all seen. How may each person seek and find?

BEGINNINGS OF GUIDANCE

How did guidance come into the picture? How did it become associated with the individual and provide a focus for education?

No single date can mark the beginning or end of a cultural force or a people's dream. Guidance can be said to have begun with that dream. Many had hoped; there were those who found the means to realize the dream.

Practical Starts

> . . . Late in the fall of 1907, Frank Parsons had formulated plans for the organization of a vocational bureau, and he sought financial support for the undertaking from Mrs. Quincy Adams Shaw, daughter of Professor Jean Louis Agassiz of Harvard. By January of the following year plans were completed, and the Vocation Bureau came into being on January 13, 1908, under the leadership of Frank Parsons as Director and Vocational Counselor. The bureau was established with a main office at the Civic Service House and branch offices in the Young Men's Christian Association, The Economic Club, and the Women's Educational and Industrial Union. Parsons maintained office hours at each of these places. [C. H. Miller, 1961:145][1]

[1] Reprinted by permission of Harper & Row, Publishers, Incorporated.

C. H. Miller's words paint a picture that can re-create the feeling of anticipation that was felt as Frank Parsons hurried between his many Boston offices. Boston was also the host for the 1963 American Personnel and Guidance Association National Convention, which provided for the golden anniversary celebration of the founding of the National Vocational Guidance Association in 1913, an outgrowth of Frank Parsons' work. The American Personnel and Guidance Association now has a membership of almost twenty thousand persons. Dozens of related organizations enroll thousands more, although many part-time and full-time workers do not belong to any organization. Guidance has hurried, guidance has grown.

One year after Parsons' Vocation Bureau opened its doors, a direct connection was established with the Boston schools. Guidance and counseling became allied with education as education used the services of the new bureau.

Since Boston claimed Frank Parsons, many now consider Boston the primary guidance center. Yet many schools were wrestling with the same problems at the same time. New York City was undertaking summer and part-time placement of boys in school. C. H. Miller (1961: 149) reports teachers serving as counselors in New York in 1909. Jesse B. Davis, working in Central High School in Detroit at the same period, initiated a weekly period for "vocational and moral guidance" in 1907. Dozens of other schools were experimenting with guidance concepts.

Colleges and universities were facing the same issues and coming to similar conclusions. The guidance function of deans of women was first identified about the same period as Parsons' work in Boston. Care, social direction, friendship, and chaperonage were offered to the girls in the dormitories. Princeton developed in 1908 a "preceptorial" program through which faculty members could serve as "guide, philosopher, and friend of the student" (Barry and Wolf, 1957:20). Colleges throughout the land were becoming concerned with the individual student seeking education. Education was seen to be more than passing on information or exercising the intellect.

Education and Guidance

Education and guidance maintained an unofficial though active relationship throughout the period prior to World War I. Officially the schools were concerned only with intellectual development and academic curriculums. Educators began to question the role of the individual student in such a process. A revolutionary report, *The Cardinal Principles of Secondary Education,* appeared in 1918 to change the focus of education on the secondary level and indirectly on all levels. This publication maintained that the whole student is the concern for education. Citizenship, character, ethics, use of leisure time, family membership, health, and vocational direction were among the concerns that broadened the basis of free public education. Guidance and education were inextricably bound together from this point.

PARALLEL DEVELOPMENTS

Guidance could never have achieved its present position within the schools without the help of other disciplines and forces present and active within the society. An awakening concern with human behavior —through psychological theory and research, a creative concept of mental health, the professionalization of and concern with sociology, and an exploding interest in individual differences—all paralleled and aided in the growth of guidance within the schools.

Psychology

Psychology served as an apprentice of philosophy for many years. The freeing of the discipline was largely accomplished by Sigmund Freud and his work in human behavior. Freud's speculative theories on motivation, adjustment, and behavior prepared the foundation for most modern psychological research and practice. At the same time that Freud was writing and practicing, American and European psychological laboratories were being established to study human behavior. These early efforts were directed at the study of psychophysical differences between individuals. The individual's capacity to discriminate between and react to weights, lights, pressures, and other simple physical factors were primary concerns.

Freud's highly tentative theories and prolific writings provided the basis for psychoanalysis and psychoanalytic theory. His early efforts also laid the foundation for the focus on early childhood and the clinical approach that have marked all guidance. Later efforts of E. G. Williamson, Leona Tyler, Carl Rogers, and others in guidance have all been built upon the clinical beginnings offered by Freud.

Early psychological research gave rise to creative efforts in experimental and scientific psychology. Individual differences became a major concern of research. Testing, measurement, and statistical inference were pushed beyond the limits that had existed for centuries.

Psychoanalysis and the study of the motivation of human behavior and adjustment developed parallel to guidance. These major streams within psychology and education were divergent from an early time, but ultimately affected guidance as much if not more than any other area. Testing, measurement, and statistics were immediately applied to guidance and counseling practice. Alfred Binet in France, just after the turn of the century, developed a measure to separate students into ability categories. Grade data, which were used to establish mental capacity, also provided the foundation for Louis Terman's later work at Stanford University, which created an intelligence test that is still used —Stanford-Binet. Edward Lee Thorndike at Columbia University had begun to explore the meanings of individual differences. The work of others such as James McKeen Cattell and Sir Francis Galton had also helped to establish foundations for modern measurement and assessment techniques.

Parsons reflected some of the emphasis on measurement in his book on choosing a vocation (1909:7). He was concerned with intelligence and the senses and with psychophysical measurements as well as association-times. The next few years saw a widespread growth of measures of individual capacity and a broadening of the approach.

World War I gave a tremendous impetus to the testing field. Arthur L. Otis, a graduate student of Terman at Stanford, began his work on a paper-and-pencil form of the Stanford-Binet. The test is still used in later forms as the Otis Self-Administering Test of Mental Ability. The Army Alpha and other group tests were attempts to help to assess the millions of men called to serve their country. The testing field suffered a boom-and-bust cycle following World War I. Similar swings have occurred in the testing and measurement field since its beginning.

Only recently have the broader concepts of clinical psychology become integrated with guidance theory and practice. Personality appraisal was the domain of clinical psychologists, and guidance workers were not encouraged to interfere, although dabbling did occur. Testing was used to assess individual talent, but there was little actual use of test data to help men understand themselves. The gap between the use of diagnostic tests and use of tests for the guidance of students left large questions to be answered (Goldman, 1961; Rothney, 1958).

Guidance has tried to serve all society by attempting to bring together these diverse strains into some of the newer national testing efforts. "Project Talent" was started to measure the performances of almost half a million high school students in all areas of achievement and life-planning. Guidance is beginning to reach out beyond the school and the community and to explore the concept of total national assessment. Present national testing programs number almost two dozen. Psychology, testing, and guidance are coming together as they operate within the school.

Mental Health

Clifford Beers in his book *A Mind That Found Itself,* first published in 1914, made a profound impression upon an awakening society and upon guidance. The individual became a concern of community and professional groups. School children were viewed as growing, developing organisms as well as pliable receptacles for rote memory tasks. The Wickman Study in 1927 provided a foundation for a comparison of teachers' and clinicians' judgments of student behavior. Since that time the views of teachers, guidance personnel, and clinicians have moved closer to a common understanding of children's problems in developing into healthy, mature individuals.

Social and Cultural Forces

Against the broad background of the industrial revolution, urbanization, and immigration arose the study of persons as members of societies. The community, the city, the family, and the school became objects of examination. The cross-cultural currents of these forces were not clearly seen and studied until later periods, but the growth of the concept of the community as a force and cultural fact provided a supporting principle on which guidance has now begun to build.

The pioneering study of comparative cultures by Ruth Benedict and the intensive investigations of individual societies by Margaret Mead have been accompanied by the examination of communities in our own country by Warner, Hollingshead, and the Lynds. These studies grew out of the uncovered issues of stratification, social structure, status, and class concepts that were in turn outgrowths of industrial revolution, urbanization, and immigration. The individual was being examined not only as he selected and entered a vocation but as he existed within the community, the nation, and the world. Examinations of such forces were independent and frequently unrelated. Guidance often ignored these developments as it attempted to understand its own role in education and in the life of the person. Guidance was a potential that could profit from the efforts of others to push back the frontiers of understanding.

PHILOSOPHICAL DETERMINANTS

The roots of guidance lie deep within the philosophical theories which helped to shape our nation. C. H. Miller (1961) traces the foreshadowings of guidance back to John Amos Comenius, John Milton, John Locke, and other old-world philosophers. There is no question that such men were concerned with the issues of education. America's contribution to education and ultimately to guidance was the development of free education for an entire society and the long search for individual freedom and responsibility through education.

The golden age of political philosophy and practice came with the birth of the American republic. The Boston agitators and the Philadelphia statesmen combined with the southern gentlemen to create a nation and to provide a philosophical basis which continues to serve our nation and Western civilization.

One of the significant contributions of the colonial political philosophers was the concern with education as a foundation for a free society. No longer were governments seen to be the masters and guardians of the state. The people were posited as guardians and heirs of power and as the purpose for all government. To permit the implementation of such a view, education has had to come to the fore as a servant of the society. Education came to embody the philosophy that defended the individual as the primary value of a society. Governments, laws, social organizations—none could draw life independently; respect for the individual has come to be the core of the institutions of a free society.

The implementation of the dreams of the colonial philosophers was a tremendous task. Many of the philosophical principles served as goals rather than as statements of demonstrable fact. Despite a civil war and countless political changes, the power as well as the desire to realize the stated goals were still in the future. Yet freedom and individual fulfillment had come out of the ivory tower of philosophical discourse. America was the arena for ideas to become real. Free will and determinism were examined on the street corner as well as on the podium and in the pulpit.

Morality

Early guidance efforts were strongly grounded in a desire to provide moral substance for students. Jesse B. Davis linked vocational guidance with moral development in Grand Rapids, Michigan. John Brewer's attempts to equate guidance and education in his book *Educa-*

tion as Guidance reflected a continued concern with the morality of guidance. The individual was seen as deriving his life and his opportunity from God. Duty, obligation, and character were basic terms encountered in such interpretations of guidance. Immanuel Kant and theology were dual roots for some early guidance practices.

Guidance retains a strong flavor of the early efforts of such men. There is no question that man is concerned with the kind of life that he must live. Ethics are vital to daily life. Private and public education alike have seen clearly their responsibility for helping to produce persons of "character." The question of what *type* of character has been the stumbling block that has prevented the assimilation of moral and spiritual philosophy into guidance. Guidance has chosen to remain a part of education and separate from religious views.

Economics

The view of man as a tool has been defended by industrial as well as political philosophers. The naturalistic view of man in his relationship to the industrial revolution stressed the picture of man as a cog in a giant machine. Guidance at first accepted but later rejected the analogy to the square peg in the square hole and the round peg in the round hole.

Morality and economics were often linked together by amateur philosophers as well as by professional guidance workers. Hard work, service to one's economic superior, and contribution to the welfare of society by finding one's place in the economic and moral scheme have long been primary planks in the "Protestant Ethic."

The economic flavor of occupational libraries, dictionaries of occupational titles, job families, and the fitting of psychological test data to the Procrustean bed of economics have been a part of even the recent past of the guidance movement.

Classical Philosophies

Guidance has been unable to fit comfortably within the confines of any of the traditional views of man and his pursuit of the good life. Idealism, naturalism, rationalism, humanism, or any combination of these views of man has not been adequate. Guidance, like education, has grown out of but is larger than any of these views.

William James and John Dewey have come closest to providing a philosophical base for guidance and for guidance as a part of education. Pragmatism has a strong claim, though seemingly paradoxically, upon the natures and dreams of Americans. Dewey similarly captured the imagination of a new society through his plea for experimentation and instrumentalism. James, though he opposed the nonpractical, leaned heavily upon religious values and the concept of truth as revelation. Dewey centered his beliefs upon the open-ended nature of the democratic society. His inquiry into morals reflected a belief in the value of scientific experimentation in unknown areas of the material world. Morality and truth were seen to be growing and developing creations of man. Man was instrumental in creating his own destiny; he was at the same time an end in himself.

Although it is becoming apparent that Dewey is perhaps the most significant philosopher to influence the development of guidance, he thought and wrote about more than guidance and individual growth, concerning himself with the total educational process in a free society. Experimentation in education was to be a means to create unknowable ends for education and for society. Dewey was not against guidance, but he looked more broadly at men and society. At that time guidance was narrow; as it has broadened its conceptual design, Dewey has become more significant. Individualism, such as that of Thoreau, has been blended with American education through James and Dewey.

CULTURAL PERSPECTIVES

Hindsight is considerably easier than prediction. The examination of what pioneers in guidance might have thought may be almost scholastic exercises. Guidance arose out of a cultural context to solve specific problems. Assistance to those seeking jobs was a very real and practical issue. To ask whether such efforts were also seen as the beginnings of a philosophical view of man and of education for free men is to ask unfair questions.

Guidance arose out of the background forces surrounding it in the early years of this century. Guidance was also paralleled by other movements unrelated to it at the time. Guidance must be viewed as an outgrowth not only of its beginnings but also of its developing dimensions.

American Education

American education is a product of developments that preceded its establishment on this continent, but it is also more than that which preceded it. The peculiar stamp of American education has arisen from the need to support and defend the basic proposition of the state—the development of the individual. The basis of a free society was seen to be necessarily an educated populace. Education became a requirement of a political system. It was adopted as an instrument to develop and to further a free society. No person could or can foresee the dimensions of the future for a free open society. Education provides the means to accomplish whatever goals and purposes may be possible. Dewey helped to reflect the dream of the founders of the country.

America was able to do more than provide free public education in "the three R's." America was and is the first large-scale society able to create and to implement the concept of free public education for all to the age of 16. Even this age limit is rapidly disappearing in many sections of the country. Opportunity for appropriate education through two and often through four years of college is becoming a reality. Barriers of economics and discrimination are falling. The picture is not perfect by any means; the goal, however, is clearly seen.

America has been the first nation to seek and to implement education for the masses; it is continuing to seek an intellectual elite, prepared through free choice, possessing a sense of responsibility to self and to a sponsoring society. The hopes which Thomas Jefferson expressed in a letter to John Adams are coming to fruition. The natural aristocracy of "talents and virtue" rather than the "pseudo-aristoi" of wealth and birth is becoming a reality. Lerner's concept of "equal access to equal opportunity" (1962) is becoming the means to establish the goals of Jefferson.

The Opportunity of Circumstance

Many thousands of years from now it may be possible to read in history books of the noble experiment that came to fruition in the distant past. Or the American experiment may be viewed as the dream that failed. The roots may be traced back to man's belief in his inherent right to be free, and those who trace it may sigh and say, "Oh, what it might have been."

Modern man enjoys material privileges that the most wealthy could not obtain a few decades ago. Moreover, the individual in America enjoys the opportunity to determine for himself his own destiny. There are no guarantees of success, and the "bitter pill of fairness" of John Gardner (1961) may be the reward for many who fail. Still, man has seldom before been privileged to try, much less to fail.

The industrial revolution, the wealth of raw materials that a fertile land has provided, and the dream of freedom that visionary pioneers dreamed—these are the elements that surround the individual as he faces the task of creating his own life and contributing to the society that has permitted him to exploit his own talents and capacities. Guidance asks to stand with man as these problems are faced, to explore and assess possible outcomes with him, although it can offer no promises of success or of failure. Guidance has been created for the task of helping man to fulfill his destiny, however it may come. Guidance with education has become the servant of the individual and of a society dedicated to the individual.

THE THRESHOLD

The year 1963 marked the fiftieth anniversary of the founding of the National Vocational Guidance Association. The publication, immediately prior to the National Guidance Convention of 1963, of Barry and Wolf's *Epitaph for Vocational Guidance* (1962) seemed impertinent. But the book served not only as an epitaph, but also as a prologue to what might lie ahead. The horse as a major mode of transportation was doomed with the advent of the automobile. Yet those who used autos traveled more effectively and efficiently. The horse became outmoded but not extinct. Vocational guidance may be dead, but vocational counseling is becoming more vital as guidance begins to understand its own nature more fully.

Vocational guidance began to die long before it received an epitaph, when the first counselors discovered that a vocation was only a part of the life of a person. The education that preceded, accompanied, and followed vocational life was involved, as were marital choices, ways of life, and personal goals and purposes. Many professional vocational counselors tried arduously to deny the facts of individual development as they were made increasingly clear. As late as the years following World War II there were discussions about using the word *guidance* without a qualifying adjective. The angels were dancing on the pinhead again. Robert Hoppock warned of the coming demise of vocational guidance. Donald Super in many writings clearly spelled out the changing nature of the field. Barry and Wolf only completed the process.

The traditional British cry of grief and joy: "The Queen is Dead! Long Live the Queen!" can help all in guidance to recognize the opportunities of the present. The past and the future are separated by a fine line. The period of mourning is over and the praise due to the founding fathers has been accorded. Guidance must look to the future. The future of guidance can be composed of the dreams of the past as well as the realities of everyday life in the second half of the twentieth century.

Equality of Opportunity

"All men are created equal. . . ." These words of Jefferson have guided and confused Americans since the creation of the Republic. What does *equal* mean? Obviously psychology as a science has helped to reveal that no two persons can ever be truly equal in talents, character, or personality. The proposition that men are and ought to be equal in the opportunity to create their lives and to seek life, liberty, and happiness has been undertaken by our society. Complete success in the safeguarding of these rights has not yet been achieved in all areas of our life. Age, color, race, religion, and other criteria have been used to deny equality of opportunity to the individual. Yet the use of federal troops to enforce law and order in several of the states of the United States, must be regarded as an attempt to defend the rights of an individual to the equality of opportunity. Equality of achievement, no; equality of opportunity, yes. Our people continue to seek the goals that Jefferson said he offered not as his own ideas, but as a reflection of what the people believed (Jefferson, 1825; quoted in Boyd, 1945:2).

Guidance has been created out of an educational and societal background to assist each individual to learn how to use this equality of opportunity. Man must learn how to use and to understand his freedom, his responsibility, and his opportunity. If preparation is not adequate, manipulation can be cloaked in the guise of delivering freedom and opportunity, and irresponsibility may result. Freedom and opportunity are then judged inadequate. Rather it is the education which has been inadequate, for the process of learning determines the quality of man's behavior.

Guidance, as the profession charged with helping the person to use his opportunity and to learn to be free and responsible, is a part of education. Guidance could not exist without education, and education as we now know it is not complete without guidance. The interrelationships of education, teaching, and guidance can now be better understood as the historical roots of guidance are understood and as guidance faces its future.

Education, Teaching, and Guidance

Many writers and workers in education have either equated or tried to equate guidance, teaching, and education. All are concerned with the development of the individual, but all have differing emphases and particular contributions to make to the total process.

Our society has attempted to help each person to come to grips with and to become a part of the world. Education provides the person with an understanding of the world. "The three R's" are part of the world, as are advanced nuclear physics, musicology, and Mark Twain. The task of teachers who specialize in one aspect of the world or its operation is to help students to understand and to learn about that portion of the world.

Subject matter and guidance are two elements within education that are neither the same nor opposed to each other. The student must have assistance in both areas if he is to accomplish what his society has safeguarded for him—the opportunity, through education, to create a life of meaning and purpose.

Teachers are facing the dual charge of teaching both subject matter and students. As such, teachers are the link between the subject matter and guidance. The student depends upon all three elements in exploiting his own potential through education.

Guidance needs to understand its specialized role within education. It has been created from within the traditional area of responsibility of the teacher. This historical process can explain the hostility that frequently greets guidance in a school or college. The age-old privilege of the teacher is being given away. Teachers may not fully understand their ambivalent feelings. They welcome the potential skill that can help the student, who is their ultimate concern. Still, teachers may also feel that their vocation is being taken away. Guidance workers need to understand their relation to teachers and to education and to recognize that teachers and subject matter as well as guidance can be instruments to help the student to realize his potential.

The issue was not clearly faced by any of the educators who charged teachers with developing students as competently prepared subject-matter specialists, and with training them to use the subject-matter learnings. Teachers have responded in a creative fashion to this dual charge. Some teachers were judged failures, not because they could not help students to learn their subject matter, but because the students seemed unable to profit and to be able to use the material. Teachers were assumed to be specialists in helping students to chart their lives and to use the learnings that education provided. Teachers have continued to wrestle with the dual task ever since the revision of the classical curriculum. Many teachers can focus upon both tasks; some teachers prefer to specialize in either subject-matter learning or student use of learning. The latter teaching task has been separated from the traditional teaching responsibility and called guidance.

Guidance has assumed, asked for, demanded, and received a specialized function of teaching that has been removed from teaching and made the province of a particular group. Teachers may continue to tackle both tasks or they may wish to focus their efforts at various times upon each of these responsibilities. Guidance focuses upon the student's use of his learnings—the understanding of the world that education helps him to obtain. As such, guidance has as its subject matter not French, algebra, nor inorganic chemistry, but student values, life objectives, and life purposes. Guidance workers need to understand that they can fail in their task of helping students just as faculty members can fail to help students to understand a particular portion of the world.

Education assumes that a total integration of (1) learnings about the world and (2) the student's application of these learnings in his life is possible. Education depends upon subject matter and guidance. In creating his own life, the person depends both upon his subject matter learnings and upon his learning to be free and responsible.

How the individual is to relate himself to the world has always been a difficult issue within education. Early classical education assumed that the process would take place naturally. The individual needed only to understand the classical languages, mathematics, some of the cultures of the past, and perhaps the changeable interpretations of the dominant religious thought of the day. The transfer of training in this scheme of education was virtually nil. The success of men and some women often seemed to occur in spite of their education. There seemed to be little if any direct connection between education and the effectiveness of the life of the person.

Education grew and began to understand more of learning and individual development. The curriculums began to reflect the dominant ideas of the society within which education occurred. Philosophy, science, and other "liberating" subjects were introduced into the curriculums. Business, technical subjects, and the humanities were also proper for the curriculums. Again the connections between the subject matter and the individual student were assumed. The subjects would automatically liberate the student. If a student studied science and learned all that he was supposed to know (according to the course standards) about science, he wanted to become a scientist. He became a scientist (or a businessman, clergyman, soldier, or electronics engineer). The implications of this educational scheme are present today in schools and colleges around the country. Teachers were charged with helping students to learn the subject matter and at the same time were assumed to be capable of "teaching students, not subject matter." Teachers may have been somewhat confused, but they could not rebel. Who could be against student learning if he were in education?

Guidance and the Future

The future is by no means secure because guidance has entered into education. Guidance has wrestled for virtually 50 years to clarify its role within education, but has only just begun to assess its own dimensions and to understand its function. Guidance can begin now to examine its own house, to seek professionalization and ethical practice. The next half-century of guidance faces the challenge of the previous half-century. If guidance can move as far ahead in the future as it has in the past, education, teachers, society, and students will be willing to accord guidance all that it may now wish to claim. The future is the test for guidance. We have an epitaph for the past.

The key to the future of guidance is the recognition of the threshold upon which it now stands. The way in which guidance seeks to move, to enhance its concept of service to students, education, and society, will determine its nature for years to come.

To help individuals learn how to create lives of meaning and purpose that can utilize the potential of an educational system and a free society is a tremendous task. Guidance must face with humility the achievements of others prior to the time guidance was available. Teachers have labored under a responsibility that no fair appraisal of work load would defend. Now that teachers, guidance persons, and all within education can relate to each other to help students, both students and education can profit. The society will be accomplishing the goals of its earliest dreamers. Guidance is a natural development of educational history within a free society. Guidance has not created itself, but has been created by those who have recognized the need.

Man's nature makes it difficult for him to be free. His experience conditions him and limits his knowledge of alternatives and choices. Education must liberate man, not condition him (Tiedeman and Field, 1962). Guidance stands with man and with education as the liberating process of education helps him to learn to be free and responsible. If guidance can fulfill its nature and succeed in the task that has only recently come into focus, the future can be brighter than the past.

SUMMARY

The historical background of guidance has been presented in order to show the total milieu out of which guidance has developed. The industrial revolution, urbanization, and immigration are examples of major forces that created needs for guidance. The events that are known as first practices of guidance have been placed within historical perspective.

Many parallel events and societal developments were taking place as guidance began its relationship with education. Psychology, mental health, sociological elements, and cultural forces are examples of areas considered.

The philosophical determinants of guidance have been analyzed. Morality, economics, and classical philosophical thought enter into the past and future of guidance. A view of the cultural perspective that surrounds guidance and an examination of the threshold upon which guidance stands have been presented.

REFERENCES AND SUGGESTED READINGS

Barry, Ruth, and Beverly Wolf, *Epitaph for Vocational Guidance,* New York: Bureau of Publications, Teachers College, Columbia University, 1962.

Barry, Ruth, and Beverly Wolf, *Modern Issues in Guidance-Personnel Work,* New York: Bureau of Publications, Teachers College, Columbia University, 1957.

Beers, Clifford W., *A Mind That Found Itself* (rev. ed.), New York: Doubleday, 1948.

Boyd, J. P., *The Declaration of Independence,* Princeton: Princeton University Press, 1945.

Brewer, J. M., *Education as Guidance,* New York: Macmillan, 1932.

Brewer, J. M., *History of Vocational Guidance,* New York: Macmillan, 1942.

Davis, J. B., *Moral and Vocational Guidance,* New York: Ginn, 1914.

Dewey, John, *Democracy and Education,* New York: Macmillan, 1915.

Gardner, John, *Excellence,* New York: Harper, 1961.

Goldman, Leo, *Using Tests in Counseling,* New York: Appleton-Century-Crofts, 1961.

Havighurst, R. J., *Developmental Tasks and Education* (2nd ed.), New York: Longmans Green, 1952.

Honeywell, R. J., *The Educational Work of Thomas Jefferson,* Cambridge: Harvard University Press, 1931.

Hutson, Percival W., *The Guidance Function in Education,* New York: Appleton-Century-Crofts, 1958.

Lerner, Max, *America as a Civilization*, New York: Simon & Schuster, 1957.

Miller, Carroll H., *Foundations of Guidance*, New York: Harper, 1961.

Norris, Willa, "Highlights in the History of the National Vocational Guidance Association," *Personnel and Guidance Journal,* XXXIII (1954), 205–208.

Parsons, F., *Choosing a Vocation*, Boston: Houghton Mifflin, 1909.

Paterson, D. G., "The Genesis of Modern Guidance," *Educational Record,* XIX (1938), 36–46.

Rockwell, P. J., and J. W. M. Rothney, "Some Social Ideas of Pioneers in the Guidance Movement," *Personnel and Guidance Journal,* XL (1961), 349–354.

Rothney, John W. M., *Guidance Practices and Results,* New York: Harper, 1958.

Super, Donald E., "Transition: From Vocational Guidance to Counseling Psychology," *Journal of Counseling Psychology,* II (1955), 3–9.

Thomas, Russell, *The Search for a Common Learning: General Education, 1800–1960,* New York: McGraw-Hill, 1962.

Thoreau, Henry David, *Walden*, Boston: Houghton Mifflin, 1957.

Tiedeman, David V., and F. L. Field, "Guidance: The Science of Purposeful Action Applied Through Education," *Harvard Educational Review,* XXXII, No. 4 (Fall, 1962), 483–501.

Vocational Guidance in Secondary Education, Commission of the Reorganization of Secondary Education of the N.E.A., Bulletin No. 19, Washington, D.C.: Government Printing Office, 1918.

THE INTERDISCIPLINARY FOUNDATION OF GUIDANCE

THE ISSUE. Guidance stands with each individual as he attempts to solve life's problems and to create a life of meaning and purpose. Guidance must utilize the knowledge and concepts of all disciplines that have helped to create and support it. The immensity of this task cannot be fully accomplished, even with the collected and ordered data that is available. Yet to ignore and not to utilize such material can result in failure for guidance before the task is begun.

Guidance has developed gradually and haltingly as a profession. The responsibilities of guidance demand that more than good will and inspiration be used to help individuals. The behavioral sciences, the social sciences, the biological and physical sciences, and the humanities can help guidance. How?

❧ ❧

Guidance is the blending of many disciplines into meaningful patterns to help individuals. The behavioral sciences of psychology, sociology, and anthropology support even the most simple activity in any guidance program. The behavioral sciences also relate to other disciplines such as economics, history, government, education, and philosophy. The humanities, as well as the behavioral sciences, give purpose and direction to guidance. These major disciplines are capable of offering not only patterns of knowledge but also sources of strength as guidance attempts to help individuals to solve problems, to be free, and to create a meaningful life.

No guidance worker can hope to be specialized in all areas of knowledge. Yet every guidance person needs to recognize, reflect, and

CHAPTER THREE

focus the contributions of many disciplines and the individual efforts of specialists in all of these areas.

Esther Lloyd-Jones has likened the guidance worker to the general practitioner in the medical field. The efforts and knowledge of physiologists, drug researchers, laboratory pathologists, neurosurgeons, psychiatrists, internists, and many other medical and scientific research specialists undergird the work of every family doctor. The task of the general physician is to recognize his debt to all who help him and to interpret their findings for his own work, to recognize his own limitations and refer cases beyond his own skill and training, to maintain and advance his own level of understanding, and in all cases to help the sick person to profit from the accumulated knowledge and facts of medicine.

The guidance worker, like the general practitioner, is the focus through which available knowledge and help can be channeled to the individual. Even as the family physician recognizes that his care cannot in itself cure the patient, so the guidance worker similarly needs to recognize that in the end it is the person himself who must secure his own present and future within a world.

Guidance rests upon the shoulders of the giants of other fields of knowledge. The most broadly educated guidance worker can only glimpse the detailed dimensions that exist within the conceptual designs of other areas. The recognition of the stature of these disciplines as they contribute to the daily work of every guidance person is an important first step for anyone concerned with an understanding of the principles upon which guidance rests. A leader in any field of human activity is more and more driven to the realization of the interdependence of human knowledge. Chemistry, physics, and biology come together in space medicine. Specialists in any area can find themselves passé and illiterate within their own lifetimes because of the inexorable march of knowledge in their own area of specialization. Guidance is a newcomer to the scene of human endeavor and the outcome of the efforts of all disciplines. Failures within the field of guidance can most frequently come when workers assume that the answers have been found, making the field of guidance static, smug, and self-satisfied.

Although it is clearly impossible to trace and to explore each discipline that supports guidance, it is clearly desirable to assess the broad dimensions of such disciplines and to examine a cross section of the knowledge that exists in each. Guidance relates to each supporting discipline in a unique fashion. As the particular nature of the relationship of a discipline to guidance is understood, it is possible to comprehend more clearly the nature of guidance and its relation to the individuals it serves and the process of education of which it is a part. Moreover, the potential guidance worker can recognize his need for a broad base of operational knowledge.

THE PROBLEM

The nature of guidance makes mandatory a thorough interdisciplinary knowledge of human behavior on the part of all guidance workers. A specific illustration can pinpoint the issue.

Pat and Maia

Pat had left high school prior to graduation in order to enlist in the service. His academic record had been average to below average and his attendance very poor. His words were: "My mother was in school more than I was. . . ." She was constantly interceding on behalf of Pat to secure his readmission after one escapade or another. The opportunity to leave school through enlistment was a welcome "out" for Pat. There was, however, no war to relieve the pressure that he felt as he said goodbye at home. "There were tears and anguished cries of me wasting my life and growing up to be nothing but a bum."

Pat served four years and left the service with no greater ambition than he had had when he entered. He looked back upon the service as four easy uneventful years in which he had simply existed and traveled around the country. He went to work in a local hat shop and settled into a routine of work and an easy civilian life. He lived at home and said that although his mother's nagging had been getting to him, it was an incident at work that had finally provided the spur to a changed pattern of action in his life.

"My job wasn't anything great but it was a good week's pay. It was that young-looking guy that had come into work after college with no experience at all. He had been given two rapid promotions and ended up as my immediate superior on a production line. I simply took stock of myself and wondered what was to lie ahead for me.

"I went back to visit with my high school guidance counselor. To hear him tell it I might as well give up; there was no hope. He said that I would have to repeat my last two years of high school and would probably not get into any college, even if I did take the two years as he had suggested. My hopes were driven down lower than the 'shoe top' level where they had been when I had hoped to do something with my life. He was a real big help and gave me a lot of 'guidance.'

"Fortunately I talked to my dentist and he suggested that I visit the admissions office of several of the colleges in town. He thought that there might be a way for me to get a special high school diploma and start college on a trial basis. He was right and I got rolling.

"What a deal; my dentist ended up as my guidance counselor." Pat was positive about his dentist and more than a little bitter about his guidance counselor.

Pat's career in college was almost meteoric. His grades were excellent and his maturity helped him in all of his classes. He was sincerely interested in learning and seemed to have discovered an intellectual curiosity that belied his early school experiences. He was, however, frequently uncertain of himself as he assessed his newfound purpose and maturity as a college student.

Pat talked about his conflicts as he attempted to look at himself and his future with his counselor in college: "You know I don't ever want to cross that bridge again after I graduate from college. The bridge leads into my neighborhood and I am almost ashamed to go home every night. I have more and more tended to draw into myself at home. Nobody ever reads more than the funny papers and the sports section. I really hate to go home sometimes. That bridge is really symbolic in my life and once I get out of there I don't ever want to go back." Or–

"You know sometimes when the family gathers at the house they all want to play 'Twenty Questions'; they think it's great sport. Actually I should feel complimented when I think of it. They all are so proud of me that they want to see all the things I know and they like to play 'Twenty Questions' for that reason. They are driving me bats." Or–

"You know this whole business of dressing up is a fraud." Pat could appear one day in dirty chinos and a sweat shirt, needing a shave and the next in a dapper pearl gray suit with an appropriate waistcoat and a light gray topcoat with hat to match. His taste in clothes was excellent and he had learned the social amenities. Still, Pat had serious questions about the whole business: "Most of these high-bred dudes are all a fake. They put on an act and really get to believe it themselves. I would take most of the crew back in the shop anytime. They don't know a Homburg from a top hat, even when they see one, but they are a hell of a lot more real as people."

It was about this time that Pat and Maia met and became attracted to each other.

......

Maia was a delicate, fair-skinned beauty. She was a year behind Pat in college and about three years younger. She was secretary of her class and a representative to the Student Council where she had met Pat.

Maia was active in many student groups and very much the belle of the school. However, she had never dated any of the boys on a steady basis and seemed to be available only at school dances or school affairs. She was something of a mystery to many of the boys and therefore doubly desirable.

Maia had confided her problems to the counselor and was attempting to struggle through a maze of social, personal, and emotional conflicts.

"I don't know what to do. I've never been able to have a real date. My parents are from the old country and they won't let me go out at all with any boy. I am lucky to get to school meetings and sometimes to other school events. I have to explain to them exactly what the occasion is and why I should be there. They both wanted to come with me in the beginning and I had a terrible time persuading them that it wouldn't be necessary.

"They were impossible in high school. My first dance at the school gym was a fiasco. Mother insisted that she should go with me; I had a tentative date with one of the fellows, but that didn't make any difference to her. I said I would try it. I ran out crying after the first few minutes when mother insisted that she would 'clear' every fellow before I danced with him. I haven't gone to another dance since. Sometimes I can get out if they aren't aware of the exact nature of the school function, but usually I don't even try. Every boy who has ever been to the house resents their attitude.

"I don't want to lie to them; what can I do?" Maia wept quietly. The men in the college simply did not see her "mysteriousness" as she did. She felt that her parents were two large millstones around her neck and that there was no hope.

Maia's social life during her high school years, with the exception of the incident at the dance, consisted only of drugstore dates at lunch time and other very superficial contacts with boys around her. College had been a glistening dream for her. She had hoped to resolve all of the problems that she had faced in high school. She realized, in retrospect, that living at home had made a solution impossible. For a whole semester she had entertained the hope of moving to the dormitory, but her parents had refused to see any sense in spending the extra money it would cost for her to live away from home.

Maia was the oldest of two children, both girls. She had been interested in nursing, teaching, and library work, but she had become depressed about her restrictions at home and her academic work had begun to suffer in her sophomore year. She had come in of her own accord to talk with a counselor about her poor grades and her lack of interests in any vocation.

Pat and Maia began to see one another between classes and to study together in the library whenever it was possible. They were becoming very fond of one another. . . .

INTERDISCIPLINARY FOUNDATIONS

Pat and Maia were of different religious faiths. Pat's name could have been Pasquale or Patrick. Maia was from a closely knit family group whose cultural roots were deeply attached to customs that are sometimes common in families with a strong rural Greek background, as well as Orthodox Hebrew, Armenian, and many other European ethnic groups. Pat and Maia were each developing as reaching, striving individuals. Each was facing crises in life that were peculiarly personal and yet were symbolic of the issues that are present in many families as college education fulfills long years of vicarious sacrifice.

Pat was able to recognize the symbolism of his crossing and recrossing of the bridge each morning and evening as he commuted to college. "You can't go home!" seemed to be the refrain that played in the lives of each of these products of family life. The paradox and the guilt engendered by the recognition of the paradox was not lost or repressed by either of these young adults. They were each struggling with the issue and had turned to guidance workers for counseling aid in solving problems of everyday living. Neither was "sick," "neurotic," "psychotic," or even, as yet, a behavior problem to the school, the family, or their peers. They were respected members of the student body, honor students at one time or another, and potentially creative graduates and citizens. They were seeking help in solving problems of living; each was seeking to be free and to be responsible. The potential tragedy in their lives was almost a daily companion as they began to seek out one another and to discuss their problems and their need for one another.

Guidance is preventive, concerned with problem-solving in the lives of normal, productive students; with helping them to become free to live up to their potential, and responsible to themselves, their families, their cultures, and their futures. How can guidance help Pat and Maia; how can counselors be of aid and comfort as such heartbreaking issues are faced and resolved? Can such issues ever be resolved satisfactorily? What are the foundations which guidance can draw upon to help such students?

A system of testing, ingenious forms for recording interviews, sumptuous offices, effective relationships with administrators, a large budget for clinic units, adequate secretarial assistance—the many issues that sometimes seem to be vital to guidance programs and guidance workers are insignificant as problems such as those of Pat and Maia are faced. The knowledge of the processes of problem-solving and the broadly based education of the counselor can be startlingly significant and useful.

No single book or treatise about man's knowledge of man and the world can include comprehensive material about all the behavioral sciences and related areas. Can a brief view of each of these areas help potential guidance workers and those who would understand guidance to appreciate the dimensions of the fields upon which guidance rests? What are the questions that can be answered by the knowledge that exists, within such disciplines?

The behavioral sciences include varying disciplines as their definitions are debated and developed. Psychology, social psychology, sociology, anthropology, cultural anthropology, and other related areas are usually characterized as behavioral sciences. Yet the social sciences of history, economics, political economy, and government, largely descriptive in past years, have become dynamic as they have drawn upon the understandings, tools, and concepts of the behavioral sciences. Studies of successful politicians, uprooted voters, obsolescent workers, and even of ancient civilizations have become startlingly different in emphasis and findings as the interplay of human beings one with another is seen to be an intervening variable in all such knowledge. The boundary lines of all academic disciplines have become less rigid, less certain. Knowledge and fact cannot be seen as static and immutable.

The social and behavioral sciences, like the physical sciences, have been changing. New issues, developments, and learnings have destroyed old shibboleths in all areas of man's knowledge about himself and his world. The new patterns that have emerged are not nearly so neat as were older conceptual designs of knowledge. Guidance, as a profession and as the practice of helping persons, is not involved in the sometimes bitter, sometimes creative conflicts that have occurred as new concepts and patterns of knowledge have been organized. But guidance workers do need to understand, study, and profit from the new interdisciplinary studies, concepts, and hypotheses as they become available. Most guidance workers are educated in one of the academic disciplines known as social behavioral sciences. Some may even enter guidance from a background of physical or biological science. Guidance persons need to be a part of, and yet separate from, all disciplines. Guidance stands with the individual as all disciplines can be made a part of his life.

PSYCHOLOGY

Psychology contributes not only to the total nature of guidance but also to the details of its every-day practice. The concept of individual development that arises out of psychology is relatively new in the scheme of man's knowledge, and yet it is at the core of all guidance. The tools of psychology are also the tools of the guidance counselor. Psychology has taught that observation and listening against a background of theory and fact can help a counselor to construct a concept of a dynamic human being, living within a constantly changing environment and culture.

Individual Development

Psychology freed man from the mechanistic systems of philosophy. Man is more than any system of knowledge and more than the product of any single or group force. Through psychology man has been recognized as the complex product of his environment and his own heredity and as the basic unit of society and culture. Man has been recognized, through the systematic study of human development, as a unique individual who is more intricate than any physical force or feature in our universe.

The interacting forces of environment and heredity produce in each person a unique combination of characteristics and patterns of behavior that separate him from all other persons and yet at the same time unite him with all human beings. The complex maturational processes within each person take place against a constantly changing cultural and physical environment. The motivational factors that lie beneath all patterns of behavior create within each person particular values, goals, and life objectives. Pat and Maia are such persons; each is a product of his or her past, present personality, and potential for growth.

The development of the individual takes place through the complex processes of learning and problem-solving. The most simple types of animal learning can still puzzle research workers whose task is to isolate the learning process and to formulate theories and laws of learning. The constant adjustment patterns, the endless problem-solving nature of life, and the environmentally and personally produced frustrations that exist in all of life create the puzzle that is man. The early successes of psychology have dramatically affected the daily life of all persons. Yet the ever-growing complexity of man and his ways have continued to frustrate research and applied psychology alike.

The science of psychology, like all other areas of man's knowledge, yields facts that often do not clearly relate one to another. The search for knowledge is constant and tortuous. Nevertheless, psychologists have undertaken the understanding of the nature of human behavior. Guidance workers are among the most immediate users of the concepts and principles that emerge about man and his nature as a complex living organism.

Dimensions of Individuality

Early psychology produced many methods and tools for the study of individual man. The attempt to assess the essential nature of individual development required the development of such tools. The exploration of man's nature continues as more and better tools have been created.

That guidance uses the very specific tools of the psychologist is not always recognized. The interview, the test, the analysis, group behavior studies, systematic case data, even the more gross procedures of simple observation, anecdotal recording of phenomena, and the use of the scientific method—all are the tools that psychology has shared with guidance.

Early psychologists attempted to assess individual differences through psychophysical methods. Weight differentiation, heat intensity, visual acuity, and similar physical factors were the early subjects for research. The individuality of man was at first a puzzle to psychological researchers. Although many false starts preceded the systematic collection of data about the characteristics that separated man from man, interests, aptitudes, intelligence, values, personality, adjustment patterns, and even career patterns eventually came to be the first concerns of the research psychologist as he attempted to delineate the ways in which man differed from man.

That each person is different from every other is a concept that is difficult to grasp. Each individual possesses traits and characteristics that may be different according to test scores and measures. Even when two individuals are represented to be virtually alike on all known continuums, they are still startlingly different in subtle and gross ways that psychological measures cannot assess.

Human Potentialities

Every person in the process of growing and developing as an individual creates personal goals and objectives. These goals may be viewed from many different perspectives. The very young child may wish that he could go to school like all of the older children who are in kindergarten. The soon-to-be-retired postal worker may dream of the books he plans to read and the formal garden he hopes to construct. Persons at all ages create plans and hopes for themselves. The potential for success in any venture that is planned arises out of individual capability, opportunity, and aspiration level. Man affects and creates societies, cultures, and civilizations in his striving for life.

The nature of man is only partially understood by the most advanced psychologist and research specialist. The animal nature of man as a physical creature, the cultural nature of man as a member of a human society, and the creative nature of man as a product of the interaction of the first two elements has already been explored. The unexplored potentials that exist in all persons are partially understood through psychology and are expanded through education. Guidance becomes a type of human investment broker as it helps individuals to understand themselves through psychology and to profit from education.

The nature of man is not static nor is it limited by the score obtained on any series of psychological measures. The potential of man rests more in what he can become, rather than in what he has been or in what he may be at any single instant of time. Psychology has begun to unlock the mysteries of the person, just as physical scientists have begun to explore the atom. What we know is far less than what we suspect or what we can barely glimpse.

Psychology and Guidance

Psychology provides the key concept of man as a developing human organism with horizons that can only be conceived in terms of process rather than content. If man is the proper subject matter for man, psychology is conducting a study that must remain uppermost in the mind of any guidance worker. Guidance depends upon the concepts, tools, and progress in research that is accomplished in psychology. The guidance worker becomes, as much as any sociologist, anthropologist, or political scientist, an applied psychologist.

The danger of psychology as a source of understanding of individual development is in the halting, uncertain nature of its progress in fact and theory. The contributions of a Sigmund Freud are still being assessed and redirected. The newest contributions of a motivational psychologist need to be evaluated along with Pavlov's dog salivating for food at the sound of a bell and with Skinner's pigeon learning to peck at a round disk in order to get a food pellet.

Guidance profits from the discoveries of psychology, and yet it must be aware, as is psychology, of the undetermined importance of many facts and contributions that come from psychological research.

Pat and Maia are building their lives. How have they developed as persons? What are the effects of their developmental experiences within a family, a community, a culture? How do they look at themselves? Psychology can begin to supply tools, procedures, and theories that can provide such data.

SOCIOLOGY

Sociology is concerned with the origins and patterns of society. The forms, institutions, and functions that individual man and men in groups can and have created are the issues which sociology studies, codifies, and conceptualizes. Man as a social animal is both affected by the society of which he is a member and at the same time is creative within, and contributory to, the society within which he lives. Society can be viewed as a part of the total culture that man creates for himself.

Pat and Maia were both members of societal groups at all levels of complexity. Each was influenced by his or her family structure and responded to the mores, customs, and forms of the family and subunits of his or her own particular society. The conflicts they were facing were not only intrapersonal or psychological issues, but were also conditioned by the lives they had lived as members of a family and of a society. The crosscurrents of neighborhood, religion, nationalistic custom, family traditions, and even social recreation patterns were beneath the surface of some of the frustrations that were felt by these two young persons and that frequently broke above the surface of everyday problem-solving. Sociology offers concepts that can help explain the behavior of these students and assess the dimensions of possible solutions to their problems.

Society

Man has bound himself to others through the creation of society as a conceptual design of life. The community of the aboriginal in Australia is structured as a design for a life, as is the small New England town. The cooperative pattern of life that a group establishes in order to perpetuate itself is a concept that crosses all racial and political boundary lines. Not only are communities of varying sizes established as societies, but subsocieties exist within every community. The social needs of groups are supplemented by the economic, ethnic, and historical facts of existence.

The City Planning Commission of New York City has attempted to map the boundary lines of approximately 87 separate neighborhoods within the confines of New York City. A city charter revision of 1963 requires completion of the task by 1968. The lines of neighborhoods flow and shift as the listed dimensions of social structure are examined. Historical roots demand one boundary, economic practices form another, ethnic similarities create a third, and the boundaries merge and diverge as other criteria are applied.

Life within each societal unit is circumscribed by customs, beliefs, value patterns, and by the institutions that have been developed within the society. Each person is subject to pressures from such a supporting environment and at the same time creates added dimensions to affect his own and others' lives within such a unit. The individual must be born, must grow, must explore and develop as a person in a society. The conceptual designs that can help guidance workers appreciate life as it is lived in varying societies are practical data that enter into problem-solving issues of all types.

FORMS OF SOCIETY. Each societal unit develops patterns of living and of problem-solving that are made up of habits, norms, mores, and customs. The definitions of such terms may vary, but all refer to ways of doing things that are not always reflected within the laws or legal history of a society. They are often held with a force equal to or greater than law. Folkways, customs, and mores are different levels of patterns designed to regulate behavior within a society. The ethical strength of these controls frequently makes them more effective than the laws which govern a larger unit of society to which the subunit belongs. Villages on political borders have frequently had their allegiances to a central government changed forcibly, but life within the villages may continue unchanged even though it may be illegal under new governmental controls. Society exists at all levels, not merely the national.

Customs of dress, speech, travel, courtship, marriage, child-rearing, and death rites are all elements of life that are controlled by a society. The young are instructed in the acceptable patterns of solving the problems that must be faced as life progresses. Limits of behavior are established and penalties are inflicted for transgression. The internalization—the acceptance of the patterns as "right" and appropriate for governing behavior—is accomplished through a type of societal "osmosis" as well as through instruction. "Osmosis" is simply a general term for the many little learnings that take place throughout life. Subliminal learnings—learnings and conditioning even below the level of conscious knowledge—can also make up a part of such behavior determination.

INSTITUTIONS OF SOCIETY. A society is organized and patterned into institutions that help order, control, and perpetuate it. The family is a primary group within almost every society. The institution of the family helps to provide for the continuation of the species, offers an arena for the instruction of the young in the ways of the society, and serves as an economic, political, and religious unit. The family may be defined in various ways in different societies. Matriarchal lines are maintained in some known societies; fraternal lines are dominant in others.

The church, government, education, military practices, and other institutions also serve the needs of the society. Patterns, forms, and even functions may vary within societies, but each known society establishes its institutions as formal structures to serve the group as a whole.

The society that establishes institutions may be as nonliterate and essentially primitive as that of the American Indians, or as modern and highly industrialized as that of Sweden. The American Indians divided themselves into many political units; Sweden is nationalistic and is geographically a political entity. The design of a concept of sociology must encompass such societal interactions. Even more significant is the analysis that can be made of subunits of larger societal groups. The neighborhoods of New York City, the ethnic settlements within the

United States, and even religious, economic, and geographical differences can help to construct patterns of life that can qualify as societies with institutions. Such are the complexities that help to determine the everyday behavior of each child within a group.

FUNCTIONS IN SOCIETY. Sociology characterizes the forms and the institutions that govern and define life for all persons. A further area of study within the field of sociology is the concept of function that exists concurrently with such institutions.

Function is the means used by man to solve a specific issue. The need to earn a living, to eat, to protect and maintain a physical organism, to perpetuate the species through reproduction, and even to relax through recreation are all examples of functions that are within the purview of the sociologist. The nature of the function and the forms, institutions, and patterns of control that are exerted within a society help to explain the behavior of the members of that society.

The occupational patterns of older European groups also illustrate function within sociology. The family traditions of craftsmanship, apprenticeship, and occupational secrets have been largely lost in the highly industrialized society of contemporary America. Yet the traditional pride in workmanship and in family guilds are frequently found in communities in which occupational opportunities are limited and restricted by geography, climate, and other economic considerations.

Functions combined with institutions and forms constitute the major conceptual designs of sociology. Societies are analyzed, profiled, catalogued, and compared in sociological studies in order to establish the particular patterns of behavioral determinants that are operative in all groups. Culture as a broader concept is a part of anthropology as well as of sociology and is examined in greater detail in a later section. The issues and conceptual designs in sociology and anthropology overlap. The issues of the design and structure of sociology as an academic discipline are complicated by disagreement on definitions and by the complex nature of many concepts. For example, caste and class, as they exist in sociology and anthropology, are forms, institutions, and norms and at the same time reflect functions in many social groups. Clear-cut, definitive statements cannot yet be made in these complex areas.

Sociology and Guidance

The emphasis on environment in some early sociological writings has helped to drive a wedge between some guidance practices and the principles that can arise out of sociology. Guidance workers have often been loath to leave the school and enter into the homes, the communities, and the institutional units of the society that surround the school. School social workers have been specially prepared to function within this area, and too frequently the guidance worker has assumed that sociology specialists cannot help in counseling, occupational planning, educational problem-solving, and the establishment of life objectives. Sociology enters into the life of every student, and if guidance workers are to aid in the problem-solving, life-constructing process, they must be aware of the dimensions of the student's life and of the issues that can and will enter into any future decision and life-construction process. Trained sociologists can and do work side by side with guidance specialists.

Although psychology may be concerned primarily with the "inside" view of the person, and sociology may be concerned with the "outside" view, the guidance worker is concerned with both views. A two-dimensional view of individuals is naïve and partial. Pat and Maia are products of the societies into which they were born, in which they grew up, and which they attempt to understand as they seek to construct lives of their own. The freedom of the person to fulfill his capacity depends upon the knowledge that he is at the same time both conditioned and free. Responsibility to oneself, a self that has been formed by life within a society, is part of the problem of creating a future concept of self. Psychology and sociology, even when combined, fall short as a foundation for providing aid to all persons in solving issues of such complexity.

ANTHROPOLOGY

Anthropology is the science of man. It is as broad as man and the world in which he lives. Although the world is physical, the world of man is more than physical. The interaction of man with his world has permitted him to create a concept of culture. Culture provides a frame of reference for man as a developing organism and as a producer of that frame.

The culture concept is complex and yet basic to anthropology and the behavioral sciences. Culture is man-made. It is the sum of all that man has created to help him solve problems, live, and give meaning to his life. Persons living in societies, creating forms and institutions, and providing for the functions of life—these are the creators of culture.

The small child who first sees all banks (perhaps because of their governmental-like structure) as "official" is wrestling with the concept of culture. As banks are seen to be private enterprises, like candy stores, they are more easily seen to be creations of man. Governments are also both the creations of men and the institutions of the society they serve. The pomp and circumstance of a religious ceremony, a military act, or even of the civil procedure for marriage are considered "right" by the persons involved. The child undergoing, participating in, or observing such cultural rites seldom sees them as related to the games for which he makes up the rules. Yet all men are like such a child, for culture is a man-made concept. As a force, culture is directing, controlling, interpreting, and gives meaning to life, but man is the one who makes up the rules and then plays the game.

Anthropologists have long studied isolated, nonliterate cultures or societies in order to examine the concept of culture in simple form. The uprooting of ancient artifacts, the archaeologist's pick and pith helmet have been caricatured in cartoons and motion pictures many times. Yet the examination of such societal units has helped to build the foundation for anthropology. Anthropology, however, is not pith helmets and picks, nor the dust and confusion of museums. It is, in the words of Malinowski (1944), the "Magistra Vitae."

Anthropology gives meaning to all the behavioral sciences, to the physical and social sciences, and to man's efforts to create life. The cross-fertilizing nature of anthropology helps to give dimension to psychology, and it helps sociology expand and provide meaning for the forms, institutions, and functions of societies. Anthropology unites archaeology, psychology, sociology, science and technology, the descriptive social sciences, and even man's creations—the humanities; anthropology is the study of man in his world.

Methods of Anthropology

Anthropology traces its history more to the biological than to the physical sciences. Anthropology is rooted therefore more in the inductive method of reasoning than in the experimental method of the laboratory. The analysis of cultures cannot be made under controlled experimental conditions. Yet as anthropology has developed it has not only shared but expanded the experimental methods of all sciences. It has utilized the projective techniques of the psychological tester, the case-study concepts of the sociologist, the descriptive narratives of the chronicler, and of course the reconstruction concepts of the archaeologist. Moreover, anthropology has used them in unified form.

The methods of anthropology are the methods of all disciplines. All processes for accumulating facts, achieving understandings, and applying results are appropriate for the anthropologist. The significant method which is peculiarly that of the anthropologist is that of total interpretative analysis and synthesis. Anthropology must assume not only the complex task of dissecting a subunit of the society of American Indian culture, but must also examine the social change that accompanies automation in modern Western civilization. The techniques that were developed in halting fashion in small units are now being transposed, refined, and applied to ever more broadly conceived areas. The instrumentality of man as a creator of culture is being examined on all levels of life. The methods are only partially adequate; the tasks are immense. Anthropology, however, is attempting to answer the questions about life and man that can neither be asked nor answered by any other discipline.

Structure in Anthropology

Methodology in anthropology is complex, and structure within the field is even more intricate in design. The evolutionary concept of individuals banding together into a group and into a society to create a civilization and a culture is basic to the nature and structure of the field. The stage, or progressing unit, method of study has helped to compile theory and explain data. The historical descriptive concept of man is similarly part of the nature of anthropology. The varying concepts of culture in different parts of the world and the issues of whether or not cultural invention or cultural transmittal explains the nature of a given society can be partially understood when historical concepts are ordered and understood. The comparative analysis of culture and societies, with all of the complex data that can be gathered from an examination of total units of society, also gives perspective and meaning to a knowledge of the individual. More recent concept-building has helped anthropology and those who work in the field of anthropology to organize the discipline as a functional approach to an explanation of life and man.

Clearly anthropology is composed of many elements organized in various patterns. The very nature of the field is confused by the immensity of the task undertaken by those who strive to order such a vast area.

Anthropology and Guidance

The scope of guidance may seem narrow when compared with the structure of anthropology as a discipline. Yet guidance, as well as anthropology, is concerned with total man. Man's efforts at problem-solving, living, and creating are at the heart of guidance and anthropology. Man must be able both to make decisions and to obtain perspective about them. Pat and Maia are individuals attempting to cope with the customs, traditions, and man-made controls on their lives. Yet these young people do not have the perspective to help their parents or their community to see the tasks that they are undertaking and the frustrations, conflicts, and problems that must be resolved.

Perhaps no counselor or guidance worker can help any person assess fully the dimensions of the issues involved in even the most simple acts of problem-solving or living as a member of a society. The persons facing the decisions frequently lack perspective and background. Can those who would help lack the same qualities?

No guidance worker can truly understand the dimensions of the problems faced by a young American Indian attempting to leave the microcosm of the reservation. The Negro who is "passing" as white, the interfaith marriages of Jews, Protestants, Catholics, Mohammedans, or Buddhists, the conflicts of the African student who is assumed to be from the American south, the southern white who is facing militarily induced integration in his community—such issues are constantly present in normal life.

The issues are present in more cases than those arising out of such grossly conflicting psychological, sociological, and cultural concepts. The confusion of the young child who fears he will be abandoned when his parents go out for the night, the adolescent who doesn't have a date for the prom, the teen-ager who smokes cigarettes in order to be adult and important, the eldest child who in college acts out his father's need for vicarious success—such problems are a part of everyday life within a society. Life is a problem-solving process conducted within a supporting culture that makes freedom possible and demands responsibility. Guidance workers who would sit with those who would be free and responsible must know and understand the dimensions and meanings of their own freedom and responsibility.

OTHER SOCIAL SCIENCES

Economics, political science, history, government, and related specialities support many aspects of guidance. The behavioral sciences serve more directly as a foundation for helping individuals grow, develop, and construct a life, but the other social sciences are also vital to areas of problem-solving.

Economics

One of the traditional and still significant functions of guidance is to help the individual select, enter, and succeed in an occupation. Economics describes the area of operation for any occupationally productive person. The labor market, automation, the rewards of work, the demands of the job, the regulations of the government—these are a few of the elements of the complex problem-solving area in which guidance is assumed to be competent to help an individual make decisions.

The nature of career-development research has changed radically in recent years. The concepts arising out of the behavioral sciences have helped to clarify the identity-seeking nature of occupational choice. Occupational development is not only an attempt to gain economic security, but is also a process of creating a plan of life, a concept of living.

The days when Benjamin Franklin was escorted around his native Boston by his father to view the available occupations are long gone. The prospective employee in today's industrialized space age may not even be able to conceive of the position he may fill when his preparation period is over. Occupational information was once a primary but known content area for counselors to discuss with students. But as the data becomes more complex each day, the task is no longer to make it available to the student, but to help him collect, order, and integrate such information into a pattern of life choices.

The economics needed by guidance workers is not a narrow textbook knowledge of profit and loss, nor even variable theories of business cycles. These concepts are only beginning points for the guidance person who must help the student enter into a world affected by economic principles. By combining both theoretical and practical economics, guidance can provide for the functional use of vast amounts of knowledge accumulated, ordered, and integrated out of the behavioral sciences and thereby affect the life of a single student.

History, Government, and Political Science

Through history the sweep of man's existence is recorded and interpreted for succeeding members of the human race. Government examines the constructs, rules, and patterns used by peoples to order their lives. Political science strives to analyze the methods used to achieve and maintain political power. The descriptive or chronicle function of these social sciences has been merged with the dynamic study of the individual and the group. Studies of the voter in the city, of the successful politician, of a period in history, of the failure of a city government—all examine the individual and the group in operation. The content areas of study can be differentiated; the behavior is that of individuals.

The functioning of persons in all areas of social science is a meaningful study for guidance workers. Such disciplines affect the lives of individuals profoundly. The very nature of individual freedom and responsibility depends upon an understanding of the historical and philosophical developments not only in Western civilization but in previous societies and civilizations as well. The concept of government in the Western world has given life to the ideals of individual freedom and responsibility. Guidance must know about the lives that have and can be created. Pat and Maia are products of specific societies with histories and patterns. They can, in turn, affect those units as they assume active roles as citizens.

THE BIOLOGICAL AND PHYSICAL SCIENCES

The biological nature of man is important to anthropology and all of the social sciences. Man cannot be divided into small pieces and put back together only in the final chapter of a textbook. The separation of the biological and physical sciences from the behavioral and social sciences is arbitrary and can be defended only as a construct to facilitate careful examination.

The scientific method is applicable in all investigations of man and his world. In the study of the material of man's world, however, it is possible to be more discrete and concrete than is possible with conceptual designs that cannot be weighed, measured, and counted.

The experimental method is the basic pattern in all science. The control of dependent variables and the investigation of the experimental variable have permitted man to assess and understand his environment, including his own physical structure. The methods of psychology, sociology, and anthropology as well as the application of all of the social sciences are dependent upon such experimental methods.

Few guidance workers are specialists in physical science, in biology, or in the applications of such knowledge. Yet these areas are among the most important aspects of modern life. Scientific investigation must be a part of man's search for knowledge. The ordering and utilization of such data permit man to know his world and to create a concept of life to fit his dreams of what it can and should be.

THE HUMANITIES

I saw a man pursuing the horizon;
Round and round they sped.

. . . .

"It is futile," I said,
"You can never—"
"You lie," he cried,
And ran on.[1]

Stephen Crane's description of man's pursuit of meaning is symbolic of all of the humanities. Man seeks, has sought, and continues to seek the dimensions and nature of the good life. Although beauty and truth are ethereal and tenuous concepts, they are nevertheless measures of man. Man creates structures, forms, patterns, even civilizations and cultures. In all these man is seeking to express his nature and his purpose in life.

The humanities encompass all of man's creations, but especially that which is beautiful and truthful. The practical elements of life can serve man, but they cannot provide a purpose for his existence. The creation of a poem, a statue, or a painting is not necessarily useful in living or in solving the problems of life. Man's capacity to live, to understand life, and to measure his own life are dimensions of philosophy, of aesthetics, of ethics—in fact, of all that is known as the humanities.

Neither philosophy nor guidance can provide a road map for life. The nature and meaning of life are riddles with which all must live. For guidance to assume that it can roughly shove philosophy out of its chair at the head of the knowledge table is not only the most ribald jest, but a puerile vision of grandeur. Guidance can only stand with the individual as issues are faced; the issues are as real with or without guidance. Guidance can only hope to give the individual a better understanding of the problem and to help him assess and choose solutions that may be appropriate for him.

[1] From *Stephen Crane: An Omnibus*, Robert W. Stallman (ed.), Knopf, 1952. Reprinted by permission of Alfred A. Knopf, Incorporated.

Philosophy

What are reality and human nature? The questions about life and its meaning, life's relation to the individual, and the dimensions of the good life must be assessed by every person as his life develops. Philosophy is no longer in an ivory tower. The issues of philosophy are the questions that each person attempts to solve as he uses his education to become a constructive member of his culture.

The questions of values, freedom, responsibility, and creativity are concerns of philosophy, of psychology, and certainly of an individual who is determining his life. A sense of existence is necessary to the development of purpose and meaning. The tasks may be ignored: an individual may become an unthinking automaton or may attempt to live according to the solutions of others. Guidance and education in America reject these alternatives as valuable outcomes of life within a responsible society, although such results are possible.

The very nature of guidance is determined by the examination of the philosophical principles that control the role that guidance assumes with an individual. What Archibald MacLeish calls the "Act of Faith" or the "American Proposition" (see Chapter One) is established and maintained by the philosophical position that has been adopted by the American society and is the major export of Western civilization to the other civilizations of the world. The faith in the individual that this philosophical view promotes is the keystone of our society. Guidance assumes a responsibility to help persons become free and responsible to themselves and to a society.

Ethics

The study of ethics and philosophy are joined by the principles of reality and human nature that are developed in the search for knowledge. Ethics depends upon the concepts that the philosopher offers those who would live a patterned, meaningful life. What are the morals that can guide behavior? What are the duties of man to himself and to his society? What is the relationship of man's nature to his actions, obligations, and purposes? These are the great issues of all times, of all societies, of all civilizations. The individual answers such questions constantly in everyday life. Education and guidance depend upon the premise that the examined life is the life worth living.

Aesthetics

The concept that the humanities deal only with the "polite" learnings has helped to separate the humanities from philosophy and ethics. The separation of these elements serves only to remove beauty and meaning from the actual business of life. The objects of the artist, whether they be of a material or nonmaterial nature, are products of a culture and reflect man's understanding of his total existence. A musical composition, a poem, a novel, a painting, a bit of sculpture, the architecture of a building, even the beauty of an age—these cannot be judged solely by their usefulness, their instructive nature, or even their balance or symmetry. Art objects must be judged as representations of man and his world, for man creates these objects of beauty. The beauty and truth of man's own life as he creates it is the supreme measure of man's aesthetic, ethical, and philosophical existence.

Guidance and the Humanities

The behavioral and social sciences serve as foundations for the practice of guidance. The biological and physical sciences help all social scientists to investigate, to assess, and to order the material world around man. The humanities, and only the humanities, can help guidance to value life and its practice. Psychology helps guidance to the realization that values are learned, but learned values must be assessed against the yardstick of man's own understanding of himself and his world. Man cannot give meaning or purpose to his life without understanding the aesthetic as well as the practical nature of human behavior.

The humanities can direct the choices of values and the solving of problems that create man's freedom and responsibility. The quality, purpose, and meaning of life are revealed as these privileges are exercised. Pat and Maia can be partially understood by an assessment of their values, ethics, and life objectives. In turn they need to assess their own values, ethics, and life objectives as they make decisions and, if possible, solve their problems.

THE ROLE OF GUIDANCE

The importance of guidance in education and life is often poorly understood and will frequently be denied even by guidance workers.

Yet if the basic premise as to the nature of guidance is accepted—that guidance stands with persons as choices are made and as problems are solved to create a life with meaning and purpose—guidance cannot deny its central role in education.

Guidance is made up of services, practicalities, bits of educational flotsam and jetsam. Still guidance is at the heart of the educational process that is dedicated to the development of the person within a free society. The task is to organize, order, and evaluate the elements of guidance so that it can accomplish its task. As guidance succeeds it helps to focus for each student not only his own nature and role in the world, but also the knowledge and wisdom that has been marshaled for all members of our society.

The task of guidance calls for humility. It may function at the center of the educational process if it can fulfill its responsibilities to persons, education, and educators, but it cannot hope to provide solutions to all of lifes' problems. Pat and Maia may find heartbreak and tragedy their measure in life. Guidance can only attempt to help persons find possible solutions from the knowledge and concepts of life that have been made available by others. As a part of all learning and knowledge, guidance cannot deny its forbears without destroying itself.

However, it can also be said that if guidance cannot accept its responsibilities to a free society, those who created guidance will find another way to accomplish their objectives. Max Lerner has characterized the Soviet society as possessing "a stick, a plan, and a faith." Our free society was described as having "an elite, an elan, and an ethos." A free society, dedicated to the revolution of the individual, will and must find a way to help persons; otherwise freedom will die. Free and responsible persons in a democratic society can help to develop individual freedom and opportunity throughout the world that is the only known boundary of man.

SUMMARY

Guidance has arisen out of and is supported by the behavioral and social sciences, the biological and physical sciences, and the humanities. The cases of Pat and Maia have been used to illustrate the meanings of these many disciplines within individual lives.

The behavorial sciences make it possible to study man as a dynamic, creative organism. Psychology, sociology, and anthropology are the major pillars of such a dynamic view of man. The social sciences as a whole examine the dimensions of life and the operations of man within his created world of society, civilization, and culture. Economics, history, government, and political science have been analyzed as they relate to guidance and the operation of guidance programs. The biological and physical sciences have been presented as ways of knowing man's material world. The humanities offer knowledge and concepts in the areas of philosophy, ethics, and aesthetics.

Guidance has been examined as a concept created out of and still a part of all of the disciplines that support a free society.

REFERENCES AND SUGGESTED READINGS

Benedict, Ruth, *Patterns of Culture*, New York: Mentor Books, 1934.

Brameld, Theodore, *Cultural Foundations of Education,* New York: Harper, 1957.

Bushnell, John H., "Student Culture at Vassar," in Nevitt Sanford (ed.), *The American College*, New York: Wiley, 1962, 489–514.

Frank, Lawrence K., *Nature and Human Nature,* New Brunswick, N.J.: Rutgers University Press, 1951.

Frank, Lawrence K., *Personality and Culture,* New York: Hinds, Hayden & Eldridge, 1948.

Frank, Lawrence K., *The School as Agent for Cultural Renewal,* Cambridge: Harvard University Press, 1959.

Frank, Lawrence K., *Society as the Patient,* New Brunswick, N.J.: Rutgers University Press, 1948.

Fromm, Erich, *Escape from Freedom,* New York: Farrar and Rinehart, 1941.

Fromm, Erich, *The Sane Society*, New York: Rinehart, 1955.

Gillin, John, *The Ways of Men,* New York: Appleton-Century-Crofts, 1948.

Hinkle, R. C., Jr., and G. J. Hinkle, *The Development of Modern Sociology,* Garden City, N.J.: Doubleday, 1954.

Hughes, E., *et al.*, "Student Culture and Academic Effort," in Nevitt Sanford (ed.), *The American College,* New York: Wiley, 1962, 515–535.

Jones, Howard M., "Education and One World," in L. Bryson *et al.* (eds.), *Goals for American Education,* New York: Harper, 1950, 213–234.

Kendler, H. H., "Problems in Problem-Solving Research," in *Current Trends in Psychological Theory,* Pittsburgh: University of Pittsburgh Press, 1961, 180–207.

Kimball, Solon T., "An Anthropological View of Social System and Learning," speech to American Personnel and Guidance Association, 1962.

Klinger, M. R., "Moral Values Across Cultures," in *Personnel and Guidance Journal,* XLI (1962), 139–144.

Kroeber, A. L., *Anthropology,* New York: Harcourt, Brace & World, 1948.

Lerner, Max, *America as a Civilization*, New York: Simon & Schuster, 1957.

Malinowski, Bronislaw, *A Scientific Theory of Culture and Other Essays,* Chapel Hill, N.C.: University of North Carolina Press, 1944.

Mead, Margaret, *The School in the American Culture,* Cambridge: Harvard University Press, 1951.
Mead, Margaret, *Social Structure,* New York: Oxford University Press, 1949.
Murphy, Gardner, "The Cultural Context of Guidance," *Personnel and Guidance Journal,* XXXIII (1955), 8–14.
Newcomb, Theodore M., "Student Peer-Group Influence," in Nevitt Sanford (ed.), *The American College,* New York: Wiley, 1962, 469–488.
Reiss, Albert J., *Occupations and Social Status,* Glencoe, Ill.: Free Press, 1961.
Sanford, Nevitt (ed.), *The American College,* New York: Wiley, 1962.
Seward, Georgene (ed.), *Clinical Studies in Culture Conflict,* New York Ronald, 1958.
Stein, M. R., *et al.* (eds.), *Identity and Anxiety,* Glencoe, Ill.: Free Press, 1960.
Taba, Hilda, *School Culture,* Washington, D.C.: American Council on Education, 1955.

THE PURPOSES OF GUIDANCE

THE ISSUE. What are the purposes of guidance; or as some may suggest, does guidance have any purpose? Various objectives and reasons why guidance does and should exist have been developed during the half-century of growth and experimentation.

Carroll H. Miller in his comprehensive treatment of the foundations of guidance states the question as follows: "What then is the basis on which it may be decided that one boy or girl shall receive this kind of education, and another that kind? Is it ability? The needs of society? His prospects based on his socio-economic position? His own choice? The choice of his parents? Or a kind of mystical 'destiny'?" (1961, p. 141).[1] Despite his broad view of guidance, Miller's answer to this question is pessimistic:

> This fundamental question of a basis for guidance has not yet been answered. Being non-directive as a technique in counseling is one thing; but offering non-direction as an answer to this question is quite another matter and amounts to an assertion of complete individualism. It is perhaps not too much to suggest that even now guidance as such has not achieved a philosophy. Rather, guidance practice simply reflects the particular educational setting in which it operates. This may be desirable, but it just passes the question back to the philosophy of the particular school or school system. [p. 141][1]

Miller charges that guidance is a process with no philosophy, either a chameleon within an institutional setting or a headless horse-

[1] Reprinted by permission of Harper & Row, Publishers, Incorporated.

CHAPTER FOUR

man pounding ahead with no concept of direction. These charges are serious and offered in sincerity. If Miller is correct, guidance is indeed the infantile discipline that some have condemned.

The problem is that guidance has had to grow and function at the same time that its basic premises were being gradually and often painfully developed. Guidance has developed concepts of purpose and philosophy as problems and conflicts have been resolved. No single set of principles has yet been offered and accepted by all persons within the field.

The pieces of a guidance philosophy have fitted together slowly. Although many pieces may still be missing, the basic design is now evident. The dimensions of a philosophy of guidance are broad; the nature of purposes in guidance is complex. Guidance must fit into the purposes of a democracy and into education in a free society. Guidance must serve individuals as they grow, develop, and choose freely their own role in a society. The purposes of guidance need to be examined; the structure and design of all purposes must be exposed and evaluated.

Guidance began as an attempt to aid students in selecting proper vocations, in providing adequate living conditions, and in maintaining their mental health. From these beginnings, actually only a few decades ago, guidance has grown into an instrument of national policy. It has become a primary element in education and a tool of culture as persons are aided to develop within a free society. Several purposes of guidance may now be identified that are significant and startling in their scope and design.

These purposes cannot be viewed as independent elements, but as interlocking premises supporting guidance while at the same time serving as goals or objectives. No single purpose is clearly more basic than any other, but guidance would be weakened if any were removed.

Five statements of purpose that guidance has developed will be examined:

1. Guidance, as a part of national effort, helps to uncover, develop, and utilize human talent and capacity.
2. Guidance provides for the individualization of education.
3. Guidance helps persons to seek self-realization and self-fulfillment.
4. Guidance aids persons to relate self-realization and fulfillment to societal and cultural purposes.
5. Guidance contributes to the extension and effective utilization of individual freedom.

NATIONAL PURPOSE AND GUIDANCE

Guidance has become an instrument of national policy in the United States. The constant challenge of the cold war following World War II helped to focus the attention of the country upon its human as well as its armament resources. Guidance has become a major tool of the educational process that is dedicated to the total development of manpower within a society.

The shortage of trained engineers and scientists in the 1950s led to a national recognition that more effective means of identifying and encouraging talent were needed. The emphasis on technology and science almost resulted in a narrow policy of centering upon the identification and selection of potentially able specialists. The exclusion of all other fields was a very real danger as the legislators attempted to help the country. The American Personnel and Guidance Association helped very materially in preventing the development of such a restrictive national policy, offering the following statement (1958):

> Faced by a tragic shortage of scientists and technologists, we are strongly tempted to solve the manpower problem by channeling outstanding high school and college students into scientific and technical careers. Here lies the danger of tampering with freedom of choice. If the top academic potentiality of this nation were to be forced into a single, selected pattern, generations of youth would lose the privilege of freely choosing their life careers—a privilege cherished by youth

throughout the history of this nation. Such a course of action might not solve even part of the problem, for a lack of educated talent persists in all areas of our national life. The solution, therefore, must be viewed from a broader perspective, and we must aim toward utilizing *every available* talent. Only then will the demand for scientists and technologists be met, along with the demand for educated talent in all fields.

Utilization of human potentialities depends upon two factors: one, the nation's decisions to turn needed educated talent to national uses; two, the maximum growth of human talent through our educational processes. This statement concerns only the latter.

Through education, it is possible to alleviate the present manpower shortage without damaging freedom of choice. This freedom can instead be enriched through the educational process, for persons can grow to the height of their potentialities when:

1. They know their potentialities, interests, and values.
2. They have the opportunity to develop them through education.
3. They know about the complex, rapidly changing career picture.
4. They are motivated to develop their potentialities and to relate them to the opportunities in our society.[2]

Guidance leaders, in the best political traditions of this country, became enlightened lobbyists and helped Congress frame the National Defense Education Act of 1958. Public Law 85–864 states in part:

> The congress hereby finds and declares that the security of the nation requires the fullest development of the mental resources and technical skills of its young men and women. The present emergency demands that additional and more adequate educational opportunities be made available. The defense of this Nation depends upon the mastery of modern techniques developed from complex scientific principles. It depends as well upon the discovery of new principles, new techniques, and new knowledge.
>
> We must increase our efforts to identify and educate more of the talent of our Nation. This requires programs that will give assurance that no student of ability will be denied an opportunity for higher education because of financial need; will correct as rapidly as possible the existing imbalances in our educational programs which have led to an insufficient proportion of our population educated in science, mathematics, and modern foreign languages and trained in technology.

Guidance has become involved in the national purpose of the country and in the construction of a society that is dedicated to the

[2] From "A Statement of Policy Concerning the Nation's Human Resources Problems." Reprinted with permission from the *Personnel and Guidance Journal,* XXXVI (1958), 454–455.

development of individual potential. Guidance is committed to helping all students achieve, in accord with their free choice, up to the level of their potential. The search is not simply for scientists or engineers to build better missiles or atomic submarines, but for development of the total resources upon which the quality of a free society depends.

An important portion of the educational policy of this country is stated in the National Defense Education Act of 1958. Some would wish for an even more definite statement. Some would cry that music or sociology has been left out. But although the bill is not a perfect document, it does attempt to fulfill the standards described by John Gardner in his book, *Excellence*. Gardner believes that a complex technological society requires not only the education of an elite, but the "development of human potentialities at all levels" (1961:71). To this goal guidance is dedicated.

Guidance personnel across the country, as well as national guidance leaders, helped to frame the National Defense Education Act. Arthur Hitchcock, the Executive Secretary of the American Personnel and Guidance Association, coordinated the efforts of key persons in all states as they wrote, discussed, and helped to guide the nation's legislators to the total task rather than to the restrictive policy of simply developing a national testing program to isolate potentially gifted scientists or missilemen. Of the national legislation Arthur Hitchcock has written: ". . . in this law the nation has declared that guidance is an instrument of national policy. The law states in effect, that in a democracy, the growth of human resources is dependent upon guidance to identify able students and to assist them in their fullest possible development" (1959:295).

The provisions of the law made possible appropriations for the establishment of institutes to educate guidance workers, both in summer sessions and in year-long programs. The bill also provided for interest-free loans to college students, to open education to all regardless of financial condition. The so called "loyalty oath" that was also included was one of the regressive features of the law. It is to be hoped that as future education bills are written it will be possible to broaden some of the legislative provisions.

Guidance has assumed, along with education, a national purpose and direction. Guidance persons are charged by our society with the responsibility of aiding students in establishing plans of education, selecting programs of study, evaluating their potential for a particular program, and in all ways, individualizing the educational process for the citizens in a democracy. The strengths of a free democratic society can, in turn, influence the development of responsible societies throughout the world.

GUIDANCE AND EDUCATION

The American school is faced with many tasks. Basic skills of reading, writing, arithmetic, and speaking are the responsiblity of all schools. Moreover, the accumulated knowledge of a culture and the acquired talent for critical thinking must be passed on to each student.

The abstract nature of these educational tasks cannot obscure the very practical problems of inducting millions of students into institutional life, feeding these same millions, and maintaining order and discipline while learning proceeds. The "babysitting" aspect of American education, which has been examined by many critic-commentators, can often deaden the most avid teachers and students. The school needs to keep all tasks in proper perspective while fulfilling its basic promises to the citizens it serves.

The Nature of Education

Education offers to students facts, knowledge, and hopefully creative views of the many academic disciplines. But student experience is frequently a conglomeration of isolated courses pungently mixed with administrative fiat and lunchroom socializing. The compartmentalization of a curriculum into tiny cubicles of courses defeats the purposes of the school and the aspiration of the learner. The administrative emphasis on deportment (be a quiet and good little boy) to secure an orderly school where "hall passes" or recess niceties are more important than learning is not lost on attuned young personalities. Guidance workers can also become entrapped by their own small goals and narrow conceptions. The guidance worker who views his task as a railroad switchman, channeling students into school and thence to college, business, or the trades shows that education can suffer and fail through guidance as well as other processes. The overriding dream of excellence on every ability level can be destroyed by mediocrity.

The Commission on Staff Utilization in Secondary Schools, sponsored by the Ford Foundation and headed by J. Lloyd Trump, has conducted a four-year study of methods of improving the quality of education. The Commission reports (1958–1961) and a series of motion pictures entitled "And No Bells Ring," produced by the Commission, have helped to create new visions of the meaningfulness that education can possess. Skilled methods of subject-matter presentation, faculty-student discussions of ideas, independent work for students, and original techniques of faculty-specialist cooperation in student guidance are examples of the possibilities for education that have been outlined. Ford Foundation funds are not always necessary to capture the enthusiasm for education that can be engendered in a community. The Swampscott, Massachusetts, school system has also ventured into such explorations, as shown in the program outlined below.

EXCITING THINGS ARE HAPPENING IN EDUCATION

WORKSHOPS

#1—"Team Teaching—Its Implications for the Future"
Dr. Robert Anderson, Harvard Grad. School of Education
Medill Bair, Sup't. of Schools, Lexington
Mrs. Ethel Bears, Principal, Lexington Franklin School
John Thomas, Senior Team Teacher, Estabrook School, Lexington
Mrs. Jane Rogers, Principal, Stanley School, Swampscott, Moderator

#2—"The Advanced Placement Program—How it Works"
Dean Catherine Williston, Assoc. Dean of Instruction, Radcliffe
Philip Hugny, Director of Advanced Studies, St. Paul's School
Miss Lillian Murdock, Coordinator of Advanced Placement, Brookline High School
John McLaughlin, Principal, Swampscott High School, Moderator

#3—"Is College the Right Goal for Every Child?"
Dean John McDowell, B.U. School of Social Work
Robert Coe, Personnel Director, General Electric Co.
Dr. Esther Matthews, Counselor in Charge, Newton South High School
J. Richard Bath, Principal, Hadley Elementary School, Swampscott, Moderator

#4—"Can the 'Lay Reader' Program Improve the Quality of Student Writing?"
Dr. Edwin Sauer, Director of Lay Reader Program, Harvard
Harold O'Connor, Head of English Dept., Concord High School
Mrs. Frances Guindon, Lay Reader, Concord High School
Philip Jenkin, Acting Sup't. of Schools, Swampscott, Moderator

#5—"Standardized Tests—Do They Really Tell?"
Dean John Palmer, Dean of Undergraduate Students, Tufts Univ.
Dr. Henry Isaacson, Director of Pupil Personnel Services, Lexington
Dr. Robert D. Forrest, Sup't. of Schools, Swampscott
Miss Rita McLaughlin, Elementary Guidance Counselor, Swampscott, Moderator

#6—"How Can We Create Favorable 'Educational Climate' in the Community?"
Dr. Harry B. Gilson, Sup't. of Schools, Winchester
Ian Forman, Education Editor, Boston Globe
Theodore Sargent, President National Assoc. of School Boards
Dr. John Clippinger, Pastor, First Church (Cong.) Swampscott
Charles Harris, Executive Director, Mass. Council for Public Schools, Moderator

MECHANICAL TEACHING AIDS WILL BE ON DISPLAY AFTER 3:00 P.M.

Sponsors:

THE SWAMPSCOTT COUNCIL FOR PUBLIC SCHOOLS (in cooperation with) The Swampscott PTA Council, The Swampscott School Committee, and the Swampscott Teachers Association, Swampscott, Massachusetts[3]

Guidance and the School

Guidance can help the pupil adjust to the school as a society as well as help relate the concept of a larger surrounding society to the individual and to the school. School in the early years is often an alien world which each pupil must enter and accept as part of everyday life. The guidance worker becomes the agent of the school charged with the proper adjustment of the student to the new circumstance. As time passes and the pupil progresses to higher grade levels, it is the function of the guidance worker to help him select educational and career goals that are in accord with his abilities, aptitudes, interests, and ambitions.

Guidance as an agent for parents, the community, and the school is also concerned with the transitions between schools that all pupils within an educational system that is larger than a one-room unit must make. Administration needs to measure new groups and their needs. However, new pupils are not manufactured goods to be accommodated upon the supply shelves until they are moved on to the next level. Guidance needs to recognize the individuality of each pupil and to provide for meaningful articulation from home to school, from school to school, and from school to work and full societal membership.

Advanced placement examinations, early school entrance through psychological testing, and an emphasis on the importance of intellectual activity are elements that guidance workers must concern them-

[3] Reprinted courtesy of the Swampscott Council for Public Schools.

selves with as school years begin. The recruiting for football teams in violation of institutionally adopted codes is not a function of guidance counselors, nor hopefully any person who considers himself an educator. The purposes of education must dictate the transitional activities that make it possible for education to get on with its job.

Guidance is concerned with the student inside and outside the classroom. An earlier view of guidance restricted its functioning to out-of-class learnings and served to divide it artificially from subject learnings. Since the development of student goals and purposes takes place within and outside the classroom, guidance is necessarily concerned with the quality of learning that takes place in all areas of the school. Guidance cannot ignore the necessity of facing standards of excellence in all types of student planning, learning, and accomplishment.

Faculty members and students often confuse educational standards of excellence. Empty football fields and full libraries are not *per se* the mark of excellence in education. Faculty members need to recognize this fact (Benezet, 1961), and must also realize that it takes more than hard work to provide the excellence that is the goal of American education. Students and alumni can confuse the excellence of a winning football team with educational excellence. Benezet's comment on this issue is biting: "To speak of a winning football team as a part of university excellence is . . . like lumping together the accomplishments of a philosopher and a performing bear" (p. 45).

Guidance workers need to join forces with faculty members in striving for "a conception of excellence which may be applied to every degree of ability and to every socially acceptable activity," in John Gardner's words (1961:131). They must join students and faculty members in demanding that the important aspects of learning be stressed on all levels and in all dimensions of education.

The concept of education as an instrument of culture demands that guidance be a part of the learning process. Individuals must do more than receive the learnings of a static society. Each individual must become able to think about his learnings and to adapt them to his own future. Although guidance is not always a one-to-one counseling process, it faces the responsibility that, as problem-solving and learning processes occur, students need to have someone who is concerned with their long-range and immediate plans. Brameld speaks of education and includes guidance within his view, although he never uses the word: ". . . education cannot be content merely to describe the phenomenon of goal-seeking. Its obligation extends further: not only to help personalities come to terms with the dominant goals of their respective cultures, but to help them analyze, express, implement, and often reconstitute these goals as fully as they are able and as comprehensible as they see fit" (1957:196). Guidance becomes the agent of education as learning is individualized and schools undertake to implement such an idea of education. Education becomes more than a lifeless passing on of knowledge, and more even than the application of critical thinking to the knowledge accumulated. Guidance and education together are able to aid students in achieving a concept of growth and development that can help them to see that they are individuals and as such are the basic units of a future society and culture.

Guidance as Individualized Education

Guidance must individualize learning if it is to fulfill the tasks that society and education have assigned to it. To be sure, it is possible for any course or teacher to individualize the subject matter being studied or the process being examined. The individualization of education through guidance implies a larger process in which each person is able to view himself as an individual within a society and within a culture—a person who must face and resolve problems, develop a sense of identity, and select a place within the society that maintains the educational process.

Some concepts of guidance have stressed a narrow service approach that concerns itself only with providing help to the student at the point of need. This view gives little thought to the overriding nature of education and society, and ignores the broader concept of education as a cultural phenomenon.

Developmental concepts of guidance focus only upon the student, ignoring the fact that education is related not only to individuals but also to the society and culture. A technical or utilitarian view of guidance, or any other aspect that can be isolated from the history of American education distorts and shows only partial patterns of guidance in education.

Guidance within a surrounding educational design can not only make possible the achievement of an individual destiny but also provide the basis for a society to maintain and to better itself. The anthropologist Malinowski, writing during World War II, saw this concept clearly: "The main argument concerning education as a cultural process makes us realize that it is one of the most powerful instruments of democracy. Its cultural value consists in that, abolishing birthright, it supplies us with the greatest opportunities to mobilize real talent. In making education universal, democracy makes possible the participation of the people in the guidance of its own destinies" (1944:150).

Education can become an individualized process through guidance and can aid persons to create their roles within not only a society but a total culture. Our society focuses upon persons and sees itself as an instrument to serve the individual. The recognition that guidance and education are processes designed to serve the person permits him to gain a broader concept of society. Persons can become not only simple, consuming members of a culture but can also influence its future development.

THE INDIVIDUAL AND GUIDANCE

Each person lives within a self-constructed world bounded by specific dimensions that are created out of his personal attributes and his experience. The individual looks out upon an outside world that seems alternately to open and close down upon him, and that he can either enter or retreat from. On beginning any grade, a student may feel lost and without purpose. Guidance can help the person as he encounters the world by blending practical advice and a meaningful interpretation of the relations of the self to the world.

Individual Life Stages

Every person develops irregularly during his life. Each phase of life creates problems and demands effective responses. The problems of warmth, air, and nutrition for the newborn infant are vastly different from the issues of an adequate house, occupational mobility, and even sexual adequacy for an adult male.

The concept of life stages has been presented by Erikson (1956) and by others. Erikson believes that, as the individual passes through the various phases and as issues are resolved, ego-identity development takes place. He concerns himself with the "epigenetic principle of gradual unfoldings"—the principle that the successive differentiations made during his life provide the person with a developmental concept of self. These "psychosocial" stages and the resulting formation of the personality occur in all persons, with a large proportion of growth and development taking place in the years from birth to young adulthood.

Guidance is concerned with the individual during these early life stages. Because the guidance worker is not emotionally involved, as a parent is, he can help clarify and interpret the problems, issues, and solutions. The development of personality, the acquisition of knowledge, the integration and application of knowledge are all dependent upon the quality of such "life adjustment." Erikson sums up his view in this statement: ". . . identity formation neither begins nor ends with adolescence; [it is] a lifelong development largely unconscious to the individual and to his society. It is self-realization coupled with a mutual recognition by society" (1956:69).

Guidance assists the individual in giving order to the "discontinuities" of development that each person must experience.

Normal and Problem Persons

Guidance has frequently concerned itself only with the slow learner, the gifted child, or the troubled child or adult. Guidance must recognize its obligation, as a part of a total educational process, to all students. Gardner Murphy sharply condemns the failure to live up to this obligation:

> Take for example, as a contrast with the stereotyped school . . . what is already done, through careful planning for handicapped children. The deaf or the polio-striken child, for example, gets as a result of specialized planning, a wide variety of incentive and assistance, gratifications and challenges, which offer a strange contrast to the rather passive and mechanical routines demanded for ordinary normal children. There is real virtuosity today in work for the deaf, and in many aspects of work for the blind. We carry out, in other words, brilliant repair work on the damaged members of our community against a rather sleazy backdrop of general fumbling with the creative potentials of our normal children [1959:173].

Some of the greatest "fumblers" have frequently been guidance workers and other specialists who sigh "would that we could but we. . . ." The nation, the educational system, and the person now demand that "guidance must!" The normal child of every class and every school is entitled to creative, meaningful guidance. Guidance has become a part of the educational process.

Individual Development

The selection of educational, career, and life goals, which is a problem for the adolescent, arises out of a background of total personal development. Guidance persons have only recently been able to view these processes as lifelong affairs with roots in childhood and implications even for old age. Malinowski again helps to place the entire developmental process of the individual within an educational and societal setting. He describes choice as a "long process, essentially social," in which the individual is influenced by others from infancy until his career choice is made (1944:142).

Guidance cannot enter the picture in the senior year of high school to help a student select a job or a college. The quality of growth and development of all the preceding years is the foundation upon which precipitating choices are made.

The demands of modern society dictate that education, through guidance, provide help to all students so that they may plan, profit, and grow as life and learning progress. The continuity and synthesis of personal development are the hallmarks of a successful person within a free society. Education and guidance are devoted to these ends. Brameld has placed the issue in a broad perspective, describing the overreaching goals of education, social science, and philosophy as ". . . social-self-realization—a term which symbolizes the desire of most men for the richest possible fulfillment of themselves, both personally and in their relations with other men through groups and institutions" (1961:93).

The directions are clear, the means of education and guidance are available. Guidance must face its responsibility to the individual, which in turn contributes to the society and the culture.

SOCIETY, EDUCATION, AND GUIDANCE

Guidance, unlike patriotism, can never become the last refuge for scoundrels. The United States, and most of the other nations which make up modern civilization, have renounced an uncaring, isolated existence. Guidance, as it deals with individuals, must be conscious of a surrounding, developing society and culture. The process of self-fulfillment and self-realization that is essentially individual is also societal.

Society, like culture, is the creature of man and should be the servant of man. But too frequently the servant can become a Frankenstein that is uncontrollable. Self-assessment and planned redirection are creative processes in both individuals and societies; guidance is a part of these processes.

Education Within Society

The power of the Hitlers, Mussolinis, the Stalins and Khrushchevs that are produced anywhere in the world can be traced to the basic concepts that are accepted by a society and transmitted by its educational system. The failure of German society to head off the nightmare of Naziism demonstrates how even single units of an educational system can be held partially accountable for a national and international tragedy. Qualitatively similar was the concern expressed by Health, Education, and Welfare Secretary A. A. Ribicoff in 1961 when he charged higher education and its highest officers with being concerned more with transitory issues, such as "scrounging for money, . . . looking for staff, . . . getting a piece of the program . . . ," than with problems of education and society as a whole. Seldom if ever has a high governmental official charged education more directly with the need to look to its entire house rather than to selfish interests. Doubtless there were many college presidents and deans that were offended. College presidents and deans dislike a public reprimand as much as does tiny Tommy who may misbehave in kindergarten. Yet educators themselves have said the same to one another.

Education is a process which is interrelated with a society from all vertical and horizontal views. Education is the primary tool of a democracy and as such is answerable to both the society as a whole and to the individual members of a nation. The achievement of individual freedom and the construction of a more effective free society are dependent upon the quality of education present in any nation.

There are some who are inclined to believe that the nature of education is not the proper concern for specialists or even for a society as a whole. Education should evolve like Topsy! Such persons look upon the functions of education as inappropriate for public discussion. But although education should not be a political issue purely to obtain votes in an election, there is no more vital issue for specialists or for the public in a free society. Education is both political, as it is implemented through national legislation, and nonpolitical in its operation. The development of guidance and education as a part of national policy occurred in the late 1950s. The aim of national educational policy was described when Herbert Hoover wrote in 1922: "that while we build our society upon the attainment of the individual, we shall safeguard to every individual an equality of opportunity to take that position in the community to which his intelligence, character, ability, and ambition entitle him; that we keep the social solution free from frozen strata of classes; that we shall stimulate effort to each individual to achievement;

that through an enlarging sense of responsibility and understanding we shall assist him to this attainment; while he in turn must stand up to the emery wheel of competition" (pp. 9–10).

Educational practice and national policy may develop slowly and imperceptibly at times. But the history of the educational program of the United States reveals a constant fashioning of education into a more effective tool for the betterment both of a nation and of an entire civilization.

Individual Guidance and Society

The individual is at the core of the free society and must ultimately be at the core of a free and peaceful world. The safeguards of human rights that governments and societies can offer to persons must be secured and enhanced by responsible persons within those societies. Guidance workers, in a most myopic view, can be described as "distributors of talent within a technocracy." How much more important it is for guidance counselors to develop a perspective on the cumulative efforts of all guidance and education. Responsible persons in a free society are the products of the rich texture of learning experiences which freedom makes possible. The talents and educationally developed productivity of a free citizenry are the greatest strengths of any nation.

American education has developed a "multiple chance" design in order to fulfill its sorting responsibility. The old concept of early selection for professions, trades, and unskilled labor, with its accompanying cultivation of an elite that ignored the nonprivileged masses, has been rejected. Free public education and free higher education in many areas, together with an increasing concern for the support of all talented and potentially creative persons, promise the fulfillment of the dream of an educational elite along with an educated populace.

The multiple chance system of educational opportunities at all levels of ability permits the individual to rise as high as he is able to within a free society. The sorting out takes place as the individual is unable to compete, as he finds that he must select an occupational and societal status that is consistent with his abilities, aptitudes, intelligence, interests, and ambitions—all honed by the "emery wheel" of Hoover. The results of educational experiments show that the gifted person can come from the hills of a rural section or from the asphalt jungles of any city as well as from the drawing rooms of the "four hundred." A new focus has been provided for all educational effort.

The freedom to succeed in an open society also carries the possibility of failure. Because the individual cannot rationalize or project the blame for his own failure upon God's will in a caste- or class-locked society, upon the tyranny of an oligarchy, or upon the "if I could" that can support so many failures, a new and fearful burden is placed upon all guidance workers. As failures occur, and as they must be accepted by a healthy personality, guidance must be of help to the individual. The acceptance of failure within a concept of self is dependent upon the ability to develop alternate and newly satisfying goals. Guidance cannot serve merely as a herald to welcome and bid adieu to the student on a narrow college-bound pathway.

Failure within a multiple-chance, sorting-out educational process is the "bitter pill of fairness and efficiency" of Gardner. Failure must be made acceptable by the attribution of plurality of values to all job and educational placement. Gardner's universally valid goal of "excellence" must be applied to the performance of all tasks in a society. There is no other way if guidance, education, and a society are to meet the challenges of personal and societal success and failure. Gardner sees such dreams as within the grasp of American education. He writes: "What we are trying to do is nothing less than to build a greater and more creative civilization. If we accept . . . schools and colleges will then be the heart of national endeavor" (1961:142).

Brameld has held that "means without ends are blind" and that "ends without means are hopeless." Society, education, and guidance share common means and ends. The task is almost inconceivable in its scope; yet is there anything which is more important to seek? Gardner is both whimsical and profound as he ends his treatise on "excellence" by saying: ". . . But who ever supposed that it would be easy. . . ."

INDIVIDUAL FREEDOM AND GUIDANCE

The modern guidance worker may have decided that the purposes of guidance require force and rigid control of persons for predetermined ends. Carl Rogers and B. F. Skinner have conducted a dialogue extending over many years about the nature of control, psychology, counseling, and freedom (see Suggested Readings). Control is accepted by both Rogers and Skinner as a means to individual freedom within a free society; each, however, defines control in a personal fashion. Rogers stresses the success that is possible to a person who feels secure, accepted, unthreatened, and free to grow and develop. The self is free to explore, to integrate, and to achieve its potential. Skinner stresses the determining nature of man's past as man's freedom, emphasizing cultural control of learning and experience as basic in producing free citizens.

Probably neither Rogers nor Skinner would accept the premise that each of them represents a part of what may be a broader concept of freedom. Man's past is man's freedom; however, at any single instant of time freedom is also the right to choose freely from the alternatives that an open society can offer.

Freedom cannot be equated with the feeling that one is free. What man can conceive is always a part of freedom, but man can only conceive in accord with his experience and his vision. Creative man is constricted or stimulated by the perceived right and privilege to choose, to determine. Man's reality is made up of himself and his world. Freedom must arise out of this reality.

A free society is as much an actual support for individual freedom as is the dark, encapsulating world which Conrad creates in *The Heart of Darkness,* symbolic of man's exploration of his own inner depths. Yet at any given moment, man must be able to sever himself from his societal background in order to make meaningful choices. Freedom is thus built upon a foundation of past experiences and learnings, while it operates by a temporary disjoinment from the past.

Malinowski and Murphy provide a parallel view of the issues raised by Rogers and Skinner. Their terms are less frought with individual connotations and are perhaps more helpful to the guidance worker who must face and resolve the issue of personal freedom daily.

Although he wrote earlier, Malinowski seems to reflect and broaden Skinner's view as he writes:

> The relation of education to freedom is clear. Exactly as culture gives mankind its integral increment of freedom through evolution, so in the life history of every individual through the stages from animal to infant, to the last word in contemporary culture, education bestows upon him the freedom of his tribal or national culture. Or else it deprives him of certain aspects of this freedom. . . . Human beings can either be trained to be free, or trained to be rulers, tyrants, or dictators, or else they can be slaves. Thus the understanding of educational mechanisms and conditions is essential to our appreciation of the reality of freedom as it occurs differentially in human societies [1944:140–141].

Murphy, a psychologist rather than an anthropologist, attacks the same issue of freedom with terms that may be more familiar to the guidance person. His views complement those of Malinowski. Murphy puts it thus:

> Freedom to choose means the operation within the person of impulses to gather information relevant to his decision and to see the issues clearly. If these impulses and this information are not present, it is difficult to see what freedom would mean; and it is difficult to see how this kind of freedom could *precede* the impulses seeking freedom. This kind of freedom arises from a human context, and to some degree we can help to find freedom for ourselves and others by providing rich contexts. But none of this is done causelessly. There must likewise be the personal hardihood and capacity to act upon the understanding of the issues. If these things are available, there is freedom [1958:242].

Murphy's italicizing of the word *precede* emphasizes the fact that a cultural backdrop, as well as freedom of choice and of individual operation, are necessary to individual growth.

Guidance persons are again concerned with the surrounding atmosphere, climate and context of education, society, and a culture as they attempt to help individual persons make free choices and reach freely the "social-self-realization" described by Brameld and Erikson.

SUMMARY

Five purposes of guidance have been listed and examined. The relation of guidance to (1) national effort, (2) the individualization of education, (3) self-realization and fulfillment, (4) societal and cultural purposes, and (5) individual freedom shows the objectives of guidance as it operates at all levels and dimensions of education.

The process of guidance is identical, although it serves many purposes; the strength of the guidance movement is revealed as its operation serves to strengthen the various areas that can profit from its activity. The individual is the center of guidance and of the many areas it serves.

Those who assume that guidance is a chameleon, serving only the immediate institution or community, underestimate and distort the true significance of guidance. Guidance is strong only as it serves the process of individual growth and development; not in serving the manipulative ends of a community, nation, or culture.

REFERENCES AND SUGGESTED READINGS

American Personnel and Guidance Association, "A Statement of Policy Concerning the Nation's Human Resources Problems," *Personnel and Guidance Journal,* XXXVI (1958), 454–455.

Benezet, Louis T., "The Trouble with Excellence," *Saturday Review,* Oct., 1961.

Brameld, Theodore, *Cultural Foundations of Education,* New York: Harper, 1957.

Brameld, Theodore, "Prolegomena to a Future-Centered Education," in L. Bryson, L. Finkelstein, and R. M. MacIver (eds.), *Goals for American Education,* New York: Harper, 1950, 341–372.

Brameld, Theodore, "What Is the Central Purpose of American Education?" *Phi Delta Kappan,* XLIII (1961), 9–14.

Brunson, M. A., *Guidance: An Integrating Process in Higher Education,* New York: Bureau of Publications, Teachers College, Columbia University, 1959.

Bryson, L., "What Should Be the Goals for Education?" in L. Bryson, L. Finkelstein, and R. M. MacIver (eds.), *Goals for American Education,* New York: Harper, 1950, 485–492.

Bryson, L., *et al.* (eds.), *Goals for American Education,* New York: Harper, 1950.

Childs, John L., *Education and Morals,* New York: Appleton-Century-Crofts, 1950.

Craig, William G., "The Student Personnel Profession: An Instrument of National Goals," *College Student Personnel,* III (1962), 161–168.

Erikson, E. H., "The Problem of Ego Identification," *Journal of the American Psychoanalysis Association,* IV (1956), 56–112.

French, Will, *Behavioral Goals of General Education in High School,* New York: Russell Sage Foundation, 1957.

Gardner, John W., *Excellence,* New York: Harper, 1961.

Geiger, G. R., "An Experimentalist Approach to Education," in National Society for the Study of Education, *Modern Philosophies and Education,* Fifty-Fourth Yearbook, Part I, Chicago: University of Chicago Press, 1955.

Havighurst, R. J., and B. L. Neugarten, *Society and Education,* Boston: Allyn & Bacon, 1957.

Hitchcock, A. A., *et al.,* "Milestones in the Development of Personnel Services in Education," in National Society for the Study of Education, *Personnel Services in Education,* Fifty-Eighth Yearbook, Part II, Chicago: University of Chicago Press, 1959, 283–298.

Jencks, C., "The Next Thirty Years in the Colleges, *Harper's,* CCIII (1961), 121–128.

Malinowski, Bronislaw, *Freedom and Civilization,* New York: Roy, 1944.

Melby, Ernest O., and F. W. Reeves, "Education and the Evolving Nature of Society," in National Society for the Study of Education, *Personnel Services in Education,* Fifty-Eighth Yearbook, Part II, Chicago: University of Chicago Press, 1959, 15–40.

Miller, Carroll H., *Foundations of Guidance,* New York: Harper, 1961.

Murphy, Gardner, *Human Potentialities*, New York: Basic Books, 1958.
National Society for the Study of Education, *Modern Philosophies and Education*, Fifty-Fourth Yearbook, Part I, Chicago: University of Chicago Press, 1955.
Rogers, C. R., and B. F. Skinner, "Some Issues Concerning the Control of Behavior," *Science*, XXX (1956), 1057–1066.
Skinner, B. F., "Freedom and the Control of Man," *The American Scholar*, XXV (1956), 47–65.
Skinner, B. F., *Walden Two*, New York: Macmillan, 1948.
Stoddard, Alexander J., *Schools for Tomorrow: An Educator's Blueprint*, New York: Fund for the Advancement of Education, 1957.
Taylor, Harold, "Education as Experiment," in L. Bryson *et al.* (eds.), *Goals for American Education*, New York: Harper, 1950, 429–448.
Trump, J. Lloyd, "Report of the Commission on Staff Utilization in Secondary Schools," in XLII–XLV of *The Bulletin of the National Association of Secondary School Principals*, 1958–61.
Warner, W. L., *et al.*, *Who Shall Be Educated?*, New York: Harper, 1944.

THE TOOLS OF GUIDANCE

GUIDANCE is more than a series of educational principles and purposes. It is a professional discipline with specific tools and procedures that can help guidance workers achieve the objectives they have established for the assistance of students.

The primary tool used by early guidance persons, an emotional and almost sympathetic involvement, has been replaced by the more scientific processes of counseling, psychological testing, group procedures in guidance, and the adaptation of the social worker's concept of the "case study."

Individual counseling has become the most direct and intimate tool of the guidance worker. The one-to-one, face-to-face problem-solving climate for decision-making that exists in counseling provides for the student and the counselor a process in which each can learn. Psychological testing provides a concrete and specific method of diagnosing and assessing the dimensions of student status, potential, and capacity. Group procedures permit counseling to take place with small

⁂ PART TWO

groups and allow the guidance worker to establish meaningful interactive situations in which students can learn to solve their own problems more effectively and to establish their own plans for the future. The case study is essentially a composite of the tools and procedures that are utilized with an individual student. As problems, causes, and proposed solutions are marshaled in each individual situation, education can become more meaningful to students.

The tools of the professional worker in guidance are no better than the skill and sensitivity that accompany their use. The user is as important as the tool. Moreover, the tools of guidance are all designed to aid the student to help himself. Again the goals of guidance are apparent as the tools of guidance are directed to the development of the free and responsible citizen.

The four chapters of Part Two examine the four major tools of guidance: (1) Individual Counseling, (2) Psychological Testing, (3) Group Procedures in Guidance, (4) The Case Study.

COUNSELING

THE ISSUE. Counseling and guidance are often assumed to be the same thing. The relationship between a student and a guidance worker that counseling makes possible is certainly at the heart of the guidance process, yet the two are not the same.

School counselors are not psychiatrists nor psychotherapists. However, school counseling is able to help students resolve emotional and personal problems as well as educational and vocational issues. The larger view of human development shows that school counseling may be more significant than psychiatric or medical treatment.

Counseling is a key concept of guidance and basic to its functioning. Whether it is viewed as a tool of the guidance worker or as the heart of the guidance process, all writers and workers in the field agree that counseling is vital in aiding students to live up to their total potential. Counseling therefore needs to be examined with care and detail.

Education is concerned with the preservation and transmittal of a total culture, while aiding students in assuming their place in a society. Guidance attempts to individualize education as students are helped to learn to solve problems and to think critically about themselves and their futures. Counseling becomes a primary avenue for the individualization of education and for the operation of guidance. The goals of education and of guidance can be focused within the life of one person through counseling.

The great potential of counseling as a process and as a tool helps to explain its significance to guidance workers, students, and parents.

CHAPTER FIVE

Guidance cannot exist, in meaningful fashion, without the use of counseling.

Counseling provides the one-to-one personalized contact that gives guidance its impact and provides education its direct connection with individual problem-solving. Through counseling an individual can be aided in the application of cultural learnings and accumulated factual knowledge. Counseling provides the arena for the person to chart his own future in light of his present, his past, and his educational acquisitions and personal potential.

To define counseling is to attempt to assess its operational significance within the lives of students. A simple definition that encompasses most of the complex and sensitive interpretations of the meaning of counseling may be phrased as: "An open-ended, face-to-face, problem-solving situation within which a student, with professional assistance, can focus and begin to solve a problem or problems."

Arbuckle (1961) offers nine separate definitions of counseling, all stressing the problem-solving nature of the process but differentiating among the varying roles played by the counselor. Gustad (1953) stresses the problem-solving or learning-orientation of a social interaction. Counseling at its most simple level of operation and yet in its most complex form is an opportunity for a person to talk and think privately and carefully with the assistance of another person who is committed to the belief that the person can be aided in solving his own problems.

Counseling is thus important in its own right as a process and is also symbolic of the larger processes of guidance and education. The protected environment of the counseling session is representative of the educational fabric of our society. The individual is aided by a professional educator (guidance worker or counselor) to become increasingly self-sufficient in working through and solving his own problems of living and taking a place as a member of a society.

The importance of counseling to guidance and education both in the past and the present has led to many confusing uses of the term. Education is concerned with the preservation and transmittal of the cultural and societal wealth of the sponsoring unit. Education is also concerned with aiding students in living effectively and in preparing for lives as free and responsible citizens. Guidance, as an element within education, is concerned with the process of thinking and problem-solving in the personal lives of students. The individualization of education and the operation of guidance depend upon the utilization of counseling as a primary tool. Counseling thus cannot be separated from its sponsoring institutional processes. Counseling that exists outside of education still depends upon past learnings and education.

Occasionally persons are inclined to equate counseling with guidance rather than to see it as a tool of guidance and of education. Guidance and education must use many additional tools in order to aid all students. Yet the importance of counseling leads some to assume that counseling is the *sine qua non* of guidance and even of education. Such views harm counseling and place an undeserved burden upon it.

The automobile depends upon the internal combustion engine. Without the engine the automobile would be a wagon or a cart. Yet to say that the engine is the automobile is to confuse the problem. Perhaps the analogy could be pushed further to point out that neither the engine nor the automobile is all that is meant when one considers the transportation industry. Education, guidance, and counseling are intimately related and interdependent, yet they are different processes dependent upon varying elements and designed to accomplish differing ends. The goal of counseling is the isolation of individual problem-solving behavior and the assistance of persons in this specific process.

COUNSELING IN THE SCHOOLS

Counseling in the schools is a process, as defined previously, designed to help students solve problems and make decisions. School counseling is appropriately related to but by no means the same as psychological, psychiatric, psychoanalytic, or legal counseling. The confusion in the use of the terms *counseling, therapy,* and even *psycho-*

therapy has helped to cloud the significant difference that exists between school counseling and the operation of a hospital clinic, a mental hospital, and other institutions where counseling occurs.

School counseling is concerned with the problem-solving issues that are common to all students. Examining lives, weighing decisions, and planning futures are common procedures in education; personality rehabilitation, emotional restoration, out-patient recovery, and such practices are uncommon within schools. The overlapping of these processes is common in all schools and yet it is important to distinguish clearly between the focus of school counseling and goals of therapy or psychotherapy.

Decision-Making and Therapy

Hospital patients with serious emotional problems are frequently treated for long periods of time and helped to function in a reasonably normal fashion. The problems of job placement, living arrangements, recreation, education, or training plans are not usually a part of therapeutic problem-solving. A hospital "guidance" worker, counselor, or often a rehabilitation counselor is called upon to assist the patient in long-term therapy. However, a "guidance counselor," a rehabilitation counselor, or, in the context of this discussion, a school counselor is not usually called upon to enter into any long-term therapeutic relationship with a student. Some counselors are interested, prepared, and free to enter into such relationships; most school counselors are not. Similarly a psychiatrist or a psychoanalyst is not interested, prepared, or free to enter into the problem-solving that must be a part of occupational or educational planning, job placement, or related activities. The functions of these various counselors are similar, but they differ in focus and in the degree of personality disorganization of the individual involved.

School counselors at all levels have frequently felt that they were more superficial and less capable than their medically or psychiatrically prepared counterparts. The entire guidance and counseling profession has long suffered from a type of inferiority complex because of the feeling of insecurity aroused by such comparisons.

The differences between the operation of these "counselors" needs to be seen in its relation to the life of the person undergoing the counseling. The emotionally or physically handicapped person or the confused, neurotic patient is incapable of making meaningful decisions about his own life. The treatment is designed to bring this person *up to* a level that makes possible the decision-making and problem-solving that is a normal part of life. The school counselor and the therapy-oriented counselor are therefore fulfilling different functions, each performing different but related service.

Viewed from another perspective, it may be said that the school counselor is primarily helping a person to deal with his present and future operation as a person. The therapy-oriented process is focused upon the removal of handicaps that preclude meaningful operation as a person. That many people are able to function normally in this area of operation is a favorable comment upon our culture, our society, and our educational system. That a school counselor should feel inferior in his functioning because he is concerned with the present and future operation of the student rather than with his past assumes that the rehabilitation of a person is more important than helping him to plan for his present and future life. Such a feeling of inferiority results from the counselor's failure to clarify his role and purposes.

School counseling operates at the heart of the process that helps persons to become and remain free and responsible persons within a society. There is no other more important goal for a counselor or guidance worker to fulfill than to help a person to be free, to solve problems effectively, to live responsibly, to live up to his inherent capacity, and to become increasingly independent in his operation in all of these areas. School counseling is focused upon the problem-solving processes of all students, not upon the emotionally or psychologically disturbed student. School counseling is thus a part of the total effort of guidance in the school, part of the educational process, and the link between all of these elements and the individual student.

The Educational Base of School Counseling

School budget allocations frequently create difficulties for the guidance program and for the implementation of a counseling philosophy. Many school counselors are unable to defend the expenditure of funds for a case load of a few dozen students out of several hundred. Although the question of time allotment is important to the school or college, the expenditure of funds is more closely related to the total instructional program. The administration must recognize that the decision-making and problem-solving that is inherent in all school counseling is part of the actual fabric of education. The aid that can be offered to normal students in fulfilling their own potentials is more significant in the school budget than is the therapy offered to a few disturbed students.

A PHILOSOPHY OF COUNSELING

"Why counsel?" is a question that must be answered as counseling is placed within a framework of guidance in a school system. The basic purpose of counseling needs to be understood as students seek counseling, as counselors function, and as school budgets are arranged to provide for such a service.

Counseling has long been accepted as being good for everyone. However, guidance personnel and even specially prepared counselors could not always explain why it is desirable.

Why should counseling be available to students? Why should a guidance program always include provision for student counseling? How can administrators and teachers serve as counselors? Or can they? These and similar issues can be clarified and partially resolved as the nature and basic purpose of counseling is understood.

The Process of Counseling

Counseling is a process designed to aid students in solving their own problems, in thinking for themselves. Education and guidance are concerned with the development of free and responsible persons. Counseling provides the environment within which the individual student can be helped to solve his problems. The person who is free to think for himself, the person who is able to solve his own problems and to be responsible for the consequences of his actions usually does not seek nor require counseling.

The fact that a student seeks counsel in solving a problem demonstrates the nature of counseling as a process and helps to clarify its dimensions. Counseling provides an opportunity for the student to obtain help in thinking through a problem and in freely determining his own actions while accepting the responsibility for the consequences of his decisions.

To aid in the problem-solving or decision-making process of students, counseling must be an open-ended, free situation. If a counselor, administrator, teacher, or even a guidance worker enters into counseling with the assumption that a specific action, decision, or attitude on the part of the student will result, counseling cannot take place. Such an activity may be an interview, a debate, a persuasive discussion, or even a plain argument, but by no stretching of guidance or counseling philosophy could such an activity be called counseling.

The nature of all counseling demands that it be client-centered. Counseling cannot take place if it is counselor-centered or even problem-centered. Whether the counselor may enter into the discussion of implications, values, plans, or outcomes is an issue of the approach used by the counselor. The problems, the issues, the solutions, the plans arising out of counseling may be a product of the mutual interaction of the counselor and the counselee, but ultimately they must be the free and responsible choices of the counselee.

Counseling is a learning-oriented process; yet many learning activities are not counseling. A teacher may work individually with a student and help the student learn more effectively the forms of a verb in Spanish. Such activity is learning-oriented, face-to-face, and problem-solving. Some persons may wish to define such a conference as a counseling conference. It can be described more accurately as a teaching conference or a learning process, one-to-one. Counseling is learning-oriented but oriented toward the operation of counselee as a person, not toward his acquired knowledge.

The counselor is skilled in aiding the counselee to examine his problems, his values, and his operation as an individual. By discussion, working through, and quietly thinking, the counselor and counselee may produce solutions, decisions, and even changed attitudes or feelings. The counselee is the person who accomplishes the behavior or attitudinal change (learning), although it is also assumed that the counselor is changed by the mutual interaction of such a problem-solving process.

The key factor in the counseling process is the mutual dedication of counselor and student to the examination of the problem-solving process. Such thinking must be open-ended unless one assumes that a counselor can dictate the thinking or provide solutions for another. When solutions are provided for a person, whether the person accepts or denies them, it is better to think of such a process as advising.

Many interviews are mistakenly assumed to be counseling sessions. An interview has a definite purpose: the exchange of information. Counseling may take place during an interview, but it is necessary for such counseling to fulfill the definition as a problem-solving process by both counselor and counselee undertaken with an open-ended, freely-selected outcome possible for the counselee.

The Content of Counseling

Counseling may of course deal with almost infinitely variable contents of subject-matters brought to it by the counselee. However, regardless of its specific problem nature, counseling is centered on the past, present, and future actions and functioning of the counselee. Counseling is always "personal." Occupational plans may be discussed in a student-counselor session. However, the occupational plans are assumedly those of the student. If the student is talking about the plans of his brother, his sister, or a friend, one would have to assume that a discussion, rather than counseling, was taking place. Counseling presumes a direct personal involvement on the part of the counselee and in turn the personal and realistic attention and involvement of the counselor.

Many guidance personnel and writers have debated about whether placement discussions, occupational information sessions, or attendance interviews can be described as counseling. Many would call such activities "guidance" or information-giving. Yet if the process is closely examined to determine whether the student's own actions, feelings, or beliefs are involved, whether his thinking is of a problem-solving nature, whether he has freedom of choice, and whether his concern is his own past, present, or future, one can determine whether or not counseling is taking place.

All counseling is therefore related to the individual undergoing the experience. Some counseling will involve more of his feelings, emotions, or personality disturbances. Such "content" in the counseling is determined by the problem-solving nature of the counselee. If thinking is distorted by an inability to face reality, this problem, or rather subproblem, must be faced and solved before the more long-range goal of counseling can be sought. Psychotherapy sessions are primarily concerned with such issues. The person seeking this type of counseling is unable to solve problems for himself, to make decisions, or to live effectively as a free and responsible person. The process of therapy in such cases is almost wholly concerned with the correction or amelioration of such personality distortions. However, when such a program has been completed, the person must begin to think for himself, decide issues, and plan for his own future.

The nature of therapy and counseling have long been debated in the professional literature and among counselors and therapists. The distinction between the two is that therapy is designed to remove handicaps to effective problem-solving or thinking, whereas counseling is concerned with problem-solving, thinking, and decision-making in everyday life. Obviously such processes overlap. Therapy, however, is more common with the emotionally handicapped or mentally ill person. Counseling is concerned with the process of problem-solving in normal or nearly normal students. The removal of handicaps, the corrections of distortions or delusions, and the facilitation of normal problem-solving behavior on the part of the client is usually characterized as therapy.

Therapy and counseling are therefore related and overlapping functions. The school counselor usually is neither equipped nor prepared to deal with the emotionally disturbed client. Frequently the therapist in a hospital or clinic is equally poorly equipped to work with normal problem-solving issues. Each field overlaps and shares operational experiences; one is not a substitute for another, nor is one more superficial. Counseling and therapy deal with differing aspects of the performing ability of the person, normal and abnormal.

The Significance of Counseling

The symbolic and practical significance of counseling within a school system is immediately apparent, although not every student may need or seek counseling. The educational and guidance experiences that are a part of everyday school life may provide the needed assistance and opportunity for each pupil to become skilled in functioning in a normal problem-solving fashion. Education in all of its aspects is concerned with the development of the thinking and problem-solving processes of students. Dewey's famous statement of the need to help students learn "how to think" rather than "what to think" is appropriate at this juncture. The total impact of education on students is concerned with providing facts, knowledge, and the methods of using such knowledge. Guidance assumes a primary concern for such a process as it affects student lives. Counseling becomes the tool available to all educators, but especially to the guidance worker, to use when students need more aid than is available within the regular curriculum.

Administrators and teachers may function in many relationships with students. Counseling becomes one of the possible relationships which a student may enter with a teacher or administrator. But the traditional concept of education and the press of daily work may prevent teachers and administrators from providing for students the protected environment and the open-ended nature of the problem-solving discussions and experiences that are known as counseling.

The process and content of counseling are outgrowths of the basic nature of education. The opportunity for students to obtain special help in problem-solving, in personal planning, and in decision-making makes counseling central to educational and guidance programs. Counseling can trace its nature back to guidance and to education as all share the common processes dedicated to the development of free and responsible persons. At the same time education and guidance need to recognize the central and overwhelming importance of the counseling process.

THE NATURE OF COUNSELING

Counseling may appear to the disinterested observer as a simple discussion between two persons. Even a careful listener may see or hear little that seems unusual in the counseling session. Counseling may appear a mysteriously simple process to a prospective counselor or even to a student contemplating counseling. Yet there is an on-going problem-solving process in operation in all successful counseling sessions.

Effective counseling demands the concentrated effort and skillful application of techniques and talents by the counselor and the sincere commitment of the counselee to the solution or amelioration of a problem. An examination of counseling in operation can strip away the mystery of counseling and reveal its gross as well as its subtle elements.

Student Problems

Counseling involves the problems that can and do occur in the lives of all persons. Any individual may be faced with confused feelings, ideas, fear, and hopes. Sometimes he has constructed tentative solutions to his problems. At other times he may be only dimly aware of any problem and may seek aid in clarifying his state of confusion or perplexity. The counselor serves to aid the individual to achieve his own solutions to problems.

High school principals may become involved in disciplinary activities, in assisting students in rearranging schedules, or even in helping students select a prospective college. Guidance counselors in junior high schools may find themselves aiding students in selecting curriculums for high school programs, meeting with parents about their children's prospective programs, or even helping individual students to solve distressing personal problems. The elementary school child frequently acts out his problems and is unable to verbalize such difficulties. The "school adjustment counselor" or the elementary school guidance worker may find himself working with parents, community officials, health officials, as well as teachers and administrators. College counselors serve students in varying fashions in dormitory life, career-planning, placement procedures, and personal problem-solving.

The scope of counseling is determined by the population served within the school, age ranges, and the nature of the problems that occur within that community. The areas of counseling are as broad as the areas of guidance, as broad as the areas of human problems. It is not possible to restrict rigidly the problem areas that occur in counseling.

Problems the student brings to counseling are frequently not the actual problems, felt problems may not be real, and unrecognized problems can develop as counseling progresses. Counseling in any given situation is determined by the needs of the counselee and the capacities of the counselor.

Counseling as a process cannot be categorized, explained, or clarified by an attempt to construct a list of student problems. The index of this or any guidance book, the autobiographies of greater and lesser persons, even the textbooks in abnormal and normal psychology contain the scope of the problems that can and do occur in the counseling sessions that take place within the schools of our country. The basic nature of counseling does not lie in what is discussed or in what problems are solved in counseling, but in the actual process of problem-solving that takes place as counselor and counselee cooperatively seek answers to the problems of life within a climate of understanding. Such a process is essentially a relationship.

Problem-Solving in Counseling

The change process in counseling has been defined by many authors as learning. Frequently it has been identified as "insight" or a different way of seeing the many factors of a specific situation. Certainly there are other methods of learning that are involved in counseling. Learning of all types is the change of behavior or the change in the attitude that is the predisposition to behave.

The actual learning process in human beings is infinitely complex and involves changes that take place within the neurological structure of the body. Another way of viewing learning is to examine the process of thinking or problem-solving that takes place as learning occurs and which involves stages or developmental periods of activity.

Problem-solving in counseling is similar to problem-solving in all of life. Groups face problems and attempt to resolve them: a class in physics is concerned with the explanation of the loss of heat in a calorimeter; an individual must select one of two possible mates for a wife —each situation is a problem and must be resolved. Counseling is often further complicated by the inability of the person to state his difficulty clearly. The student who replies to the counselor's question "And what is your problem?" by saying "If I knew what my problem was I wouldn't be here" demonstrates an obstacle that is frequent in counseling.

DETERMINING THE PROBLEM. To select out of all areas of personal existence, the single problem that is most important is often impossible. Life doesn't permit such an organized and logical step. Seldom also is it possible for a person in need of counseling to isolate any single problem. Most of life's problems are made up of layers, corollaries, or unwarranted assumptions. However, the task in counseling is to seek out the problem. Again the need of the counselee to make such a selection is vital. Diagnostic procedures may be important in clinical psychological interviews or even in a medical clinic, but counseling depends upon the counselee's freedom to examine and select the area of discussion upon which he wishes to focus.

The problem may never be isolated. Students may not be able to indicate what is bothering them because they do not know. Counseling is possible even if the counselor accepts this attitude. Frequently after counseling is over the student may state that he has made real progress in one area while still denying that such an area was ever a problem. He may be completely correct and still be unable to recognize specific progress in any area as being related to discussions in another area. Important counseling results arise out of the satisfactions and changed behavior or attitudes of the student.

Collecting Data. The dimensions and the background of the problem are often the data that are necessary for the counseling process to proceed. The facts of personal existence that can influence a problem are limitless. A guidance program may supply additional data that can be of aid to the student in counseling. The issue of whether the student acquires such data from the counselor or as a normal part of the guidance program is entirely methodological. The inclusion of such data and its significance is determined by the student. Counselors can spend many hours introducing vast amounts of test data that the student does not see as important. The student's privilege to ignore such data must be preserved in counseling.

The counselor may or may not be an active participant in this stage of counseling, depending upon the orientation from which he operates. Research has not supplied an unequivocal answer. The student will need to be aided in collecting all relevant data. This process may be assisted by a reflective, nonprobing attitude and behavior on the part of the counselor. The student may take the lead in determining when data are adequate or when continued searching is necessary. Even when the counselor participates in the active process of collecting data, it is the student who must decide when adequate data are present.

Ordering Data. After data have been collected, they must be ordered and organized. Patterns of meaning can appear out of a mass of data or out of partial facts. Again this process must be controlled by the counselee. The generalizations that may be developed out of counseling must come from the efforts of the counselee. Interpretative generalizations on the part of the counselor may or may not be valuable to the student. Again the student's thinking and problem-solving is at issue, not that of the counselor. To be sure, there are many cases where counselor-supplied patterns or relationships can be accepted and utilized by the student. The key question is not whether such ideas, such insights, such generalizations are the original property of the student. The source of the principles is not the issue; the utilization of them is.

Achieving Conclusions. To decide that a conclusion drawn from a set of data is appropriate is a natural consequence of the problem-solving nature of counseling. Plans for the future, changed ideas about past experience, or even a revised feeling about the present may be classified as a conclusion in counseling.

Again the important element is that such conclusions or plans must be the result of the thinking or problem-solving processes of the student rather than of the counselor. The nature of any conclusion is an outcome of the patterning of the data used. The usefulness of the conclusion will determine its validation by the counselee.

Evaluating Conclusions. As conclusions are obtained there is an automatic need to evaluate or test out their adequacy. The counselor may help the student here by being able temporarily to represent reality, the testing-ground upon which such plans or conclusions must be viewed, or he may assume a nonparticipating attitude and posture. Regardless of the specific technique that is used by the counselor, it is important to realize that it is the student who must test and evaluate the conclusions developed.

It must be recognized that disorganization in the steps or stages of counseling can occur. The student who is capable of organizing his thoughts, problem, and answers adequately and whose feelings support his decisions may not need counseling. Actual practice of counseling shows that the sessions may ramble through all of the stages in a few minutes. Or it may be that several sessions are devoted to only a small portion of one of the stages. The steps in problem-solving are merely a construct of the process involved in counseling. Even if a student is never able to organize the stages he has completed chronologically, counseling may have been successfully concluded. Again the counselee is the one who evaluates and profits from whatever takes place in counseling.

The Climate of Counseling

The climate or atmosphere necessary to counseling has been apparent in all of the previous discussion. The acceptance of the counselee as a person of worth and dignity is basic to counseling. Easily said but exceedingly difficult in operation, such a principle supports all that must occur in counseling, and its denial can destroy anything that could be accomplished.

Carl Rogers, Dugald Arbuckle, and many other writers concerned with the client-centered approach to counseling clearly stress this principle. They state that the relationship based on such acceptance is the raw material out of which any counseling progress must arise.

Acceptance and respect for the person in a counseling relationship also demands that a positive and warm atmosphere be established. The atmosphere begins with the establishment of rapport. Rapport is often thought to be the result of simple or friendly beginnings or even small talk on the part of the participants. Rapport is important to the entire process of counseling and is best understood as a relationship rather than as a feeling that occurs within a few minutes of the beginning of a session. One student told of his experience in counseling and the attempts of the counselor to establish rapport:

> I was plenty scared when I went in to see the counselor. He had called me in to see him and I was afraid that I had done something for which I was going to get the devil. As soon as I got into the office he started talking to me about baseball. I guess he wanted to make me feel at ease. Yet I knew absolutely nothing about baseball and had always avoided any discussion. By the time we talked about baseball for five minutes I was really scared. Was he softening me up for the final blow or what?

The interview turned out successfully and yet one wonders if the counselor was ever aware of what had made it so difficult for the session to get started. What the counselor believes to be small talk or relaxing may not appear to be so to the student.

Counseling depends upon an open-ended structure. The problem-solving and personal planning that comes out of counseling must be encouraged by a warm, accepting climate that reflects respect for the counselee as a person of dignity and worth. Such principles and strictures are easily offered and easily accepted on a superficial basis. Yet without such foundations counseling is doomed to relative or absolute failure. Counseling and a counseling attitude is a demanding and difficult skill. Some persons are never able to learn to be counselors because they are unable to live up to such requirements. The superficial observation or listening technique that one may acquire while learning about counseling can obscure the necessity for these principles in successful counseling.

Ethics and Practicality

Many school personnel may accept any or all of the principles offered about the nature of counseling and yet state that to apply such ideas is impossible within any normal school situation. To be sure, it is necessary for all students and counselors to live within the commonly recognized limits of human behavior and societal regulation. Freedom is never a totally unrestricted concept. Freedom to exist as a person presupposes the right to similar freedom for all other persons. Responsibility demands that one must both accept the consequences for his actions or decisions and recognize individual and societal responsibilities. Counseling is a primary avenue to help students accept their nature as members of a society while creating for themselves a contributing responsible role within the laws and limitations of that society.

Referral Procedures

Counselors must be capable of recognizing and referring the serious problem cases that may occur in all school or college situations. The potential suicide is common in college, as is the withdrawn, repressed student in elementary school. The school counselor and the guidance program as a whole is responsible for providing aid and assistance to students, parents, teachers, and administrators as such problems occur. Counselors may not normally deal with such problems and may wish to refer the student to other professional persons. Yet just as teachers must be informed and knowledgeable about more than they teach, so counselors must not be limited by their education and experience. The preparation of school counselors must involve experience in dealing with problem cases as they occur. The section on the professional preparation of guidance persons will deal in greater detail with this issue.

COUNSELING ORIENTATIONS

Radically different schools of counseling methodology existed in the early years of counseling. The beginning of psychology saw "schools" develop each claiming to represent the true path to knowledge. Although early counseling approaches never openly claimed that their own system was the chosen method, they certainly insinuated such ideas.

Directive, nondirective or *client-centered,* and *eclectic* are terms that have been used in many writings about and by counselors. Actually such clear-cut dichotomies seldom existed in fact. The early history of counseling showed influences that were directly traceable to the medical, legal, and theological professions. Each of these fields was long established and had created a climate for the specialist advising the sick, the uninformed, or the parishioner. The distinction between the adviser, counselor, or physician and the client or patient was a vast one. Specialized knowledge was needed in order to advise or to cure. Early counseling approaches were significantly influenced by such related professional climates.

Some early counselors attempted to advise students about vocational choice, personal problems, and even emotional problems in the manner of a specialist. The very spelling of the word *counselor* was debated for many years because of the legal spelling which dictated *counsellor.* Other workers attempted to seek methods of helping persons to help themselves. No clear patterns existed.

Carl Rogers exploded upon the counseling scene in 1942 and questioned many of the most precious beliefs held by counselors of that day. His book *Counseling and Psychotherapy* advocated a new system of "nondirective counseling." Rogers, in his later writings (1951), and Arbuckle (1961, 1962) have preferred to call such a system *client-centered.* Rogers' impact needs to be seen and understood within the context of counseling as it was understood at the time of his early writings. In that period many guidance persons and educators, as well as physicians, lawyers, and theological persons, believed that it was their responsibility to tell others what was best and to help them by directing them into the most proper actions.

The uproar of Rogers' early writings has subsided as specialists in counseling have come to recognize the importance of helping students to help themselves. But Rogers' ideas have continued to be misunderstood and often maligned in medical and psychiatric circles. Many of these specialists are only partially informed about the writings and work of Rogers and are seldom inclined to consider his recommendations seriously. By leaving the counseling center at the University of Chicago to become a Professor of Psychiatry and Psychology at another midwestern university, Rogers has attempted to carry his teachings into the medical and psychiatric fields.

A Counseling Continuum

Rather than attempt to divide the many approaches to counseling into schools, camps, or even approaches, it is more meaningful to consider counseling methodologies on a continuum from client-centered to counselor-centered. Client-centered counseling stresses the student's control of the counseling. Counselor intervention in the active discussion of problems, background, or related data, or even in an evaluation of planned actions is avoided. The important elements in client-centered counseling are the establishment of a warm, permissive, and accepting climate within which the student can feel comfortable and is able to progress in his problem-solving at his own pace, aided by reflection, understanding, and restatement on the part of the counselor, but with little if any intervention or interpretation.

Counselor-centered, directive, or even eclectic approaches to counseling—the counselor-centered end of the continuum—encourages the active intervention and participation on the part of the counselor. The open-ended, problem-solving nature of counseling is still defended by so-called counselor-centered groups, at least within school settings, but there is an assumption that the counselor is able to bring to the counseling sessions knowledge, experience, and data that can be of aid to the student. The counselor is more an active partner in the counseling process.

Some persons have questioned the use of the term *client-centered* because they believe that all counseling grows out of the needs of the individual. The issue is primarily one of participation and involvement on the part of the counselor in the process of counseling. Clinically trained counselors and those who have been well schooled in the adjustment processes that are involved in personality-formation and personality-functioning are inclined to participate more in the actual counseling process. Diagnosis, interpretation, and such other techniques as well as the more commonly accepted methods of reflection, permissiveness, and understanding are characteristics of such counselors.

School Counseling

Counselors within school systems have been educated in many fashions. Clinical psychological training, social work backgrounds, guidance training programs, and even theological training have been offered as qualifying a person for the role of counselor within a school system. The conflicting orientations to counseling in schools have stemmed from the varying backgrounds of the counselors and the assumption that school counseling is similar or identical to hospital, clinical, or even psychiatric counseling.

School counseling is counseling with reasonably normal functioning members of society. As previously explained, the techniques appropriate to dealing with such persons are quite different from those used on a psychiatric ward of a hospital. To be sure, there are many disturbed and emotionally ill individuals who will turn up in the office of the school counselor, and he must be able to recognize such problems and to obtain or recommend proper types of treatment for such disorders. But the school is not and cannot be either a hospital or a mental health clinic. The individual who does need treatment for a serious disorder cannot be allowed to take over the total time and efforts of the school counselor. The very real problems of educational and occupational planning, the resolution of personal difficulties, the acquisition of jobs, the resolution of behavior problems in the classroom, and similar problems are the natural province of the school counselor.

Teachers and Counseling

Many strong words have been spoken and written about the issue of whether or not teachers are, should be, or can be counselors. Administrators may recognize that inherently they are also involved in such a controversy. A definition of counseling is vital if one is to bring any type of order out of the many diverse positions that have been advanced and defended in the past.

Teachers, administrators, and all school personnel have long been concerned with the development of individuals who are able to think for themselves, solve problems and to make decisions. These goals are a part of all of education and are normal objectives of all educators. Too frequently such developments are expected to be a natural outcome of a course in math, speech, or even Latin. Such outcomes of education are not inherent in the subject matter of any course. Teachers of talent and sensitivity have long recognized that, as they deal with students and attempt to help them become educated and responsible for themselves within a society, more than a subject-matter learning is involved. It is important to recognize that teachers, administrators, and school personnel have long been involved in counseling. The effectiveness of providing an accepting, permissive, warm, and understanding climate for students to talk over problems and to come to conclusions on their own is not the discovery of the guidance profession or of counselors. Counselors have extracted this area as one in which they seek special training and hope to have special competence. Recognizing that teachers, principals, superintendents, and frequently librarians, coaches, and others involved with students can and do counsel, is simply a recognition of the current and historical functioning of such persons in our schools.

The issue of whether or not teachers are or can be effective counselors is inherent in the methods they use in discussing problems with students. If teachers attempt to dispense advice, to solve problems for students, or to manipulate individuals, they are not functioning as counselors. However, students have received assistance in the offices of teachers throughout the history of education. These teachers are those who have been able to accept the student as a person, to recognize his dignity regardless of his age, and to realize that even the youngest student needs to function independently and efficiently as an individual. Free and responsible persons must be able to solve problems and to make decisions. Teachers, administrators, and any school personnel can function as counselors, and they do engage in counseling as they help students to become such mature individuals.

Counselors and guidance persons have extracted for themselves a historical function that has been fulfilled in the past by teachers and educators. To turn now and say that such persons cannot and moreover should not counsel is perhaps the "unkindest cut of all." Guidance and counseling have seldom prospered in a setting in which all counseling is presumed to occur only in a counselor's office or only by appointment with a director of guidance.

COUNSELING ISSUES

In the area of counseling many issues exist that can and do plague the counselor and guidance worker in their work with students. The relationship of counseling to psychiatric treatment, the applicability of Freudian theory to school counseling, the use of diagnosis in counseling, and the relevance of past histories of students are typical of the many problems that are involved in school counseling. Three issues seem to cut across all other problems in counseling and perhaps need to be faced, even in a book directed to guidance as a whole rather than solely to counseling. The discussion of these issues is pertinent to all of guidance as well as to counseling. The principles that have been developed out of counseling have become useful in all areas of guidance. The three issues are: (1) intellectual versus emotional processes, (2) the role of values in counseling, and (3) immaturity and maturity in counseling.

Intellectual Versus Emotional Processes

Early writings in the nondirective counseling area stressed the importance of responding to the feeling content as expressed by students rather than to the so-called intellectual words or ideas that were used. If, for example, a student spent several minutes describing his attitudes and ideas about his father, the counselor was encouraged to respond to the feeling that was expressed. The counselor frequently responded by saying such things as "You feel that your father is unfair or. . . ." Feelings were held to be the only important element for counselors to recognize and to deal with. The emphasis upon the response to the feeling counteracted a tendency for the counselor to be superficial and to respond only to the words and to the offered ideas of the student or the client.

However, the counselor's need to respond to feeling has been overemphasized. Counselors sometimes seem to believe that if they can use the word *feel* in responding to a student a magical process will take place. Arbuckle explains the operation of the response to feeling as he writes: ". . . the client-centered counselor has as his primary means of verbalization the reflection of feelings of the client. This reflection of feeling, it should be noted, might in some ways be described as a method, and indeed might well become a method for a student counselor. If one is actually going to become a client-centered counselor, however, it ceases to be a method and becomes, rather, the means of a human approach to another person, a means of communication, comfortable for both the counselor and the client, and effective for the client . . ." (1961:151). Arbuckle goes on to cite six examples and show how feeling responses by client-centered counselors seem to be superior to feeling responses by other types of counselors.

The fetish of using "you feel" has misled beginning counselors and has made the training of so-called client-centered counselors appear almost tedious.

Counselors need to respond to the actual thoughts and ideas expressed by students. Feelings may or may not be accurate reflections of the actual or total condition of the person at any given moment. Psychology has taught that the total individual reacts to any stimulus. In any action or expression of self, be it words or behavior, the total person is involved. Counselors need to be concerned with understanding, reflecting, and incorporating into the counseling session all of the reactions, words, feelings, values, philosophies, and attitudes of the person seeking aid. There is no question that when the counselor attempts to understand and reflect the actual feelings of the person he can begin to approach the total ideational expression of the person. Yet a slavish dependence upon a method or the excessive use of a single word is harmful to all counseling and particularly to school counseling.

Feelings are reflections of ideas, values, successes, or failures in thinking, problem-solving, or even simple behavior. Feelings as such are a person's own reactions to other elements within personality. These feelings are clues and lead back to the first-level experience of the person. But feelings are not the primary problem-solving tools of the person. Whatever one's feelings may be, they are the result of the value or the worth that one places upon an idea, a construct, a behavior, or even any aspect of the self. Open-ended counseling with students needs to stress that the total organism is involved in problem-solving. One cannot solve problems with only one's emotions, although they can serve as guides, clues, and evaluations. The counselor must help the student to uncover and resolve the very real issues and problems that have led to the feelings that are described in counseling.

Whenever a person has problems, the total person is involved. Feeling, values, actions, beliefs, and guilt are outcomes of human behavior. Counselors are concerned with total human beings and cannot assume that problems only affect emotions and can only be solved through a concentration upon feelings. Carl Rogers (1961:23–24) speaks of the total experience of the person as being a "touchstone" of validity. "Experience is for me the highest authority." Although Rogers is speaking of his own experience in this quotation, he clearly alludes to the importance of understanding the total experiences of a client. Still speaking of himself, but continuing to stress the counselor's understanding of a client, he says, "It is to experience that I must return again and again, to discover a closer approximation to truth as it is in the process of becoming in me."

Values in Counseling

Counselors have long been advised to avoid coloring any counseling session with their own value structures. The fear of the imposition of values upon an unwary student has led to an attempt to keep counseling devoid of any counselor values. Actually such an attempt is always doomed to failure. The values by which a person, counselor or counselee, lives are available and obvious in all his actions, behavior, and words.

Teachers and educators at all levels have faced this problem throughout the years and frequently have been more realistic about its resolution than have counselors. Teachers often must reveal their own biases as they discuss and study a topic. Students with creative teachers are not expected to ape or adopt a teacher's value system, but must create and develop their own. Teachers have recognized that it is often impossible for them to cover or deny their values while waiting for students to explore, evaluate, and adopt their own ideas and values. But teachers who have permitted students freedom in learning have helped create more effectively educated persons able to determine for themselves their learnings, ideas, and most of all values.

Counselors are dealing with each student in the personal raw material of his life—his past, his present, and his future. Values are guides to behavior. To ignore them and to assume that they can be eliminated from the counseling session is to assume an ostrich-like view of the process of how problems are solved and of how persons guide their own lives.

Counselors' attitudes and values are only one side of the issue. The necessity for counselors to be able to admit to their own feelings and values has been stressed by Rogers and other nondirectivists. The concept of congruence—acting and behaving as one actually feels or believes—demands that the values of the person who serves as counselor be faced and recognized. The issue is not whether the student is aware of these beliefs and values, but whether he is free and confident that the counselor is not attempting to force these values or beliefs upon him. Counselors who are able to face and know themselves honestly can also begin to face and understand the values of others.

Student values are major issues in all counseling. Early experiences with meaningful persons and institutions are the raw material of constructed values. That values are learned is common knowledge; that they must be evaluated and judged as adequate or inadequate to the tasks that are undertaken is less clearly understood. Students' concepts always contain value judgments that are deeply rooted within their own self-concepts. These value judgments are critical in determining the solution of any problem, in planning for any career, or in attempting to create a life.

Values become the road maps, the limits, or even the commandments by which each person lives. To examine such basic elements within personality, within the structure of the self-concept that a student may have, is to examine the paths that he may follow in the future and to help explain why various actions have been taken. The school, the church, the family, or perhaps a guidance worker may attempt to help students adopt a certain value, philosophy, or way of life. Counselors may examine values with students but not necessarily teach values to them. Counseling can provide the environment within which values may be examined, rejected, reinforced, or modified in new directions, However, the actions or modifications of values must take place within the student rather than within the counselor.

The freedom to examine, to cast aside, and to adopt values is one of the most precious freedoms within the entire concept of counseling. Counselors who consciously or unconsciously manipulate students are assuming privileges that simply do not belong to them. The need to protect the value-examination part of the counseling process is vital to its success. Only slowly will students be able to evaluate their own reasons for having done or wanting to do something. Career choice reflects a value structure, college or work after high school is a composite of past values interacting with present experience, marital choice or even selection of a dating partner is similarly a reflection of the value structure of the person. Counselors, if they are to help students in solving problems of human behavior—and there are no other types—must become involved in examinations of values.

A student sometimes cannot face the unusual behavior patterns that may be discovered in the self. The student who has been doing poor work in college and who has obviously been using his failure in school to strike back at his parents can be frightened by the discovery. The conflicting values that permit such behavior are common in many students, and are deeply involved in overlaid value patterns such as "love thy parents," "strike back at those who hurt you," "independence is valuable," or "I must be responsible for my own actions." A diagnostic specialist in the psychological interpretation of personality may be able to trace through such convoluted value patterns, but such a diagnosis does not help the student until he is able to arrive at an understanding of his value pattern on his own.

Student Maturity

Counseling provides the experience of determining one's own ideas, plans, and actions. Many counselors are concerned, as are parents, that such an opportunity can be abused by students. There is no question that in our society there can be no freedom for a 7-year-old to drive an automobile or to plan for marriage. The counselor, in helping students to assess their own problems and to plan solutions, does not fulfill the role of a town policeman, a justice of the peace, or an arresting citizen. The facts that the student may need in order to plan a course of action may be supplied by the counselor. Frequently a counselor must help a student to assess the outcomes of a particular course of action. This function on the part of the counselor is to represent reality, as clearly as he can understand it, for the student. But the counselor himself is not reality; he merely represents it.

College planning is a typical problem area. It is not the responsibility of the counselor to gain admission for any student, regardless of parental pressure. Students may wish to apply to various schools or colleges where they would not be accepted because of their psychological test scores. The counselor will need to help the student to face the reality of the action the admissions officer may take. A counselor may wish also to help the student to consider other colleges that may be within his aspiration level. Whether to apply to the college that may turn him down must be the decision of the student. The facts and the interpretations of fact which the counselor makes are elements for the student to consider within the total framework of the conference session. The counselor cannot coerce the student into any action, but must give him freedom of choice. The counselor is not the parent of the pupil and may not assume responsibility for him. Parents may, if they so decide, try to force, demand, or forbid actions of one type or another. The behavior of the student may or may not conform to the rules established by the parents. But the counselor cannot function as a substitute parent in the name of guidance.

There are many methods that will impress the student with the limitations that must be faced as any behavior is contemplated. The freedom to examine all possibilities within a counseling session can add to the maturity of the student. The responsibility that the student must assume for his own actions and plans are similarly a part of the counseling experience. The counselor cannot ignore such problems, although again the ultimate action on the part of the student and his responsibility or lack of it must be his own province. Counseling attitudes are often adopted by parents as they help their children face and resolve questions of decision and responsibility. A 7-year-old child cannot be given the freedom to drive a car, but he can be allowed to decide whether he wishes to play little-league baseball or to attend a cub scout meeting. A 15-year-old boy may not be free to decide whether he may drive the family car. The same 15-year-old can be free to decide the afternoon activity or his clothing accessories, and he has every right to be included in any discussion of his future education and occupation. That such a boy may wish to discuss the reasons why he cannot use the family car with a counselor is certainly legitimate. Although he is aware of the laws in his state or community, he may wish to explore the reasons and assumptions behind such laws. The counselor need not assume the parental or police role with the student. Counseling provides an opportunity to grow in the process of thinking and problem-solving.

GROUP COUNSELING

Counseling has long been thought to be simply a one-to-one process within the private, protected environment of an office or room. Recent efforts in the medical and psychiatric fields as well as experimental work in educational institutions have helped to identify a process which is becoming known as group counseling.

Small groups of four to eight students have been brought together to discuss and attempt to solve similar or related problems. Some of the groups are larger than this size and some serve heterogeneous problem groups. Many techniques are being tried and research is being reported upon in many publications. Some groups meet together for only a few meetings; others may remain together for several months while problems are discussed and individual progress is sought by group members.

Research in group procedures has shown that many types of problems previously restricted to one-to-one counseling sessions can also be undertaken in small and medium-sized groups. The issue of whether or not groups may be used on occasions when individual counseling will not work has not been solved. Similarly it has not yet been established whether there are problems or types of student situations that can be handled in individual sessions but cannot be approached in a group setting. Differential research on these issues has not yet been made available.

The group-counseling field has been hampered by the same semantic problems that have occurred in the individual-counseling field. "Multiple counseling," "group therapy," and similar phrases have grown up around the use of groups in a counseling framework. Most frequently such groups are designed to achieve results similar to those expected in individual counseling. Students are invited to attend group sessions on the basis of expressed need or desire to work on problem situations. On some occasions it is profitable to undertake individual counseling along with group counseling for some members of the group. At other times it is found that individual counseling may serve as a follow-up to several group sessions.

The counselor in a group counseling session functions similarly to the counselor in an individual session. However, the introduction of the forces and pressures that naturally develop when a group is organized changes the environment for the students and for the leader. Counselors who attempt to enter into group counseling sessions are usually and desirably those who are skilled in the use of groups in other areas of a guidance or school program. The nature of groups requires a sophistication in group dynamics that parallels the need for a counselor to understand human growth and development as well as personality functioning.

Group guidance activities are a type of catch-all in many schools. *Group guidance* is a confusing term that is often used to describe almost any type of guidance activity that is carried on with more than one student. *Group counseling,* however, is a specific technique clearly related to individual counseling and involving more than one student at a time.

The future of group counseling in school systems appears to be bright. When counseling first became available as a tool, use of "group-guidance techniques" was avoided by most guidance workers. The growth and development of counseling along with the later development of the group as a tool for guidance has helped counselors as well as guidance workers work efficiently with increasingly large numbers of students. Group counseling and individual counseling are by no means identical in process and use. But the use of both techniques in advanced, well-staffed guidance programs is beginning to develop patterns that may be expanded into other school systems.

COUNSELORS AND COUNSELING

School counseling has been outlined as a process of working with individuals or groups of students to help them solve more effectively the problems that are a part of their normal educational and personal development. Counseling is a part of guidance, but it cannot be equated with it. It is more meaningful to view counseling as a specific tool designed to accomplish a special task—to help students solve problems in an open-ended, accepting, and protected environment.

A guidance program for students depends heavily upon the counseling process. All students are possible counselees, and yet it is important to recognize that a functioning guidance program may make it unnecessary for some students to seek counseling. The normal educational and guidance program of the school may provide the necessary assistance in adjusting to the school or institutional environment and enable students to become increasingly able to apply the educational experiences in their own lives.

Since counseling is viewed as a process, it becomes important to recognize that counselors function in a special relationship with students in counseling sessions. Testing or other types of assessment procedures in schools, occupational or educational planning sessions, and notices of placement openings are not counseling. There may be times during the larger guidance or educational program when a counseling type of relationship is established. The placement counselor may serve in a counseling relationship to a student as possible placement is discussed. Interviews simply to tell students of employment opportunities or to explain how to fill out forms are not counseling, although they may be necessary parts of the total guidance program.

All guidance workers are theoretically skilled counselors. However, all guidance work is not counseling. Broadly defined, in terms of aid to students, it is clear that almost all counseling is a part of guidance but that guidance activities may precede, accompany, or follow counseling. Large guidance programs with a large staff may be able to employ counselors who are not expected to participate in other types of guidance activities on a full-time basis. However, in many systems, usually in the smaller communities and districts, only a single guidance worker is employed. When such a person attempts to be all things to all people, problems can arise. Although he should be available to work as a counselor with students as the need arises, demands of other types of guidance programing may make it impossible for him to function always as a counselor. He can be handicapped by issues of budget, by the previous training and skills of other workers in the guidance program, by the expectations of the administration, the students, or the parents, and even by his own view of guidance and counseling. Specific issues of educational preparation for counselors and for guidance workers will be included in Part Five of this book. In that section the specific requirements of various states, professional recommendations for certification, and related topics will be presented in detail.

SUMMARY

Counseling is a primary tool of guidance. Counseling provides the warm and permissive climate within which an individual or members of a group can solve problems with the assistance of a trained and experienced person. Counseling is concerned with helping students to make decisions and to solve problems about themselves and about their educational experiences.

The process of counseling involves the student and the counselor in the open-ended assessment of proposed actions or behavior on the part of the person seeking help from a counselor. The subject matters of counseling are the content of the lives of students who seek help. Counseling is significant for individuals since it enables them to examine their own value systems and to assess their own planned actions or behavior changes in a protected and accepting environment. Counseling is a vital element in education and guidance because of its personalized learning and problem-solving nature.

Student problems may come from any and all areas of an individual's life. Regardless of the content, the essential nature of counseling involves a counselee in the process of collecting and ordering data about a problem so that a possible conclusion may be reached. Such conclusions can then be evaluated and examined in light of future experience. The accepting and permissive climate of counseling promotes problem-solving and permits the individual to solve problems according to the limits of individual freedom and responsibility and to the nature of the sponsoring society.

Historical approaches to counseling, as well as present methodologies of counseling, have been examined. All counseling is presented as student- or client-centered. The intervention or participation of the counselor in the problem-solving processes of the student may differ along a continuum of counselor involvement in counseling.

Three significant issues concern the role of counseling within guidance and education. The need to respond to total student behavior rather than to any single element, such as intellectual or emotional content, has been stressed. Additional issues concerning the role of values in counseling and the nature of maturity in students have also been presented.

The developing field of group counseling has been outlined, with a comparison of group methods with individual methods. The functioning of the counselor as a member of the guidance program staff concluded the chapter.

REFERENCES AND SUGGESTED READINGS

Adams, James F., *Problems in Counseling: A Case Study Approach,* New York: Macmillan, 1962.

American Psychological Association, Division 17, *The Scope and Standards of Preparation in Psychology for School Counselors,* Washington, D.C., 1961.

Arbuckle, Dugald S., *Counseling: An Introduction,* Boston: Allyn & Bacon, 1961.

Arbuckle, Dugald S., "Counselor Education—Philosophy and Objectives," *A Progress Report on Standards,* Washington, D.C.: American Personnel and Guidance Association, 1962.

Arbuckle, Dugald S., "Five Philosophical Issues in Counseling," *Journal of Counseling Psychology,* V (1958), 211–215.

Calia, V. F., "The Guidance Counselor: The Miracle Man in Education?" *The School Review* (1956), 429–431.

Carter, Thomas M., "Professional Immunity for Guidance Counselors," *Personnel and Guidance Journal,* XXXIII (Nov., 1954), 130–135.

Farwell, G. F., and H. J. Peters, *Guidance Readings for Counselors,* Chicago: Rand McNally, 1960.

Fiedler, F. E., "A Comparison of Therapeutic Relationships in Psychoanalytic, Non-Directive, and Adlerian Therapy," *Journal of Consulting Psychology,* XIV (1950), 436–445.

Fiedler, F. E., "The Concept of an Ideal Therapeutic Relationship," *Journal of Consulting Psychology,* XIV (1950), 239–245.

Hoyt, Kenneth B., "What the School Has a Right to Expect of Its Counselor," *Personnel and Guidance Journal,* XL (1961), 129–134.

Hudson, George R., "Counselors Need Teaching Experience," *Counselor Education and Supervision,* O (1961), 24–27.

May, Rollo, *The Art of Counseling,* New York: Abington, 1939.

McGowan, J. F., and L. D. Schmidt, *Counseling: Readings in Theory and Practice,* New York: Holt, Rinehart & Winston, 1962.

McKinney, Fred, *Counseling for Personal Adjustment,* Boston: Houghton Mifflin, 1958.

Patterson, C. H., *Counseling and Guidance in Schools: A First Course,* New York: Harper, 1962.

Patterson, C. H., *Counseling and Psychotherapy: Theory and Practice,* New York: Harper, 1959.

Patterson, C. H., "The Place of Values in Counseling and Psychotherapy," *Journal of Counseling Psychology,* V (1958), 216–233.

Penney, James F., "Counseling: Its Causes and Cost," *Journal of Higher Education,* XXXII (1963), 402–404.

Pierson, George A., and C. W. Grant, "The Road Ahead for the School Counselor," *Personnel and Guidance Journal,* XXXVIII (1959), 207–210.

Rogers, Carl R., "The Characteristics of a Helping Relationship," *Personnel and Guidance Journal,* XXXVII (1958), 6–16.

Rogers, Carl R., *Client-Centered Therapy,* Boston: Houghton Mifflin, 1951.

Rogers, Carl R., *Counseling and Psychotherapy,* Boston: Houghton Mifflin, 1942.

Rogers, Carl R., *On Becoming a Person,* Boston: Houghton Mifflin, 1961.

Rogers, Carl R., "A Theory of Therapy, Personality, and Interpersonal Relationships, as Developed in the Client-Centered Framework," in Sigmund Koch (ed.), *Psychology: A Study of Science,* III, Study I (1959), 184–256.

Rogers, Carl R., and R. F. Dymond, *Psychotherapy and Personality Change,* Chicago: University of Chicago Press, 1954.

Samler, Joseph, "Change in Values: A Goal in Counseling," *Personnel and Guidance Journal,* XXXVIII (1960), 32–39.

Sechrest, C. A., *New Dimensions in Counseling Students,* New York: Bureau of Publications, Teachers College, Columbia University, 1958.
Strupp, H. H., "An Objective Comparison of Rogerian and Psychoanalytic Techniques," *Journal of Consulting Psychology,* IXX (1955a), 1–7.
Strupp, H. H., "Psychotherapeutic Technique, Professional Affiliation, and Experience Level," *Journal of Consulting Psychology,* IXX (1955b), 97–102.
Super, Donald E., *et al.*, "The Role of Counseling in State and Regional Programs," in American Association for the Advancement of Science, *Identification and Guidance of Able Students,* Conference report, 1958.
Trueblood, Dennis L., "The Counseling Role in a Group Activities Advisory Context," *Journal of College Student Personnel,* I (1960), 13–17.
Tyler, Leona, "Theoretical Principles Underlying the Counseling Process," *Journal of Counseling Psychology,* V (1958), 3–8.
Tyler, Leona E., *The Work of the Counselor* (rev. ed.), New York: Appleton-Century-Crofts, 1961.
Vance, F. L., and T. C. Volsky, Jr., "Counseling and Psychotherapy: Split Personality or Siamese Twins," *American Psychologist,* XVII (1962), 565–570.
Warman, R. E., "The Counseling Role of College and University Centers," *Journal of Counseling Psychology,* VIII (1961), 231–237. (Comment by Ralph F. Berdie, 237–238.)
Watson, Gladys H., "An Evaluation of Counseling with College Students," *Journal of Counseling Psychology,* VIII (1961), 99–104.
Williamson, E. G., "The Fusion of Discipline and Counseling in the Educative Process," *Personnel and Guidance Journal,* XXXIV (1955), 74–79.
Williamson, E. G., "Value Orientation in Counseling," *Personnel and Guidance Journal,* XXXVI (1958), 520–528.
Williamson, E. G., and J. Foley, *Counseling and Discipline,* New York: McGraw-Hill, 1949.
Wrenn, C. Gilbert, "The Ethics of Counseling," *Educational and Psychological Measurement,* XII (Summer, 1952), 161–177.
Wrenn, C. Gilbert, "Status and Role of the School Counselor," *Personnel and Guidance Journal,* XXXVI (1957), 175–183.

PSYCHOLOGICAL TESTING

THE ISSUE. Tests are tools. Test results are facts. Tests can be either used or abused; tests can help as well as hurt.

The test in American schools is probably the most discussed and confusing element in the methodological kit of tools of the guidance worker. What tests are, how they can and should be used, and the significance of test data are issues that transcend even the boundaries of guidance and education.

Truly, test results belong first of all to those whose performance is being measured. Yet students whose behavior is assessed through testing are frequently the last to learn about the meaning of their performance. The student has primary rights to the interpretations of his efforts but seldom receives such information. How can such an anomaly exist?

The test and the results of testing have rightful places in guidance and education. What is this place? The paradoxes that have grown up around and within the field of testing require examination and discussion.

❦ ❦

Each person born into our world is separate and different from every other. This fact of individuality is frequently overlooked, educationally distorted, and even occasionally denied by persons who are concerned about their uniqueness. Psychological tests are a major tool of the guidance worker and educator who wish to explore and understand the individual characteristics of each student. Psychological tests yield measures of the differences among individuals. But although

CHAPTER SIX

psychological tests depend upon the belief in individual differences, they also depend upon the tendency of most individuals to be alike.

The mystery of the intelligence or personality test has been exposed for all to see in our psychologically curious culture. The early efforts of school personnel to uncover the various differences of individual students has blossomed into one of the million-dollar industries in our society. No teacher or administrator, much less a guidance person, is untouched by psychological testing in the schools. Required courses in testing are common in all educational institutions preparing teachers and professional school workers. Yet guidance has become the primary user of psychological test data. Such data frequently reveal new dimensions of the individual student. The guidance worker must perforce be a specialist in the theory and application of psychological tests.

TESTING AS A TOOL

The thousands of tests that are now available for use in education show the growth of the testing movement during the last half-century. Tests can provide data in almost all areas of human knowledge and performance. A test is a controlled scientific experiment. Significant variables are controlled and the dependent variable is the response of the subject.

Tests have become so widespread in education that their nature and structure is often overlooked by the users. Guidance programs are particularly involved in the use of tests as tools. Tests provide an appraisal of student performance. Future courses, educational plans, occupational hopes, and even personal adequacy often depend upon the outcomes of tests. Testing is thus a powerful tool in the kit of the teacher, administrator, and particularly the guidance worker. The structure and nature of tests must be understood by all guidance personnel.

The improper use of any tool is possible and may be inherent in the nature of the tool. A knife, a fire, and a hammer are simple tools that can often accomplish remarkable results when wielded by a skilled user. Yet it is evident that such tools can also be instruments of destruction, harm, and even murder. Tests can be misused and can destroy, hurt, and at times even kill the spirit of a student.

The misuse of counseling as a tool can similarly hurt and destroy a student. The outcomes of counseling, however, are less clearly visible than those of testing. Testing is more precise in its use and in its potential danger. An examination of the principles of the uses of testing in guidance can only scratch the surface of its use as a part of all American education. As it is a tool that is important in the lives of students, it is vital that its nature and advantages, as well as any dangers and disadvantages, be faced and understood. Experts in testing have understood that the same care is needed in the use of their potent tools as is necessary for the surgeon with his scalpel or the physician with an antipolio vaccine. The misuse of a tool can lead to as much hurt as its proper use can lead to effective help.

Knowledge is the key to proper utilization of testing as a tool. The most sophisticated users of tests are those who are most aware of the drawbacks and limitations of their tools. The discussion which follows is an attempt to approach tests as tools in guidance at their most basic level. The concepts which follow are applicable to all tests, to all test users, and to virtually all situations within which tests may be appropriate. The principles of test usage in guidance programs depend upon detailed factual knowledge about any test that may be used. A discussion of principles that attempts to treat all tests cannot hope to deal exhaustively or even superficially with any single test. It is best to remember that attitudes about the use of tests in guidance can arise out of an examination of the strengths, weaknesses, advantages, and disadvantages of any or all tests that can be used with students.

Testing is a major tool of any guidance worker; the more effective and skilled the use of such a tool, the more meaningful will be the guidance that depends on it.

A RATIONALE FOR PSYCHOLOGICAL TESTING

The scope of psychological testing in American education can be seen in the introductory statement of a recent textbook in psychological testing: "Anyone reading this book today could undoubtedly illustrate what is meant by a psychological test. It would be easy enough to recall a test the reader has taken in school, college, in the armed forces, in the counseling center, or in the personnel office" (Anastasi, 1961:1). Anastasi is perhaps too restrictive in believing that only readers of her book would recognize the meaning of a psychological test. Testing is a part of every school level and is utilized in all schools. Some tests may be homemade but most are standardized, nationally available instruments. Early entrance into a school program, retardation, acceleration, and normal progress are partially determined by the use of test results. Almost every major school decision now is, in part, dependent upon a test result.

What a psychological test is, how it is used, and most importantly why it is used are questions that must be answered prior to the acceptance of such a widely used technique in education. The "what" and the "how" are relatively easy to answer out of current practice in schools and programs at all levels. The "why" is perhaps the most difficult to define and certainly is the most important issue to resolve if one is to understand the role of testing in education and more specifically in the guidance program.

The "What" of Testing

A psychological test in its simplest sense is a sample of human behavior. "An apple is a fruit that is round, red, sweet, and grows on trees"; this answer to a vocabulary item establishes the fact that he knows the meaning of the symbol "apple." The question is asked and the answer is given. This tiny slice of human behavior in itself is not significant. Other questions need to be answered by the test administrator in order to evaluate such a response. What is the age of the child giving the answer? How many other children of this age are also able to answer this question? Is this answer related to the child's ability to answer similar questions of words of equal difficulty? Would the child be able to answer this question if it were to be repeated a few weeks later?

Psychological testing depends upon the measurement of individual human behavior and the comparison of this behavior with that of other persons. The task is to establish clearly the particular behavior of the person being tested; the comparison must be made in order to analyze the significance of his behavior. The complexities of these tasks may seem to obscure the actual simplicity of the process. An intelligence test measures the ability of the person to answer specific questions. Word definition, verbal problem-solving, numerical manipulations, verbal reasoning, and problem-solving involving the use of hands and eyes are common elements in most intelligence tests. The person is asked to supply a specific answer to a specific question. Achievement tests in algebra, history, social studies, and like areas are based upon similar processes. Personality tests such as the Rorschach Test ask for the subject to tell what is seen in an inkblot; interest inventories ask whether the testee would like to dissect, mount, or paint butterflies. The principle in all testing is the same: the individual responds to a problem situation; the response is compared with the responses of other persons.

Test results are composed of multiple responses of the subject. It is important to recognize that no matter what the test, what the area covered, what the conclusions reached, or even what the decisions made based upon the tests, the test score is derived from bits and pieces of individual human behavior. The conclusions that are developed out of this behavior must be related back to the behavior measured.

Users of tests, particularly psychologists, can become exceedingly skilled in using the data produced out of a psychological test. Skill in using such data is often a result of an understanding of human behavior and the application of observations produced through the testing. The actual test results are simple records of the way that a person has responded to a problem that has been presented for solution.

Many persons have compared psychological test results to a series of photographs of a person. The analogy is an apt one. Photographs show the characteristics of a person in many different poses. Seldom if ever would a person be willing to state after looking at one picture, "That's the way I would like to look," or "That isn't me at all." Test results are similar in that they are largely isolated pieces of human behavior that are placed together in a particular pattern so that meaningful conclusions can be obtained through an analysis of the results. Just as a person does not wish to be judged by one photograph, so it is equally dangerous to be judged by a single test score. The skilled tester is able to say: "What kind of an intelligence score would you like me to get for you? Would you like to have a high IQ? Would you like to have a low IQ? Would you like to have a test result that will show a well-adjusted person; or would you like to see a maladjusted person?" The humor in this type of statement is often frightening to the neophyte in testing. A person who is familiar in the testing field is very similar to the skilled photographer who is able to create the desired effect through a manipulation of the background, the lighting, or through the use of filters. Hopefully, the test user does not attempt to produce particular test results, but is able to interpret the results of any given test through a related analysis of the test's weaknesses, its strength, and its distortions.

Psychological testing is then, at its simplest, the collection of individual bits of human behavior that are patterned, analyzed, compared, and interpreted according to the skill of the test maker, the test user, and the background information that is available about the person taking the test and others who have taken it before.

The "How" of Testing

After the "what" of psychological testing is established, it is necessary to become concerned with the "how." The earliest testing provided for the individual examining of the student by the test giver. The names of Galton and Cattell, among others, are associated with the early efforts to develop tests of mental capacities. Their work in psychophysical and perceptual processes helped to show the way to later more complex tests. Alfred Binet and his co-workers were the pioneers in intelligence testing. Rough measures of intelligence were obtained in France, early in this century, by asking students to solve problems of increasing difficulty. Student performance was compared with normal, feeble-minded, and retarded children. Three scales were developed by Binet before his death in 1911. The tests were designed to yield a "mental age." L. M. Terman at Stanford University first developed the concept of the "Intelligence Quotient" by comparing mental age with chronological age. The Stanford-Binet Test is still used today throughout the country in a form that stems from the original adaptation of the Binet scale.

Achievement, aptitude, and personality testing soon followed the development of intelligence testing. The challenge of World War I and the need to measure the qualifications of millions of men led to the development of paper-and-pencil counterparts to the individual measures of intelligence. The advance to paper-and-pencil testing provided the means by which later developments of achievement testing, aptitude testing, and personality testing took place. Individual as well as group pencil-and-paper forms were commonplace in all of these tests. Following World War II the lines between intelligence, aptitude, and achievement tests seemed to blur. The classification system had been too neat and it appeared that by measuring the same behavior one could infer various results if proper care were taken to analyze the results properly.

The key to methodology in psychological testing has been the development of standardized questions, instructions, time limits, and common practices for administering the test. The variable to be measured was the response of the test subject. The standardization of all procedures made it possible for results to be compared from group to group. Tests that had been "standardized" on groups of students that were no larger than a few hundred were common even as late as a decade ago. Larger and larger samples have been developed so that student performance can now be compared with literally thousands of students of similar ages, school experiences, and test conditions. Testing has become a scientific tool, mass-produced in a technical society, and merchandised to school systems across the land.

The original nature of test data, as human behavior under standard conditions, has become largely lost in a welter of statistics, derived scores, self-interpreting profiles, and decisions based upon superscientific numbers. *The Organization Man* (Whyte, 1956) helped to highlight the uncritical acceptance that tests had obtained even in the business world. *The Brain Watchers* by Gross (1962) highlights some of the half-truths that have developed in testing.

The "Why" of Testing

School officials and guidance workers alike are often confused and uncertain when they are asked *why* they use tests. It seems as though it is the thing to do. Test data are collected and stored on permanent record cards, decisions are influenced by test scores, parents expect the results to be available, and tremendous sums of money are expended to develop and maintain testing programs.

Essentially, test programs must exist in a school system in order to produce factual information about students and to provide for the meaningful use of such data. The use of the data depends upon a continuing recognition of the actual nature of the data.

Mary has an intelligence quotient of 110; Mary successfully answered 51 of the 75 questions on the paper-and-pencil test. These facts about Mary are identical. Although the score does not provide a new insight into Mary, it does describe a particular series of facts about her. The meaning of these facts must be derived by combining them with all other facts known about her. Mary may be convinced that she is physically slow, intellectually slow, and considerably less capable than her classmates. Mary's view of herself contradicts the factual information supplied by the test score. The problem exists regardless of what the test score fact may be. Mary's attitude is as much a fact as is the test score recorded on her permanent record card in the office.

Psychological test scores provide facts about students. What is done with these facts, how they are incorporated into the educational program, how a guidance program can use them to aid students in learning and thinking about themselves and their futures, how they can help parents understand and aid their children—these developments in a school or college program depend upon the effective utilization of test data. Psychological testing can provide facts that cannot easily be obtained in other ways. When the facts have been carefully obtained, appropriately evaluated, and accurately recorded, it is possible for test data to be used in a school. Test scores and psychological tests can provide the basis for many aspects of a school and a school guidance program, but none of these uses is inherent in the tests themselves or in the scores obtained. Test data are raw, crude material. The effectiveness of the raw material depends upon the use to which it is put.

TYPES OF TESTS

Psychological tests may be classified as individual or group, verbal or performance, as well as by the subject matter included in the test. Recent books about tests have attempted to classify them into broad categories such as intelligence, aptitude, achievement, and personality. The issue of multifactor theories of intelligence versus a general concept of intelligence was common only a few years ago. Recent research in testing has actually helped to cloud these issues. Aptitude tests are now viewed as achievement tests and at the same time as measures of intelligence. Personality tests have remained as a broad category of testing, but data about the personality of a test subject have always been an outcome, even if secondary, in all types of tests and test situations.

A meaningful type of test classification for a guidance worker in a school system is provided by the terms *content testing* and *person testing*. Content testing measures the things which the person knows or has learned. Person testing attempts to characterize the patterns of actual behavior or predispositions to behave by the individual. Even these broad labels are imperfect and overlap as specific tests are analyzed. Yet such a system helps to focus upon the purposes to which the tests are to be directed in their use in a school or guidance program.

Individual and Group Tests

The actual collection of psychological test data can be accomplished by a test administrator assessing the reactions or responses of one person or by simultaneously testing from two to several hundred students. The issue of whether a single student or a large group is to be tested is determined by the nature of the test and the use to which the results are to be put.

Subject-matter or content testing such as achievement in mathematics, history, or science can be accomplished through large group testing. Similarly it has become possible to assess aptitude potential, or promise for future success in a number of areas, through large group testing. The National Merit Testing Program, the Scholastic Aptitude Test of the College Entrance Examination Board and similar types of tests are normally administered to very large as well as small groups. Most content tests in the various grade levels are also group tests. The Iowa Tests of Educational Development, the Metropolitan Test Series, and other grade-level achievement tests are administered to classes within the schoolrooms.

Individual testing is necessary whenever it is desirable for the test administrator to know not only what answer is given by the subject but also the methods and techniques he utilizes to obtain the answer. Other types of individual tests are used whenever it is felt that diagnostic problems may exist as an individual student is considered. The Stanford-Binet or the Wechsler Intelligence Scales are commonly used to establish individual intellectual capacity. Personality tests are administered to groups, but usually with little confidence in the results or in the validity of the conclusions drawn. When personality factors are seen to be significant in the student's problem-solving, it is desirable to obtain the results through a face-to-face, one-to-one testing situation. The test administrator can then observe and record all significant behavior as well as the particular responses of the subject.

Content Tests

Content tests attempt to assess and compare the knowledge or factual information possessed by one subject as compared with appropriately selected comparison groups. Content tests permit a fact to be established about a student such as:

1. Student A scored in the top 10 percent of all students tested in the X test of social studies.
2. Student B scored in the bottom quarter of all students who took the literary appreciation test Y.
3. Student C scored in the bottom or first stanine in clerical aptitude. The test measure was standardized (established) by measuring the clerical aptitude of employed clerical workers.
4. Student D had an IQ of 135.

or,

1. Student A scored in the first decile in the social studies section of the X achievement battery in the second grade.
2. Student B had an IQ of 125.
3. Student C achieved a "college board" score of 640.

It is important to note that all of these "facts" are simply different ways of saying that the student correctly answered a certain number of questions on a content-type test.

Content-type tests can provide a large amount of data about the qualitative and quantitative dimensions of a student's knowledge. Sampling techniques in all of the major subject-matter areas make it possible for data to be obtained in minutes about a student's learning in a subject that may have extended over 12 or 16 years. Similarly a profile of the aptitudes and intellectual capabilities of a single student can be compiled that could not be obtained without test usage.

It is startling to note the power that is put into the hands of the test user by content-type tests. Tests can provide for educators and for guidance workers a bird's-eye view of the entire educational history of the student as well as much data about the informal unofficial learnings he has accumulated. The significant question about such test data is "And what will be done with this information?"

Person-Centered Tests

Person-centered tests attempt to compile data about the way in which a person behaves or about his manner of problem-solving. Contrasting with the content-type tests, concerned with what a student may know or believe, a person-centered test characterizes the attitudes toward the self and others, the pattern of intellectual reasoning, and the skill with which symbols of all types are manipulated. Person-centered tests are designed to compile a profile about the way of life or the personality of the individual in a gross sense.

1. Student A tends to think in global rather than discrete fashion.
2. Student B values power more than the accumulation of property.
3. Student C uses his intelligence in open, creative ways rather than attempting to circumscribe his thinking.
4. Student D fears the control his parents exert over him.

The series of statements that can arise out of the use of person-type tests is remarkably different from those statements that can be compiled from content-type tests. However, there are many types of tests that do not fit neatly into either of these categories and perhaps yield data in both classifications.

Tests that are clearly person-type tests are those which measure the personality characteristics of an individual, such as the Rorschach Test, the Thematic Apperception Tests, and many tests of abstract reasoning and concept formation. Additional person-type tests are the attitude inventories, value measures, and most of the interest inventories.

The person-type test has never been as clearly or widely developed as the content-type test. It is easier to test the comparative level of knowledge in American history or algebra than it is to pinpoint the individual's characteristic pattern of problem-solving or personality structure. The content-type test is a reflection of discrete facts and the specific, even if involved, interrelationships between or among such facts. The person-type test reflects knowledge about the personality or problem-solving processes within an individual.

The use, the application, and the purposes of the tests are even more important in person testing than in content testing. The facts that are obtained about a person are more intimately related to the individual test subject. Success in testing of this type always depends upon the person's willingness or capacity to know himself. What is to be done with the raw material of the test data is the most significant issue for both content and person testing.

TEST DATA AS FACTS

Tests can be used to collect facts or interpretations of fact in many different areas of academic performance. Any classification, such as the content- versus person-type test is more likely to provide general information about the test than to reveal the types of data that can be acquired. The areas of student knowledge and student operation that are outlined below are in general accord with an older classification of tests according to the areas tested.

The topical areas that are to be described are offered not as a scheme to classify tests as instruments, but rather to clarify the types of test data that can be obtained for use in guidance. Intelligence tests are also achievement tests and aptitude tests. However, when a test instrument is used to assess intelligence, it is assumed that for some reason it is desirable to obtain an estimate of the intellectual level of the subject. What can be done with the data after they are collected will be discussed in a following section. Guidance uses test data in many ways, but any use depends upon a careful gathering of factual material in as accurate and appropriate a manner as possible.

Intelligence Data

Intelligence data can be obtained through the use of either individual or group tests of mental ability, mental capacity, or any of the tests that have developed in this area. The inference of an intelligence level—and an inference is all that is available from any test—is constructed out of the answers a subject gives to problems of a verbal and performance nature that have been developed and standardized in a particular test.

Vocabulary, verbal reasoning, mathematical manipulation of digit symbols, verbal analogies, memory, and similar tasks have been used most frequently as problem areas for an assessment of verbal intelligence. Picture problem-solving, block design, spatial relations, decoding, reasoning through pictures, and similar tasks have been the raw material for performance measures.

Individual administrations of such intelligence tests provide for a clinically close situation in which not only specific answers can be obtained but a subject's methods of problem-solving may be observed. Group tests have succeeded very well in creating similar tasks that can be scored by the use of paper-and-pencil answer sheets. Although the unavailability of clinical data about the subject's performance on a group test is a weakness, such data can often be obtained through other sources.

The nature of intelligence tests depends very much upon the standardization procedures that have been employed by the test maker before the test is used in a school situation. An intelligence measure compares a particular student with others of similar age, grade placement, experience level, and even cultural background. If the standardization group has not been adequately studied, any inference about a person's relative standing on the results of the test is meaningless.

The statement "He is just not college material" is a common judgment made on the basis of the results of an intelligence test. That colleges of all types, willing to admit students of virtually all levels of ability, exist as accredited institutions belies such a statement. Moreover, it is often not made obvious that in such a statement the speaker is assuming that the performance of the college students with whom the hypothetical student is being compared would be at such and such a level. The assumptions inherent in this statement would frighten a logician and chill the many test specialists who have wide and varied experience with such problems.

Intelligence test scores supply important data about a single student, a group of students, a class, and a school population. The nature of measurement dictates that the significance of an average test score increases as it is derived from larger and larger numbers of subjects. Such factual material about a student population or a community level can be used in curriculum construction, homogeneous or heterogeneous groupings, and occupational analysis, as well as in educational planning. By comparing intelligence test data with achievement test data, particularly when both are obtained in test batteries, the tester can compare the performance and capacity levels of individuals or large groups.

Intelligence level estimates provide facts that are difficult and often impossible to obtain in any other fashion. The opportunity to assess such dimensions of an individual or a group has changed the type, character, and creative possibilities of the schools that have been able to collect and understand the significance of the facts available.

Aptitude Data

Data on the aptitudes of students can be collected in the same fashion as intelligence test facts. Despite the wide variety of aptitudes that have been identified and supported, use of individual tests of aptitude has not been widespread. Recent developments in the testing field have, to the contrary, stressed the use of integrated (commonly standardized, or administered to a common sample group) aptitude test batteries. The Differential Aptitude Test Battery of the Psychological Test Corporation has been used throughout the entire country. Other batteries, similar in design and structure, have been created by other test publishers.

The types of aptitude usually assessed in school situations are verbal or vocabulary manipulation, numerical and mechanical aptitude, spatial relations, and verbal reasoning, as well as the more special aptitudes relating to music, spelling, clerical techniques, and English usage. Some aptitude tests have been constructed to measure potential for an occupational field such as accounting, nursing, or law. These latter tests have proved to be only partially successful and have not spread to other fields.

The similarity of aptitude and intelligence is immediately apparent. No clear-cut theoretical position has been advanced to clarify such a situation. The early view of persons as possessing a general or even multifactor intelligence and overlaid levels of aptitude in many conceivable areas has fallen like a house of cards upon test makers, users, and confused students. Research is progressing in test publishing houses, research institutes, and universities. Experts agree upon a complexity level that was only dimly seen in the early days of test construction. Such problems are common in all scientific investigation and characteristic of a dynamic and responsible professional field.

The present theoretical confusion need not obscure the very real and valuable facts that can be marshaled when aptitudes are related to vocational choice, course selection, college planning, placement procedures, and many other guidance and educational efforts. The analysis of actual performance by employed workers, students attending technical school, and successful career specialists have helped to provide a background of meaningful data for comparison with the results of any aptitude test.

A special type of aptitude test has recently developed within American education. The National Merit Testing program is typical of several areas of such testing. Students are measured on tests of scholastic aptitude (variously defined as aptitudes usually appropriate for academic success), and are compared with students across the country. Scholarships, grants, fellowships, and other types of rewards are offered to chosen students. A significant feature of such tests is the broad comparison that is possible. Instead of the hundreds or occasionally thousands of students previously used in comparison groups, it is now possible to compare a single student's performance with hundreds of thousands of similar students. Research productivity, needed acclaim to scholarship rather than merely to athletic laurels, a renewed interest in the reasons for academic success, help for needy and qualified students, and many other praiseworthy results have grown up out of such nation-wide testing.

National testing has been hindered by many of the same problems that handicap all types of testing. Scores seem to acquire magical qualities, one degree between two scores is used to distinguish between important scholarship and honorable mention. The scores on these tests, just as the earlier IQ's, "College Boards," and similar tests have become entities in themselves, rather than scores based upon the actual behavior of the subjects on a series of problem-solving questions.

Achievement Tests

Achievement tests are measures of currently possessed, demonstrably available information in varied content areas. Early tests of achievement were keyed to discrete items in relatively narrow subject-matter areas. Developments in achievement test usage after World War II have stressed broader testing in conceptual patterns of knowledge such as the humanities, social studies, and science. At the same time test makers have attempted to stress the acquisition of "developed skills." Developed skills are abilities or intellectual habits of thinking in specific areas of study: problem-solving in science, symbol manipulation in mathematics, reading comprehension, map reading, and similar techniques. Single tests of achievement have also been supplemented by integrated batteries for various grade levels.

Youngsters at an early age begin to tell their parents, "Today is the day we take our Iowas." The tests may be any of the various Iowa Tests of Basic Skills or Educational Development. Other children may talk of the "STEP," the Sequential Tests of Educational Development, or the "Metropolitans," the Metropolitan Achievement Tests. But although these tests are widely used, they are only representative of the many tests available.

Almost all achievement tests measure word usage or vocabulary in one way or another. Mathematical skills are also included. The overlapping content areas in intelligence, aptitude, and achievement tests are confusing to all who use, make, or take them. The concept of "acquired intellectual ability" is offered as a foundation for newer types of achievement tests, yet all test makers will support the similarity of the tests labeled intelligence, aptitude, and achievement.

The key to the conceptual difference between these tests seems to lie in the types of questions that the test user wishes to answer about the results obtained from the subject. Future success (aptitude potential) can usually be judged from the possession of certain levels of achievement at certain ages; the younger the possessor of most factual data or developed abilities the higher the aptitude indicated. Similarly intelligence, or the results of intelligence, can be assessed through an examination of possessed factual data and compared age levels. The important consideration is the relationship among acquired facts, age, grade level, previous education and training, and other securable data. Test users need to recognize that it is the behavior and the problem-solving responses of the subject that are being manipulated, compared, totaled, and interrelated to obtain the desired pattern of knowledge from test data.

Achievement test data are exceedingly useful in determining the level of educational development that a subject has attained. Class or group levels may also reveal patterns of achievement for different schools within the same school system, community, or state. The uses which guidance makes of achievement tests can parallel use by the schools and also help focus information for individual self-knowledge and decision-making. Achievement tests are particularly appropriate as they can be compared with and related to measures of intelligence and aptitude for the same student, class, or large student group.

Personality Tests

Personality tests or inventories are similar to other types of tests in that they measure subject behavior but are different from other types in that, rather than assessing content possessed, they measure attitudes, characteristics, or beliefs about the subject himself. This difference is a significant variation, since no objective standard of evaluation for personality exists. The distance from Paris to New York can be determined and the answer compared with the response of the person taking the intelligence, aptitude, or achievement test. A feeling of inadequacy may exist within a person, as reported by the person, or it may not. The person may be reporting a fact about the self that cannot be verified, or even a false fact that the person believes to be true. The difference between a content- and person-type test, as earlier described, causes significant problems in many personality tests.

Some tests of personality do not depend upon the subject's direct report on the aspect of personality being measured. Projective tests, such as the Rorschach or the Thematic Apperception Test or some of the broader situational-type tests, attempt to assess personality through an analysis of the product of a person's attitudes toward himself, others, and the world around. Theoretically, it may be true that a person may see the world in a particular fashion owing to his own feelings, attitudes, or personality characteristics. However, the measure of personality through subject responses that are "twice removed" from actual existence makes validity in such testing even more difficult to achieve. Specialists in individually administered tests of this type have obtained variable results, sometimes exceedingly effective and at others only partially valid. Accurate school use of most personality tests is considerably more difficult than other types of content tests.

A type of personality or person test widely used in academic areas is the interest inventory. Students are asked to indicate what types of activities they prefer to do, observe, or perform. Because there is usually little desire for normal individuals, who understand the purpose of the inventory, to fake or falsely answer such questions, valuable attitudes about work and occupational patterns can be obtained. Yet the validity of such testing is always questionable. The test user must understand the nature of the assessment and the dangers that are inherent in the measurement as well as in its subsequent manipulation.

Interest inventories, attitude surveys, sentence completions, or even word association tests can become useful tools in the hands of experienced users such as clinical psychologists or specially trained guidance workers. However, caution must always be exercised in examining the relationships of such tools. Interests do not always correlate with aptitudes or achievement patterns. Similarly it is not always true that where ability, aptitude, or skill exist interest or positive attitudes will be found. Experienced test users as well as students are often misled into improper reasoning when mixed person- and content-type test data are analyzed.

Many of the common paper-and-pencil type personality inventories attempt to assess traits such as the student's outgoing nature, friendliness, family problems, and emotional state. These personality traits are frequently undergoing a process of change through school development and seldom if ever are directly related to the specific problem that the student is given. The reliability and validity of such instruments is seldom very high, and caution needs to be exercised in the use of such instruments.

Problem inventories face the practical issues listed above and simply ask the student to check his problem areas. Such a survey tool as the Mooney Problem Check List can help to assess the broad problems of a large group, to initiate a group counseling relationship, or to aid in individual counseling. The behavior pattern tapped by any personality tool is so far removed from any specific of personality structure that its usefulness is determined by the skill of the user rather than by the test or inventory itself.

TESTING IN GUIDANCE

Test programs may be initiated within a school or a community by administrative leadership, attempts at curriculum evaluation, or perhaps by the emphasis on individual help given by a guidance program. Reading programs, study courses, and other such program items may also spark the adoption. Regardless of who has been responsible for the beginning of the program, all groups within the school setting may profit from the uses of the test data. The need for cooperative use of test results underscores the importance of planning in the operational details of any testing program.

Although it is beyond the province of guidance to examine, in detail, the use of tests in administration, curriculum construction or evaluation, or other specialized areas, the guidance worker should be willing to share the use of test data, cooperate in the administration of such a program, and share the budget responsibility for any program. A guidance program can utilize the results of virtually any test that is administered within a school. Test data is information about students that can help students to know themselves better. Students can incorporate test data into a conceptual design about themselves and their present and future plans. The facts that come from tests are facts that arise out of the measured behavior of students. Students, through guidance, can be helped to profit from knowledge of such test information.

Cooperative Testing Purposes

The existence of a testing program within a school immediately raises questions about the uses of the data that are gathered. Early-entrance decisions may be based upon individual administrations of an intelligence test and an interview to assess social maturity. Achievement test results collected from the senior class in a high school can help to establish the attainment levels of the average student in a community as well as individual ranks for each student. Each situation, each separate test, each individual community establishes its own pattern of testing, test usage, and interpretation. The immensity of the task of understanding the multiple uses of any single testing program is difficult to describe. However, an examination of the principles involved in the cooperative use of a single test may help to highlight the responsibility that is assumed by all groups in a school when testing takes place.

The early-entrance test that permits an underage child to enter kindergarten or first grade has solved an administrative problem. Any or all of the following uses may also be made of such an individual intelligence test:

1. Tentative readiness for reading group placement.
2. Assumptions about the relationship of intelligence and social maturity to school readiness.
3. Teacher judgments about progress in school adjustment, subject mastery, and potential for special help or aid.
4. Diagnostic judgments about reading, speech, or general behavior problems.
5. Promotion decisions for the first several years of school based upon effort, achievement, and intelligence.
6. Determination of the level of all first-grade pupils in the community in order to select a graded series of reading books.
7. One example of intellectual level for a college admissions officer or placement interviewer attempting to assess school records for college or work potential.

The jump from item number 6 to number 7 may seem large, and yet it would be easy to supply other uses to which the test data could be put during the years of attendance at the same or other community schools. A single record of behavior, obtained through psychological testing, can be useful to everyone within a school system who is capable of understanding or applying the results. But the test score belongs primarily to the child from whom it was obtained. The score may be inaccurate, spuriously high, inconsistent with later results, or a clear indication of feeble-mindedness or unusual ability. The school person who administered, recorded, stored, or transmitted the data does not own the test. All who are involved in the education of the child will be partners in the use of the data, partners with the child whose behavior is the test score.

The multipurpose use of tests demands that cooperative procedures be used in collecting, recording, transferring, or utilizing the data that arise out of a psychological test situation. Elementary schools that refuse to transfer the records of their students to secondary schools are guilty of educational quackery. Yet how many instances of such selfishness have been recorded? A more subtle form of selfishness may exist in dealings with the student himself. However, the student has paid for his privilege to attend school, public or private, and has the right to assume that all of the information collected about him will, or at least can, be used to aid him.

Test data about students form a basis for considering all issues in curriculum-building and revision, administrative decisions, supervisory procedures, and guidance programing. Guidance as one of the major groups in education needs to enter into all appropriate efforts to collect, order, and utilize such data

Student Self-Knowledge

The facts that can be collected about students are facts that need to be shared with them. Frequently, test data are viewed as school property to be recorded, stored, and treated like grades. Actually, grades are stored, recorded, and used for students. The concept of the student as the center of the educational process dictates that testing merely for record-keeping be an empty, expensive process.

Students may profit from an indirect use of test data, particularly in the early grades. Intelligence test scores can be used to establish reading levels and in other types of decision-making that may not include any direct consultation with students. Similar use is made of achievement and aptitude test data. Yet common practice allows students and their parents to become involved in the understanding and use of achievement test information in the very early grade levels. Students are interested and eager to know about their own progress. Although there has been little use of intelligence or aptitude test data with younger students, older students are slowly being permitted to know about their own progress in these areas of testing. Perhaps creative programing will provide ways to involve even younger children in an analysis of their own status with regard to intelligence and aptitude data.

Principle would seem to dictate that test data of all types be usable with students of all ages. The development of new techniques will permit guidance programs to extend such test knowledge into younger and younger groups.

Self-study and self-knowledge for the purpose of self-analysis, all dedicated to making it possible for students to make effective decisions about themselves and their future, is still a relatively new concept for many schools. Colleges have frequently pioneered in these guidance activities, perhaps because it was felt that the more mature student could profit more effectively. Recent research programs and publications (Katz, 1960, 1962) have demonstrated the desirability and possibility of extending detailed self-knowledge and self-analysis for decision-making down into the seventh, eighth, and ninth grades. Casual references have been made about random activity of this type in elementary school programs, but no detailed programs yet exist.

Self-knowledge, self-analysis, and effective decision-making can be encouraged, aided, and made meaningful as test data are made available and understandable to students in all levels of education. Guidance must face the primary responsibility for such programing. Guidance personnel need to face their tasks in the area of testing and attempt to take the lead in helping students to know themselves better so that more meaningful decisions about themselves can be made. Meaningful decisions about the self underlie the development of effective life plans.

Guidance Programing

The responsibility for testing can be divided among several educational groups. No single administrator, curriculum specialist, guidance worker, or even a highly trained specialist in a narrow area such as reading, speech, or home visiting would want to have sole responsibility for all testing within a school program. Guidance, however, is one of the logical responsible sources for a coordinating type of leadership in the testing field. Intelligence, aptitude, personality, and related tests have traditionally been associated with a guidance effort in the school. Achievement testing has commonly been the responsibility of administrators or curriculum supervisors. However, many cooperative arrangements are possible.

A meaningful organization pattern is possible when guidance assumes the primary responsibility for helping students understand and utilize their own test results, leaving other uses to administrators or others. Parental understanding of test data is closely associated with student growth and understanding, and is a normal related activity for counselors. Guidance workers are frequently members of curriculum committees consulted on administrative procedures based on test interpretation. Therefore student and parental use of test data can be the primary area of operation for guidance workers.

When student and parental understanding become primary issues for guidance in the use of tests in schools, it is possible to avoid some of the unbalanced programing that exists. Community X spends a large sum of money each year to test all grades from 3 to 8 on an achievement battery, but schedules few intelligence and no aptitude tests. A more balanced testing program would help the students know themselves better and still accomplish the over-all goals of the school system.

GROUP PROCEDURES. Group procedures are a resource that can be used to help students learn about themselves at all levels. The group process can extend the content of test data into a meaningful program. Elementary school pupils are aware of the individual differences in talent, capacity, interest, and education necessary for various projects. Discussions about such projects can involve measures of these characteristics. Teacher-pupil, teacher-parent, and teacher-pupil-parent conferences can offer the means of transmitting test data to students and parents. Guidance specialists with responsibility for elementary school programs need to work with such established types of activity to help teachers, pupils, and parents profit from knowledge of tests.

Many schools have experimented with group programs that involve parents in discussions of tests and other school procedures. Actual data about their own children may or may not be made available in these meetings. Counseling can and probably should be used to supplement any such group program.

The necessary information about what tests are, how they are scored, and what the scores mean must be shared with any consumer, parent or child. Group procedures can be effective in bridging the gap between what lay consumers believe about test data and what may actually be true. Measurement techniques are possible subject matters for groups, classes, or parental meetings and are important facts for any person attempting to understand testing and test results. The chapter on group work as a tool of guidance (Chapter Seven) and other writings about groups such as those by Glanz (1962) and Warters (1960) also provide specific methods for using group techniques in helping persons to understand test facts.

COUNSELING. Counseling is a primary avenue for sharing and utilizing test data with students. The objective reality of a test score can recede if a student is incapable of accepting it. Self-attitudes may conflict with measured "fact." Skilled counselors are quick to recognize that the student's belief about himself is the primary influence on his behavior. The most imposing array of "factual" information can be ignored by the student with a need to ignore such data. Counselors must be able to help a student incorporate test data into his knowledge of himself over a period of time as far as is desirable, possible, and appropriate.

Counseling, like group work, is a tool that can be used to help students to think, solve problems, and make decisions about themselves and their futures. The interplay of these techniques depends upon a thorough knowledge of their effectiveness, advantages, and weaknesses. Counseling becomes the most intimate and important avenue for helping students who cannot help themselves through other means. The counselor needs to be aware of the entire program of testing and, in fact, the entire educational effort if he is to be able to work with students in helping them solve problems and become effective persons.

SUMMARY

Psychological testing is a third major tool for guidance workers. The concept of testing as a tool has been examined as the "what, how, and why" of testing were presented. The details of any testing program involve the understanding of individual and group tests and the differences between "content" and "person" tests.

Test data may be considered as facts that can be gathered in the areas of intelligence, aptitude, achievement, and personality. After the data are effectively gathered, they must be used. The many uses which guidance makes of test data concluded the treatment of tests as a tool of guidance.

REFERENCES AND SUGGESTED READINGS

Anastasi, Anne, *Psychological Testing* (2nd ed.), New York: Macmillan, 1961.

Cass, J. C., and D. V. Tiedman, "Vocational Development and the Election of a High School Curriculum," *Personnel and Guidance Journal,* XXXVIII (1960), 538–545.

Cronbach, L. J., *Essentials of Psychological Testing* (2nd ed.), New York: Harper, 1960.

Darling, R. J., *et al.*, "Using Test Results to Identify Student Needs for Corrective Instruction," *Educational Bulletin,* XXII, Monterey, Cal.: California Test Bureau, 1962.

Droege, Robert C., "GATB Norms for Lower High School Grades," *Personnel and Guidance Journal,* XXXIX (1960), 30–36.

Flanagan, John C., *et al., Design for a Study of American Youth,* Boston: Houghton Mifflin, 1962.

Frankel, Edward, "Effects of Growth, Practice and Coaching on Scholastic Aptitude Test Scores," *Personnel and Guidance Journal,* XXXVIII (1960).

Freeman, Frank S., *Theory and Practice of Psychological Testing,* New York: Holt, Rinehart & Winston, 1955.

Getzels, J. W., and P. Jackson, *Creativity and Intelligence,* New York: Wiley, 1962.

Glanz, Edward C., *Groups in Guidance,* Boston: Allyn & Bacon, 1962.

Glanz, Edward C., and J. F. Penney, "A Cooperative Research Project for Curriculum Validation," *Journal of Higher Education,* XXVI (1961), 39–44.

Glanz, Edward C., *et al.*, "The Measurement of Aptitude and Achievement Growth in the First Two Years of College," College Research Report No. 2, Boston University, unpublished.

Goldman, Leo, *Using Tests in Counseling,* New York: Appleton-Century-Crofts, 1961.

Gross, Martin, *The Brain Watchers*, New York: Random House, 1962.
Gysbers, N. G., "Test Profiles Are for Counselees," *The Vocational Guidance Quarterly*, IX (1960), 9–12.
Katz, Martin, *You: Today and Tomorrow*, Princeton, N.J.: Educational Testing Service, 1959.
Lyman, Howard B., *Test Scores and What They Mean*, Englewood Cliffs, N.J.: Prentice-Hall, 1963.
Marsolf, Stanley S., *Psychological Diagnosis and Counseling in the Schools*, New York: Henry Holt, 1956.
McCauley, John H., "Reporting Results of the Standardized Testing Programs to Parents," *Personnel and Guidance Journal*, XLI (1962), 56–58.
Pallone, N. J., "Effects of Short- and Long-Term Developmental Reading Courses upon S.A.T. Verbal Scores," *Personnel and Guidance Journal*, XXXVIII (1960).
Ricks, J. H., "On Telling Parents About Test Results," *Test Service Bulletin*, LIV (1959), 1–4.
Ross, C. C., "Should Low-Ranking College Freshmen Be Told Their Scores on Intelligence Tests?" *School and Society*, XLVII (1938), 678–680.
Shaw, Merville C., and D. J. Brown, "A Review of Scholastic Underachievement of Bright College Students," *Personnel and Guidance Journal* (1957).
Stalnaker, John M., "Research in the National Merit Scholarship Program," *Journal of Counseling Psychology*, VIII (1961), 268–277.
Super, Donald E., *et al., Scientific Careers and Vocational Development Theory*, New York: Bureau of Publications, Teachers College, Columbia University, 1957.
Super, Donald E., *et al., Vocational Development: A Framework for Research*, New York: Bureau of Publications, Teachers College, Columbia University, 1957.
Thistlethwait, D. L., *College Press and Changes in Study Plans of Talented Students*, Evanston, Ill.: National Merit Scholarship Corp., 1960.
Thurstone, Thelma G., *Reading for Understanding*, Chicago: Science Research Associates, 1959.
Thurstone, T. G., *et al.*, "Your Child's Intelligence," *N.E.A. Journal*, L (1961), 33–48.
Vernon, Philip E., *Intelligence and Attainment Tests*, New York: Philosophical Library, 1961.
Viaud, Gaston, *Intelligence: Its Evolution and Forms*, New York: Harper, 1960.
Warters, Jane, *Group Guidance*, New York: McGraw-Hill, 1960.
Whyte, W. H., *The Organization Man*, New York: Simon & Schuster, 1956.

GROUPS IN GUIDANCE

THE ISSUE. The individual is the central focus for guidance. The group can provide an effective avenue for aiding the individual. The seeming paradox of groups being used to maximize individual growth and development is resolved as the nature of the group is examined.

The seeming simplicity of the group arises out of its widespread involvement in all human interaction. Yet upon detailed study the group is seen to be a complex unitary concept that has a structure and process regardless of the content area with which it is employed.

Groups are a tool for use in guidance. How the group can help the individual is the basic issue for the use of groups in guidance.

❦ ❦

Psychological testing, counseling, and group procedures form a pattern of specific professional tools that can be used in all areas of guidance. Testing and counseling are more widespread processes in schools and colleges, but recent research and newer applications of group work have made it as useful an instrument as counseling and testing at all levels of guidance programing.

The history of groups in guidance shows an early interest in group activities followed by a period of disinterest and disenchantment. Recent research in many disciplines has permitted group work to become more scientific and objective in its operation and application. Guidance has again become a primary user of group procedures. Groups have been analyzed and understood as a social unit with a particular method of operation. The subject matters that can be used within a group are exceedingly variable and make it necessary for guidance workers to

CHAPTER SEVEN

explore the particular applications that are possible. The complexity of the operation of groups—the group process—has led to the development of training procedures for group leaders and guidance personnel. The issues of the place of groups in guidance, the process and content of groups, and the development of skill in the use of groups are the major elements that must be understood by those concerned with guidance.

THE TOOL CONCEPT

The concept of a group as a tool is not widely understood or accepted as useful by guidance personnel or those in other areas of social science. Groups are almost too natural for the unsophisticated user. The ubiquitous nature of the group in our society, our schools, committees, work units, and games helps to mask the complex nature of human interaction within groups.

The early history of guidance shows the definite application of so-called "group guidance." Yet careful examination shows that the use of groups was distorted and frequently naïve. Guidance workers were faced with large numbers of students, and the tools of counseling and testing were only partially developed. Psychological testing was in its infancy, and counseling was assumed to be virtually the same as advising. Guidance counselors were assigned to classroom units, and whenever a "guidance" topic was discussed, "group guidance" was assumed to be taking place.

Guidance was an unknown quantity, and teachers and administrators of a willing and unwilling nature were assigned to guide students. This atmosphere prevailed as "group guidance" was developed and applied in the schools. Many situations became unbearable for students and guidance personnel alike. It was easy to blame the process of "group guidance" and to condemn all guidance as well.

Counseling became the more meaningful and appropriate tool for guidance workers to use in the schools and colleges. The individual approach to students took the guidance worker out of the classroom and into the counseling office for private and personal conferences. The entire group concept was quickly discarded, often with considerable pleasure. Psychological testing was progressing rapidly at the same time that counseling was receiving intense study. Specialists in research and theory development were working in both areas. Testing and counseling became the major methods of guidance in the school. Groups and group work had been largely discarded by many as inappropriate and distinctly distasteful to students and faculty members alike.

Research in Groups

Prior to, along with, and following the abortive use of groups by guidance, many other professional persons were attempting to assess and to describe the significant dimensions of the group as a unit within our society. Research into the nature of "dyads"—the two-member group, the natures of small and large groups, the cut-off points for size descriptions, patterns of communication within groups, and many other areas of group operation began to provide a sizable background of significant information on the group as a social unit.

Individuals were seen to behave differently in groups than when alone. Significant research projects were undertaken to examine and to attempt to explain such phenomena. While the total behavior of members of groups was under scrutiny, it was found that variables of leadership and purpose also affected the productivity of a group. What had seemed superficially simple had become complex. The group was a dimension of everyday life that was different from but as significant as the previously discovered facts of individual behavior.

Groups were seen to vary in effectiveness as size variables were manipulated. Frequently smaller groups were more effective than larger groups, and yet it was found that for some tasks smaller groups were less effective. Research demonstrated that in certain tasks, where it had long been assumed that a small group was more effective, very large groups could be equally successful. The data began to accumulate in mountainous piles. Groups, simple and widespread as they had seemed, were not simple.

Social scientists from the fields of sociology, anthropology, psychology, and other disciplines became involved in a study of the group as an interactive tool within human relations. Cartwright and Zander (1953, 1960) summarize the significant research studies completed in this period of tremendous growth. Recent reports of work in political science, community planning, welfare, and in the more traditional disciplines are testimony to the current dependence upon the concepts of group development that have been created through research.

Groups in Guidance

The period within which group research was progressing so rapidly was roughly the period in which guidance was concentrating upon counseling and testing as primary tools. Group guidance had been tried and found wanting, and guidance had turned its back upon the developments that research in group activity was producing. Scattered attention was given to the use of groups in guidance; however, most use was vague, inspirational, and unrelated to the research findings that were accruing in other fields.

There has recently been a resurgence of interest in group activities within guidance circles. Not only have guidance workers begun to use group principles in occupational planning, in educational information sessions, and in widely different program areas, but counseling had also turned to explorations in group sessions. Research had raised many questions about the attempt to bring together more than one person to solve personal problems. Guidance workers, slowly and even grudgingly, began to recognize that earlier judgments had perhaps been hasty and ill-timed in light of creative efforts of interdisciplinary and professional research.

Helen Driver's books (1954, 1968) attempted to return the group to a meaningful position within total guidance programing. Additional text materials were also becoming available to guidance counselors and to educators for use in helping to prepare guidance workers. Warters (1960), Lifton (1961), and Glanz (1962) are more recent works on the subject that stress the contributions made by research specialists in other disciplines that could be adapted for use in guidance programing. The continued publications of the National Training Laboratory in Bethel, Maine have also stressed the scientific use of groups in all areas of human relations and personal development.

The new use of groups in guidance was of a different order and quality than that of the early days. No longer were large numbers of students brought together into an auditorium and made to suffer through long lectures in the name of "group guidance." Groups were seen to be variable tools to be used in unusual ways in the usual areas of the guidance program. Orientation programs were structured in small groups with faculty and student leadership. Upperclassmen were brought together and trained in the techniques of group leadership. Leaders were not only permitted to analyze the content of the group, but they were also urged to examine and learn about the process of group activity that took place. Student government groups were helped to understand the principles of group behavior that applied in committees and in parliamentary sessions. Problem-centered groups were established to discuss personal and emotional problems. *Group counseling* became a term, along with *multiple counseling,* that was legitimate in a guidance program.

Group work had returned to the guidance scene. However, the group that is currently used in many advanced guidance programs is thoroughly understood in its generalized and particularized structure. The components of the group—such as its structure, leadership, task orientation, channels of communication, and patterns of progress—are a part, and a significant part, of the concept of group work in guidance. No longer is it simply referred to as *group guidance.* Groups can be used in all areas of guidance. The issue that must be faced is: "In what area and in what fashion are groups being used?" Group work has been recognized as a specific tool that can be employed in varying ways and in variable situations. Group work has grown up and guidance workers have learned to harness its potential.

GROUP STRUCTURE

The uncritical use of group work in the early days of guidance and the more recent recognition of the dynamics of groups as an appropriate area of study for a guidance person have emphasized the understanding of the nature of groups by all who use the concept. The structural nature of a group demands that recognition be given to the separation of the content of a group's discussion and the process through which the discussion takes place. The distinction that can be drawn between the content, or the *what* of a group discussion, and the process, or the *how* of a group discussion, helps to establish the primary basis upon which group work can be demonstrated as an independent area of study and application.

Process

Some groups are able to organize, select their task, order their procedures, collect data, and develop conclusions with speed and efficiency. Other groups bog down at the first meeting and degenerate into gossip sessions or personal vendettas. The difference between such groups does not lie in the area of concern or the task that must be performed. Such breakdowns in process can occur in sewing circles or in status-laden international committees charged with tasks that affect nations. The destructive element frequently lies in the procedures, the processes, and the methods that are used to accomplish the task at hand.

Group process may be viewed from many perspectives. The nature of a group is so complex that patterns of structure and operation differ greatly. Five major issues may be separated out of the many that could be offered in examining group process: (1) Group formation and structure, (2) Leadership and membership in groups, (3) Words and meanings in groups, (4) Human behavior in groups, (5) Problem-solving in groups.

Voluminous research has been completed in all of these areas. It is beyond the scope of the present treatment of group operation in guidance programing to examine in detail the state of research in group process. Cartwright and Zander (1953 and 1960) offer a thorough review of all related research. Warters (1961) examines much of the data that relate to guidance, and Glanz (1962) follows the outline presented in this chapter in describing the findings from all major sources of research data appropriate to guidance.

Each of the indicated areas of group process will be briefly developed to expose the nature of group process in operation.

FORMATION AND STRUCTURE. Groups may be formed through the spontaneous action of the participants or of others who serve as organizers or even manipulators. Groups can be formal or informal and will take some of their characteristics from the nature of their development. The formal groups are governed by constitutions, by-laws, or rules of procedure. Nonformal associations may function as action, study, or discussion groups. The nature of the group determines in part its purpose and function. A political-action group of the League of

Women Voters dedicated to increasing the vote in an election is not the same as the board of trustees of a hospital. The principles of operation stem, in part, from the nature of the group. Frequently members of groups are not aware of the nature of their group and become confused in their proposed tasks. Groups establish objectives and purposes as they organize or are organized. These reasons for existence may be clearly understood or only dimly seen by members. Some groups may establish unrealistic levels of aspiration or may be too skilled for the tasks that leaders or organizers offer. The agenda that is adopted by groups reflects their understanding of the nature of the task they are undertaking. Even as progress is made in creating an agenda, it may be possible for a group to become disorganized if members attempt to subvert the group to their own personal ends or for "private agenda" items.

The strength and vitality of a group depends upon the attractiveness of the group for the members, which may stem from the public function of the group or from its private usefulness to the members. Participation and involvement breed a cohesiveness that can hold the members of a group together as it faces difficult or demanding tasks.

Leadership and Membership. The leader in a group situation can exert a strong influence upon the functioning and perhaps the success of a group. Leadership was a subject about which much was written, but little research was done until recent times.

The classical concepts of leadership—authoritarian, laissez-faire, and democratic—have been identified and examined in detail in the well-known research projects of Lewin, Lippitt, and White (1939), replicated by Guetskow, Kelley, and McKeachie (1954). Additional leader classifications such as the functional concepts of participatory, supervisory, bureaucratic, and consultative are also operative in groups.

Leaders of various types perform in differing fashions in their groups. The autocratic or authoritarian leader assumes responsibility for the direction of the group and the tasks of the members, and in short becomes the dominating figure in all of the group's activities. The laissez-faire type leader is virtually the reverse of the autocratic type. This type of leader can generate as much frustration and tension within a group as can an authoritarian leader. Participatory leaders, democratic in orientation, serve as members and leaders of the group to which they belong. Supervisory leaders are usually more skilled in certain areas of operation of the group and attempt to develop leadership among group members.

The leadership roles that are offered, foisted upon, or created out of the group are important factors in its life and effectiveness. The performance of the members is affected by the activities of the leader, and through members the leader can exert various influences. Such overt factors of all groups need to be understood clearly, for the leader or even members can assume leadership functions that are not obvious to the group and yet are significant in its functioning.

Members of a group are the "forward wall" of the team. If the leader can be considered as the backfield, the analogy of the football team fits rather well. All sports fans know that the most capable quarterback still depends upon a skilled and effective line. The members of the group have specific functions to fulfill within the group. Student workshops at all educational levels, as well as political action groups, have recognized the importance of the unit leader, the recorder, and the process observer as special roles that must be adequately fulfilled by members. Simple membership also carries with it the responsibility to work for the purposes and objectives of the group.

WORDS AND MEANINGS. Members and leaders in groups frequently do not say what they mean or mean what they say. Communication problems exist even as two persons attempt to relate one to another, and the complexity of the problem of understanding increases in geometric progression as the size of the group increases.

Each member of a group exists in a world that is bounded by limits that are self-determined and self-interpreted. The task of the leader, the members, and in fact the group is to bring order out of diverse levels of meaning and participation. The fact that a group can succeed in such tasks is a tribute to the group as a concept.

The problem of the intellectual and emotional content of verbalizations is a common one to the counselor who attempts to understand and accept the issues raised by the student in an individual counseling session. The problem is essentially the same within a group, but its complexity is increased. Moreover, members of the group will attempt to understand and influence one another even when they are operating upon varying premises and approaches. The leader again becomes an intermediary, an interpreter, and even a decision-maker.

Some groups are able to work most effectively as cooperating units, while others are more effective when factors of competition are introduced. The person who would use a group in a particular situation must be aware of the conditions that can be introduced to promote effectiveness.

HUMAN BEHAVIOR. The adjustment process underlies the behavior of individuals as they perform everyday tasks and solve problems. Similarly the need to overcome frustrations in order to achieve stated and unstated goals exists within groups. Groups offer unique as well as common opportunities for individuals to solve their own problems and clothe their lives with meaning. Groups offer immediate satisfactions for persons seeking membership and recognition. Similarly it is possible for a group to bestow power, status, acceptance, and prestige, and to fulfill many of the common needs of individuals.

The structure of any group depends upon the opportunities for the individual members to find satisfying outlets for their talents, ambitions, needs, and motivations. The necessity to provide opportunity for each individual to learn and profit is the same both within and outside groups. The nature of the group, the effectiveness of the leader in recognizing the needs of the members, and the productive capacity of the group as a whole are only a few of the elements of the learning potential that can be created within a group.

The recognition of the self as a functioning unit within a group is one of the significant learnings that need to take place as a person begins to understand the concept of group process. The National Training Laboratory in Bethel, Maine has long stressed this concept of self-awareness and constructive self-consciousness. The need is for an awareness of the self not merely as an egocentric unit, but rather as a human being with needs, fears, capacities, talents, and deficiencies. As individuals are able to see themselves in operation, they begin to recognize that similar behaviors can occur in others.

Learning potentials can vary in groups as purposes, membership, leadership communication patterns, and tasks are varied. Cooperative groups can produce greater levels of learning, while competitive groups may interfere with the learning process; the reverse is also true as tasks, procedures, and outcomes are changed. Large groups, small groups, student-centered or teacher-centered groups, and other such variables all differ in their potential effects on learning.

PROBLEM-SOLVING IN GROUPS. The progress toward the solution of a problem that is possible in a group is dependent upon its skill in the problem-solving process. The issues, tasks, and operational functioning of groups may differ from similar problem-solving in individual behavior. Yet the problem-solving process is the same in a group as in an individual. The isolation of a problem, the collection and ordering of data, the development of tentative conclusions, their evaluation, and the ultimate application of the conclusions to the present and the future are the steps in problem-solving process both in groups and in individual experience.

Problem-solving is a cyclical, recurring process in groups. Seldom if ever is a single problem the only concern of a group. Corollary issues are constantly being encountered, and ancillary issues frequently arise out of the partial or full solution of the original problem.

Decisions in group situations may be accomplished by several methods. Authority decision-making is widely encountered even in school groups. Consensus or total agreement, compromise, and even partial consensus of a group within a narrow area, known as "block and gap consensus," can also be used by groups to resolve an issue. No single method of decision-making is appropriate in all groups and it may frequently happen that the group is unable to resolve an issue.

The skills of leaders, members, and groups as units are necessary to develop group skill in problem-solving. Experience as a productive member, experience with a productive group, and experience as a productive leader can breed future successes with increasingly difficult problem areas.

Content

The "what" of a group discussion may be as variable as the issues and problems that human beings face within a socially constructed culture and environment. Sunday school groups can discuss the New Testament. A crime syndicate executive meeting (an action group to be sure) can be concerned with new methods of raising revenue. The content of a group is determined by the wishes of the leaders, the participants, or those who assume the responsibility for its organization. Guidance programs may utilize groups to examine the content areas of vocational exploration or educational planning, or even involve students in group counseling sessions that delve into personal and emotional areas.

School orientation is an issue that is significant for all areas of school operation. The transitional periods between kindergarten and first grade, elementary school and junior high school, junior and senior high, and senior high and college are all areas of concern for guidance workers and are usually included within the planning and programing of a school system. The content of the many groups that may be included in the guidance program reveals the variable uses to which groups can be put and the variable content areas that can be included in the orientation area alone. An example of the varying content for orientation groups is given on page 156.

SCHOOL ORIENTATION: MAJOR GUIDANCE UNIT[1]

Specific Group Topics	*Probable Leaders*
1. Curricular programs	1. Faculty members
2. School services	2. Guidance personnel
3. Student activities	3. Upper-class students
4. Study habits	4. Reading specialists
5. Student-teacher relationships	5. Faculty members and upper-class students
6. Personal goals	6. School counselors
7. Rules and regulations	7. Student government leaders
8. Grading procedures	8. Faculty members
9. Psychological testing	9. Guidance personnel

Orientation is but one area of guidance within which groups may be used. A later section of this chapter will attempt to outline in further detail the many uses to which groups may be put. Such uses can be thought of as "content areas" for groups.

GROUP WORK TRAINING

The need for special training in group work is clearly seen as the essential nature of groups is examined. The research findings show that the utilization of group procedures demands more than mere passing acquaintance with the principles of group operation. The accumulation of research data on group functioning has also made it possible to examine the procedures that are appropriate for the preparation and training of group leaders and members. The National Training Laboratory, college workshops, community training programs, League of Women Voters conventions, and even camp counselor training programs have all investigated and codified data on the preparation of leaders and members for group operation.

On-the-Job Training

Group work training history has shown a refreshingly realistic approach, in contrast to the so-called "armchair" methods used in other areas of guidance training. Counseling has for many years been stressed

[1] From Edward C. Glanz, *Groups in Guidance,* Boston: Allyn & Bacon, Incorporated, 1962, page 22.

as an important element in the preparation of guidance workers. Yet only recently has practical training been available for potential counselors. Counseling was talked about, read about, and debated about, but frequently counselors were graduated with no supervised work experience in the concepts and techniques of counseling. Leaders, members, and group specialists of all types have long been developed out of actual group experience. The "T"—or training—group has been developed as an instrument to help persons become familiar with the process and content of groups. Actual groups are formed from the members of a class, a student leadership training unit, or even a community human-relations study group. The prospective group leaders and members are participating in the process of working, evaluating, and experiencing group activity as they talk about the process.

The usual training practice calls for each group to undertake a task, frequently chosen by the group, which involves the normal problem-solving process of group action. The members rotate as leaders and evaluate their daily, hourly, or weekly progress. The critique session, a down-to-earth discussion of the group's progress, immediately involves the participants in an evaluation of themselves as group members and leaders, and of the process of group work as a problem-solving procedure.

Guidance programs are now assuming an obligation to help student leaders and elected officials of school organizations understand and work as group leaders. School activities for many years emphasized popularity, and school elections often turned upon personality or athletic prowess. Student experience in the working of groups has helped them begin to assess their candidates in a more realistic manner.

Human Relations

Many training programs have been organized in schools and communities to help persons become more aware of the issues and problems of human relations. The opportunity for individuals to understand themselves and their co-workers as human beings with particular capacities and problems helps them to work together more effectively.

Human-relations training programs have frequently utilized group work techniques to aid the members of the workshop or conference in understanding human-relations problems. The intimacy of the small group discussion—the opportunity to examine one's own attitudes, behavior, and performance in an unthreatening atmosphere with co-learners—has produced more sensitive, perceptive persons, who are more effective as group members and leaders.

Member Roles

Research into group procedures has identified certain patterns of participation that help the group to function more effectively as a unit. Various populations that use the group process use different terms to refer to such roles. "Unit leaders" are common in the League of Women Voters, "resource specialists" in human-relations training programs, and rotating "process observer" roles in all types of groups are examples of such specialized use of members in groups.

A most widely accepted pattern of member specialization in groups of all types is the appointment of a recorder and a process observer. Each of these member roles will be examined in greater detail.

The Recorder. The recorder in a group is charged with the task of maintaining written evidence of the progress of the group in its content area. The recorder is similar to the secretary in most social, fraternal, or business groups. The recorder is almost always considered to be also a working member of the group. The leader can call upon the recorder to summarize the progress of the group, to report to a larger unit from which the subgroup has been drawn, or to prepare written reports to be submitted to nonparticipants.

The Process Observer. The process observer is the group member charged with observing and recording the process by which the group attempts to solve its problems. The process observer needs to be a specialist in group process and skilled in charting the communication patterns among group members and the group leader. The leader of the group may call upon the process observer at any time to report to the group on its success in achieving progress or in problem-solving.

The process observer leads the group in a discussion on the group as a group. Frequently the discussion can be vital to the continued success of the group. Members are reminded of their own responsibility as members and as participant observers.

USING GROUPS IN GUIDANCE

Once the concept of the group as a tool is understood and accepted by guidance workers, it is possible to use groups as a complementary concept to counseling and testing procedures in a school program. The use of groups does not conflict with any previously discussed or described pattern of counseling or testing. Actually it is possible to merge and mix the various basic tools of guidance in the construction of program plans.

Groups, as they are used in a guidance program, must be closely related to the counseling and testing approaches that are adopted by a school or college. The following discussion of the use of groups assumes the close coordination of all three tools. The examination of groups in a relatively isolated view may seem to indicate that groups have little or no relationship to counseling and testing. Actually, the isolation of the group process is only intended to emphasize its importance.

Articulation and Orientation

Group procedures have a long history in the meetings held by college admissions officers with high school students. A "college night" program provides students with lectures and presentations about college life. More meaningful programs have made it possible for students to talk with alumni from the surrounding areas and to meet with other prospective students to discuss issues, questions, and information. Admissions or articulation at all school levels provides additional opportunities for group use.

Orientation at all levels of school and college has already been used as an illustration of an area in which groups may be effectively employed. The use of student leaders has been widespread, for guidance workers have recognized that students one year removed from the experience being completed by new students are capable leaders and can help them as much if not more than a professional worker or teacher. The guidance staff and the faculty of the school or college can supplement the efforts of students in the orientation program and can make the entire process more meaningful.

Student Activities

A natural consequence of the use of groups and student leaders in an orientation program is their use in their own organizational and activities program. The use of groups and group procedures throughout an entire school year gives students an opportunity to learn the techniques and skills that will be required of them in their work. The development of a leadership training program or a human-relations skill-training program can not only provide an impetus to such an activities program, but also serve to improve and strengthen student involvement in their areas of concern and operation.

Psychological Test Interpretation

The importance of communicating psychological test results to the students, expressed in detail in an earlier chapter, suggests that group procedures are a prime technique for involving students in the understanding, appreciation, and application of the data that is available about them. Groups that can be formed for discussing test results are a midpoint between classes oriented towards testing and guidance and individual counseling. The group provides a more comfortable atmosphere for students to examine and discuss their own scores.

Measurement principles are appropriate topics for groups that are concerned with understanding test results. It is not effective simply to present data in a lecture-like atmosphere. The intimacy of a group session demands that the students be prepared to understand as fully as possible the data that are being offered to them about themselves. A program to help students master minimum measurement principles must be prepared according to the level of the student group. College freshmen are capable of dealing with all the statistical material including such issues as a standard error of measurement, if the group leaders wish to enter into such detail. Seventh-graders are not so sophisticated, and yet it is possible to present them with measurement data that can aid them in interpreting their own test scores. Katz (1959), in his book *You: Today and Tomorrow,* provides a guide for junior high school students entering into group processes in test interpretation.

No single method of interpreting test scores to students has been found satisfactory in all respects. The issues of involving students in understanding their own test scores through groups and other techniques is reviewed by Goldman (1961:343–363). Goldman favors involving the individual in the interpretation process (1961:358), although he stresses that research is by no means clear in supporting this position.

The need to use test data more effectively and appropriately is being only partially faced in the guidance field. As new techniques and new research data are reported, it seems reasonable to assume that group techniques will become more important.

Educational Planning

The educational careers of students are developed, patterned, even created as they progress from level to level in our educational system. The kindergarten child that is certain that his ultimate goal is to be a policeman may or may not select, enter, and succeed in his objective. The patterning of educational experiences is guided by and a reflection of many factors. The research of Super (1957, 1960), Tiedeman (1958), and Roe (1956) and the experiences of counselors at all educational levels have helped reveal the many elements which enter into the career and educational planning of students.

Parents and students alike are vitally concerned with the educational choices that are made as school progresses. The availability of language instruction in elementary school, the special team systems provided for gifted and retarded children, and advanced reading groups are only simple examples of the issues that must be decided early in school careers. The choice of a curriculum at the end of the eighth or ninth grade, the selection of electives, the selection of colleges—the choices are constant at all levels of educational operation. Group discussion with students, led by counselors, involving parents, and geared to the needs of particular groups of students provide only one approach to the many issues that can and should be examined as these choices are made.

Mature and thoughtful students are able to assess their own capacities, aptitudes, interests, and values, and to relate such data to educational goals. The creation of such individuals is a goal which is as appropriate for guidance at elementary school levels as in the last year in high school. To aid students in achieving such levels of operation is not easy. Groups can be combined with testing, counseling, and other guidance procedures to help the students to achieve such maturity, freedom, and responsibility.

Occupational Planning

Occupational planning is closely related to and dependent upon educational development. Career objectives can often determine educational choices. The occupationally confused student is often confused in educational planning and decision-making. Groups are able to assist students in investigating, evaluating, and assessing themselves against the requirements, opportunities, and rewards of a career.

Occupational research has long been a portion of guidance programs at all school levels. The elementary school field trip, the junior high school career day, college nights, and even research papers on specific occupational choices or on broadly defined occupational fields are common activities of the guidance program. The group concept can add dimension and depth to such activities. Rather than isolated research or investigation, the group provides shared, cooperative data collection and evaluation. The student who unrealistically appraises himself and an occupation can be aided by group discussion with his peers. The use of student leaders in such areas can provide additional development for students and more effective program planning by the professional staff.

College entrance does not end the need for students to explore their occupational plans. Frequently college students experience the most severe conflicts as they ask themselves, "Am I in the right program?" College guidance programs need to help students assess their present status and redirect their choices if they find that an inappropriate choice has been made. Again the concept of the group as a tool can aid college counselors, counseling bureaus, and even faculty advisers and departmental seminars. The "pyramid plan" established and evaluated at Pennsylvania State University demonstrated the usefulness of such techniques in great detail (Davage, 1958).

Guidance Courses

The concept of the guidance course has had a varied and cyclical history. The homeroom program, the "group guidance" effort, occupations courses, core guidance units, and even psychology courses have all attempted to relate guidance objectives and operation to the classroom atmosphere. The superficiality of many text materials has been a major hindrance to such efforts. Efforts to supply curriculums for these courses by such varied sources as drug houses, makers of sanitary products, and even manufacturers of combs, clothing, and hair tonic have frequently been disastrous. Recent publications have remedied many of these problems, and variable content units and methodological approaches have been suggested.

Katz's book, *You: Today and Tomorrow,* filled a major need for meaningful content for guidance courses in the junior high school. Other sources have also helped to fill the void or replace the less than professional efforts in some schools. In the newly directed efforts to use course or classroom programs as guidance units it has been possible to utilize group activities in almost all areas. Hoppock, in 1957, reviewed many of these efforts in his book, which traces the development of occupations courses for many years. The data on meaningful course contents with professional staff programing have consistently supported the use of such techniques.

GROUPS IN COUNSELING

Counseling was seen, in an earlier chapter, to be an open-ended, face-to-face, problem-solving process within which a student, with professional assistance, could focus and begin to solve a problem. This definition of counseling does not restrict such an activity to a one-to-one situation. There is no question that *face-to-face* seems to imply a one-to-one relationship and yet such is not necessarily the case.

Counseling is a complex process calling for professional training, practical experience, and an ethical knowledge of procedure and policy. When counseling is possible in group situations as well as in one-to-one relationships, the issues of competence, developmental training, and ethical practice become infinitely more complex. Yet research continues to demonstrate that in many areas group counseling activities seem to work as well as individual approaches. No data has yet been accumulated on a systematic schedule to demonstrate the efficiency of one procedure over another in specific guidance situations (Hoyt and Moore, 1960).

When group work and counseling procedures are examined, it becomes increasingly clear that, even though it is theoretically possible for group efforts to be directed to problems that have normally been reserved for individual counseling, their relationship is more than merely additive. The demands upon the group counselor are those impinging upon any group leader; such issues as leadership, membership, communication, motivation, power, and status operate in a group counseling session just as they do in any group. Yet the counseling nature of the group demands that positive recognition be offered to the counseling issues of personal, emotional, and often intimate concern to students.

That group work and counseling can be combined is attested to by an overwhelming number of research reports. The issue that must be faced by guidance personnel is the level of competence that is required if ethical and meaningful service is to be rendered on a professional basis. Group counselors assume that they are specialists not only in group work and in counseling but in the combined use of these two tools.

Individuals in guidance must face such professional issues if they hope to establish clearly the right to a professional standard for the use of groups in school activities. If guidance personnel are specialists in the areas of counseling and group work, it would be more than reasonable to assume that they can and need to become skilled in offering group counseling for students as a regular part of any guidance program. The issues of professional preparation and professional standardization will be examined in greater detail in a later section of this book. Suffice it to say at present that group counseling assumes certain things by the very meaning of the two words. Guidance workers face the responsibilities that are inherent in their functioning as professional persons. Groups and counseling must stand on an independent and interdependent foundation.

SUMMARY

Groups have a long and varied history within the guidance field. Early experimentation with group efforts were abortive. Recent reexamination of the group process has led guidance to reincorporate the group as a tool in programing. The structure of a group and the related use of groups in guidance demands the effective understanding of the nature of group operation (process) and the varied subject matter (content) that can be used in a group situation. Five major areas were examined as elements within the process concept of groups (1) formation and structure, (2) leadership and membership, (3) words and meanings, (4) human behavior, and (5) problem-solving.

The use of groups in a guidance program requries that personnel be trained in the use of group techniques. Various methods of training leaders and members have been examined.

The application of groups within a guidance program raises the question of the areas within which groups can be used. Groups have been offered as appropriate for inclusion in articulation and orientation, student activities, psychological testing, educational planning, occupational planning, and guidance courses. The importance of groups to a counseling effort concluded the examination of groups as they are used in guidance.

REFERENCES AND SUGGESTED READINGS

Allen, Richard D., *The Inor Group Guidance Series*, I–III, New York: Inor, 1952.

Bass, Bernard, *Leadership, Psychology, and Organizational Behavior*, New York: Harper, 1960.

Bach, George R., *Intensive Group Psychotherapy,* New York: Ronald Press, 1954.

Becker, S. L., *et al., Teaching by the Discussion Method,* Iowa City: State University of Iowa, 1958.

Bellows, Roger, *Creative Leadership,* Englewood Cliffs, N.J.: Prentice-Hall, 1959.

Bennett, Margaret E., *Guidance in Groups* (rev. ed.), New York: McGraw-Hill, 1963.

Bissex, Henry, "Newton High School, Newtonville, Mass., Completes Four Years of Large-Group Instruction," *Bulletin of the National Association of Secondary School Principals,* XLV (1961), 101–114.

Bonner, H., *Group Dynamics,* New York: Ronald Press, 1959.

Broedel, John W., *et al.,* "The Effects of Group Counseling on Gifted Underachieving Adolescents," *Journal of Counseling Psychology,* VII (1960), 163–170.

Calia, V. F., "A Group Guidance Program in Action," *Junior College Journal,* XXVII (1957), 437–442.

Cartwright, Dorwin, and Alvin Zander (eds.), *Group Dynamics: Research and Theory,* Evanston, Ill.: Row, Peterson, 1953 (rev. ed.), 1960.

Cunningham, Ruth, and M. Roberts, "It Takes Experience," *Childhood Education,* XXIII (1948), 208–213.

Cunningham, Ruth, *et al., Group Behavior of Boys and Girls,* New York: Teachers College, Columbia University, 1951.

Damrin, E. E., "Russell Sage Social Relations Test: A Technique for Measuring Group Problem-Solving Skills in Elementary School Children," *Journal of Experimental Education,* XXVIII (1959), 85–99.

Davage, R. H., "The Pyramid Plan for the Systematic Involvement of University Students in Teaching-Learning Functions," Division of Academic Research and Services, Pennsylvania State University, 1958.

Davis, Keith, and W. G. Scott (eds.), *Readings in Human Relations,* New York: McGraw-Hill, 1959.

Driver, Helen, *Multiple Counseling,* Madison, Wisc.: Monona Press, 1954.

Driver, Helen, *et al., Counseling and Learning Through Small-Group Discussion,* Madison, Wisc.: Monona Publications, 1958.

Durrell, D. D., "Implementing and Evaluating Pupil-Team Learning Plans," *Journal of Educational Sociology,* XXXIV (1961), 360–365.

Durrell, D. D., *et al.,* "Adapting Instruction to the Learning Needs of Children in Intermediate Grades," *Journal of Education,* CXLII (1959), 1–78.

Fiedler, Fred E., *et al.,* "Quasi-Therapeutic Relations in Small College and Military Groups," *Psychological Monographs,* LXXIII, No. 3 (1959).

Flanders, Ned A., *et al., Teaching with Groups,* Minneapolis: Burgess, 1954.

Gates, C. D., *et al., Group Guidance Resource Units, Eleventh Grade* (rev. ed.), Rochester, N.Y.: Board of Education, 1960.

Glanz, Edward C., *Groups in Guidance,* Boston: Allyn & Bacon, 1962.

Goffman, Erving, *Encounters,* Indianapolis, Ind.: Bobbs-Merrill, 1961.

Goldman, Leo, *Using Tests in Counseling,* New York: Appleton-Century-Crofts, 1961.

Gribbons, W. D., "Evaluation of an Eighth-Grade Group Guidance Program," *Personnel and Guidance Journal,* XXXVIII (1960), 740–745.

Guetzkow, H., *et al.,* "An Experimental Comparison of Recitation, Discussion, and Tutorial Methods in College Teaching," *Journal of Educational Psychology,* XLV (1954), 193–209.

Hare, A. Paul, *Handbook of Small Group Research,* Glencoe, Ill.: Free Press, 1961.

Hoppock, Robert, *Occupational Information,* New York: McGraw-Hill, 1957.

Hoyt, K., and G. D. Moore, "Group Procedures in Guidance and Personnel Work," Review of Educational Research, XXX (1960), 158–167.

Katz, Martin, *You: Today and Tomorrow,* Princeton, N.J.: Educational Testing Service, 1959.

Knowles, M., and H. Knowles, *Introduction to Group Dynamics,* New York: Association Press, 1959.

Lewin, K., *et al.,* "Patterns and Aggressive Behavior in Experimentally Created Social Climates," *Journal of Social Psychology,* X (1939), 271–299.

Lifton, Walter M., *Working with Groups,* New York: Wiley, 1961.

National Society for the Study of Education, *The Dynamics of Instructional Groups,* Fifty-Ninth Yearbook, Chicago: University of Chicago Press, 1960.

Olmstead, Michael S., *The Small Group,* New York: Random House, 1959.

Puffer, J. A., *The Boy and His Gang,* Boston: Houghton Mifflin, 1912.

Reber, Kenneth W., "South Bend, Indiana, Develops Educational Broadcases of Group Guidance," *Bulletin of the National Association of Secondary School Principals,* XLV (1961), 167–178.

Rinn, John L., "Group Guidance: Two Processes," *Personnel and Guidance Journal,* XXXIX (1961), 591–594.

Roe, Anne, *The Psychology of Occupations,* New York: Wiley, 1956.

Roethlisberger, F. J., *Management and Morale,* Cambridge, Mass.: Harvard University Press, 1941.

Roethlisberger, F. J., and W. J. Dickson, *Management and the Worker,* Cambridge, Mass.: Harvard University Press, 1939.

Rogers, Carl R., *Dealing with Social Tensions,* Danville, Ill.: Interstate Printers, 1948.

Shimberg, B., and M. R. Katz, "Evaluation of a Guidance Text," *Personnel and Guidance Journal,* XLI (1962), 126–132.

Siegel, S., and L. E. Fauraker, *Bargaining and Group Decision-Making,* New York: McGraw-Hill, 1960.

Steese, P. A., *et al., Group Guidance Resource Units, Ninth Grade* (rev. ed.), Rochester, N.Y.: Board of Education, 1960.

Strang, Ruth, *Group Work in Education,* New York: Harper, 1958.

Super, Donald E., *The Psychology of Careers,* New York: Harper, 1957.

Super, Donald E., *Scientific Careers and Vocational Development Theory,* New York: Bureau of Publications, Teachers College, Columbia University, 1957.

Super, Donald E., and P. L. Overstreet, *The Vocational Maturity of Ninth-Grade Boys,* New York: Bureau of Publications, Teachers College, Columbia University, 1960.

Super, Donald E., *et al., Vocational Development: A Framework for Research,* New York: Bureau of Publications, Teachers College, Columbia University, 1957.

Taba, Hilda, *et al., Intergroup Education in Public Schools,* Washington, D.C.: American Council on Education, 1952.

Tagiuri, R., and L. Petrullo (eds.), *Person Perception and Interpersonal Behavior,* Stanford: Stanford University Press, 1958.

Tannenbaum, R., *et al., Leadership and Organization,* New York: McGraw-Hill, 1961.

Thelen, Herbert A., *Education and the Human Quest,* New York: Harper, 1960.
Thrasher, Frederic M., *The Gang,* Chicago: University of Chicago Press, 1927.
Tiedeman, David W., and R. P. O'Hara, *Position Choices and Careers: Elements of a Theory* (Harvard Studies in Career Development, No. 8) Cambridge, Mass.: Harvard Graduate School of Education, 1958.
Warters, Jane, *Group Guidance,* New York: McGraw-Hill, 1960.
Weschsler, I., and J. Reisel, *Inside a Sensitivity Training Group* (Industrial Relations Monograph No. 4), Los Angeles: Institute of Industrial Relations, U.C.L.A., 1959.

THE CASE STUDY

THE ISSUE. The "whole student" is a real issue of guidance and education. No single student problem or aspect of student life can reflect the total nature of student behavior, nor can growth or development in a single life area represent all of education.

The cyclical popularity of testing as a tool to understand human behavior has paralleled the steady growth of counseling theory and practice. Group work has returned to the professional guidance scene. Only case-study work has been eclipsed for a long period of time as a primary tool of guidance. The concept of the case study is actually more basic to guidance than any single tool. The case study provides an encompassing design for providing help of all types to the individual student.

How the case-study concept can serve all guidance is an illustration of integrated professional practice with the tools of guidance. Counseling, testing, group work, and other tools can and must be a part of a pattern of case-study work. Guidance personnel cannot avoid functioning as caseworkers; guidance work builds upon casework.

A CASEWORK PHILOSOPHY

The case study and its accompanying structural pattern of casework has developed in many professional disciplines. The medical profession has viewed patients and their problems as cases. The patterns

CHAPTER EIGHT

of diagnosis, prognosis, and treatment have been a part of the methods of physicians for centuries. Lawyers have not only worked on cases of individuals, but have codified their precedents and judgments in casebooks and records. Psychologists and psychiatrists have adapted case-study procedures from the medical field. Wallace Brett Dunham helped to introduce the "case method" into business education at the Harvard School of Business Administration. The entire profession of social work has depended upon casework and the use of the case study. Social workers are often known simply as caseworkers.

Again guidance stands upon the shoulders of those who have pioneered in methods, techniques, and theory validation. Case techniques cannot be seen as original, unique, or even private prerogatives of any profession. Guidance needs to recognize its debt to other disciplines while it seeks to apply a valued technique to help students within a particular environment, the school. R. I. Watson (1951:37) specifies the significance of the case study for guidance workers: ". . . the case study is the technique *par excellence* for dealing with the individual as an individual in all his uniqueness." If guidance is concerned with individuals as they profit from and progress through an educational experience, can guidance ignore the case study as the unifying concept within all of its work?

The behavioral problem, with a past, a present, and a future is a natural case study within the guidance and educational setting of any school or college. The gifted child who needs further challenge and opportunity is a case problem for teachers, administrators, and guidance personnel. The retarded child, the truant, the underachiever—the list can be inexhaustibly continued. Yet the normal child, the everyday pupil, is also a case subject. Individuals are cases and can be the subjects of case studies. Guidance is concerned with individual persons and thus must be concerned with individual cases.

Groups of students with similar problems may be collections of similar case studies. Thy emay also form patterns for helping students with related or similar problems. Groupings cannot destroy the integrity and the dignity of the individual if guidance is to fulfill its essential nature within education.

Some theoreticians and practitioners may claim that no case history is necessary prior to, or even along with, a counseling relationship. Carl Rogers popularized the counseling technique that stressed "start where you are." Yet, as counseling continues and as the counselor maintains records or protocols of practice, case-study concepts become a part of even nondirective or client-centered counseling.

Case-Study Structures

A case-study pattern exists whenever an individual student is isolated and helped. Parallel case-study patterns may exist when identical approaches are used with different students or when similar students are brought together in a group. The individual is still the center of the concept of the case study. A group must be a collection of individual case-study patterns if the leader looks beyond the group to the individuals that compose it.

Longitudinal and horizontal concepts of person analysis establish the essential nature of case-study work. Observation at any single instant of time cannot be a case study, but longitudinal repetition can begin to establish such a concept. The cross-section study of the person for a given period of time can extend the case-study concept across varying dimensions of behavior. Length and breadth are the two dimensions that pattern case-study work. Although emphasis may exist within a single case upon either dimension, thorough case-study patterns will take both dimensions into account.

Caseworkers

Any person who attempts to study an individual becomes involved in casework. The major activities of such a caseworker are observational, quantificational, and historical. The caseworker observes and quantifies behavior and seeks perspective through historical and biographical techniques. Every tool for knowing and learning about persons can be integrated into the approaches of the caseworker. The caseworker is distinguished by an integrative view which seeks, in scientific fashion, to tie together and to explain all data.

Guidance persons may function as counselors, group workers, and even specialized test administrators. Whatever tools are utilized, it becomes necessary to view all information and learnings in an integrated fashion. The guidance worker differs from other professional workers who are caseworkers in that case data are not used simply to treat, advise, restructure environments, or even to arrive at a diagnosis. All of these activities may be appropriate for guidance. The most important activity for the guidance worker as a caseworker is to use case data to help the person to help himself.

THE CASE-STUDY OUTLINE

A structured outline for the collection and ordering of data about an individual person can be both a help and a hindrance. Any outline of categories of data is only a skeleton around which the full data are organized. Skilled caseworkers in many disciplines prefer to collect and order data in accord with the problem and the nature of the individual. Other workers use an outline to help obtain balance and perspective in the accumulation of data. Case-study work is not a precise step-by-step operation. Flexibility in approach and comprehensiveness in understanding the individual are the key concepts that must guide any person undertaking a case study.

The following areas of study and data collection are offered as suggested guides to action. Every school or college situation will dictate that changes and different emphases be made as specific problem situations are faced.

1. *Presenting Problem*
   Whose problem is the focus of the study? Is it seen and presented by the student or by those who feel that the student has a problem? Behavior problems, discipline issues, and underachievement may or may not be seen as problems by the students involved. What is the history of the problem, and how has it developed and manifested itself?

2. *The Person*
   The case-study worker should know the name of the subject, his address, date of birth, age, place of birth, sex, race, national origin, religion, and other pertinent data.

3. *The Family*
   Who are the members of the family? For all family members it may be desirable to know: name, date of birth, age, place of birth, sex, race, national origin, religion, occupation, education, health (and medical histories), personality characteristics, attitudes toward other members of the family, sibling rivalries, and attitudes toward the case subject.

4. *Environmental Conditions*
   What are the specific facts about the immediate environment within which the subject lives? Socioeconomic factors about the home, occupational patterns of the neighborhood, town or neighborhood traditions, problems, and aspirations, language and ethnic identifications, and the financial status of family may need examination.

5. *Cultural Pattern*
   What is the cultural pattern within which the subject and the family exist? What are its cultural identifications, the customs, mores, and traditions of its major cultural force, its attitudes toward education, work, marriage, and family? What has been the sociological and cultural movement of the family through its recent and past history?

6. *Medical Status and History*
   What is the present state of health of the case subject? What are the significant factors about his medical history: the results of any recent thorough physical examinations, his physical development, disease and injury history, and sexual development?

7. *Developmental History*
   What are the pertinent facts about the maturational history of the subject? The caseworker may need to study the subject's prenatal period and birth, early developmental patterns, speech performance, emotional development and temperament tendencies, emotional maturity and integration throughout maturational history, social-skill learning, and performance.

8. *Intellectual Capacity*
   What determinations can be made about the intelligence, capacity, aptitudes, and potential of the subject? What other data are available, such as psychological test results, test data records, behavioral dimensions of capacity, or special talents and skills? Special attention may be directed to conceptual skills, creativity, memory, judgment, and insight.

9. *Educational History*
   What is the pattern of education completed and proposed by the subject? Facts about formal and informal educational development can include entrance age for school, acceleration or retardation in grade placement, special-class membership, level and trends

of all school grades, behavioral problems, special achievements and awards, school adjustment and citizenship patterns, and educational aspirations.

10. *Economic History*
    What has been the occupational development of the subject? Career development facts may be gathered, such as early interests and fantasy choices, attitudes toward work and career development, earnings on summer and part-time jobs, occupational success or failure in specific work situations, nonpaid work experience, hopes for career development, and ambition.

11. *Philosophical and Ethical Patterns*
    The codes and philosophical acceptance patterns of the subject can provide clues to behavior and motivation. Factors that may be investigated are: ethical codes and attitudes of the family, religious affiliations and attitudes of the subject and his family, peer identifications and gang loyalties, value adoptions and patterns, and significant behaviors that can reveal or infer philosophical and ethical patterns.

12. *Legal History*
    What history of official and unofficial delinquencies exist? Other legal facts that may be obtained are: court history or actions, and the subject's attitudes toward legal involvements.

13. *Leisure and Hobby Patterns*
    What collections or projects have been completed in school and in play? What attitudes and performances are characteristic for the subject in reading, manual hobbies, sports, and creative efforts? What is the character of the subject's fantasy and daydream life? What are the remote and practical hopes for leisure-time use?

14. *Objectives and Purposes*
    What life objectives and purposes have been established by the subject? Dimensions of life purpose that can be examined are: family hopes, personal aspirations, career hopes, marital expectations, self-concept patterns, and self-awareness and introspective patterns.

CASE-STUDY TECHNIQUES

The collection, ordering, and synthesizing of all case-study data is a task that calls for the professional skills of persons in many differing disciplines. Physicians and social workers may provide historical as well as current data. School administrators, athletic coaches, and school nurses may also enter into the process. The collection of data may require the cooperative efforts of all who are informed and wish to offer help to the subject. Attempts to diagnose and evaluate data, propose treatment, and follow up on casework are elements of professional guidance practice at its best.

Information about an individual can be gathered in three major ways—observational, quantitative, and historical. The data can then be collected, ordered, and synthesized. Conclusions need to be drawn from synthesized data and from proposed actions as well. Evaluation of tentative conclusions and the formulation and evaluation of new conclusions provide the basis for continued follow-up.

The Collection of Data

Data that provide the raw material for a case study can be obtained from many sources. School records (discussed in the next section) can provide a substantial initial source. Interviews, counseling results, psychological test programs, special test periods, and field visits are also usual and useful patterns of data-gathering.

The outline offered in the previous section can be used in all of its dimensions, but more frequently requirements will dictate that sections and partial studies must be made. The problem that is under consideration is a major factor in the structure of a case study, the ordering of data, and the methods to be used. No single approach or pattern of data collection can be applied to all situations.

It is better for the collection of data to err in the direction of completeness. Problems have a tendency to become more complicated than they appear at first examination. Full and complete data permit an exploration into areas of study that may not have appeared to be necessary at first.

Ordering Data

Data can be ordered as they are collected, but care must be taken not to close the process of organization before all information is available. The essential task in ordering data is to relate one element to another in a meaningful way. The outline of the case study attempts to integrate all data into appropriate categories. Yet overlap occurs. Creativity may be viewed as a dimension of intellectual capacity, a philosophical view of life, or even as a part of a family tradition. Creativity may overspread all of a person's life and individuality. The widespread occurrence of creativity is a significant fact in itself. To force a talent into a narrow constricting pattern is to defeat the nature of the case study and to deny its flexibility.

Patterns must be sought as data are ordered. Examination of the relatedness of information can lead to the establishment of patterns that may not be initially available to the subject or to the caseworker. Rigid expectation of patterns such as overprotection or rejection in the family, sibling rivalry, or inadequate resolution of an Oedipus complex reveal the biases of the caseworker. However, such difficulties may be overcome by case conferences, which provide opportunity for several workers to examine the data from different perspectives. Flexibility and intuition may be most important in the ordering of the data in a complex case study.

A commitment to the scientific method for the study of human behavior is appropriate to the ordering of data. Many interpretations of data may be possible, depending upon the meaningful patterns of data that can be established to support possible conclusions.

Synthesis

The collection and the ordering of data lead to a synthesis. The scientific method again provides a model for the caseworker. Creative thinking about data can lead to new and more meaningful interpretations of previously known information. The interrelation of all facts needs to be developed as synthesis thinking progresses.

The scientist's task of explaining all known data by the simplest hypothesis can guide the caseworker who seeks to understand and synthesize the variable factors that influence a single person. The past experience and the education of the caseworker become practical tools to use with case data.

Conclusions

The old German expression of "so," pronounced as if the "s" were a "z" and inflected to become "zo . . . ooh?" describes a useful attitude for the caseworker seeking conclusions. The modern teen-ager might express it as effectively by saying, "So what?" The question is meaningful regardless of the language of the person who asks it. Scientific skepticism must be a part of the tool kit of the modern guidance person who attempts to understand the most complex organism known to man, man.

Diagnosis, prognosis, treatment procedures, offers of counseling, evaluation, and follow-up techniques will all be subsumed as conclusions are drawn from the ordered data available in the case study. Some cases may call for no action at all; no action is still a decision and a conclusion. Other case studies will lead to referral to community resources or to outside specialists. The proposed actions are outgrowths of the conclusions that are based upon the collected and ordered data of the case study.

Follow-up

The concern for future progress and development shown in the case study belies the static and backward view charged by some professional workers. The case study helps to understand the past, to deal effectively with the present, and to be prepared for the future. The follow-up depends upon the earlier elements of the case study. No rigid concept of follow-up can fit all case-study situations. The nature of the case, and more significantly, of the person will determine the style and substance of the follow-up.

Methodology Versus Substance

The case study is appropriate for dealing with student problems at all school levels. The nature of the problem, the tools used to gather and order data, the conclusions and follow-up are functions of the nature of the individual who is the subject of the case study. The case study is simply a tool or a method that can be used by professional persons. The case study does not answer a student's questions nor can it solve problems for the caseworker or the student. The student and the guidance worker can face issues more directly and resolve problems more effectively when case study procedures are recognized as scientific approaches to human problems. The case study needs to be seen as a means to an end, the end being the problem-solving process of the person who is the subject.

SCHOOL RECORDS

The provision of school records is a recognition of the existence of the case-study principle. The regular collection of data permits the development of further case-study procedures whenever the need arises.

Record-keeping can be divided into two elements. Data needs to be collected in an accurate and appropriate fashion and it needs to be used. The case-study concept provides meaning for the process of keeping records.

Modern electronic computers are often termed "thinking machines." It is true that such machines can be programed to solve problems for which the needed data exists, when the techniques for problem-solving can be built into the mechanism. The machine can function no more effectively than the available data will permit, and of course, no more efficiently than the problem-solving techniques that are programed. Answers that are not expected may be obtained, but it is doubtful that any machine will ever be able to engage in problem-solving processes that are not constructed into it by the manufacturers.

School records are the data that can be used in problem-solving. The techniques and tools of the guidance worker, as well as those of other school personnel who use the records, are the problem-solving techniques that can be applied to the data that is available.

A Philosophy of Records

School records are a reflection of the performance of the pupil, whether he graduates or not. The records tell a story of the actual behavior of the student. Such records should of course be as complete and accurate as possible. They should, moreover, be cumulative, flexible, and creative, in order to reflect the nature of the person who is undergoing the educational experience. Records are symbols of behavior and experience.

The grade level of the student will dictate the content and much of the process of the record system. Marital status is not an appropriate question for kindergarten students, but it is becoming increasingly important as an issue for college freshmen. Whatever content is deemed important in records is a reflection of the behavior of the student. Budgets for school administrators can be seen as promises to realize the dreams of a community. School records need to be seen as dimensions of individuality and as demonstrations of what is considered important in the lives of students.

Specific Records

Specific forms for recording student behavior can be obtained from many guidance publishers. The *Guidance Cumulative Folder* of the Chronicle Press and the structured folder put out by the American

Council on Education are examples of traditionally used forms. State departments of education and regional education associations have also sponsored forms that are frequently appropriate. Local needs can determine the form selected and variations in its use.

The Educational Testing Service is experimenting with the use of cumulative record forms that can be maintained by electronic calculators and be made available upon demand. No matter what form is adopted or what type of recording process is used, it is vital that their accurate recording and appropriate use be defended.

The "Cumulative" Concept

Cumulative records have been designed to follow and to reflect accurately the progress of the student in school. Although previously some schools have been guilty of chauvinistic paternalism in jealously guarding their records, modern practice has permitted the school to retain needed records and at the same time to serve students by forwarding useful and meaningful information. Public school systems have solved the problem within their community, but frequently have not faced the issue in serving transfer students. Colleges have been even less successful in examining high school graduates and in serving graduate schools.

Records are a reflection of the student's behavior and of the school's understanding of him. Yet records that accompany transfer students from one school to another and to college or graduate school seem to imply that only grades in specific courses are appropriate reflections of student behavior. Newer transcript forms have attempted to supply additional data about psychological test scores and recommendations through rating scales. But who would wish to have years of his life symbolized in such a sparse fashion? Creative work still remains to be done in adapting record-keeping to live up to the case-study concepts of guidance and education.

CASEWORK

The view of the guidance person as a caseworker is not commonly accepted or seen in professional practice. Yet the guidance person who would understand and aid the whole person is a caseworker. A guidance worker may not be able to conduct a physical examination, to determine whether brain damage has hindered school performance, or even to characterize the sociocultural background of the student. Nevertheless, the utilization of such data in an ordered form to achieve conclusions and to help the student help himself are the tasks of guidance.

Whether a bricklayer sees himself as a man putting cement between two bricks or as a man helping to build a cathedral is a matter of internal attitude or set about the nature of his task. Guidance workers must be concerned with the total student, and as such cannot afford to be simply "test givers," counselors, group leaders, or record keepers. They must try to be skilled and capable in using all of the tools and instruments of guidance. Casework provides one such tool to aid guidance workers to understand and help the whole student.

Tools and Cases

Any guidance tool can be used to help construct a case study of an individual student. Test data need to be seen in perspective. Counseling can help students understand issues and treat problems. Group situations can provide diagnostic data and at the same time can provide the means for problem-solving.

The nature of all guidance tools demands that the guidance worker maintain a perspective about student behavior and about the provision of help for the student. The guidance person stands with the student at the center of all the data that has been collected, ordered, and synthesized. What is to be done, what conclusions are to be developed, and what actions are to be taken? The problems of the case are at the same time problems of the student and the guidance worker.

"Others"

The "others" in a case-study situation can be those from whom the data is gathered, with whom data is ordered, or who will help to implement the conclusions and planned actions of the case study. Parents, teachers, peers, administrators, and all school personnel can be and may have to be involved in the case study. How the guidance worker relates himself to such persons and how he can help the student relate to them are crucial questions for every case study.

The case conference, which will be analyzed in the next section, is a device for furthering the objectives of the case study. It is also a method through which one guidance person can serve effectively as a coordinating force for all elements of the case study and for the student who is the subject.

The Student and the Case Study

The early use of the case study to determine eligibility for community or state aid has helped to develop the impression that casework is manipulative. Data will be collected on the student, such data will be ordered, and syntheses will be developed. The student seems to be the passive subject of the entire process, rather than an active participant.

Case-study work can create and foster manipulation of students. However, guidance workers who seek to help students become free and responsible persons cannot use case-study and casework methods in such a fashion.

Students need to be involved in their own case studies. They can not only be aware and participating partners in the process, but can also on occasion sit down with a case conference group to assess and plan actions. The attitude of the guidance person toward the student and his development determines the quality and connotations of the techniques utilized.

THE CASE CONFERENCE

The case conference is a part of case-study procedure and is at the same time a separate guidance tool that can be used effectively in many different situations. A sensitive understanding of the nature of individuality is inherent in the case study and is made explicit through the use of case-conference procedures.

The potential value of the case study to the individual may be lost or vitiated if specific methods are not developed to exploit its various aspects. The case conference provides a technique for focusing the efforts of a guidance staff or school to help the individual. The case conference in a school or college guidance program can also serve to coordinate the efforts of specialists, improve the effectiveness of the professional guidance staff, provide an environment for the involvement of faculty members in the guidance program, offer a device for in-service training of regular faculty members, establish a firm base for the referral of disturbed students, and involve students in positive action to solve their own problems.

The various forms of the case conference provide one of the most useful tools for guidance. The case conference needs to be examined in detail so that its variable applications may be fully presented.

Definition

The case conference is a face-to-face discussion of case-study data about an individual by the persons who have collected the information or who will be concerned about the possible actions arising out of the case study. The case conference permits guidance workers to meet with administrators of the school or college, physicians, nurses, physical education instructors, faculty members, parents, community representatives, and even the student subjects of the study. Although a single case conference will seldom include all of the listed persons, flexible use of the case conference technique will probably see the involvement of all such persons at one time or another.

The case conference permits cooperative effort in the study, discussion, and ordering of all assembled data, and in the synthesizing of the information into conclusions. The actions proposed can be followed up by additional meetings of the entire group or of selected members. The chairman of the case-conference discussion may be any person who participates. The guidance worker can and should serve as chairman if other persons do not wish to do so. But guidance workers need to recognize that the specific problem may determine who should serve as chairman. The responsibility for chairing the discussion may also be rotated among all participants.

The case conference may be used for a single situation, but it is more effectively utilized as a regularly scheduled portion of the guidance and educational program. The conference may be informal or structured, according to the needs of the meeting. Visual aids can be used to heighten the immediacy and impact of all considered data.

Subjects

Case-conference meetings may consider gifted students within the institution, retarded children, underachievers, behavior problems, discipline cases, or Science Fair winners. In fact, students of all shapes, sizes, and natures are appropriate subjects for a case conference. The purpose of the technique is to help students solve problems more effectively; all students may have problems that must be solved.

Several decades ago, the undergraduate men's college of Columbia University scheduled regular case conferences which brought together the faculty advisers of all undergraduate men. The advisers were permitted to suggest any student as a subject for the conference. Many students were discussed during the meetings and problems of all types naturally occurred. Visual aids were used to portray grades, psychological test scores, and other significant data drawn from school records. Many public schools schedule regular case conferences twice a month to accomplish similar results.

The variety of subjects that may be brought into regularly scheduled meetings assumes that every student can profit from the concerted efforts of those who are close to his development and growth.

The Responsibility of Guidance

Any person in an educational institution can express an interest in and attempt to provide for a case conference. Guidance, as the aspect of an educational program that is primarily responsible for individual student growth and development, has the prime responsibility for initiating the case conference. The guidance program of any institution can be strengthened and made more useful to students by the use of case conferences of all types. The wide range of student problems and issues often overwhelms both the potential and the experienced guidance worker. The case conference can be made a part of the regular staff meeting of all guidance personnel. Some authors have preferred to label such intrastaff case conferences as "staff clinics." The specific term is not significant, but the use of the case conference is basic to professional guidance practice.

The use of case conferences within a broader environment of the school or college can serve the interests of students, the primary concern of all guidance programs. Guidance persons can supply data, systems of data ordering, and assistance to faculty members, administrators, and other school personnel. The attitude of the guidance person is a key to the ultimate success of the case conference technique. A "Jehovah" complex (Hutson, 1958), can defeat and destroy the concept. The guidance person who assumes that he knows all the answers and can solve all student problems himself clearly indicates that he neither needs nor cares for the assistance of other persons within the school. Such an assumption labels the guidance worker both arrogant and foolish.

Leadership by guidance workers needs to be of a supervisory and democratic nature. Such leadership (Glanz, 1962) attempts to make it unnecessary for the leader to continue to function. Independent operation of the case conference is the goal of guidance persons in working with teachers, faculty members, and all others in the school or college.

Coordination of Specialists

Specially trained educators frequently have difficulty in communicating with one another. The school psychologist and school social worker may often use terms or develop concepts that are alien to each other. Faculty members are sometimes prone to complain that they do not understand the work of the school-adjustment counselor or the psychometrician. The student is the loser whenever any person in education is unable to share with co-workers knowledge and suggestions for interrelated action.

The case conference provides a design within which varying approaches may be brought together and focused upon the problems of a single student. All of the work of a single specialist cannot possibly be shown to advantage in every case conference. Still, as continued conferences are scheduled, it is possible for cooperating specialists to learn more of the nature of each other's work and to profit from mutual interchange. Specialists are also better able to understand and appreciate the work of the faculty, while faculty in turn can see the role of specialized assistance in an educational effort.

Research has shown that vocabulary problems can interfere with the communication process. Studies have revealed that similar diagnoses and proposed plans of action can be developed by persons from very different disciplines and backgrounds. The vocabulary used to describe the diagnoses and to express the planned actions may be widely different, but the actual ideas and concepts expressed are very similar. The case conference helps each participant to view other persons of the group not only as interested and appropriate members but also as partners in the total process of helping students help themselves.

Faculty Involvement

Invitations to faculty members to attend and participate in scheduled case conferences can provide a method for the practical involvement of faculty in the problems of individual students. The faculty member often finds it difficult to understand and appreciate many of the elements of a professional guidance program. The high level of professional training in a specific subject that marks all faculty members may establish a barrier to detailed understanding of the work of guidance. Faculty members, like guidance workers, seldom wish to display their own lack of background or unawareness of an area that seems to be important to all within an institution. The case conference provides a method for the faculty member to observe the process of understanding and providing help to students, while also permitting him to participate and to help in a manner and at a rate that he can determine for himself.

Case conferences of the guidance staff may extend invitations to other faculty members to sit and participate. However, most faculty members will feel isolated if they are the only "outsiders." Physical education teachers, coaches, librarians, administrators, and other school personnel can also be invited to attend. A mixed group will provide a feeling of security for any member of the case conference who is attending for the first time.

The case conference needs to be structured and implemented so as to avoid requiring the participation of new members. However, willing participation can be made possible through summaries and invitations to new members to add to the understandings or plans of the group. Faculty members will frequently demonstrate their interest by offering to help with student problem-solving. Often a faculty member will offer to follow up a problem or to engage the student in a discussion of the problem area. Natural relationships are thus routes for extended problem-solving. The teacher can become involved with the student and see the case conference as an extension of his own relationship.

All experienced members of a case-conference group will usually enter into the discussion and planning of action. The group atmosphere places a premium upon universal participation without coercion or direct expectation. The effort to gain cooperation may go no further than the stating of the belief that the faculty members understand the student under discussion and that any actions or future relationships may be colored by their willing participation in the case conference.

Faculty participation needs to arise out of real and vital relations with students. Whenever faculty members feel, correctly or incorrectly, that they are being exploited by guidance workers or by any administrative officer of the institution, involvement becomes superficial and forced. Guidance persons who understand the nature of the case conference do not need to worry about the participation or involvement of the faculty. A response to an invitation is all that is needed; a properly conducted case conference with a cooperative atmosphere can virtually guarantee faculty involvement and participation. Few other guidance techniques can promise and deliver so much in terms of school involvement and faculty interest in guidance, students, and problem-solving.

Faculty Growth

"In-service training" is a phrase that has often been used by guidance workers who hope that a faculty member can be helped to understand and to assist in many guidance functions within the school or college. Actually the very term has helped to alienate faculty and to insure a low level of involvement in guidance activities.

Faculty members resist the idea that they are unskilled workers who need to be trained to do a task. Frequently guidance workers have come into a school and attempted to "train" senior members of the faculty who have long been interested and concerned with students. The resistance that is encountered may not be understood by the person who wishes to promote special types of faculty interest in students. The guidance person may miss or not understand the sincere commitment of faculty members. He may be devoted to a specialized vocabulary and to narrowly defined techniques that are, in reality, only variations of previous faculty practice.

The case conference permits faculty to continue to operate with their own methods while learning something of newer or different techniques. The guidance person, at the same time, may be able to learn more about the traditions, mores, and customs of the faculty and about the work with students that preceded the establishment of a formal guidance program. Faculty members and full-time guidance persons can come together and learn about each other's activities through case-conference techniques.

Psychological test procedures, group-work skills, and counseling can be seen in perspective by faculty members through case-conference meetings. The tools of the guidance worker are not completely alien to the faculty member. Testing, counseling, and group work of many types have been employed by faculty members in a general way throughout their careers. Case-conference work permits faculty to incorporate new learnings and to build upon older traditions without the threat of "training." Guidance has been extracted out of the educational process that is wholly familiar to skilled, sensitive, and experienced teachers. Rudeness and insensitivity have often marked the efforts of guidance workers to involve teachers in processes that have been a part of their everyday practice and personal philosophy.

Case-conference meetings permit questions to be raised about the interpretation and the use of data. Testing, group work, and counseling become understood in a pragmatic fashion rather than as subjects to be taught to professionally competent faculty members. Teachers may ask for help in becoming better counselors and advisers as they see techniques that are not known to them. Testing becomes a tool that can help a faculty member to understand his own student better. Faculty members are interested in students, or (in most cases) they would not be involved in education. Guidance persons need to establish and structure case conferences so that the natural interests and skills of faculty members can be extended and developed.

Referral Procedures

Students who need the assistance of specialists such as psychiatrists, physicians, or reading clinicians can cause procedural and jurisdictional disputes within an institution. Administrators and guidance persons need to work together in providing students with the opportunity to obtain the needed help. Faculty members need to be informed and aided in understanding the processes of referral and follow-up.

Creative use of case-conference techniques can help to establish policy in such cases. Precedents can be established, not to be followed slavishly but to serve as guides for future action. Faculty members will learn how and where help for certain types of problems may be obtained. Case conferences will also call for the establishment of data channels feeding back to the referring teacher or group. The two-way street of communications is an expected outcome of case-conference work.

Student Involvement

The methodology of the case conference is sufficiently flexible to permit the involvement of students in the solving of their own problems. Creative use of educators' talents and of institutional records can allow for the solution of problems that may seem to be impossible at first. An example of student involvement may help to illustrate not only the potential of student participation but much of the material presented about case conferences.

> . . . Our team has often brought students into discussions and into problem-solving of a personal type. Our faculty team of five persons works together as a matter of course throughout the year. We hold weekly meetings to discuss our subject matter and to understand the progress and achievement of all of our students.
>
> Early in the year we schedule informal meetings of a semisocial nature for small groups of the students. We serve coffee to seven to ten students and for the faculty members. Our discussions vary with every group. We do not attempt to make them rigidly academic or social. Current events and school activities often can determine our topics. The students begin to become comfortable with us as persons not just as teachers. We see the pupils as persons and they see us as human beings.

The "warning period" often causes distress with some of our students. The guidance person who is a member of the team often will meet individually with students who are in academic difficulty, but the problem is also one for the team as a whole. We have used several approaches and found varying methods that can help students.

One of the most successful procedures we have found is to discuss the students in detail in our team meeting and then to bring the students in to meet with us as a team. Sometimes we will bring in students who are similar in their problems (at least it may seem they are similar; we are often surprised) and on occasion we will bring in one student at a time.

At times the students feel that they are being "called on the carpet." Seldom does this attitude hold true for all the students. Our meetings earlier in the year have helped the students to see that as a team we are interested in the students as individual persons and not merely as performing academicians in the classroom. In any case we spend considerable time in working on this problem to assure the students that it is not a disciplinary conference. Before long one or another student in the group meetings will enter into an analysis of his own problems on a voluntary basis. The very real concern that the faculty has for the student soon shows to the individual, and to the remainder of the group. The meeting is designed to help and not to judge or to preach. Students perceive this. Before long we do not have enough time to spend on each student and we have to terminate the meeting. Some students seem to be affected merely by the realization that we as faculty members are vitally interested in their progress. It is often most surprising for students to learn that student success or failure is also faculty success or failure.

Sometimes we meet, as a team, with one person. Usually we have found that the student is overwhelmed by facing all of his faculty members at the same time. The type of student problem will determine how we will establish student contact with the team. In all cases the guidance person works along with the team to prepare the student and team for the meeting and to follow up on the meeting. However, not only the guidance person will schedule conferences with the student. All faculty members usually offer their services and it is not uncommon to see students take advantage of such offers and be working with several faculty members concurrently.

Our team meetings are used for many other types of student contacts besides the discussion of poor academic achievement. We have often called meetings of the advanced students and tried to stimulate them to even higher levels. Discipline cases may also involve student meetings with the team. We have found the team system indispensable to our entire educational program. It has colored our academic work and all of our guidance operations. It is amazing what can be done as faculty members, guidance counselors, and other specialists, can be brought together to help themselves [Team Coordinator].

The "team system" is a variation of the case-conference technique. The team meeting becomes a regularly scheduled case conference. Whether or not the term *case conference* is used is unimportant. The team meets, and the educational program, the students, and the educational staff can profit.

SUMMARY

The case study has been presented as a fourth major tool of the guidance worker. Case-study work is an "umbrella" type tool that permits the incorporation of testing, counseling, and group work into an over-all framework of guidance.

Guidance persons were examined as caseworkers and as users of the case-study technique. A detailed case-study outline was presented to be used partially or totally within a guidance program. Case-study techniques were listed and developed to show how the data in a case study can be collected, ordered, and synthesized.

School records have been offered as systematic techniques that can be and are used in case studies in every school system or college. Records have been examined as reflections of student behavior and as the raw material for helping students on an individual basis through case-study approaches.

The case conference is closely related to the case study. The case conference offers a method for collecting, ordering, and synthesizing data at all school levels. Subjects for case conferences can be found in all areas of educational activity. The responsibilities of guidance workers as well as faculty members were placed within a total perspective of case conference and case-study work. Additional uses of case-conference concepts were explained in detail. These additional uses include the coordination of specialists, faculty involvement, faculty growth, referral procedures, and student involvement.

REFERENCES AND SUGGESTED READINGS

Adams, James F., *Problems in Counseling: A Case Study Approach,* New York: Macmillan, 1962.

Allen, Richard D., *Case Conference Problems in Group Guidance,* New York: Inor, 1933.

Andrews, K. R. (ed.), *The Case Method of Teaching Human Relations and Administration,* Cambridge, Mass.: Harvard University Press, 1953.
Barr, John A., *The Elementary Teacher and Guidance,* New York: Henry Holt, 1958.
Cassel, Russell N., "A Clinical Procedure for the School Psychologist," *Journal of the National Association of Women Deans and Counselors,* XXIV (1960), 23–27.
Castore, G. F., and F. D. Berrien, "A Student Evaluation of a Case Method Course," *American Psychologist,* V (1950), 149–151.
Cottingham, Harold F., *Guidance in Elementary Schools,* Bloomington, Ill.: McKnight, 1956.
Freeman, Stanley L., *Case Studies in Student Orientation* (ed. D), New York: Teachers College, Columbia University, 1952 (unpublished dissertation).
Glanz, Edward C., *Groups in Guidance,* Boston: Allyn & Bacon, 1962.
Gragg, Charles L., "Because Wisdom Can't Be Told," in K. R. Andrews (ed.), *The Case Method of Teaching Human Relations and Administration,* Cambridge, Mass.: Harvard University Press, 1953.
Hefferman, Helen (ed.), *Guiding the Young Child from Kindergarten to Grade Three* (2nd ed.), Boston: D. C. Heath, 1959.
Hollis, Florence, *Casework: A Psychosocial Therapy,* New York: Random House, 1963.
Hutson, Percival W., *The Guidance Function in Education,* New York: Appleton-Century-Crofts, 1958.
Hymes, James L., Jr., *A Child Development Point of View,* Englewood Cliffs, N.J.: Prentice-Hall, 1955.
Knapp, R. H., *Guidance in the Elementary School,* Boston: Allyn & Bacon, 1959.
Linton, Ralph, *The Cultural Background of Personality,* New York: Appleton-Century-Crofts, 1962.
Mahoney, Harold J., "The Team Approach to Pupil Personnel Services," paper presented to Interprofessional Conference on Pupil Personnel Services in the Public Schools, Washington, D.C., Sept., 1961.
Millard, Cecil J., and J. Wm. Rothney, *The Elementary School Child–A Book of Cases,* New York: Dryden, 1957.
Raines, Max R., "Helping College Freshmen Identify Problems Through a Case Conference," *Personnel and Guidance Journal,* XXXIV (1956), 417–419.
Sarason, Seymour B., *et al., Anxiety in Elementary School Children,* New York: John Wiley, 1960.
Traxler, Arthur E., *Techniques of Guidance* (rev. ed.), New York: Harper, 1957.
University of the State of New York, *Manual on Pupil Records,* Albany, N.Y.: State Education Department, 1962.
Walton, Wesley W., "The Electronic Age Comes to the Schoolhouse," *Systems for Educators,* VIII (1962), 3–10.
Watson, R. I., *The Clinical Method in Psychology,* New York: Harper, 1951.
White, R. W., *Lives in Progress,* New York: Dryden, 1952.
White, Verna, *Studying the Individual Pupil,* New York: Harper, 1958.

GUIDANCE IN OPERATION

GUIDANCE IS a process within education. Various services are included within any guidance program. Each aspect of a program or a service needs to be organized as an effectively operating unit. Yet guidance is always greater than the sum of its individual services.

Guidance focuses upon the individual within education. The implementation of individual goals, personal aspirations, and development plans through self-understanding becomes the major purpose of guidance. Student growth and development can take place within all areas of education as well as within any specific service unit.

Guidance begins with preschool preparation and continues throughout the life of the person as he relates to education and to

PART THREE

learning. Educational and vocational planning, personal problem-solving, discipline issues, student activities, records, articulation and orientation, and placement are the major areas of operation and service in a guidance program.

Patterns and philosophical constructs of guidance have appeared in public and private schools. School boards, boards of trustees, administrators, and even parents can select the particular program patterns that they feel to be appropriate to their community.

Guidance in operation is the focus of Part Three of this book. The major topics highlighted in each chapter in this part are: (1) Self-Understanding, (2) Guidance Services (divided into Parts I and II), (3) Patterns of Guidance.

SELF-UNDERSTANDING

THE ISSUE. Philosophers have long proposed that man himself is the proper object of study for man. The complexities of man's behavior are confusing to students of all ages; the study of oneself poses an additional intervening variable for the student. The study of human behavior becomes personal and immediate.

Education is concerned with the content of man's accumulated and potential knowledge; it is also concerned with the person who learns. Guidance centers upon and stands with the person. Self-understanding is thus the single most basic service of guidance and at the same time is a foundation for all guidance programing.

The nature of self-understanding, the elements of the self that each student can study, and the means guidance can provide for self-study and self-understanding are pivotal points to consider in viewing guidance as an operational process. Only through self-understanding can the person become truly free and capable of responsible action.

The most significant integration of education takes place within the individual. Correlated and interdependent subject matter courses have characterized the general education movement and curricular advancements on all school and college levels. The development of the individual, however, rather than subject matter, is the ultimate purpose of education. The final testing-ground for education is the meaningfulness of knowledge in life. Education must be incorporated into the life of the individual. Self-understanding has been recognized as an important goal for all effective programs. However, the assumption that academic investigations into the behavior of man will lead to self-understanding is most questionable.

CHAPTER NINE

The subject matter, or the curriculum, and the individual are two major focuses for education. The almost naïve belief that studying other men will, necessarily, help a person to understand himself is a sacred cow of many programs. Guidance calls this assumption into question, and at the same time offers principles and a methodology that can help the person to study and learn about himself.

GENERAL EDUCATION

The issue of general versus special education has raged for centuries. Modern societies in particular are concerned with producing an educational program geared to the development of citizens and also capable of producing trained, specialized technicians.

There are many differences between specialized and general education. The most essential difference lies in the proposition that general education is education for life as a whole, whereas specialized and technical education is preparation for earning a living. General education is one of the special provinces of the public schools of America. The private school systems of a special religious, military, or preparatory bent may add particular dimensions to their program, but they also reflect a concern for offering a sound general education to all students. Our legal codes reflect such doctrines and principles. Higher educational units attempt to provide for all students a continued preparation in learning to live as well as in learning how to make a living. On the other hand, technical, specialized education, of the type offered in a medical or law school or in an apprentice-type, anteroom school, provides training and skills only for those students who can profit from and utilize such experiences.

Guidance can and must aid students in both the general and specialized educational programs that may be offered by the school. The nature of guidance service in specialized education is particular, specific, and determined by the nature of the program. But guidance is a full partner in the general educational program, for it can provide the means and tools for students to achieve the educational goal of self-understanding.

Education and Personal Integration

The glimpse of education that is provided by visiting "citizen educators" as they survey and study school programs can reveal or conceal its true nature. However, professional educators and citizen members of the local school board should recognize that education must produce knowledgeable students who are effective persons. The simplicity of the twofold nature of education belies its importance. Education must provide the facts and knowledge necessary to life in our world. Yet it is the person who must live that life. Knowledge and fact cannot maintain themselves in a suspended state. Facts can reside within the covers of a book, the walls of a library, or a bookshelf. But education is more than facts, more than knowledge. The static accumulation of facts can, at best, be classified as a library. Even libraries will deny that their accumulated matter is static. The person who can use and apply knowledge is as important to education as the knowledge itself.

Early educational programs stressed the acquisition of the "polite learnings." Young girls were assumed to be well educated if they were able to recite a poem or two and look erudite when the Greek dramatists were discussed. Similar though more complex hopes were entertained as education assumed that men of the cloth, of government services, and of the military could be prepared both for life and for specialized services. American education rests upon no such set principles. The school board of any local community can serve to defend this statement if defense is needed.

Education can exist only if the person is involved and affected by the experience. The nonactive, file-cabinet concept of education is a part of educational history rather than practice. Integration of education is not merely a static intertwining of concepts, ideas, or facts across disciplinary lines. Education must relate and connect its parts for the student, yet education that is connected and even interlocked must become a part of the life of the student. Integration of the subject matter of education in the life of the person is the ultimate concept that defines and determines the basic nature of education.

Self-Understanding

The concept of self that is developed as a person grows and creates a life is viewed from the outside as a personality. The individual viewing himself conceives of himself as a person of a changeable nature, but with consistencies and interrelated operational patterns of problem-solving. The self-concept is an internal controlling view of personality.

The person who undertakes the study of personality and more specifically of his own personality as it operates and serves his own goals and life objectives can help to integrate his own educational experience. No person can ever understand or accept fully all the elements and dimensions that make up his personality. Still, the goal of self-understanding through self-study and self-analysis is a primary educational concept and one that is approachable through guidance. A positive view of self-understanding states that each person through self-study and self-analysis can begin to know and appreciate successfully his own personality. Self-understanding can promote critical thinking, educational growth and development, and an effective consideration of the future. Guidance seeks to help students achieve these objectives. The ultimate goal is to help students accomplish such activities on their own, through self-discipline and self-direction.

SELF-STUDY

The behavior of man has become the province of psychology and anthropology. Man and his interactions with other men have been discovered to be the results of drives, needs, and complex patterns of motivation. The frustrations that can occur as man seeks and creates goals and life purposes are also areas of study for the social and behavioral sciences. Guidance is concerned with man as he studies himself within an educational environment.

The term *self-study* can also be applied to therapy and special types of therapeutic approaches in a hospital or mental health clinic. Yet, within the structure of education, self-study and the accumulation of self-knowledge need to be seen as totally normal, expected experiences for all students. Self-study provides the means for achieving the self-understanding that stands coordinate with the other knowledge that can be accumulated through education.

Several major areas of self-study are involved in the usual pattern of educational experience. The methods, levels of study, and content principles may vary among schools and levels of education, but the areas are constant and almost universal. Various terms may be used to designate these areas of self-study within education, but such semantic issues can be resolved as common concepts are extracted. The usual areas of self-study are: (1) individual differences, (2) interests, (3) aptitudes, (4) capacities, and (5) values.

The indicated areas of self-study are applicable to various life situations as well as to the school. Educational planning, career development, placement procedures, marital choices, and even family and community life are outcomes of successful or unsuccessful self-study and self-understanding. The areas of application of self-study will be examined in the chapters on guidance services within education. The appropriate application of the areas of self-study depend upon their careful and meaningful delineation.

Individual Differences

The diversity of the individual has been noted for many centuries. Plato, as well as the ancient Hebrews, attempted to classify persons and to educate the members of the appraised society appropriately. Contemporary psychology is rooted in an appraisal of individual differences. Measures of differences in mental ability, capacity, and interest have been built upon earlier psychophysical concepts of reaction times and physical differences among individuals. Studies of differences within the individual in the performance of tasks or in demonstrating capacities of all types were also made.

Individual differences are expressed through a vocabulary of measurement and descriptive statistics. The measuring of individual differences is the sophisticated enlargement of the original concept of Plato and the ancient Hebrews. All mental and physical characteristics of human beings can be understood to fall into a pattern of normal distribution, expressing the concept of individual differences in terms of measurement capacity. The normal curve (Gaussian, bell-shaped) is a conceptual description that represents the standard of measurement against which all individual differences need to be measured.

The intellectual construct of individual differences and their measurement is not only a conceptual fact that needs to be studied in psychology, mathematics, and education, but also a meaningful fact that needs to be introduced into the life of each student. Students frequently reveal their ignorance of such differences in schools, although they recognize their existence outside of school. The student who cannot understand why another student is able to study less and yet achieve more is easily able to understand the ability of one student to excel in football. The threat that is present in intellectual evaluation of all types is frequently suppressed with the connivance of teachers and guidance persons. However, the individual student may be fearful without cause or may be distorting the facts about himself through the adjustment mechanisms that operate within human personality. The availability of data on individual differences and its interpretation through meaningful understanding of measurement techniques are contributions which guidance should make to the area of self-understanding.

The measurement principles that are appropriate for advanced research psychologists are not desirable for use with junior high school pupils. But graded use of measurement tools can be meaningful at all school levels. Elementary school children can react to generalizations and the conceptual patterns of derived scores such as quartiles, half-classes, and even deciles. The terms need not be technical, and the concepts can be studied and mastered in elementary school arithmetic. Katz (1959) offers beginning instruction in measurement principles for junior high school pupils. Mahoney and Engle (1962) and other authors are providing material for use with secondary school students. College students have long studied and been helped to assess themselves through measurement techniques.

Individual differences and measurement principles form the foundation that supports later learnings about the self in the areas of interest, aptitudes, capacities, and values. To ignore the foundation upon which these potential learnings rest is to distort them before they are begun.

Interests

Vocational and personal interests provide a key area for involving students in an examination of themselves. An interest is primarily a mental set about a special type of activity. Interest may involve likes, dislikes, and tendencies to engage in or avoid certain behaviors.

Early experimentation in vocational interest produced two of the oldest "testing" tools used by guidance. The *Kuder Preference Record* and the *Strong Vocational Interest Blank* are not psychological tests in the true sense, but structured inventories that attempt to assess the student's interest patterns. These measures divide vocational interest into major types or families. The Kuder record assesses interest areas such as mechanical, musical, and outdoor. The Strong inventory may be scored for job groups such as management, technical, or agriculture. Personal-interest inventories virtually assess personality traits and characteristics of interest that are not strictly vocational.

Interest, vocational or otherwise, needs to be seen as a variable of personality. The consequences of interest are not necessarily vocational success. Aptitude and capacity may not correlate with interest, nor are they necessarily infallible guides to interest areas. Students and counselors are frequently misled by assuming that a correlation exists. Achievement depends primarily upon aptitude or capacity; when interest is in accord with such variables, the achievement can be high. However, when interest alone is present and aptitude and capacity are missing, achievement is extremely difficult.

Since interest is a variable of personality, it is desirable that explorations of interest areas be available to students as early as elementary school. The wide experience that can be provided through a curriculum, social activities, and home stimulation can be combined with specific exploration projects scheduled and aided through guidance efforts. Field trips, curricular emphases, and work projects are meaningful in this area for the early school years. In junior high school, secondary school, and college interest can be used as a basis for the study of individual differences, measurement principles, and the self. Interests can help students to begin thinking seriously about educational planning, vocational exploration, curriculum choice, and eventually about career development.

Interest cuts across the levels of education and the services that can be offered by an entire guidance program. The concept that students can and do differ in personality and mental traits is easily demonstrated through an analysis of interests and can lead to the further examination of aptitudes, capacities, and values. The student who understands not only the concept of interest as it affects persons in general but also as it affects him personally is ready for and frequently demands to study related issues.

Aptitudes

Aptitude has long been defined as a potential capacity to learn. *Skill* is a presently available ability to do something. Aptitude deals with the future, whereas skill is a concept of the present. Aptitudes are therefore one of the most significant elements of education and more specifically of guidance.

Aptitudes are derived from the complex interaction of heredity and environment. According to research, heredity establishes the limits of a potential skill while environment determines the opportunities available to the person to develop his potential. Beethoven might have had difficulty becoming a musician in a society and culture that offered no opportunity for musical expression. Similarly a tone-deaf, musically untalented child may be forced to take piano lessons for many years and become only a passably proficient pianist.

Many varieties and classifications of aptitudes have been offered by psychological research. Early efforts isolated musical, artistic, and mechanical talent, and even manual aptitudes. Individual measures of each of these areas have been available for many years. Scholastic aptitude—the specific application of intelligence to an academic situation—has been one of the most widely studied aptitude concepts.

The idea of vocational aptitudes was appealing to many and much research was accomplished in this area. The dimensions of occupations such as law, nursing, and accounting were studied and actual tests constructed to assess a person's potential to enter and succeed in such an occupation. The problem can be understood more clearly as a simple job, such as that of a tool- and die-maker, is examined. Scholastic, manual, mechanical, and spatial aptitudes are needed for any person who hopes to enter and succeed in such an occupation. In any, even a semiskilled, occupation it is necessary to possess various aptitudes and to combine them with interest, motivation, values, opportunity, and financial ability to determine the likelihood of success. Aptitude measures are most accurate when they are restricted to relatively narrow areas of potential performance.

Research and test developments since World War II have provided integrated measures of specific aptitudes. The *Differential Aptitude Tests*, the *California Aptitude Test*, and others have made it possible to assess student aptitudes at many age levels in a reliable, valid fashion. Aptitude-test measures have made it possible not only to measure aptitude, but also to make data available for students to use in developing their self-understanding.

Aptitudes can be measured at all ages with various types of tests. The overlap between aptitude and intelligence measures will be discussed in the next section. It is necessary to recognize that a reliable measurement of highly specific aptitudes cannot be obtained before the subjects are 9 or 10 years of age. Earlier measures provide only general guidelines. The junior high or upper elementary school years are the natural period for the careful assessment of aptitude potentials.

It is also possible at this time to begin to measure the general interests of students. The parallel development of aptitudes and interests can provide a meaningful basis for students attempting to collect data about themselves.

Capacity

Intelligence was one of the earliest variables studied by research psychologists. Binet in France created a rough measure of individual intelligence in the early years of this century (see Chapter 6). The issues of definition and measurement have been continuously debated since that time. The "IQ" has been alternately assessed, sliced, correlated, and buried for over half a century.

Recent studies have cast a cloud over the concepts of aptitude and intelligence. Earlier research, by such men as Spearman, Thorndike, and Thurstone, offered a choice of a "multifactor" concept of intelligence or a "G" (general) factor combined with more specific special aptitudes. Clear-cut answers were not obtained. With continued development, multiple-aptitude measures, combined into total individual assessment procedures, began to overlap into the area previously defined as intelligence. Currently it is thought that aptitude measures and intelligence or capacity measures differ only in the specific areas covered (sometimes only in the names chosen to refer to these areas) and in the normative data that are obtained in the standardization.

The use of intelligence tests which produce only a single score is not widespread. Most intelligence or capacity measures attempt to assess at least two factors of verbal, nonverbal, or performance capacity. Many tests that offer two scores (with a combination of the two to render a third) can be divided into subparts that closely resemble the current aptitude battery tests.

Such terms as *verbal aptitude, verbal intelligence,* and *scholastic aptitude* seem to refer to almost identical concepts of capacity. Scholastic aptitude may be divided into parts, such as verbal and mathematical, or verbal, quantitative, and verbal reasoning. The conceptual area of capacity to reason, to deal abstractly with verbal symbols, seems to refer to the same general area of individual capacity as the area of verbal ability. Such is the problem of confused theory that is translated into equally confused practice.

The uncertainty of present theories of capacity and intelligence has had a salutary effect upon school practice. Early concepts of intelligence led to a single IQ score that teachers and guidance workers often assumed to be the sole appropriate characteristic of the individual. However, the early tentative concepts of social, mechanical, abstract, concrete, and even mathematical intelligence have now been confirmed and broadened. School practice has become freer and more inclined toward the study of each individual child rather than toward allowing a single test score to describe his intellectual dimensions.

Whatever measure of capacity is used within a school system, it is possible to relate capacity measures to aptitudes and interests. The potential "G" factor of intelligence may be incorporated into the scholastic aptitude concept, since all types of learning seem to be related and depend upon individual potential. Future research may clarify such issues for guidance, but until research data are available it is desirable and necessary to buttress all measures of so-called intelligence with supporting assessments of major aptitude areas. Individual counseling and more general guidance activities can help each person incorporate the patterns of such data into his concept of himself and into his general plan for life.

The interpretation of capacity to students is potentially dangerous. The uses and abuses of the IQ have rubbed off on all of American society. The child fears that his intelligence will not measure up, will not be considered "college material," or will be inadequate for his possible plans. The concept of a capacity can best be handled by a guidance program after the student has been helped understand the concepts of interest and aptitude and explore the dimensions of each of these areas as they exist within himself.

The longitudinal case-study concept of interest, aptitude, and capacity can help students to obtain perspective as they examine these issues. The conceptual pictures that are available from cumulative records and consecutive psychological-test profiles can help to allay the fear of a single score that may determine all of life. Group techniques can permit students to explore general meanings and to apply results to group areas. Individual counseling can help each person understand and integrate data as he grows and develops through education. The process is necessarily gradual and halting, but the goal must remain clearly in focus.

Values

The issue of individual values has long been ignored by guidance and education. The premises of education within a free society have seemingly forbidden the indoctrination of any value or set of values. Frequently teachers, counselors, and guidance workers have avoided any involvement with values.

The tendency to back away from such issues has hurt the potentially productive and sensitive student who must assume a responsible role as a citizen and member of society. Education that depends upon the indoctrination of a specific set of values is certainly inimical to the traditions of a free open society such as exists in America. Yet the controlling nature of values and their overwhelming importance in determining the nature and quality of a life demands that they be examined by education and guidance.

The teacher and guidance worker are often considered as models for students. The pressure for individual educators to establish patterns of behavior that students may use as models has been inherent at all levels of education. The rigid conformity that has been placed upon teachers in many school systems can only be explained psychologically by the "model" concept. The forcing of value patterns upon students has thus been once removed, but has certainly been present as a system of indoctrination. The quality of indoctrination and the values that are to be held highest, fortunately, have varied and have been freely interpreted by local school boards or school officials.

Values can be introduced into the curriculum and the guidance program without attempting to indoctrinate or enforce rigid conformity among students. The role of values and the significance of adopting guideposts for living can and should be examined.

The ethical concepts of a responsible person within a society depend upon the adoption of values that guide behavior. Hitler, in training students for duty to the state, demanded that the moral responsibility to the state be greater than the filial obligation that had so long existed in Western civilization. This state-determined value was propagated by the schools and the youth groups and inculcated in all persons. This value was a guide to action. Children were expected to turn in traitorous mothers and fathers, and they did turn parents over to the Gestapo! Values are not only the fabric of ethical responsibility but are practical everyday commodities that lead to specific customs.

Guidance programs need to help students examine individual values, sets of values, and conflicting and interrelated value patterns. The guidance worker cannot deliver values to students, nor can he, within a free society, distribute official or unofficial approval and disapproval. Yet if students can be helped to understand that values are guides to their own behavior and that such guides and behaviors will lead to certain probable results, they can better determine for themselves what values must be held and which may be cast aside. The issues of freedom and responsibility loom large in the everyday concepts of individual and group counseling, in group activities in a seventh-grade guidance program, in career planning—throughout guidance and education.

Recently a few newer psychological assessment techniques have been created which are designed to measure values. Several discussion techniques can be developed that rest upon older value assessment tools [Allport, Lindzey, and Vernon (1960)]. Although values have been avoided in guidance and counseling theory for many years, it may be possible that newer techniques will create an aroused interest in value discussion and assessment.

A pioneering attempt to introduce values into the everyday conduct of a guidance program was demonstrated in the chapter "Your Values" of the textbook *You: Today and Tomorrow* prepared by Martin Katz for student use in junior high school (1959). The headings in this chapter, prepared for student use in a guidance course combining group, individual, and testing techniques, are as follows:

1. Why Must You Weigh Odds, Risks, and Values?
2. How Can You Examine Your Values? What Part Do They Play in Your Decisions?
3. Would You Rather Play It Safe or Take a Chance?
4. Will Your Values Change?
5. How Can You Keep Track of Your Values?
6. How Do You Connect Values with Choices?[1]

This chapter is written at a junior high school reading level and contains detailed fill-in workbook material. The author examines issues that are vital to the lives of students and subjects them, in systematic fashion, to an examination of values and their implications for social activities, the choice of friends, vocational aspirations, and parent-child relationships.

Values direct the personality of any person. However, it is possible to develop conflicting or even mutually exclusive values. Guidance needs to stand with students as values are studied and as interests, individual differences, aptitudes, and capacities are assessed and weighed against a personal future. The "cultural osmosis" of values is deceitful in its dominating nature. The person believes and defends what he believes. But he often does not know how he came to believe, why he does not believe the contrary. To examine the values one holds at present is only the first step. Students involved in the creation of their lives need to be aided in understanding the process through which values can be acquired, changed, and tested. Guidance must enter into the process of studying values with students and helping them relate value learnings in their own lives. When values assume their normal po-

[1] Reprinted by permission of the Cooperative Test Division, Educational Testing Service.

sition within personality and the student can understand their role, he can begin to integrate his related knowledge of interests, aptitudes, capacities, and the entire issue of individual differences.

A CONCEPT OF SELF

Personality has been a popular area of study for high school and college students in psychology and human relations courses. The concepts of personality studied have frequently rested upon the trait theory. Students are introduced to characteristics such as "superiority or inferiority attitudes, altruism or dominance in traits." The students often respond with enthusiasm to such discussions, but they are not helped to integrate such learnings into any broader pattern of school learning or life-planning.

Self-concept theory, while not denying any major theoretical position or speculation about personality, is more amenable to student study and use. The mysteries of personality have been partially simplified and the confusion of advanced theory has been taken out of the undergraduate classrooms.

The Structure of the Self

The concept of "the self as seen by the self" is offered by Combs and Snygg (1959). Many authors have recognized this internal view of personality as a meaningful and constructive approach for the guidance worker, and one which can help students to understand better their own value system and their own development of life-purposes and objectives. The formation of personality depends upon drives, needs, motives, and learning. The process of adjustment and problem-solving helps to structure and guide the later development of the person. The learning and differentiation processes help the student to select out of his environment and his personal reactions to experience those elements that are most meaningful for his future development. The interactions and interrelationships among all the factors of personality are dynamic and interdependent. The opportunity to see the self-concept as a directing force of personality can help the individual student view himself as an active agent in determining his own future. The purist view of the person as determined wholly by environment has been discarded in all behavioral disciplines. The individual, who can affect and help to determine his own future through his decisions and choices, can construct a life.

The elements of a self-concept view of personality that are important for all levels of guidance are diagramed below.

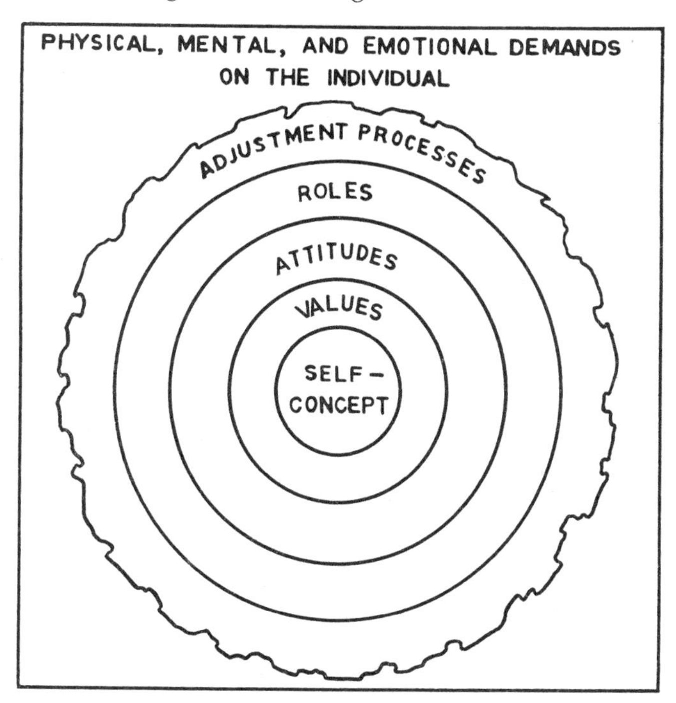

Where the adjustment and processes meet the environment world of existence, personality is observed in action. (From Edward C. Glanz and Ernest B. Walston, *An Introduction to Personal Adjustment,* Boston: Allyn and Bacon, Inc., 1958, p. 77.)

No psychologist at any level will be satisfied with such a simplified view of personality. However, the description of personality that is offered is for everyday use with students to help them achieve a degree of self-understanding. Research psychologists and theory-constructing psychologists or sociologists will construct a more sophisticated view of the personality. But the significant issue is that personality must be seen and partially understood by students studying themselves. Varying approaches to this concept of self-study and personality knowledge are presented in text materials for junior high, high school, and college levels. All agree that the self-concept theory can help guidance persons integrate their own view of personality while aiding students in self-understanding.

The Process of Self-Understanding

The process of helping students develop understanding begins on the first day of school and continues throughout the educational experience. The actual efforts of guidance personnel in this area may be direct or may be conveyed through the actions of other school personnel. How the concept of respect for the individuality and integrity of the student can be realized is the problem that is inherent in all efforts to help students to achieve a mature understanding of themselves.

Self-understanding can be aided or distorted in many ways. The first grade class groupings of "bluebirds, robins, and squirrels" may relate to the reading readiness or vocabulary levels of the pupils. The actual basis of the division must be honestly faced and interpreted to the students, for they will soon find out if the teacher is using the nice names to cover a very real difference between the groups. The names that are offered to the students are perfectly appropriate, but they cannot be used to cover the essential facts to which the students are entitled.

No student will be a "bluebird" or a "robin" for the rest of his school life and hopefully not for the entire year. Flexibility in school programing and changes in groupings which reflect student growth can help students recognize their own problems and limitations as well as their potentials.

The first step toward success for a college student may be his recognition of the need for a special remedial English or speech course prior to or along with the regular curriculum. The student cannot be deceived into believing that he is the same as all other students, for he is aware of the differences between himself and others. Although the individual student may or may not be able to name the differences or to establish their causes or effects, they are nevertheless real. The most important aspect of the recognition of differences among students is the need to value all students as potentially creative and productive. The differences in where they begin and in the areas of future self-change are practical as well as philosophical, and must be faced, resolved, and integrated into future development. Students who are different are not necessarily of differing value as persons or as potentially successful graduates of the kindergarten or the college.

The concepts of integrity and honesty must always be appropriate in dealing with students. Similar integrity and honesty must characterize all guidance efforts. Life plans and objectives cannot be built upon shifting distorted self-concepts created by the student or reflected by those who help him. The ends and the goals of self-analysis can and must be open-ended; the facts and learnings that are available to the student are the raw material out of which he can construct a future.

The goals of students may or may not be realistic. The right and privilege of the student is to be unrealistic if he wishes. The responsibility of the guidance person is to be honest, fair, and understanding. Allowing students to incorporate counselors, group leaders, and guidance personnel of all types into their distorted concepts of self can only hurt the student and the guidance worker. Guidance persons need to help students face the reality of the world as it is, not as the student may wish it to be. The guidance person may need to represent the world for the student and then, figuratively, return to stand by his side as the implications of his facing that world are explored. But the guidance person is not the reality that the student has to understand, and the counselor who symbolizes himself as a part of this reality cannot help the student to understand it.

Counselors or guidance personnel who assume a personal affront whenever a student is unable to recognize and understand the reality of a school world of rules and regulations, an admissions office, or a student court are identifying with the world that is around the student. This world is confusing, perplexing, and real; the guidance person only confuses the student more when he assumes that he is the world for the student. Self-understanding cannot be aided by a guidance worker who becomes the same as either the student or the world. He is neither; he is a guide and helper to the student.

PROGRAMING FOR SELF-UNDERSTANDING

A program for self-understanding that cuts across all levels of education and all types of schools or institutions assumes that there are procedures that can be adopted and utilized to help all students at varying ages. Age is perhaps the most basic determiner of the degree of sophistication that can be established in a program designed to develop self-understanding.

Elementary School

The children in the early school grades are not directly accessible to verbal counseling. However, activity group work, play therapy of all types, and clinical assessment can help others understand the child.

The attempt to help the child at these levels to understand himself needs the most intimate cooperation between guidance personnel and teachers. The teacher provides the most direct contact with all but seriously disturbed or referral cases. The stress needs to be placed upon the normal nonreferred child.

Teachers can foster and create an environment that will permit students to build concepts of self that are in accord with their own knowledge of themselves. The curriculum provides a tremendous resource for students to explore the dimensions of the world and to assess themselves against a backdrop of reality. Occupation field trips to nearby locations; curricular exploration of vocations such as those in government, civics, science, and language; school projects and fairs such as are currently available in science; creative festivals which permit students to exhibit their artistic works and efforts of all types—such types of creative teaching and curriculum development can help students to establish a foundation of self-understanding that can serve them through all later school years.

Guidance personnel can help to establish and implement classroom activities. Additional activity by counselors or guidance persons can bring teachers, students, and parents together for group and individual conferences. A planned schedule of parental, teacher, and pupil conferences can be programed and coordinated by guidance persons. The opportunity for the pupil to participate with the members of his adult world can help him to recognize that he is not merely an object to be manipulated. Creative work of this type is just beginning to appear in research and experimental elementary school programs have begun to arise. Team teaching and programs for the gifted or creative child have revealed the success that can lie in this direction. New theory-building will hopefully include the normal average child for whom all education and guidance must be equally creative.

Junior High School

Gigantic strides have been made in junior high school programing for self-understanding. Junior high school efforts often have been well beyond even the theoretical design available to the secondary schools. Guidance publications from many sources have stressed the need for involving the student in the process of studying himself. Earlier efforts toward "personal adjustment" and efforts in "group guidance" were abortive in the schools. Pupils, teachers, and guidance personnel were dismayed at the superficial attempts to gloss over real and significant knowledge about students. Dating and standards of dress were frequently the "vital" areas of such programs. The National Forum series attempts to help students assess themselves in five different areas throughout their junior high school guidance program. These areas are: (1) Educational Planning, (2) Personal-Social Relations, (3) Group and Family Life, (4) Boy-Girl Relations, and (5) Vocational Planning. More precise units in self-study and self-understanding are available in the Educational Testing Service Booklet, *You: Today and Tomorrow:* (1) The Mirror of Tomorrow, (2) How to Ask the Right Question, (3) Your Abilities, (4) Your Values, (5) Your Interests, (6) Occupations, (7) Education, and (8) Making Choices (Katz, 1959). A quotation from *You: Today and Tomorrow* can offer more of the flavor of how seventh- and eighth-grade pupils can be involved in self-understanding. The following section is written for the pupil who is studying himself and facing decisions about his own future:

> You started off by recognizing the need for three kinds of information:
>
> —about yourself,
>
> —about the courses open to you next year (your immediate decision),
>
> —about the kinds of work and schooling to which they may lead your long range choices.
>
> As a step toward knowing yourself, you have learned what is meant by abilities, values, and interests. You have some idea of how to observe them in yourself. You have some understanding of the part they may play in the decisions you make, of how they may be connected with the different choices open to you now and in the future. . . . This book has already shown you some ways in which different kinds of schooling are connected with different occupations and with different abilities, values, and interests.
>
> Of course, all this is only a start. There are many other topics you will want to include as you go on with the study of yourself and your opportunities. Perhaps you have begun to recognize that your understanding of yourself and your knowledge of possible choices should continue to grow as you grow. At each point in your life where decisions are to be made, you will do the best you can in the light of what you already know about yourself, about your possible goals, and the path that may lead to those goals. Then if you make good use of your time and experiences, when you reach the next choice-point, you will have learned more about all three types of information. You will have additional knowledge and understanding to help you as you approach each new time for decision [p. 91].[2]

[2] Reprinted by permission of the Cooperative Test Division, Educational Testing Service.

Group counseling programs with parents and pupils have also been pioneered in junior high schools. The opportunities to integrate the various tools of guidance are great at this level of education. Group work can provide a wide involvement of students, educators, parents, and guidance workers in aiding students. The additional maturity of the student in symbolic processes of communication make counseling more effective than it is in the elementary school. Test programs are widespread at this level and aptitude, capacity, interest, and problem inventories are available for integration into the over-all guidance program. Students and guidance persons can initiate case-study procedures, and the student can begin to assess and understand himself in a mature fashion.

High School and College

High school and college programs of guidance and personnel work can build upon the efforts of the junior high school. All of the tools of guidance may be integrated into school-wide and community-wide patterns. Too frequently high school or college guidance workers have been unaware of the earlier experiences of students and either repeat or fail to build upon earlier student growth in self- and social understanding.

Home-room programs, occupations and psychology courses, case-conference designs, and human relations programs can all reflect significant previous learnings and build toward the solution of future problems and toward student development. Guidance theory and practice is still growing, and specific patterns are neither available nor valid for each new situation. The concepts of guidance are developing as creative uses are found for traditional and newer guidance methods. The pluralistic pattern of the present can be encouraged by the development of new designs. As basic concepts are developed for each level and type of school or college, it may be possible to specify more detailed designs to be used by guidance workers.

SUMMARY

Self-understanding has been presented as the basic service that can be offered by guidance programs and methods. The nature of self-understanding has been explored as it relates to the educational goals of a society. Education must ultimately rest on and be utilized by the individual. That the person must understand himself and relate himself to education is axiomatic in a society that values the individual and the education of that individual. General educational goals and the growth of the individual have been examined as examples of the intimate relationship between the person and education.

Many areas of self-study exist for the student. The goal of self-understanding can only be reached by the examination of specific elements of personality. Individual differences, interests of a vocational and personal nature, aptitudes, capacity, and values are the major areas of the self that have been presented.

The self-concept view of personality that can help students to integrate their own learnings about themselves is related to the individual personality dimensions that students study. The concept of self provides a means for studying the self and relating all data in a meaningful fashion.

The chapter concluded with specific applications of self-understanding at varying levels of educational practice. Elementary school, junior high school, high school and college programs are all shown to depend upon student growth in self-understanding.

REFERENCES AND SUGGESTED READINGS

Allport, Gordon, *et al.*, *Assessment of Human Motives,* New York: Grove, 1958.

Baughman, E. E., and G. S. Welsh, *Personality: A Behavioral Science,* Englewood Cliffs, N.J.: Prentice-Hall, 1962.

Brandt, R. M., "Self: Missing Link for Understanding Behavior," *Mental Hygiene,* January, 1957, 24–33.

Brown, Judson S., *The Motivation of Behavior,* New York: McGraw-Hill, 1961.

Christensen, T. E., and M. K. Burns, *Resource Units in Self-Approval and Careers,* Worcester, Mass.: Public Schools, 1954.

Combs, Arthur W., and Donald Snygg, *Individual Behavior* (rev. ed.), New York: Harper, 1959.

Cooper, Russell M. (ed)., *The Two Ends of the Log: Learning and Teaching in Today's College,* Minneapolis, Minn.: University of Minnesota Press, 1958.

Drews, Elizabeth M. (ed.), *Guidance for the Academically Talented Student,* Washington, D.C.: National Education Association and American Personnel and Guidance Association, 1961.

Eddy, Edward D., Jr., *The College Influence on Student Character,* Washington, D.C.: American Council on Education, 1959.

Erikson, E. H., "The Problem of Ego Identity," *Journal of the American Psychoanalytic Association,* IV (1956), 58–121.
Fisher, M. B., and J. L. Nobel, *College Education as Personal Development,* Englewood Cliffs, N.J.: Prentice-Hall, 1960.
Glanz, Edward C., and E. B. Walston, *An Introduction to Personal Adjustment,* Boston: Allyn & Bacon, 1958.
Glazer, N., "The Wasted Classroom," *Harpers,* CCXXIII (1961), 147–153.
Goodlad, John I., "Individual Differences and Vertical Organization of the School," in *Individual Differences,* Sixty-First Yearbook of the National Society for the Study of Education, Part I, Chicago: University of Chicago Press, 1962, 209–238.
Gould, R. M., "An Experimental Analysis of 'Level of Aspiration,'" *Genetic Psychology Monographs,* XXI (1939), 3–115.
Hall, John F., *Psychology of Motivation,* Chicago: Lippincott, 1961.
Havighurst, R. J., *Growing Up in River City,* Chicago: University of Chicago Press, 1962.
Hopkins, L. Thomas, *The Emerging Self,* New York: Harper, 1954.
Jacob, Philip E., *Changing Values in College,* New York: Harper, 1957.
Jersild, A. T., *In Search of Self,* New York: Bureau of Publications, Teachers College, Columbia University, 1952.
Katz, Martin, *You: Today and Tomorrow,* Princeton, N.J.: Educational Testing Service, 1959.
Kvaraceus, W. C., *The Delinquency Proneness Scale,* Tarrytown, N.Y.: World Book, 1952.
Landis, M. A. M., "Creativity, A Precious Possession," *Childhood Education,* XXXVII (1960), 155–156.
Lane, H., and M. Beauchamp, *Understanding Human Development,* Englewood Cliffs, N.J.: Prentice-Hall, 1959.
Leeper, R. W., and P. Madison, *Toward Understanding Human Personalities,* New York: Appleton-Century-Crofts, 1959.
Lloyd-Jones, Esther, and Margaret R. Smith (eds.) *Student Personnel Work as Deeper Teaching,* New York: Harper, 1954.
Mahoney, H. T., and T. L. Engle, *Points for Decision* (rev. ed.), Yonkers, N.Y.: World Book, 1961.
Moustakas, C. E., *Psychotherapy with Children,* New York: Harper, 1959.
National Education Association, *Annotated Bibliography on the Academically Talented Student,* Washington, D.C.: The Association, 1961.
National Society for the Study of Education, *Individualizing Instruction,* Sixty-First Yearbook, Part I, Chicago: University of Chicago Press, 1962.
Neill, A. S., *Summerhill, A Radical Approach to Child Rearing,* New York: Hart, 1960.
Nixon, Robert E., *The Art of Growing,* New York: Random House, 1962.
Redl, Fritz, *Understanding Children's Behavior,* New York: Bureau of Publications, Teachers College, Columbia University, 1949.
Redl, Fritz, and W. W. Wattenberg, *Mental Hygiene in Teaching,* New York: Harcourt Brace, 1959.
Sarason, I. G. (ed.), *Contemporary Research in Personality,* New York: Van Nostrand, 1962.
Shoben, E. J., Jr., "Work, Love, and Maturity," *Personnel and Guidance Journal,* XXXIV (1956), 326–332.
Stephenson, R. R., "Occupational Choice as a Crystallized Self-Concept," *Journal of Counseling Psychology,* VIII (1961), 211–216.

Strang, Ruth, *Guideposts for Gifted Children Themselves,* New York: Bureau of Publications, Teachers College, Columbia University, 1958.
Strang, Ruth, *Helping Your Gifted Child,* New York: Dutton, 1960.
Super, D. E., "Some Unresolved Issues in Vocational Development Research," *Personnel and Guidance Journal,* XL (1961), 11–14.
Super, D. E., and P. L. Overstreet, *The Vocational Maturity of Ninth Grade Boys,* New York: Bureau of Publications, Teachers College, Columbia University, 1960.
Taba, Hilda, *With Perspective on Human Relations,* Washington, D.C.: American Council on Education, 1955.
Taylor, C. W., "Creative Individual: A New Portrait in Giftedness," *Educational Leadership,* XVIII (1960), 7–12.
Tiedeman, David V., "Decision and Vocational Development: A Paradigm and Its Implications," *Personnel and Guidance Journal,* XL (1961), 15–20.
Tiedeman, David V., and R. P. O'Hara, *Position Choices and Careers: Elements of a Theory,* Harvard Studies in Career Development, No. 8, Cambridge, Mass.: Harvard Graduate School of Education, 1958.
Torrance, E. P., "Explorations in Creative Thinking," *Education,* LXXXI (1960), 216–220.
Torrance, E. P., *Guiding Creative Talent,* Englewood Cliffs, N.J.: Prentice-Hall, 1962.
Trump, J. Lloyd, *et al., Images of the Future,* Washington, D.C.: National Association of Secondary School Principals & National Education Association, 1959.
Weaver, Anthony, *They Steal for Love,* New York: International Universities Press, 1959.
Wilhelms, Fred T., "The Curriculum and Individual Differences," in *Individualizing Instruction,* Sixty-First Yearbook of the National Society for the Study of Education, Part I, Chicago: University of Chicago Press, 1962, 62–74.
Witty, P., *et al., Creativity of Gifted and Talented Children,* New York: Teachers College, Columbia University, 1959.
Wrightstone, J. W., "Demonstration Guidance Project in New York City," *Harvard Educational Review,* XXX (1960), 237–251.
Wylie, Ruth C., *The Self Concept,* Lincoln, Neb.: The University of Nebraska Press, 1961.

GUIDANCE SERVICES: I

THE ISSUE. Guidance is not only a philosophical principle with specific tools, but also a working program which operates in many varied areas within institutions. These areas of guidance operation have been called "services." Guidance serves students in many areas as it fulfills its nature within an institution and attempts to help students succeed in a particular educational environment.

What are the so-called "services" of guidance? How does a service concept fit into an over-all guidance philosophy? The isolated services on many college campuses and in many public school systems are testimony to the virility of the "services" concept of guidance. The functions of such services need to be understood clearly as they contribute to the personal success of students and to the development of their individual purposes.

The individual services are content areas within which the basic process of guidance and the fundamental concern for values, life-objectives, and purposes may be worked out by students. The circumstance of each service may appear to be unrelated to the nature, and purposes of guidance; yet if such services are unrelated or only independently significant, they cannot be included within the conceptual operation of a guidance program. The two issues that must be faced as each guidance service is examined are (1) what is each service of guidance and how does it work? and (2) how does this service relate to guidance as a whole?

CHAPTER TEN

SERVICES AND GUIDANCE

The relationship between the words *guidance* and *personnel* has been much debated. "Personnel services" is a common phrase in current use. The long history of these two words *guidance* and *personnel* cannot be simply explained, nor the conflicts about their use easily resolved. Barry and Wolf (1957) trace the issues in detail. The two words are often used synonymously, but *personnel* has more of an industrial or business connotation, while *guidance* has been purely an educational term. *Personnel* is also a more common word on college campuses. More significantly, the personnel concept has stressed the multiple-unit nature of the program offered.

Whenever a total program or effort within a program is denoted, it seems desirable to use the term *guidance.* Whenever the separate, sometimes disparate or independent, units are emphasized the word *personnel* seems more appropriate. These definitions and preferences are general, and perhaps reflect the biases of the writer. Yet both Alice in Wonderland and scientists demand that words be defined and used in accord with stated definitions.

Arbuckle has written about personnel services on both college and high school levels (1953, 1962). He stresses the particular units that make up a guidance or pupil personnel program, but he also sees the total concept of guidance and personnel work as a unifying factor in any school. Certainly *personnel* or *guidance* may be used as the reader wishes. The essential issue is the recognition of the importance of the varying arenas within which guidance can and must operate. The discrete units must be unified into a total program reflecting the best efforts of all involved personnel.

Historical Concepts

The concerns of writers, practitioners, and even students are involved in the underlying concepts of personnel services versus guidance. The strength of individual service units, such as a veteran's counseling bureau, an admissions office, a placement director, or even a tests and measurement specialist, has led to resistance to a unified concept of programing. Moreover, the central office responsible for guidance was unable to function in an effective manner in all of the areas of specialized service. Guidance and personnel work have finally begun to achieve maturity, and the need for effectiveness in both areas has been recognized to be more important than the words chosen to symbolize them. *Guidance, personnel work,* or *pupil personnel services* refer to both (1) help to students in the total concern of making decisions, solving problems, and becoming free and responsible persons, and (2) individual services designed to offer practical assistance and aid in a variety of areas.

Guidance—A "Gestalt"

Guidance is more than the sum of its parts. It is made up of related units of service, performed by professional persons, united in a concern for student's progress in self-understanding, adjustment, and problem-solving. It is intimately involved in the student process of constructing life objectives and purposes through the experiences of education. Guidance is made up of parts, persons, and a basic philosophical purpose. Yet it is more than any of these related units, independently considered. The total picture or "gestalt" attempts to bring together these areas and to construct a whole that can also encompass all of the interrelated parts. Guidance is the process of aiding students to become free and responsible; this student growth can take place within many service areas.

ADMISSIONS

An admissions office often brings to mind the understanding interview completed on the college campus with a mature, effective Dean of Admissions. The college admissions officer has become almost a symbolic figure in America. Yet he also symbolizes a process that takes place as a child enrolls in kindergarten, transfers to elementary school, to junior high school, to senior high school and from college to graduate school. An employment office could even be termed an "admissions" office.

Admissions is a process rather than an event restricted to any level of school or life. The very word *commencement,* used to designate the final ceremony of a specific school, refers to the admissions process—one is being admitted to another stage of life and must "commence" to function in that area upon the completion of the graduation rites.

Admissions has become a status-laden area within our society. The admission to a status college, the ability to say "Yes, I'm attending ______________," has become the replacement for what was once simply college attendance. Few if any colleges refused to admit a qualified candidate prior to World War II. Since that time specific colleges have been raised in status as competition for places became greater.

College admissions are not the only area of status-seeking within a status-conscious society. Special kindergartens, private schools, team-teaching units in the fifth grade, and multiple secondary schools within a community have all been areas to which status has been attached. The motivations of the students and their parents, peer pressures, and similar concepts of psychology, sociology, and anthropology are relevant to the issue of admissions as it applies to the life of a single student.

Many statements have been offered about what admissions, particularly college admissions, should not be. However, little has been made available to guidance workers about the responsibilities of the admissions process at all levels of school operation. A positive view of what admissions can accomplish for students and for education can help to reveal the role of guidance in such a service.

Admission to What, by Whom?

The test of age is frequently the criterion test for admission to kindergarten or first grade. Yet age is seldom the sole proper test for such admission. Early admission often depends upon demonstrated intellectual potential shown in individual intelligence tests and upon social maturity tested by the school interview. Additional factors such as reading readiness and physical maturity are also used to group the new students "homogeneously." School psychologists, school social workers, adjustment counselors, and of course the principal or superintendent are usually involved in decisions of this type. These admission procedures are decisions made about students by educators. But too frequently only the unusual student is so considered. Guidance principles stress the importance of examining the issues for every student.

Admission to succeeding grade levels and promotion to ascending levels of difficulty within a school system involve similar concerns. Achievement becomes a necessary added dimension in the evaluation of grade level work. Although the child who felt himself a failure on the first day because he could not read was overly worried about his achievement, he must advance within broad patterns in order to progress to a higher level of education. Curriculum specialists, administrators, and other educational personnel enter into these decisions made about students. But the guidance person needs to become involved in considering the student's own view of his progress. Otherwise, only manipulative decisions are possible.

"I was held back" is a cry that is heard often in some schools and never in others. The philosophical premises of the school often determine such decisions. Yet student progress in the appropriate curriculum is the only defensible basis upon which they can be made. Because the student must be the center of this concern, the guidance person needs to be involved. Frequently the failure is that of the school in being unable to provide an appropriate or challenging program for the student. Education and guidance can offer little help to students if false assumptions of progress are maintained despite contrary evidence. Long-term damage is done to the student and to the process of education if such organizational fictions are permitted to replace integrity. Education as an instrument of society is obliged to provide meaningful opportunities for all students if the law of the state insists that attendance is mandatory. The gap between what educators assume a curriculum to offer to a child and what it actually offers is the basis of much "delinquency" and maladjustment at school. The guidance worker cannot avoid an intimate involvement in decisions so important to the lives of students. The guidance worker is neither a defense attorney for the student nor a prosecuting attorney for the school administration, but rather stands with the student as issues are faced and resolved. The guidance person can help the student (and parents) solve the problems that are encountered and make the decisions that are called for when practice falls short of theory within the school.

College admissions, or better, post-high-school program admission depends upon the nature of the educational program and the talents of the student. The principle of admission at this level is identical to the one which applies at the first-grade level: can the student profitably complete the program and can the institution offer what the student seeks? Although the criteria are infinitely more complex than those existing at the younger age levels, the operational concept is the same. The area of post-high-school admissions has become an area of specialization for guidance and personnel. The admissions dean of the college is matched by his counterpart in the technical institute, the business school, the conservatory, or the secretarial or hairdressing school. What principles can guide these diverse persons and also relate appropriately to all levels of education?

Principles of Admission

A professional guidance service in any area of admissions must depend upon principles and practices that cut across types, levels, and natures of educational institutions. Entrance into the institution assumes that student growth and achievement has occurred, and that the programs of the institution have merit. The "fit" of student with the institution is the key concern that must be faced by each guidance person and each educator concerned with the area of admissions.

STUDENT. Any student who enters an institution, public or private, at any level assumes that if he is permitted to enter he can grow, develop, and profit from the experience. Moreover, his achievement through attendance and effort must be honored by an institution. A private nursery school where children are herded and tended is as much malpractice as is the diploma mill which offers doctor's degrees in self-therapy. The mandatory attendance for students under 16 at a school where no appropriate program is offered is similarly a type of malpractice. The institution bears a responsibility that needs to be interpreted to the student by the admissions officer.

The student must offer to the institution the potential to profit from the available program. The nature of the institution must determine such qualifications. The institution establishes the criteria, and the student must offer to qualify on the established measures.

The student assumes and offers. The admissions officer must aid in decisions that must be made as these assumptions and offers are evaluated.

THE INSTITUTION. Any institution offers a program of study, a course of experience, that must be extended to potential students as worthwhile to those who can qualify and profit from it. The accrediting agencies of all types are designed to assess the degree of fulfillment achieved by an institution.

The institution must assume, through the assessment of all candidates, that the admitted candidate is capable of profiting from the educational program that is offered. Each institution is entitled to establish assessment procedures that will enable it to determine the legitimacy of its assumption.

Thus the student and the institution each assumes and offers. The offer of the student is the assumption of the institution; the offer of the institution is the assumption of the student. Guidance must stand with the student as his determinations are made. Professional practice dictates that the student is the client, and that regardless of the pressure or expectation of the school or student, a "fit" will be possible. Although the guidance person is employed and reimbursed by the institution, he must realize that neither the student nor the institution can be served by a forced "fit."

All other determinations about the institution or the student are secondary to the issue of mutual appropriateness of decision. The status of the school, the intellectual potential of the student, the cost of the institution, the scholarship aid available, the football talent of the student, the placement service of the college, even the law regulating attendance age are all secondary issues. The requirement to attend until a certain age has been promoted by state legislatures. The law must be obeyed, but problems occur if the other primary principles are also not fulfilled.

Admissions Methods

Interviewing, psychological testing, case-history and record assessment, recommendations of teachers, counselors, administrators and friends are appropriate methods for an institution to evaluate a candidate. All guidance tools are needed. But the institution is skilled in assessing students, while the student is relatively unskilled in assessing the institution and needs as much aid as the institution in making a decision. Guidance workers need to respect the equal right of each party to full knowledge and appropriate recommendations from meaningful sources.

The problem-solving nature of guidance and the need for freedom and responsibility are inherent in admissions work and services. The guidance person needs to help the student collect and order data. The values of the school, the person, and the program, and all related values need to be assessed. The decision to seek admission must be made by the student and his parents. The responsibility for this decision is not that of the admissions officer or guidance worker. Students and parents can often seek admission to an inappropriate nursery school, private school, or college. The recommendations of the guidance person are usable and perhaps may be helpful, but the decision must be that of the parent and student. Similarly, the admissions officer must be free and responsible in making his decisions. The professional decision is the responsibility of the professional worker.

Each party to the determination must respect the other's freedom to make a decision. Self-understanding and personal planning may not meet the test of reality. The student and the institution must be free to be judged as adequate or inadequate; admissions agreements demand equal satisfaction on the part of both parties.

The methods of guidance permit and demand that a guidance service be concerned also with the student who does not complete a contract. Referral, consultation, and reassessment are the methods of follow-up for each student. The future of the student is the concern of the guidance worker, and each student needs and deserves such total assistance from a personnel service.

ARTICULATION AND ORIENTATION

The issues of articulation and orientation, like those of admissions, extend throughout all levels of education. The transition of the child from elementary school to junior high school may be as important as the move from secondary school to college. The orientation to first grade is qualitatively perhaps more significant than any other orientation process. The possible principles that can be offered to govern articulation and orientation need to apply at all levels.

Physical Factors

"My hat, my coat, my rubbers, my room, and my seat" are worries for the young child on the first day of school. Similar concerns exist when a college freshman arrives on a new campus. The dormitory room, dining hall tickets, and class schedules are physical items that surround the beginning student at all school levels. Guidance programs or student personnel programs—the level of operation seems to determine the title of the service—must assist all students as the school and the individual are brought together.

Planning for the opening of school and for the actual physical needs of all students demands careful attention to the many details that soon become routine in the life of every student. Attention to these areas permits intellectual and academic issues to be attacked with more effectiveness. At the same time the necessity for meaningful incorporation of each student into the society of the school is a recognition of the degree of involvement demanded by the school and the person, one with another. The hours and days of school stretch into months and years. The mutual relationship of the school and the person, on a physical basis, supports the parallel involvement of each in all areas of school and learning.

Emotional Factors

The experience of beginning school at any level is an adventure. The student's thoughts and plans are filled always with mixed emotions. The anticipation of pleasures and excitements is overlaid with anxious fears of the unknown, and with uncertainties about personal adequacy. Knowledge of institutional requirements and provision for physical needs can help alleviate and control the anxieties of many students. But the concerns arising out of fears of personal inadequacy are of a different order.

The efficiency of an admissions procedure, based on an expectation that the needs and capacities of the student can be matched with the needs and capacities of the institution, offers a basis for meaningful articulation between the levels of personal growth and institutional operation. Acceptance of the unknown by the student and the institution and an examination of the mutual unknown are powerful tools that can provide for emotional security.

> Mothers and fathers are permitted to bring the children to school on the first day. We know the fears that young children have on that day. Some children prefer to come alone and we certainly do not expect that parents will have to escort the children. Either method still leaves the child with a very real fear of the unknown on the first day. The teacher faces this issue in class in varying ways. The initial adjustment to the expectations of school life are difficult and our teachers are the key persons in helping children to know what is expected and to fulfill the expectations that we have. [Elementary school principal]

The young child found weeping after school on the first day was unhappy because he had not learned to read and write. Such fears and unfounded expectations can establish barriers to learning at all levels. The first day at kindergarten has many of the same emotional dimensions as the opening day of "Freshmen Week" at the state college.

Guidance services that bring together the student and the faculty to talk about the expectations of the institution and of the individual can help to provide a secure emotional base for school operation. Outlets of a social, friendly nature can also help establish the foundation for an emotional acceptance of a new situation. Special meals and affairs in the school cafeteria, recess plans, and homeroom meetings are the counterparts of the "Freshmen Hop," "Matriculation Days," and "Faculty at Homes." The nature of the problems will change as the emotional issues are faced; solutions provide acceptance, understanding, and a warm friendly climate for learning to take place.

Intellectual Factors

The importance of learning, the actual purpose that is basic to education at all levels, is frequently neglected as guidance workers and others within a school attempt to help students become accustomed to the nonintellectual demands of a new academic environment. Such a program is similar to a sumptuous dinner party at which decorations, hors d'oeuvres, stemware, silver service, and other accoutrements are all available, but dinner is never served. Students are often not in a position to recognize that they have been cheated, but the uneasy feeling that may prevail after early school experience can be evidence of physical and emotional readiness lacking any academic involvement.

The central role of learning in school requires that faculty and students be brought together to assess the dimensions of the future that will be the mutual task of both. An entire course or curriculum cannot be explored in the few hours of orientation that may be available. The faculty and the student body, however, can begin together. The quality of learning, the actual taste of knowledge about an imperative current issue, or even an appreciation of the scope of learning that lies ahead can excite and involve the new student in the basic stuff of education.

> Eight of us sat around the professor for about an hour and a half. We all talked about the headlines of the morning paper. None of us had any idea of the complexities of the issue as he helped us to explore its meaning. We all contributed to the discussion that followed as we tried to develop possible "next steps" that could be used to help to solve the problem. We were all anxious to continue the discussion, but our time ran out. All of us were looking forward to our classes after that meeting. [College freshman]

> Boy! This fourth grade is going to be a lot tougher than last year's work in third grade. We're going to study about a boy who lives in South America, spelling lists every day, elevens and twelves in the multiplication table, French on TV, and the principal is going to be our teacher in science. Boy! [Fourth-grade pupil after first day of class]

The excitement and personal rewards that can occur are too often crushed out of an enthusiastic student when everything except learning is stressed. The articulation process and the student's total orientation depend upon the physical, emotional, and social adjustment to *learning*. The embittered student who "hates school," counts the minutes until the day is over, and dreads the end of summer vacation is untouched by the scope and sweep of learning that is inherent in all grades and all subjects. Such attitudes are a reflection of the inner feelings of an individual, but are also a reflection of experiences, past and present, that bode a boring, distasteful future. Education, intellectual exploration, studying, and learning are tasks that involve both students and educators.

Programing

The establishment of articulation and orientation programs depend upon the cooperative efforts of faculty members and guidance personnel. Frequently it will be necessary to enlist the support of persons from different schools, and even beyond school districts. The success of methods utilized in a comprehensive articulation and orientation program within a school district is described in detail by Fitzpatrick and Plattor (1958).

The tools of guidance, counseling, group work, testing, and at times even case-study procedures must be integrated in the planning of detailed programs. The administrative leadership of guidance personnel is also required, as complicated arrangements are often the necessary rule rather than the exception in this area of guidance services.

EDUCATIONAL PLANNING

Although early school experience is relatively standard for most students in public schools, the later years show many variations that are planned for the developing needs of students with varying talents and capacities. The process of decision-making that must be accomplished as students progress within an educational pattern calls for effective collection and utilization of appropriate data. Individual knowledge of interests, aptitudes, and values and complementary knowledge about opportunities are the raw materials out of which mature decisions can be made at all age levels.

Points of decision occur within the lives of all students from the preschool child to the graduate student. The principles of decision-making about educational planning and the role of guidance in this service area are intimately bound together. Educational decision-making is an important area within which guidance has long been assumed to be competent and effective.

The decision to seek early or delayed entrance, to "stay back," to transfer to another school, or to seek specialized help are typical necessary decisions that must be made as individuals enter and progress in a school system. Guidance focuses upon the individual and the content area of the decision in offering service to individual students, to parents, and to a school system.

Elementary School

An accurate assessment of the individual pupil is vital to early educational decisions. The limits to individual freedom in such decisions make it impossible for the young pupil to determine the dimensions of the experience that will help shape his development. American society demands that school experience of an appropriate type be mandatory for all students capable of profiting from such an offering. The key in such early decisions is to provide freedom where it is possible and to recognize the limits that are not subject to mediation or even discussion.

In the eyes of the society and the law that represents a society parents must act for the pupil in determining early experiences. Guidance services can help parents make more meaningful decisions by providing knowledge about the capabilities of an individual. Testing of all types may be appropriate and counseling with parents can transmit the meaning of such data. Counseling with parents is a further service to aid decisions. The guidance person or even the educational administrator cannot make the decision for the pupil or the parent, but help in assessing the dimensions of the decision can be offered.

> I never imagined the help that the school could give me as we had to decide about the future of my Sarah. She had always been a slow and deliberate child, but I certainly didn't question her ability to be-

> gin school with her playmates on the street. We talked about her social development, her dependence upon me, and her ability to carry the required school work. The school provided us with the facts and said we could do as we wished. My husband and I decided to wait a year before Sarah entered into the first grade. I really think that it will work out better for Sarah in the long run. [Connecticut parent]

Delayed entrance is not the only type of educational decision in which individual data are mandatory. Special referral for speech assistance, remedial reading, hearing examinations, or advanced placement within a special group are additional areas requiring knowledge of the varied psychological, social, and cultural dimensions of the individual. The guidance worker stands with the parent as data are presented about the child and also helps to interpret the dimensions of the environment in which the child must function.

Educational decisions depend upon an accurate knowledge of opportunity and of the demands that the opportunity lays upon a participant. Advanced placement in team-teaching units may require skills and attention spans that are beyond the talents of an otherwise very bright and highly motivated child. Parents have frequently complained in recent years about the placement of children in situations that are beyond their abilities. The need to inform the parent fully and perhaps even to take the attitudes and desires of the child into account are as important for such placement as for remedial reading and speech assistance.

Decision-making about educational planning must be a three-way process involving the parents, the school, and the child. Guidance workers offering such a service must be skilled in interpreting the forces that impinge upon all of the participants. Particular care is needed in nurturing the freedom of the young child. The child cannot, perhaps, be free to decide whether or not remedial reading help is necessary. But once such a need is discovered the child's involvement, even if only in the decision of when such help is to be obtained, is vital to its ultimate success. Progress in reading, speech, hearing, and of course in grade level depend upon the attitudes and the freedom of the child to be an independent person with rights, privileges, and responsibilities. The foundations of success and of a free and responsible life are laid in the early experiences of the child in elementary school.

The creative teaching in many kindergartens and primary grades would astound teachers and guidance workers who are associated only with secondary or junior high school programs. The attention given to the integrity and independence of the child, even on the first day of kindergarten, is a key to the ultimate success of the educational experience. Kindergarten and primary teachers have recognized this fact and are experienced in applying its implications. Freedom, integrity, independence, and responsibility must begin on the first day of school if they are to be present on the last.

Junior High School

The upper grades of the extended grammar school or the special transition years termed "junior high school" present many opportunities for guidance to enter effectively into the lives of pupils, parents, and educators. The father of an eighth-grade pupil, uncertain of the progress being accomplished by the guidance program, expressed his doubts: "My son has always known what he wants to be. I've told him and he has accepted the importance of being what I couldn't be. This whole program of asking him to look at his interests, values, and capacities has confused him. I don't think this guidance business is going to help him at all. Why don't you let it be for the students who do not know what they want? Leave alone those who know what they want." The "examined life" has its painful moments, and often casts a negative light upon those close to the "examined."

The need for individual self-knowledge and for full information about the opportunities facing the person is intensified in the middle years of schooling. Decisions are traditionally made in these years that determine future educational courses and clearly influence later occupational choice patterns. Freedom as the right to choose is exemplified in the decisions that are made about courses to be studied in secondary school.

Choices of a curriculum for secondary school are not irreversible, but they are effectively binding upon the prospective graduate. *College preparatory, business, technical, scientific, shop,* and *general* are common terms used to describe the avenues of academic travel, although the names vary with the locale and the historical influences of the community.

OPPORTUNITY KNOWLEDGE. The traditional school process wherein simple forms indicating the choice of a program were sent home for parental approval provided decision-making out of ignorance rather than knowledge. Parents with no experience in secondary education were asked to guide their children's choices about what lay ahead. Experience was not in the past of the parents and was in the future of the student. Such blindfolded choices are not exercises in individual freedom.

Parents and students are capable of and wish to make meaningful decisions. School administrators may now be more aware of the need to help parents and students but may still be encouraging "blind freedom" to families unaware of the complexity of modern education.

More and more attention has been focused upon the junior high school years as a vital period in educational planning. Specific programs involving students in study groups, guidance classes, and individual and group counseling has helped to fill the void in the educational decision-making process at this level. Detailed analysis of the curriculum patterns that may be chosen and of the implications of such choices is the responsibility of guidance programs. Career information is also important to the decisions of prospective secondary school pupils.

Knowledge of opportunity and of the implications of choices is the subject matter of guidance programs and is legitimately a part of the curriculum in appropriate years. No clearer example of the concept of guidance as being concerned with life objectives and with examining them with students could be offered.

PERSON ASSESSMENT. The freedom of decision-making about educational plans, with their concurrent implications for occupational plans, can grow out of knowledge about opportunity. But such decisions must also depend upon effective awareness of personal talent, values, interests, and capacity. The combination of self-knowledge and opportunity information is complex, and distortion of the elements out of which decisions are made must lead to distorted decisions.

Self-knowledge is a goal of guidance throughout education and in later life. The decisions about curriculum choice in junior high school provide a practical area of application. The tools of guidance can help provide knowledge and to make such knowledge available to students in usable form. Cumulative records, testing programs, guidance classes, group discussions, and individual and group counseling are means that can help students establish appropriate ends for themselves.

> We spend a whole year working on a simple "plan sheet" that goes into the student's file. Our guidance class is divided into an examination of the four curricula in the high school and into areas of self-knowledge that students (and parents) need to make their choices. Our testing program, group discussion plan, teacher-counselor program, and homeroom program are all integrated into this program of curriculum choice. The whole business ends up with student choices and plan sheets for the next three years. [Junior high school counselor]

Secondary School

Educational planning in the secondary school is two-sided. It involves repair work and sometimes major revisions of earlier decisions and also looking ahead to post-secondary school educational or career issues. Secondary school must serve both as a foundation for future education and as terminal training for those who plan to work after graduation.

The overemphasis upon college-bound students has been a blot upon guidance for many years. Community pressure and budget issues have caused such problems, but they certainly do not explain the lack of professional performances by guidance personnel. A balanced program of service to all students is the only principle that guidance as a profession can defend.

NONCOLLEGE PROGRAMS. Students not enrolled in college-preparatory programs need assistance in selecting, advancing, and completing the courses of study designed to help them learn to work and to live as citizens upon graduation. The complexity of technical-training programs available in modern industry is as significant an area of concern for students and guidance personnel as is the selection of a college.

The challenge of the noncollege student is the area of performance in which guidance will be judged as a newly created technical society wrestles with automation and with an almost unbelievable industrial growth. The apprenticeship programs of the past were relatively simple and straightforward in creating jobs and careers. Psychological-testing programs, combining aptitude measurement and industrial worker norm data, are often only partially exploited as devices to help students sort out the complexities of an industrial or business career.

Flexibility is needed in all secondary school programs for the preparation of citizens. The time-worn inflexible lines between curriculums, with the resulting status differences, must be made more plastic and serviceable to all students. Guidance workers can serve students and parents by helping to influence curriculum committees, administrators, and faculty members to create new curriculums and flexibilities within current programs.

The relationships between curriculums and work possibilities need to be fully explored within the educational experiences of the non-college-bound student. "Career Days" need to be more than exhibition days for prominent visitors. A carefully designed group program, extending over an entire year, is more meaningful and practical for the students.

Noncollege programs may also lead to college. The student who is not planning on a liberal arts program can later change his mind and seek a technical or even a liberal arts college. Guidance needs to recognize that the educational choices made in junior high school or elementary school and confirmed in secondary school may still be inappropriate for the student. The freedom of choice, within the imposed institutional limits of a society, still exists for each student in planning an educational pattern. Guidance personnel need to know the dimensions of this freedom fully.

College Prep Programs. The traditional college preparatory course has many possible variations of emphasis in science, the humanities, or even language. The choices within a preparatory program are as many-sided and complex as in the business, technical, or general program. The recommendations of James Bryant Conant, Admiral Hyman Rickover, and various curriculum review teams continue to effect changes in what was once assumed to be a static, classical curriculum.

Aptitude and capacity measures of students are helpful in allowing each individual to compare his own standing with other students across the country. "College Boards," "Pre-College Boards," and even Freshman and Sophomore preparatory tests have been developed to aid in this process. Scholarship help attached to National Merit Testing and a supplemental status "lift" given to the serious student are also outgrowths of this testing process. Guidance persons need to be fully aware of the limitations of their tools in attempting to help students plan for college. Research programs (Glanz and Penney, 1961; Glanz, Calia, and Smith, 1963) and the newly written histories of many junior colleges and western community colleges belie any rigid interpretation of aptitude or achievement test data for student planning.

College-bound students need assistance not only in the selection of an institution but also in financial, scholarship, and part-time work plans. Family planning is tied up with college attendance, and the need to involve the family in the selection processes parallels the family involvement in the entry of the pupil into the first grade. Programs of group-testing procedures, individual counseling, and case-history techniques need to be combined with conference and consultation with students, parents, school authorities, and often college or university officials.

Programing Designs

The concept of educational guidance is among the oldest and most honored in all of guidance literature. The stress placed on college preparation and selection has led to detailed development of varying plans for serving students at this level. A broader view of the process of decision throughout the school experience requires that planning be extended into the lower grade levels and be coordinated with secondary school procedures. Individual self-understanding and training for critical thinking automatically fit into educational decision-making. Test programs, counseling efforts, and group techniques become instruments for assisting pupils in specific areas of problem-solving. Each pupil becomes the subject of a case history. The program design of guidance can permit or preclude the cooperative aid from teacher-counselors, advisors, and families. The resources of the guidance program and of the entire school need to be marshaled to help each student look beyond the present to a broader view of his future.

VOCATIONAL PLANNING

Aid to students and young people in the selection of an occupation has been historically another primary role for guidance. The National Vocational Guidance Association was one of the organizations that helped to form the present American Personnel and Guidance Association. Vocational guidance is still an important process in educational guidance, but it no longer exists as an isolated substantive area of guidance service.

The conceptual design of vocational guidance was established long ago. The attempt to fit the person and the occupation together in a realistic pattern was characteristic of the writings of guidance pioneers. The development of subsequent research and theory has helped to clarify the forces that affect and mould the person as he makes a choice of career as well as to delineate the complexity of career planning as opposed to occupational choice. Vocational development has been clearly demonstrated to be a process rather than an event. Individuals are constantly making and implementing choices that lead toward a career rather than, at any single moment, choosing an occupation. Career development has also been defined as an arena for identity development. Individuals are able to express their concept of self and to clarify their own understanding of their relationship to a culture through the development of career patterns that extent over a lifetime. Barry and Wolf describe the entire process in their book, *Epitaph for Vocational Guidance.*

Definitions

Few persons select, enter, and succeed in a single job. The normal changes that accompany experience on the job, changed work conditions, industrial development, and even normal promotion and job advancement make the "job versus career" issue unreal. The fluctuations of duties within any position also contribute to the construction of the concept of a "career" rather than a "job" or even an "occupation."

Time is the major element that separates a job or an occupation from a career. The development of personal talents, interests, and aptitudes and the changing requirements and opportunities during a lifetime create a growing, changing pattern of work.

The variations in any work position and the developmental patterns of both the self and the career demonstrate the interrelatedness of individual growth and career patterning. The young child and the aged adult must constantly re-evaluate themselves and their opportunities. The dynamic interrelationships of these elements have given rise to the modern understanding of career development rather than occupational choice.

Process and Content

Career development involves a relatively constant process operating within highly variable circumstances. The successive decisions made by a child in adjusting to life and its problems establish a pattern or way of life that is later placed within the work world. The personality is formed throughout life; career functioning is an outgrowth of such personal development.

The young child faces and solves problems within his environment. Research has shown that budding scientists collect and order their environment at a very early age. Something is always being collected and ordered—stones, bugs, worms, batteries, or tools. Another child is always organizing, planning, and implementing. The content may be an "animal fair," a hike, a team, or an outing. The process is clear.

The simplified examples of the budding scientist or manager may gloss over the greater complexities inherent in all career development and planning. The person interacts with his environment and makes choices, indicates preferences, and exercises his talents and aptitudes. The opportunity for such processes is provided by the entire surrounding environment and culture. The young child plays school in anticipation of school entrance. The organizer of such a game may play the teacher, the truant officer, or the parent. The child, even at such an age, is limiting his opportunities to interact with his environment. Such activities, piled, heaped, and jumbled throughout life represent the process of the child dealing with his environment, selecting out particular patterns of operation that appeal to him and satisfy him. Life progresses and offers choices, opportunities, and materials with which an individual can interact. The individual chooses, rejects, approves, and constructs patterns of problem-solving. The content of the interaction is represented by the opportunity, whether it be a game of playing school or the offer of a position as teacher intern to the graduate student.

Teachers, counselors, and parents often mistake partial success in dealing with an opportunity as indicative of long-range choice. The young child is frequently told: "You did so well in that chance to ______________, that you must be a natural ______________." The reverse may also be assumed: "You'll never be ______________; you can't feel that way and be a ______________." The reader can supply suitable statements out of his own life. Incidents can be indicative, but they are seldom if ever definitive. The collection of many experiences, effectively interrelated and integrated, offer the raw material out of which a career development plan can be constructed. Guidance workers need to become service specialists in the patterns and issues in career development, not soothsayers. The guidance worker is standing with the individual as issues are faced, as experiences are understood, and as choices are made for present and future development.

Vocational Foundations

The foundations of vocational development and career planning are created in the individual's total experience from the first few days of life on into career success. Entrance into a structured learning program of primary and elementary school grades can help extend and broaden such an early foundation. Junior high school experiences provide an opportunity for the young person to begin to assess himself against a backdrop of the broadening vocational world; secondary school experience begins the actual testing of choices and a process of constant reassessment as variable opportunities are encountered. Higher education of all types, from short-term on-the-job training to formal professional schools, is an extension of the testing process.

Part-time and summer jobs also help to establish a background for vocational thinking. Vicarious experience can be achieved through an awareness of the work of others. The danger of vicarious experience is in the selective factors, negative and positive, that may be operating in the reporting. Television and the motion picture have helped extend the vicarious experience level of growing, reaching youngsters; however, harm is frequently done by glamour and misrepresentation. The assistance of the family, school, and guidance program can help provide a balance for such reports.

School subjects can provide direction to the child seeking clarification of talents and aptitudes, while school activities provide an environment for testing ideas of the self. The world of the school is an actual world of peers. The performance of the child within this world is life and not preparation for life. Career development is created out of such living.

The concepts of process and content can help in the examination of the many sources of vocational raw material. Parents, school officials, and particularly guidance workers need to help give such foundations meaning and to relate the actual life experiences of developing persons to the constructed or manufactured experience.

Concept Development

The issue of developing a concept of a career is replacing the question of an isolated decision. The breadth of the life before a child or an adolescent is difficult to conceive. Yet to delay the achievement of goals and to create intermediate as well as long-range goals are marks of a mature personality.

Education postpones and yet broadens the base from which career pattern choices can be made. Some graduates at all levels may be frightened by the prospect of testing a concept of self against the reality of the nonschool world. Fear of such testing can cause both delay of the reality testing and the opening of further avenues to career planning. The fearful or unsuccessful construction worker may become a successful physician. Guidance persons need to understand the processes that characterize the person making decisions, rather than judging or approving of decisions. The faith in education, seemingly blind at times, is an expression of the belief that education is one of the roads to a better life in an open society.

Career concepts develop in halting reversible fashion. The development of personality is not only analogous to career planning, but is actually a part of it. The immature person conceives of immature vocational concepts, but the mature person can relate himself to the world in a total fashion. Occupational planning and career development is very much a projective technique within which the personality can be assessed and understood. Diagnostic patterning of the person as immature or mature is not enough; psychological understanding is involved in guidance as a helping, not merely diagnostic, profession.

Earlier theory building by Ginzburg (1931) helped to lay a foundation for more recent conceptual designs of career patterning. Ginzburg highlighted the phases or ever increasing maturity level that was required to characterize the vocational concepts of the person. Tiedeman (1961) and Super (1957) have broadened and extended these earlier concepts and shown the total identity-seeking nature of career patterns. Roe (1956) has examined individual vocational choice development and related it to life styles and personal objectives and purposes. Vocational theory has grown from the concept of round and square pegs and holes. Such a simple theory was never actually characteristic of guidance as a profession, but the distance between early and modern theory and practice shows the influence of all those behavioral sciences that have supported and guided guidance.

Programing

The concepts of vocational and career development can provide a definitive element within guidance programing at all school levels. Occupational information, whether it be obtained through group field trips in elementary school or occupations courses at the secondary level, are recognizable "hooks" upon which students can hang their investigations and growth.

Elementary schools offer the opportunity for guidance workers to coordinate their efforts with those of teachers, curriculum supervisors, and others interested in enriching and broadening the scope of the curriculum experience of young children. Group plans within the curriculum can stress vocational units, field trips can provide education out of school time, and other means can be found to include material that can broaden the horizons of the students.

Junior high school programs begin to relate vocational and educational planning. Students can be helped to see more clearly the aspects of life after formal schooling. Self-assessment and curriculum choices in the middle grades can be placed on a firmer foundation as vocational ends are related to educational means.

Secondary school programs need to provide for revisions and repair work on educational and vocational planning while continuing exploration for the uncertain student. College selection and educational planning for postsecondary experience must relate the educational and career concepts. Entrance into higher education units of all types does not signal the end of all career confusion. The price of revised objectives is raised for college students who wish to retrack themselves. Guidance and counsel on these levels is as essential as on any other. The assumption that all engineering students are committed to engineering has been proved false in too many schools. Engineers and all specializations share the problems of student confusion and goal reassessment.

All of the tools of guidance are significant in vocational and career planning throughout education. The case history becomes a tool that can provide analytical insight to the student as he reviews his own history and past work experiences. Groups, testing, and individual counseling are the building blocks that guidance workers can use in the construction of a program for their institution or school system. The entire scope of career planning needs to be reflected in such programing. Occupational testing by an employment bureau in the last year of high school may seem closely related to job selection; but elementary school field trips and curriculum investigation of occupations may be more significant. A professional guidance program reflects the broad understanding that is necessary in providing a background of meaningful experience out of which student choices and patterns may be created.

Some guidance workers state that their "program arises to meet the needs of students as they occur." The fluid program that can recede into the walls as student needs disappear and then reappear as new problems arise is a figment of the imagination of a short-sighted or understaffed guidance director. The historical roots of guidance demand that career development planning, more than any area of guidance service, be an integral identifiable element in the guidance programing within the institution and system.

SUMMARY

Guidance provides many services to all educational programs. The issue of whether guidance is simply a collection of services, or whether it is also more than the individual services that are included in a guidance program has been examined. A concept of guidance as an educational pillar and as a collection of services is presented.

The major areas of guidance services are examined in this and the succeeding chapter. Admissions, articulation and orientation, educational planning, and career development are the four areas of guidance service presented.

Admissions has been offered as a process designed to match and adjust the needs and offerings of a student to the needs and offerings of an institution. Articulation and orientation are physical, emotional, and intellectual processes that support and extend the educational process. Educational and vocational planning are areas within which students seek to examine their own lives and to plan for their own objectives and purposes. The guidance worker is able to stand with the individual in these processes as variable content areas of education and career are experienced.

REFERENCES AND SUGGESTED READINGS

See end of Chapter Eleven.

GUIDANCE SERVICES: II

THE ISSUE. Guidance services form the standard basis for a total program. The services that involve the major tools of guidance are included in such a pattern. Counseling, testing, group work, and case-study procedures are usable as tools in all service areas, and yet each also forms a separate program unit.

Student activities, athletics, and discipline are sometimes established as independent services within a school or college program. These areas are also a part of the conceptual design of guidance.

The separation of such areas from guidance is a reflection of educational policy and practice, while the connections between student activities and guidance are practical and appropriate. The distance between student activities and athletics is not great, but to many the distance between guidance and athletics is. Student activities can form the relating link. Counselors often do not wish to be involved in discipline; yet if discipline is concerned with the adjustments of the person to his situation, guidance must be concerned with it.

The issue is how a guidance concept can encompass such diverse areas.

Earlier writers in guidance were inclined to define three areas of education—the curriculum, business management, and guidance—symbolized by three overlapping circles with a common center. Other theorists have attempted to construct detailed diagrams showing dozens of diverse guidance problem areas. The extreme definition of guidance, represented in each of these conceptual designs, is difficult to defend. Guidance needs to examine its essential nature and attempt to

CHAPTER ELEVEN

establish locally appropriate service units wherever education or the student can profit. Each school or college can divide the school program in its own fashion. Remedial reading can be an integral part of a counseling service or it can grow out of the English department. After-school "detention" supervision or college dismissal policies may be interpreted and enacted by guidance workers or by other educational administrators. The nature of the program and the philosophy of those responsible for its implementation are the essential characteristics which determine the organization and the success or failure of such units.

Admissions, orientation, articulation, educational planning, vocational development, and placement were described as areas of guidance in the previous chapter. The service areas arising out of the tools of guidance, the programs of student activities and athletics, discipline, studying and learning, research, and evaluation will be investigated in this chapter. These various units form the major "service" areas in most guidance programs at all school levels.

TOOL SERVICE AREAS

Guidance depends upon the procedures of counseling, testing, group work, and case studies. These processes must take place somewhere and in a special fashion: they cannot exist in limbo. How and where will counseling be made available? When will test programs be administered? Who will be brought together to form groups? Who will organize and present case studies? Who will choose suitable subjects? Practical questions such as these make obvious the need for structured and specific plans. The guidance worker who was earlier noted as having a group program that "met the needs of students as they arose" failed to recognize that programs need to be planned, budgeted, staffed, and implemented as regular elements of every school year.

Counseling Programs

Schools or colleges can offer counseling services through clinics, faculty, specialized counseling programs, or even planned problem-solving at educational and vocational decision points. Many designs are possible.

Clinic arrangements can offer specialized counseling to elementary school children in reading, speech and hearing, and general diagnostic services. Referral cases can be dealt with by teachers and supervisors who participate in case-study conferences throughout the year. Faculty guidance programs can also serve elementary school pupils by helping teachers to understand each child as a separate entity. Effective counseling in elementary school depends upon both specialized clinic arrangements and sensitive teachers. The inability of young children to symbolize and to verbalize their problems makes traditional counseling almost impossible. Clinic services, play therapy, and counseling services of all types can be coordinated with sensitive teaching to provide for elementary school programs.

Junior and senior high schools and colleges are freer to experiment with program designs in counseling. Clinic arrangements can continue and may be supplemented by teacher-counseling programs, or by educational, vocational, or personal counseling. Specialized types of counseling are normally available through specially trained guidance counselors who support and integrate their services with those of teachers. Team systems, faculty adviser programs, and guidance courses can be related to any and all of these designs.

The questions that need to be answered in discussing counseling at any level of the institution are:

1. Is counseling available through a particular design, at all levels within the school or college?
2. Are specially prepared counselors and sensitive teachers involved in the counseling program at all levels?

3. Are referral techniques known and accepted by students, teachers, and specialized counselors?
4. Are parents, teachers, pupils, and administrators knowledgeable and sensitive to the existing counseling program?
5. Are planned efforts completed on a regular basis to insure that the counseling program is meeting the needs of students, not after but before they arise?

Testing Programs

Test programs frequently span all grade levels. The ubiquitous achievement-test battery seems to have established itself throughout the American school system from the third grade upward. Every year students are measured and compared with local, state, regional, and national norm groups. The expenditure of funds in this area seems to be beyond legitimate question. Administrators seem to feel that curriculum assessment is an annual rite that cannot be foregone, even in the event of a budget shortage. "Other test elements may have to go; our achievement battery must stay."

Scholastic aptitude measures of all types are a second "sacred cow." Administrators and guidance workers face the dilemma that the community demands that this testing be available, while professional practice demands that a testing program reflect a balanced effort to assess students and to help them profit from such assessment. Community expectations can be considered, but the student must be the center of the educational process.

Students who must devote tremendous numbers of hours to test-taking can become jaded and blasé about the process. Student involvement through self-study and self-understanding can partially overcome such feelings. An integrated test program can help students recognize that their school is concerned about more than merely grade level achievement and college potential.

Testing programs need to be assessed in terms of the following standards:

1. Are test budgets reasonably apportioned among achievement, aptitude, capacity, interest, and specialized tests?
2. Are all levels of a school system or of a college or university adequately represented in all assessment areas of the testing program?
3. Are *use* budgets designed along with assessment budgets?
4. Are funds expended for testing programs comparable with funds allocated for counseling, group work, and case-study procedures? Are these allocations a reflection of the institution's philosophical beliefs?

Group Work Programing

Group work has traditionally been a part of the everyday life of the elementary school pupil and teacher alike. One group may be working on advanced reading while another group concerns itself with addition. The teacher is skilled in training elementary school pupils to work independently in supervised groups. Student independence and responsibility is highest at this level of institutional experience. After the primary grades, pupils seem to lose this skill. Perhaps it is because they are no longer given the opportunity to be responsible for themselves. Although this change in the methodology of school life is often viewed as progress, perhaps it is better seen as a blacksliding.

The same pupils who saw group work in the early grade levels as natural and expected view it with suspicion as high school students or college freshmen. These students seem to need to relearn techniques that they have mastered in elementary school. Students who start group work at any level of school experience need to build upon and extend their talents rather than relearn such skills each year.

The important questions to be considered in group work are:

1. Are groups used in fulfilling guidance functions and services at all levels of school or college programing?
2. Are groups used to offer a wide range of content areas?
3. Are group activities integrated with the counseling, testing, and case conference processes?
4. Are guidance workers who serve as group leaders in the guidance program properly prepared to serve and to train faculty members and students at all grade levels?

Case-Study Programing

The concept of case-study programing can extend to all student problems and to all levels of education. Case conferences about elementary school pupils are remarkably similar to those concerning college students. The process is identical and even problem areas overlap considerably.

Case-study programing may be a regularly scheduled every-two-week process or planned on other bases. Student problems may be drawn from varying sources that can include teachers, administrators, maintenance personnel, or even students themselves. Case conferences may also be a regular item whenever a referral to persons outside of the school is made.

School or college records provide a means for organizing case-study data whenever faculty meetings or administrative planning requires them. Research and evaluation often rely upon available student records. Follow-up studies serve both research and evaluation functions for guidance and institutional programing.

The use of case studies as a service of guidance assumes professional answers to such questions as:

1. Are adequate and appropriate records available on all students?
2. Are students of all grade levels within the institution or system included in planned case-study procedures?
3. Are varied problem areas scheduled as a matter of policy?
4. Are case conferences a regular portion of case programing?
5. Are specialists from among all types of school personnel invited to participate in case studies, case conferences, and planning sessions? Are all teachers invited as a matter of course?
6. Are guidance staff meetings devoted to case-study discussions and staff case conferences?
7. Are students involved, directly and indirectly, in case-study procedures and case conferences?

STUDENT ACTIVITIES

The issue of "extracurricular" versus "cocurricular" activities has been debated and resolved many times within many schools. Confusion about this issue also arises in professional guidance meetings. A recent critic of the "sad state of affairs in education" raised this issue when he questioned equality in the minds of students of football achievement, "social skill" (what is meant by this term is not clear), and academic achievement. Sarcastic suggestions are usually offered about adding basket-weaving and square dancing awards when such discussions take place.

The issue of whether equality exists between the academic curriculum and the social, hobby, or club activities of students is an unfair statement of the problem. *Cocurricular* cannot imply such equality. However, it must be recognized that student learnings in student activities may be as significant as those in the formal academic curriculum. Wisdom can be achieved by losing or winning a chess match as well as by studying Latin.

Guidance persons need to understand fully the learnings that can arise out of student activities. The school or college government, the intrafraternity council, the "Pep Club," and even the debating society can justify their existence only if they provide for meaningful student learning. The student government may provide for hall monitors that keep order between classes, but hall monitoring is not the *raison d'être* for student government. Similarly the activities of all student groups need to be assessed against the principles of learning and education.

Guidance philosophy and goals are practical components of any student activity program. Student activity programs that are not subjected to careful, professional scrutiny on a regular basis may become independent functions that can exist in limbo, leading to undesirable exploitation of students, the curriculum, or learning.

A positive view of student activities would stress the development of a program at all levels that can provide for:

1. Student learnings in and out of class environments.
2. Equality of opportunity for student involvement.
3. Social and physical outlets of a desirable nature.
4. Experience in financial, social, and organizational climates that can extend the horizons of all participants.
5. Opportunities to apply academic learnings in non-academic situations.
6. Opportunity for growth in personal freedom and responsibility.

Social Activities

The college hop with the raccoon coat and the flask are now a part of college history and tradition as well as of the folklore of America. The student of the modern world may frighten his elders by recalling that Hitler was someone about whom something was said in history class. But perhaps he may also surprise his elders by preferring to wrestle with the current effects of authoritarian society rather than swallow goldfish or do the latest version of the Charleston or the Twist.

The atom age brought about a type of student reassessment that has worked major changes in recreational forms. The ivory tower concept of college may explain the attitudes of earlier generations of students toward recreation and fun. However, the world is very much with today's pupil of all age levels. Modern communication systems have brought the newest space explorations into the everyday lives of students from kindergarten to graduate school. Contrary to the cries of the critics, the student of today seeks relaxation within a more mature and concerned frame of reference. He neither wants nor defends an ivory tower concept of education.

Many students may still see school or college as an escape from reality or as a haven from home, work, or the world. The goldfish swallowers may still be seeking new fish, but the over-all temper and tempo of student activity has changed.

Elementary school pupils have discovered the joy that can come from a science fair. High school science fairs now rival the efforts of the colleges and graduate schools of a few decades ago. A book fair, where books from one's own treasured stock can be exchanged or sold to others, has become at least as respectable as the defacing and destruction of elementary school textbooks. The public or private school "music man" can help each hamlet have a school band and orchestra. Elementary school pupils can join with junior high school pupils in special concerts for parents. School dances are less popular; social group discussions with faculty members and teachers have taken their place in the "extracurriculum." Visiting speakers are challenging the concepts presented in out-of-date textbooks. Parents, pupils, and teachers are learning that they are all seeking common goals and that cooperative efforts are possible. Student government groups are wrestling with social issues both inside and outside the school.

Frequently a parent, teacher or administrator is distressed and frightened by the zeal and seriousness of students in their "fun" activities. Many persons close to students seem to yearn for the old days when raccoon coats and dancing schools were popular, not civil rights petitions, embarrassingly capable young scientists, and students who ask why and why and why!

Guidance workers, like others close to students, have been surprised and shaken by the developments in student groups. The cultural forces that arise out of television, jet planes, inexpensive pocket books and strangely well preserved used cars are real and ever-growing. Guidance workers, more than any other group within the school or college, need to be able to interpret and understand the cultural and social changes that color and determine everyday school life. Student social activities within a school or college are a part of the subject matter of the guidance person, just as additions to the periodic table are appropriate concerns for the chemistry teacher.

Students at all levels are seeking meanings and relationships through their social activities in a fashion that was unknown only a few decades ago. The overwhelming change brought about by the influx of veterans into colleges after World War II has continued to grow and to affect all succeeding students. College campuses have never regained the effervescence that seemed to mark a world removed from reality. Even on the elementary school level the change is evident. Changes have extended throughout the educational system from the tremendously significant postwar years of 1946 to 1950.

Athletics

The athletic policies of many public schools and colleges seem to promote open defiance of supposedly accepted societal values, despite the lip service they pay to trusted and tested value patterns. Students who see coaches, teachers, alumni, fellow-students, and parents act as though nothing matters but victory for the school team cannot help being influenced. The damage is often deep, below a conscious level, and can be most serious because there is no opportunity for students to question, to challenge, or to understand. Acceptance of twisted values and codes is demanded, along with a silence and a support that touches the student at the core of his personality and character.

The student who sees others following the dictum "win at any price, as long as you are not caught" often questions whether he is the kind of person who can accept such a guide to behavior and to life. But perhaps no one seems seriously to question or challenge the view. The general attitude seems to be "who am I to question, if this be accepted and condoned?"

The blatant abuses of athletics within American schools are not restricted to college or high school football. Bribed athletes and thrown games have touched all areas of education. Ethics may be as confused in the Little League as in the backroom bookie's office.

The community gets what it wants. The community demands that a coach be paid, that a coach be fired, that a team win. Schools and education have often reflected the worst rather than the best elements within society. The judge in New York City who condemned the college president as most guilty in a basketball scandal recognized the obligation and responsibility of education and its most respected leaders to stand and to be judged.

Qualitatively identical but concealed by the protecting walls of a school or college, is the school's failure to provide for the physical activity of every student. Parental upheavals over a failure to provide stalls for a girls' shower room echo throughout the nation periodically. But the fact that the physical activity that makes a shower necessary is not available is seldom greeted with such outcries. The attitude of the community may support a code of privacy while frequently ignoring the total physical development of the child.

The recent attack upon physical fitness on a national level has resulted in a similar confusion. Charges of gross physical unpreparedness have been based upon narrow fitness tests that stress push-ups, chin-ups, and sit-ups. But physical fitness is more than the completion of such teachable skills. Education, not students, needs to be condemned for not giving individuals the opportunity to perform skills that are well within their potential. Although corrective action may be planned as a result of the condemnation, an ethical cry needs to be raised in the names of the students adjudged inadequate.

Athletics are a student activity. The total scheme of education cannot value the winning of a football game more highly than the intraclass chess tournament. Who is to determine that football is more important or intrinsically more valuable than debating? The proceeds from football games may help to support other athletic events, but the cost of Big League football may be more than dollars. Sportswriters seeking to invent clever copy have begun to call the Harvard-Yale football game "THE game." How many sportswriters or subway alumni are as concerned about the literally hundreds of persons engaged in the intercollegiate and intramural contests that surround and support this varsity football game? College activities of all types are legitimate and proper during a full weekend. "THE game" may be important, but the colleges have not lost their perspective in this case.

Athletics, even varsity football and basketball, are a proper province of the chief guidance officer in any school or college. The basic premises of all student activities, offered earlier in the chapter, also fit all athletic activities. There can be no comfort for the guidance person, the principal, or the school board who permits or condones the operation of athletics as an independent department, responsible only to the superintendent, principal, or college president. The ostrich-like attitude that says "What I don't know can't hurt me" marks the frightened educator as well as the confused student.

DISCIPLINE

No area of guidance has provoked more confusion and conflict than discipline. Counselors have been exhorted to avoid discipline at all costs. They have been advised equally strongly to recognize that all discipline problems are adjustment problems and that they must be involved. Highlighting this issue is the experience of one guidance person. The following (in edited form) was one end of a telephone conversation in early October:

> I didn't know what to do. I called you when it got to this point. . . . I need some help. I am new on the job in this school system and I want to get along with the principal and the teachers. . . . Shortly

> after school began the principal called me in and said that I was to be in charge of all discipline. All the teachers were to send their problems to me and I was to take care of them. I was to hand out "detention" hours, suspensions, dismissals, and separations, handle court cases, serve as judge, jury and counselor. You name it I am in charge of it.
>
> My explanation to the principal about my attitude was vehement and he knows how I feel about it. . . . I think he is just trying to dump a nasty job off on me. He admits that he hates to do it and was glad that I came into the school as a guidance director and could take it over. . . .
>
> We discussed it for a long time and he wouldn't change his mind; I'm it. . . . Finally I told him that I wouldn't do it.
>
> I told him that counseling and discipline don't mix. You know, what's his name's book says so anyway! Well, to make a long story very short and painful we are having a school board meeting next week about the whole business. The principal has insisted that I have to take over the job and that if I don't he is going to fire me. I claim that he has no right to make me be the disciplinarian. He just wants to get out of a dirty job. . . .
>
> My call is to ask you to recommend some books that I can use to quote to the school board. I think I have a good case, but I don't know where I can put my finger on the exact statement that I need.

Many observations might be made about this conversation. This person is involved in a disciplinary case of his own as he attempts to establish the dimensions of his new position. His thinking about the "dirty job" seems to be a reflection of the attitude of the principal. Perhaps the students are the real losers in this "behavior problem."

Definitions

George Marshall, General of the Army during World War II, once defined *discipline* as the adjustment to the situation within which the person found himself. An older use of the term equates it with "instruction." In academic circles, the term *discipline* serves to describe an area of study.

Discipline may also be viewed as training and experience in learning to operate more effectively. *Teaching* is a reasonable synonym for *discipline* in the sense most appropriate for education. *Punishment* is the act of inflicting penalties or exacting retribution. Discipline and punishment are as different as are a school and a jail.

It is questionable whether any judge personally punishes or "penalizes" even the most hardened criminal. The duly constituted judge, as separate from the "kangaroo court" judge, is supported by law and is acting for society. The judge may or may not be personally condemning or passing sentence, but he is primarily an appointed or elected agent of a society. Some judges may confuse their roles and assume that they are law, jury, and prosecuting attorney all in one. However, a free society must support government by law and not of men.

Discipline is therefore closely related to the problem-solving, adjustment process. Intrinsic to discipline is instruction and aid in learning. Punishment, on the other hand, is the imposition of penalties or retribution. Judgment in both areas is a responsibility of society executed by chosen agents and based upon its laws, rules, regulations, or principles of living.

Discipline and Education

All institutions in a culture are interested in declaring and defending the basic tenets of their beliefs. It is obvious that education has a special responsibility to a culture in this area. Yet how frequently educators equate discipline activities with acts of a police force, a penal system, or a criminologist. Education must be interested in the futures of students and only incidentally interested in inflicting punishment or in exacting retribution.

Guidance, as the agent concerned with the individualizing of the educational process, has no choice; it must be intimately involved in discipline. Counselors may be involved in helping students understand the issues and problems. The rules and regulations of a school or college are consonant with the laws of a society. The guidance worker, as a member of that society, is involved with such rules. That all persons affected by a decision should share in its making is a prime tenet of a democratic faith. Teachers, students, supervisors—all share with guidance the responsibility for the establishment of a code of societal behavior. Each subgroup of a larger society may establish patterns of behavior that are approved and encouraged. Penalties for willful or accidental infractions of rules are inherent in such mores. After a group establishes its life patterns and its penalties for violations, it is necessary to choose an agent to act for them. Again the group has a stake in such a choice and may wish to determine the agent for judgment.

Guidance must be concerned with a meaningful interpretation of discipline within an educational structure. The individual is at the heart of the process of education and of discipline. Guidance personnel have more of a stake in the disciplinary processes of an institution than any other group of educators. This interest needs to be practically applied by the early establishment or periodic review of the regulations that support institutional mores and customs. It is also necessary to select an enforcing agent. The principal, the dean, the president, or anyone else may be so constituted. A committee may also be charged with such a responsibility. Such a committee may involve students, but a joint committee is not always necessary or desirable. Students are prone to be harsher and less understanding than faculty members or administrators. However, students may be placed in such a cooperative relationship with group agents at other levels of operation. Appeal, referral, and preliminary judgment processes can invoke students equally well.

When the groundwork has been established, the guidance worker must again resume his concern with the individual and with the educational process that can help create free and responsible citizens. It may be undesirable for the guidance worker to be the sole agent for the society, particularly if he feels that such an assignment is personally difficult. However, such is not necessarily the case. Many guidance workers have been able to act both as an agent of the school as a societal group, and as a person concerned above all with the individual.

The "dean of boys," "dean of girls," or "dean of students"—common titles for guidance persons who may assume such dual roles—can become the most popular faculty member within a school. Students and parents alike recognize the creativity involved in such an accomplishment.

Counseling is the one-to-one or group process devoted to solving student problems. Behavior issues, rule violations, and willful flaunting of a group's code are certainly student problems, and the counselor needs to be involved. Whether or not the counselor can also be the agent or judge of the group whose laws are being violated is the crucial issue. The skilled person can separate the two roles and help students understand the entire process better by recognizing that punishment is impersonal and that discipline through counseling and guidance is the goal of the judge. Most persons neither want to nor are capable of fulfilling such dual responsibilities. Theoretically, the roles are separate and can be fulfilled by the person capable of understanding the entire process clearly. But a guidance worker needs to ensure that his counseling role is not confused in the mind of the student with his role as judge. Student confusion in this area often arises out of and reflects faculty or counselor confusion.

Regardless of whether or not the guidance person becomes involved in the judicial function, it is desirable to stress the learning process that can occur in counseling. Counseling is problem-solving;

discipline involves adjustment to a specific situation. The counselor needs to stand with the person to help him to understand his behavior and to make choices, to achieve decisions, and to learn.

Operational Guides

More specific suggestions may be desired by potential guidance workers who will face issues of discipline within a college or school situation. The philosophy of discipline, outlined below, can lead naturally to operational guides that are appropriate for most schools.

A Philosophy of Discipline. An institution needs to examine its own attitudes toward student and faculty behavior. Without direction the "six hundred" can ride off toward six hundred points of the compass. Such an examination of the goals of a discipline philosophy will demand that discipline be placed within an educational framework.

The institution may believe that students need to be punished because they are inherently "bad." If this view of students prevails, it follows that punishment will serve the expiation of the "badness." A philosophy of discipline arises out of the basic beliefs of an institutional unit.

The administration of an institution will need to develop policies that reflect its most basic beliefs in citizenship, education, and personal development. A code of behavior, specific rules and regulations, agents to act for the students and for the school, and the place given to guidance will arise out of the basic stand which is taken by an institution.

A Code of Life. "How are we to live?" is a legitimate question that each student, faculty member, or parent is entitled to ask as he enters a new situation. "Students will be ladies and gentlemen at all times" is the code offered by some schools. Detailed honor systems have been constructed to implement the institution's particular concepts of discipline. Honor systems may be used at all school levels to reflect the basic discipline beliefs of the members of the community.

The establishment, codification, and revision of behavior codes are cooperative projects. Constant revision is necessary if new students are to understand the rationale of the codes; the ideas of student, faculty, and administrative groups are needed as such concepts are developed. The very process of developing standards can help to provide a positive climate for a philosophy of discipline. Some school communities have involved maintenance personnel, food service personnel, and others in such a process. Definitions of involvement may or may not include such persons in "community government."

Each generation of students should be offered the opportunity to examine and revise the stated principles by which they live. Tradition may have its place in the codifications of behavioral patterns; however, such traditions need to be renewed and accepted by each individual. The "drumming-out ceremony" of the United States Marines and some private military acadamies may have been an appropriate custom at one time, but few if any such traditions are presently honored.

AN AGENT OF THE GROUP. It is desirable for the group to have an opportunity to elect or appoint its administrators, and to judge their responsibility. Some groups elect a student honor board, others construct jointly elected and appointed student-faculty committees, still others may wish to discuss, dispute, or approve of the authority of an appointed official.

Administrative agents such as school boards or the United States Congress may pass rules to govern the participation of subsidiary groups in the recognition of their authority. The crew of a United States battleship cannot elect the cook to be the captain of the ship, nor can a school principal appoint the bus driver or the head custodian to be the judge of student conduct. Such extreme examples help to illustrate the problem. The issue must be decided by the group within the over-all limits of the local situation.

School procedure has often permitted student groups to assume original jurisdiction over certain types of infractions. Additional groups of faculty members and students may provide a second disciplinary agency. Most often a final authority will rest with the chief administrative officer of the group. Guidance persons may serve on such committees at any level or may assume such responsibility in isolation. To counsel the student who is subject to the judgment of the counselor or the group is difficult but not impossible. The recognition of the principle underlying disciplinary action can permit various satisfactory solutions to be developed.

More frequently the guidance person serves as an *ex officio* member of the group. Practical experience often leads the committee or the single person who acts as an agent for the group to turn to the guidance service for advice regarding proposed action. Counseling will often be needed to help the student understand the total situation and to provide the facts for appropriate action. Counseling will also be a necessary follow-up to all discipline actions.

THE ROLE OF GUIDANCE The role of guidance in discipline is to help the student understand that the discipline of reality is not personal judgment or retribution. Guidance may help all students through group sessions, and it may help groups through orientation and articulation plans. Guidance must stand with all students as policies of discipline are developed, interpreted, and implemented.

The Student

The student must be the central concern in all discipline. No group within a free democratic society can sacrifice the welfare and well-being of a single individual to the group with impunity. Group codes and ethical decisions that prevent the individual from learning from his experience are to be condemned as contrary to the ideals of education, freedom, responsibility, and democracy. Some may say that such an array of concepts should not be marshaled in the discussion of every single act of discipline. But if such concepts are not routinely a part of every decision, the erosion and destruction of the rationale of all such concepts will result.

The goals of discipline are learning, instruction, and a better tomorrow. Retribution may right past ills, but it begets revenge or other sicknesses that can destroy the meaning of discipline. The individual student is again the center of the total education process. Guidance must be concerned with individual students and with all policies that affect individual students or groups of students.

STUDYING AND LEARNING

The need to assist students in solving problems of studying and learning is a practical issue in most schools. Advice concerning study habits, note-taking, reading skills, outlining, précis-writing, and related tasks is frequently offered jointly through the sponsorship of a guidance department and the English faculty. Counseling in such language skills is complicated by a need to understand the diverse motivational problems that can and usually do accompany study-habit problems. Joint efforts in this area are generally more effective than unilateral action by either sponsoring group.

Study habits have been analyzed in psychological experiments; recommended procedures are available for students to examine, to follow, and to profit from. However, many students will voice a plea that they are unable to concentrate, that they spend more than adequate time on their studies and obtain only poor results. Specific prescriptions that may work for many students are not always appropriate for Johnny, who is unable to concentrate.

Johnny may have an orderly desk in his room. His light may be of the proper candlepower and shine over his left shoulder. He may have an adequate supply of paper and sharpened pencils. He is free of distractions. There are no pictures on the desk, no radios or televisions in the room, and the desk faces a wall instead of a window. Still Johnny may spend four hours in his room every night and learn very little.

Johnny may be rebelling against the authority of the parents who have provided such "perfect" study conditions. He may be acting out his aggressions against his parents through a defiance of their expressed wishes. Johnny may not even be aware of this deeply rooted hostility. He may have been forced to deny its existence and to use school and study as a scapegoat for his anger. Study-habits recommendations that treat only symptoms and do not attempt to understand the learner as an active participant in the process can be fruitless.

Study-habits programs should include most or all of the following:

1. Referral processes for teachers, students, and counselors.
2. Diagnostic study provisions for problem analysis through psychological tests, interviews and surveys, and student self-study and analysis.
3. Cooperative programs designed by the English and guidance departments.
4. Provisions for remedial reading training, speech and hearing therapy, and all appropriate remedial actions.
5. Case-study and case-conference opportunities.

RESEARCH AND EVALUATION

Professional guidance work demands that guidance personnel be capable of and engage in projects of research and evaluation within the school that supports them. Landy (1962), in suggesting standards of research competence for counselors, defines research and all types of evaluation as processes concerned with the orderly and appropriate attempt to question that which is not known.

Tool Research and Evaluation

Guidance persons are called upon to use various tools and procedures. American education has not yet, and hopefully will never, become standardized to such a degree that tools or approaches can be utilized in a precise or exacting fashion. If instruments cannot be used precisely, relative merits must be attached to local use and practice. Group work, counseling, testing, and casework can be employed differently by persons of varying skills and training. The local student and faculty population can help determine the relative effectiveness of varied uses of such tools. Research projects into the active evaluation of all tool concepts can provide the means for improving the broadening guidance activities as a professional service.

Student Follow-up

The outcomes of education can be measured directly as the lives of students are examined after the completion of their formal education. Follow-up studies may reveal the student's occupational choice patterns, his evaluations of curricular offerings in light of post-school experience, and his relative assessments of the services offered to him while he was in school. Data of this type need to be gathered routinely for use by students, faculty, and administration.

Program Experimentation

Guidance programing, like guidance tools, has not yet reached the stage at which definitive answers are available about best program plans. The organization and administration of guidance services and total program approaches need experimental validation. Assessment of student involvement and student growth and development can provide substance for such an evaluation of program plans.

Psychological Test Profiling

A significant service can be rendered to students and to all other groups within a school by the development of local norm charts for all test instruments used within an educational system or a higher education unit. Local and individual class norms are also of value to test users. Many of the statistical and scoring bureaus of test publishers now offer such services along with normal scoring. Guidance workers can help teachers, pupils, parents, and administrators use such information.

> Our elementary schools provide two or three meetings per year for parents. The teachers meet with all parents who attend, discuss the program of instruction, student problems, and planned activities, and consult with individual parents. Specific problems are handled through appointments that are established for after class hours later in the year.
>
> The achievement battery that we use in our system has been very helpful in aiding parents to understand the growth and development of their children. We keep cumulative test profiles that show grade achievement each year. We also provide the parents with norms for the classroom, for the other grades within the school system, for the community as a whole, and on a national basis [Massachusetts Parent].

Teachers who are able to help parents fathom the local norms of a class, school, community, and region are those who have been helped to understand the data and their applications.

SUMMARY

Additional services guidance provides for education have been outlined. The tools of guidance provide means for building a program of services to all students. Counseling services need to be available at all school levels to help in all types of problems. Testing programs can be integrated into the total educational design of the school while also serving student needs for self-study and self-understanding. Group programs and case-study procedures have also been examined as they serve students of all ages and grade levels.

Student activities form a major element in all academic surroundings. The changes in types of activities from one age level to another are dependent upon a common set of principles that can guide the establishment and development of nonclass learnings. Athletics of a varsity type and of an intramural type are student activities and have been described as expected portions of a guidance program.

Discipline has been examined in detail. Student behavior is a primary concern of a guidance program. Discipline provides a conceptual design for the operation of guidance in a policy-making area and in student learning. Punishment, codes of behavior, and group agents or judges have been analyzed in the light of their guiding principles. Study habits and learning have been analyzed as cooperative efforts of the English and guidance departments. The varied types of research and evaluation that are an expected part of all guidance programs have been briefly examined at the close of the chapter.

REFERENCES AND SUGGESTED READINGS

Alltucker, M. M., "A Counseling Plan for Bridging the Gap Between the Junior and Senior High Schools," *School Review*, XXXII (1924), 60–66.

Arbuckle, Dugald S., *Counseling and Guidance in the Classroom*, Boston: Allyn & Bacon, 1957.

Arbuckle, Dugald S., "Integrating Occupational Materials into the Curricular Process," *Personnel and Guidance Journal*, XXXIX (1960), 120–123.

Arbuckle, Dugald S., *Pupil Personnel Services in American Schools*, Boston: Allyn & Bacon, 1962.

Arbuckle, Dugald S., *Pupil Personnel Services in Higher Education*, New York: McGraw-Hill, 1953.

Baer, M. F., and E. C. Roeber, *Occupational Information: Its Nature and Use*, Chicago: Science Research Associates, 1958.

Bailard, Virginia, and Harry C. McKown, *So You Were Elected?* (2nd ed.), New York: McGraw-Hill, 1960.

Baker, Harry J., *Introduction to Exceptional Children* (3rd ed.), New York: Macmillan, 1959.

Barry, Ruth, and B. Wolf, *An Epitaph for Vocational Guidance*, New York: Bureau of Publications, Teachers College, Columbia University, 1962.

Barry, Ruth, and B. Wolf, *Modern Issues in Guidance-Personnel Work*, New York: Bureau of Publications, Teachers College, Columbia University, 1957.

Bonser, F. E., "The Curriculum as a Means of Revealing Vocational Aptitudes," *Education*, XXXVII (1916), 145–159.

Borow, Henry, "An Appraisal of Courses in Vocational Planning," in H. T. Morse and P. L. Dressel (eds.), *General Education for Personal Maturity*, East Lansing, Mich.: Michigan State University Press, 1959.

Borow, Henry, "Curricular Approaches to Personal Development: Some Problems of Research," *Journal of Counseling Psychology*, V (1958), 63–69.

Borow, Henry, and R. V. Lindsey, *Vocational Planning for College Students*, Englewood Cliffs, N.J.: Prentice-Hall, 1959.

Clauson, H. A., "Mattoon Illinois High School Tries Team Teaching and Science Orientation," *The Bulletin of the National Association of Secondary School Principals*, XLV (1961), 93–99.

Cottingham, H. F., and W. E. Hopke, *Guidance in the Junior High School*, Bloomington, Ill.: McKnight & McKnight, 1961.

Crites, John O., "A Model for the Measurement of Vocational Maturity," *Journal of Counseling Psychology*, VIII (1961), 255–259.

Crow, L. D., and A. Crow (eds.), *Readings in Guidance,* New York: David McKay, 1962.

Farwell, G. F., and H. J. Peters, *Guidance Readings for Counselors,* Chicago: Rand McNally, 1960.

Fitzpatrick, R. E., and E. E. Plattor, "The Role of a Comprehensive Program of Orientation in a New School District," *Bulletin of the National Association of Secondary School Principals,* XLII (1958), 154–161.

Furry, R. D., "Springfield, Illinois Teachers and Students Study Guidance Services," *The Bulletin of the National Association of Secondary School Principals,* XLIV (1960), 45–48.

Ginzberg, Eli, *et al., Occupational Choice: An Approach to a General Theory,* New York: Columbia University Press, 1931.

Glanz, Edward C., and J. F. Penney, "A Cooperative Research Project for Curriculum Validation," *Journal of Higher Education,* XXVI (1961), 39–44.

Glanz, Edward C., *et al.,* "The Measurement of Aptitude and Achievement Growth in the First Two Years of College," College Research Report No. 2, Boston University, 1963, unpublished.

Hoppock, Robert, *Occupational Information,* New York: McGraw-Hill, 1957.

Johnson, W. F., *et al., Pupil Personnel and Guidance Services,* New York: McGraw-Hill, 1961.

Klopf, Gordon, *College Student Government,* New York: Harper, 1960.

Kobliner, Harold, "The Effects of a Pre-Entrance Orientation Course on the Adjustment of Sixth Grade Pupils to Junior High School" (doctoral dissertation), New York: New York University, 1959. (Abstract in *Dissertation Abstracts* XX, No. 2, 588–589.)

Kobliner, Harold, "Literature Dealing with Vocational Guidance in the Elementary School," *Personnel and Guidance Journal,* XXXIII (1955), 274–276.

Landy, Edward, "Research Preparation for Counselors," *Proposed Standards for Counselor Preparation,* Washington, D.C.: American Personnel and Guidance Association, 1962, pp. 52–57.

Mackay, Charles B., "Senior High Orientation for Parents," *School Executive,* LXXVII (1958), 36–37.

National Society for the Study of Education, *Personnel Services in Education,* Fifty-Eighth Yearbook, Part II, Chicago: University of Chicago Press, 1959.

Roe, Anne, *The Psychology of Occupations,* New York: Wiley, 1956.

Super, Donald E., *The Psychology of Careers,* New York: Harper, 1957.

Super, Donald E., *Vocational Development: A Framework for Research,* New York: Bureau of Publications, Teachers College, Columbia University, 1957.

Tiedeman, David V., "A Paradigm of Decision in Career Development and Its Implications," *Personnel and Guidance Journal,* XL (1961).

Williams, H. F., Jr., "The Town Tells Teens About Jobs," *Personnel and Guidance Journal,* XXXII (1954), 266–269.

Williamson, E. G., "The Fusion of Discipline in the Educative Process," *Personnel and Guidance Journal,* XXXIV (1955), 74–79.

Williamson, E. G., *Student Personnel Services in Colleges and Universities,* New York: McGraw-Hill, 1961.

GUIDANCE PROGRAMS AND PATTERNS

THE ISSUE. Guidance has been involved in a dynamic developmental program for over half a century. Although it is still growing, guidance is now an accepted part of education. Communities that support educational programs through taxation, parents who look to schools to help their children, and administrators who organize and direct programs of education are all seeking answers to the question of how guidance can be included in the educational program.

The recent decades of guidance program growth have stressed the importance and desirability of guidance for students and the school. The initial acceptance of guidance has been secured. The professional responsibility of guidance is now to offer patterns and programs that can fit various school systems. Guidance cannot continue to stress its own importance, but must offer professional designs that can fulfill the functions that education, parents, and the community have accepted.

Although guidance is a unitary concept, it must be specially patterned to meet the particular needs of each level of school or college and of the specific educational units that have been developed in communities of all sizes and types. What are the patterns, the constructs, the designs that will help particular school units? How can these models be implemented?

❦ ❦

The designs of guidance that may be offered for professional use cannot be transplanted full-blown into any educational unit. Problems of initiation and implementation are practical issues that must be faced if guidance is to fulfill its potential, and must therefore be ex-

CHAPTER TWELVE

amined prior to any study of the major patterns of guidance. The administrative needs that arise following the adoption and "fitting" of a guidance concept into a school can color the operation of any type of program. The constant evaluation and adaptation of principles of guidance is necessary to keep a guidance program functioning in a dynamic fashion. Moreover, it is necessary to view the personnel who will staff the program and relate it to the other members of the educational community and the student body.

Each of these major issues will be examined in turn. An examination of program development will precede the presentation of guidance designs. An outline of important models and a study of the problems of administering a guidance program will follow. Evaluation and staffing issues are the two final topics of the chapter.

PROGRAM DEVELOPMENT

Many schools can pinpoint in their records the time when guidance was formally introduced into the educational program. Preliminary efforts often centered on a teacher who was freed from part of a classroom assignment to counsel students about their vocational or educational plans. Frequently it is also possible to determine when standardized testing began to be woven into the fabric of the curriculum. In some schools, however, the beginnings of a formal guidance program cannot be recalled. Guidance has taken on an independent existence of its own in such schools.

Guidance can thus be seen to have beginnings, attributes of design, and ultimately an independent existence that requires personnel staffing and regular reassessment. This is the life cycle of guidance within a school system. Repeating patterns may occur as newer designs or developments replace the old.

Initiation

Guidance needs to start somewhere. Student demand, parental desire, enlightened administration, teacher concern, or even professional certification procedures for the entire school or college unit are among the forces that may initiate a guidance or personnel program. The development of such a program depends upon the firm foundation that the school has previously established. Self-study, professional awareness, and student needs are three aspects of a local situation that can determine the nature of the program to be developed.

SELF-STUDY. An institutional self-study may take the form of detailed analysis by outside specialists who help local administrators examine the school's assets and liabilities. More frequently a self-study is a local attempt to understand current needs and programs while outlining future developments. Regional and national accrediting bodies have recognized the importance of the self-study concept and have included it in most types of institutional accreditation. The idea of total accreditation depending upon an outside specialist coming into assess and to rate a system was considered inimical to the traditions of American education. The judgments of outsiders are not assumed to be unneeded, but such outside evaluation must depend upon prior self-study.

Objectives, procedures, policies, and planned outcomes are traditional items that need to be included in any self-study. Guidance becomes involved as educators recognize the importance of individualizing the total process of education. Cooperative effort by school personnel can permit guidance to become an element within the total educational offering of a school system. It is desirable to examine the cost of guidance, to establish its objectives, and to plan for program designs that will "fit" a local situation.

PROFESSIONAL AWARENESS. Educational institutions must also be thoroughly aware of what guidance can do. The nature of guidance as a professional discipline and as a significant portion of education must be known if guidance is to be measured against local needs. The administrative officials of a school or college are normally responsible for being aware of such issues. Local committees may help gather up-to-date information, but the prior preparation and education of the leaders of the school unit will be the determining factor in the understanding of guidance.

Many teachers and most administrators have had professional courses in guidance, and some may be qualified to serve as specialists in various areas of guidance operation. Such persons may become resource members of a study group or committee. Current literature and research can supply data for more adequate study.

The objectives, policies, procedures, and program designs of guidance need to be examined and related to local needs. The self-study and the investigation of guidance as a profession are therefore corollary issues. Joint evaluation of study results can bring together the data from these two areas.

STUDENT NEEDS. A third element in the establishment of a guidance program is the quality and nature of student needs within the community. A study of the needs of students of various ages and backgrounds can help to establish a background against which local needs can be assessed. Individual student needs are not bounded by city or state lines. However, the needs of a highly intelligent but indigent Negro student from the slums of New York City are different from those of a skilled wood craftsman graduating from a technical high school and entering his father's furniture manufacturing business in a small town in Michigan.

Each community is peculiar unto itself. The fishing traditions of Rockland, Maine, are clearly separate from the farming patterns of central Iowa. Children growing up in these communities will have different cultural patterns of life that must be understood. These patterns are more complex than a study of local industry will indicate. The sociological, cultural, economic, and philosophical roots of any community will give character and meaning to the lives of every youngster who grows and develops within its environs.

An institutional self-study, professional awareness of guidance as a construct in education, and a detailed knowledge of student needs within a community can provide the basis upon which local planning for guidance can be established. The complexity of this process is often misunderstood. Guidance is bought as if it were a bit of yard goods that can be easily made to fit any community, school, or child. But the variations in community and educational patterns prevent such a simplified concept of guidance from being effective.

Program Planning

Available patterns of guidance can be compared to the assessed needs of the institution and the students. The decision to institute a guidance effort within a school leads to the need for a form or pattern. Guidance is a tailor-made item and cannot be ordered from a catalogue.

The basic decision to examine the varied patterns of guidance involves the observance of particular local educational traditions and developments. A community that has decided to build an elementary school especially for team teaching will have different views about their physical needs than the community that is renovating an ancient high school for use as a junior high school. Education is unitary within a community, and it must reflect not only the ideas of administrators, teachers, and parents, but also the character and structure of the culture surrounding and supporting the school system.

Guidance operates differently at various school levels. Vocational counseling is not needed in a kindergarten, but college planning may hinge upon the quality of the remedial reading program available in the third and fourth grades. Any investigation into the possibilities for a guidance program must involve the entire scope of educational effort in a community. Early guidance programs centered their effort in the secondary school level. Inadequacies at lower grade levels often hampered the effective functioning of a guidance program in the senior high school. Actually, guidance may be initiated at any level within a school. The issue that needs to be faced is that all levels of guidance must be interrelated and integrated. A student graduate may in retrospect prefer the seventh grade to the fourth grade, but he would seldom argue that he should not have had to attend the fourth grade. Students recognize the unity of their own educational experiences. Educators need similar perspective as they organize and plan for guidance.

Implementation

Although cooperative study and program development need to mark the adoption of any educational idea into a specific school, it is not usually possible to initiate a new idea full-blown. Gradual beginnings are more normal. Hopes and plans can provide the stimulus for a beginning; only in the minds of those who dream may there be a clear picture of what the future can hold.

The need for self-study, professional awareness, and an understanding of student needs as well as for the selection of a program design exists in a school attempting to establish a guidance program or to build upon previous beginnings. Guidance has developed sporadically out of necessity. That necessity no longer exists, and preplanning is desirable whenever a new program is contemplated or when existing efforts are to be assessed and expanded.

The reassessment and expansion of a guidance program is sometimes easier than a new beginning, but sometimes it is more difficult. The presence of guidance personnel can help the total system to be more aware of school needs, to learn more about available guidance concepts, and to be alert to student needs. But the inadequacy of earlier guidance may prejudice the future of a guidance program.

PATTERNS OF GUIDANCE

Confusion has been great as guidance, counseling, and personnel work have been discussed and recommendations developed to focus the efforts of guidance workers within education. Wrenn (1962) prefers to view guidance as a philosophy or a point of view that characterizes the individualization of education for the student. This view is consistent with everything that has been offered in the previous eleven chapters of this book. Wrenn however, representing the Commission of Guidance in American Schools (sponsored by the American Personnel and Guidance Association), recommends that the term *guidance services* be abandoned. He believes that the counselor becomes confused when he is viewed as a "guidance worker." To be sure, it is important that counseling and guidance be separated and understood as different functions. Whether a particular set of activities are called "personnel services" or "guidance services" does not set the problem aside. The major issue is the confusion between counseling and guidance. Counseling, although a major concept of guidance, is still a tool approach within a total guidance or personnel program. Whether the term *guidance* or *personnel* is used does not seem to be vital, but counseling and guidance or counseling and personnel work must be separated.

Guidance, unlike Gaul, has been divided many times into many pieces. In 1951 the United States Office of Education provided a breakdown of pupil personnel or guidance services (both terms were used) into nine distinct areas. In 1959 Frank Sievers, speaking for the United States Office of Education, reduced these nine areas to six, and

1960 saw a policy statement issued by the Council of Chief State School officers that further reduced guidance services to five major units. Lowe (1962) again raises the number to ten! Outside observers may wish to liken the situation within guidance to Alice's "Wonderland." Each person says that guidance or personnel services will be what he says it to be.

It seems impossible that a specific number of areas can ever be defined as "the" guidance services. Each local educational unit will need to determine such issues as whether school attendance is a guidance service or perhaps a part of the assistant principal's job. Guidance personnel should recognize that many patterns of services may or may not be included within a program. That there *is* a program is more significant.

School administrators and local school boards seldom wish to be involved in jurisdictional disputes between guidance and other school workers. These problems can be mediated and solved when objectives rather than personal status are kept foremost. School administrators and community representatives are interested in the general plan of guidance that may be appropriate for their school or college. The basic patterns or models of guidance that have developed during the history of guidance that Wrenn calls "jerry built" need to be examined. What are the choices that are available?

Four major historical patterns of guidance or personnel work seem to be available from which schools and colleges can choose. The names chosen are arbitrary, and other titles may be appropriate. Nevertheless, the concepts seem to be consistently observable within present and past educational practice. All approaches depend upon the four major tools of guidance and can operate within varying dimensions or service areas.

The four conceptual designs to be presented are (1) generalism, (2) specialism, (3) curricular models, and (4) human relations and mental health. They are not diagramed and spelled out in an organizational chart. Various individual interpretations of these designs are possible. To assume that one particular organizational pattern must follow the adoption of a design is to negate the basic purpose of identifying such models.

Generalism

Early programs of guidance stressed the significance of a point of view and the need to understand students as individual persons. The revolt and reform nature of guidance stemmed from these beliefs.

The movement was established upon the premise that all persons in education were necessarily involved in the understanding and guidance of students.

The foundations of the generalist approach to guidance have been the assumptions that (1) the total learning climate within an institution affects the quality and quantity of student learning, and (2) that every person can contribute to the development of the individual student. These foundations have been accepted by all education. Few persons can realize the significance these concepts had when they were first offered to the more sterile and rigid educational process that then prevailed.

CHARACTERISTICS. Several characteristics of generalist programs may be identified. The teacher-counselor was an important pillar in early programs. The *importance of the teacher* remains as a significant element in all such programs, even though his specific counseling contributions are currently viewed in a different light.

Decentralization is a further hallmark of generalist programs. Large central administrative units have usually been avoided; their functions being fulfilled by a guidance coordinator. This person might be a full-time guidance worker or a teacher working in guidance only part-time. Committees, often with rotating leadership, have also been charged with the development of policy and practice for each school or college as well as for the total system.

All specially trained persons are usually brought together in an *integrated program* of activity. A test specialist is assumed to be responsible to a guidance committee or to an appointed "head of program." Counselors are appointed and often serve on a full-time basis, although guidance is still assumed to be the overriding concept within the school or college. Many current difficulties derive from such issues.

The *philosophical approach to learning* was and is still the single most distinguishing characteristic of the approach of the generalist. The breadth of current guidance and personnel work is due to the emphasis developed by this approach to education. School attendance, health services, research and evaluation, and even remedial education were easily encompassed within a generalist's view of the nature of guidance. Individual services were all seen to be important, but were still a part of the total approach known as guidance.

STRENGTHS AND WEAKNESSES. The strengths and weaknesses of the generalist view of guidance are related. The very comprehensiveness of the concept weakens its internal structure. The development of highly specialized guidance tools such as testing, counseling, group work, and case-study procedures made it difficult for a single small committee or a partially trained person to comprehend or implement them. The principles of guidance that were developed have remained. Newer methods of providing leadership and administrative coordination for a total program have managed to change many of the original generalist concepts.

Another weakness of the generalist approach to guidance was the tendency of some guidance personnel to assume that one person could be all things to all people. Adequate training in all major tool and service areas of guidance were beyond the experience and often the opportunities of early guidance administrators and school personnel. Counselors who were adequately prepared were forced by circumstance or attempted of their own will to be and do everything. The needs of the small school often helped to induce conflicts that finally forced the recognition of the specialist as an important element within a guidance program.

The greatest strength and contribution of the generalist approach has been its stress upon basic principles and a broad philosophical view of all of guidance. The conceptual designs of many early generalist writers have withstood the onslaught of time and specialism.

CURRENT STATUS. The generalist view of guidance continues to provide the most widely accepted and stable concept of guidance. Current recommendations for counselor preparation and for the education of guidance workers (Wrenn, 1962) point to the need for more than purely technical and practical skills. Psychology and the social and behavioral sciences are recommended as appropriate for one-third to one-half of the preparation of a counselor. A guidance worker, who needs to be more than a counselor, will certainly need as much if not more general educational preparation.

The generalist view provides a basis for administrative leadership in many guidance programs. The specialist has been incorporated into the program and functions effectively in narrowly defined areas. However, individual service units, whether they are called "pupil personnel services" or "guidance services," need to be seen as parts of a total concept. School superintendents and college presidents may wish to try to supervise and understand the work of seven to fifteen different specialists. Better practice promises that pupil personnel or guidance be programed and organized as a total concept.

The generalist view of guidance has retained its vitality and has changed with the demands of newer practices. The specialist has been incorporated and utilized to strengthen the total program. The contribution of the teacher-counselor is backed up by specially prepared school counselors. The teacher's role in group work, in casework, and in testing has been similarly respected, but it has been also augmented by adequately educated guidance workers. Service units have expanded or contracted as needs have developed within schools, colleges, and the profession. The concept of guidance as a unitary process has been maintained through the foresight of those who believed guidance to be more than any single guidance service.

Specialism

The development of guidance as a force within American education was characterized by the influence of the generalist concepts previously described. At the same time pressure for specialized service was beginning to appear. Even Frank Parsons' early work can be viewed as a specialized service.

The testing field, research and practice in clinical psychology, studies of remedial reading, and ultimately the services offered by medical persons, nurses, social workers, and school psychologists—all influenced the specialist view of guidance developed in the schools. The employment of a single person with specialized skills was often a factor in the directional development of a guidance program within the school system. The need to identify a student problem and to provide aid and assistance to the student served as a stimulus to all who developed as specialists.

CHARACTERISTICS. Specialism has long stressed the *individual unit service,* such as counseling offices or bureaus, remedial reading programs, test and evaluation services, professional school social work, and school psychology. Each of these individual services has been concerned with the over-all development of the educational system as well as with the individual child. However, the relationships with other specialized units have often been tenuous. All guidance and personnel work was seen through a single focus, the viewing end of the telescope being held by the specialist.

The *centrifugal tendencies* of the specialized units often created the need for a strong central administrator. Rivalries, budget competition, and rigid lines of authority and responsibility were almost constant results. Cooperation among diverse units was sometimes achieved, but the nature of the approach often prevented integrated action and programing.

A *devotion to knowledge* and advanced practice has always

characterized specialized service units within a school system. The high quality of service was a natural outgrowth of such respect for professional functioning. At the same time the very press for quality led to a shouldering aside of some of the less distinct guidance functions within education. The strength of narrowness has led to a traditional *disinterest in the broader problems* of guidance and education. Such problems as discipline, student activities, orientation and articulation, parental needs, and human relations training for student leaders were and still are ignored by the specialized service unit. Teachers, administrators, parents, and students are left to sort out the "in-between" areas that are not the concern of specialists.

STRENGTHS AND WEAKNESSES. The strengths and weaknesses of the specialist approach to guidance and to personnel services have grown out of the essential nature of the philosophical design. The teacher was viewed as unprepared to help students in many areas, and was encouraged to stick to his teaching and leave the specialized services to the specialists. The resulting split between guidance and the teachers, the curriculum, and the administration was deep and has not yet been healed in some institutions and communities.

The quality of the service offered to individual students is a strength that has sustained all specialized bureau concepts. Whenever the community was able to afford all of the services and the services were coordinated a guidance program of high quality could result. But the cost and availability of specialists has been a problem of this approach.

CURRENT STATUS. Most programs of specialized services have been coordinated through the selection of a centralized administrator. The centrifugal tendencies have thus been limited. Occasionally a single bureau or service will slip away or come in unnoticed, and the fur flies while administrators argue about budget and personnel control. A school psychology or school social work program may seek a place outside of other personnel services; a tests and evaluation office may become an independent force within the school or college. The task of coordination is constant.

The specialized services concept within guidance has helped to promote a respect for quality in professional practice. Combination developments have often occurred in schools or colleges, joining a philosophy of generalism with the functioning of specialists. The totally independent units of specialism are seldom seen in current guidance practice. The synthesis of these two views is frequently possible.

Newer program designs with a coordinated pattern of specialist and generalist views are among the most hopeful signs for guidance in the future. As newer designs are developed and as students are better served, guidance can begin to gain new respect in the eyes of the community, parents, and school administrators.

Curricular Guidance Programs

Guidance has been placed in the curriculum at all levels. The desire to have guidance as a part of the organized curriculum has often exceeded the effective methods available to accomplish the task. Early experimentation with group guidance, vocations courses, life adjustment programs, and social and personal orientation units marked early efforts to bring guidance and counseling into a curricular structure.

A lack of meaningful subject matter was a major stumbling block for early courses in guidance. Students seldom accepted a hodgepodge of dating, personal grooming, and courtesy procedures as a useful course to be taken for credit and for a grade. This problem often hampered otherwise adequate programs. Psychology, sociology, and anthropology have evolved newer interpretations of individual growth and development that have given guidance courses a more substantial subject-matter base to meet the tests of student interest, curriculum structure, and evaluative measures.

The usual guidance course now contains units in most of the following areas:

(1) Self-concept study
(2) Individual differences
(3) Motivation and learning
(4) Societal and cultural determinants of personality
(5) Interests, aptitudes, and intelligence
(6) Vocational and educational planning
(7) Self-analysis
(8) Values

CHARACTERISTICS. Most curricular approaches to guidance are marked by *regularly scheduled classes* taken for credit and usually for a grade. Many orientation courses are offered for short periods of time, with no credit or grade, although they may be required. But such efforts are not full-fledged curricular units of guidance. Many of these programs have been extended into regular courses by the addition of meaningful content and other modifications. Half-year or full-year courses are the most desirable patterns.

A *structured content* is a foundation for the course. Textbook assignments are usual, and examinations are used to assess progress and to assign grades.

Student insight and personal growth cannot be graded in such courses. The results of the course are measured in *subject-matter testing* rather than by personal growth assessment. The course generally covers material that can aid students in personal insight as well as in total growth and development, but such progress cannot be assumed for students nor serve as a basis for grading. However, counseling, group work, and individual course conferences can help to provide for student application of the course data.

The persons who teach such a course are *specially prepared guidance personnel or counselors* who are interested and able as teachers. The classroom climate that is established has much that is similar to a counseling session. The descriptions of classroom learning presented by Nathaniel Cantor in his two books, *The Teaching-Learning Process* and *The Learning Process*, are particularly appropriate for guidance courses.

Curricular guidance programs are also characterized by the *integration of the tools of guidance*—counseling, group work, case-study procedures, and psychological testing efforts—with course efforts. Such an integration strengthens the application of these tools to all guidance service units.

Strengths and Weaknesses. The concept of classes in guidance is difficult for many guidance workers to accept. Still the advantages are many. Guidance allies itself with teachers, and guidance persons become regularly functioning members of the faculty. Students are able to relate their growth as individuals to their growth in knowledge in all the other areas of study.

Adequate staffing is an important element in the administrative planning for curricular guidance. It is impossible for guidance persons to serve three or four hundred students in a guidance-teaching relationship. However, guidance teachers will seldom carry a load of classes comparable to those in the mathematics or history departments. Adequate guidance departments can staff classes and serve counseling, group work, and testing needs as well as function in the many areas of service demanded for a guidance or personnel program. The continuing need for students to learn about themselves and to apply their learnings helps to prevent guidance or counseling from becoming a "one-shot cure."

The strength of the curricular approach to guidance also serves to highlight a weakness. The approach is not inexpensive, and well-trained persons must be utilized to insure that it functions well. Poorly prepared persons can fall into the traps of giving "group guidance" to several hundred and offering a subject matter that may be available from drug houses in the form of public relations movies, free samples, and advertising copy.

CURRENT STATUS. The present state of curricular approaches to guidance owes much to the continued efforts of "occupations" courses. These programs have continued to grow and broaden their base (Hoppock and co-workers). Narrow vocational concepts have been supplanted by more basic approaches, and students have profited. High school courses in psychology, human relations, and mental health have also helped advance the principles of a curricular approach. College courses have paralleled the growth in other levels. Whenever guidance workers have recognized that the goals of guidance are involved in such programs, they have offered their help as instructors. However, when guidance persons have narrowly defined their own tasks, they have often refused to participate in such courses.

Experimental work by the Educational Testing Service has produced a source book to be used for guidance courses in the junior high school years, *You: Today and Tomorrow.* It includes material that is appropriate for this age group in all of the areas previously listed as normal content.

School administrators, guidance personnel, and budget-makers on the school board or college board of trustees have begun to discover that no single approach to guidance is entirely adequate. Curriculum efforts have been paralleled by counseling bureaus, advanced testing programs, and group efforts. Guidance has begun to apply its efforts in an integrated fashion, and the student has profited.

Human Relations and Mental Health

A fourth, more diffuse and varied model of guidance exists in education at all levels. The stress upon mental health and upon human relations has produced remarkably similar programs than can operate at any level.

Efforts to improve the mental health of students have been provided by social studies programs in the sixth grade and in human relations centers on the college campus. There is no single central concept that pervades such approaches except the belief that persons can be more effective as individuals if they become able to understand and apply principles of mental health and human relations. Such programs have been under the sponsorship of teachers, administrators, and even community groups. Frequently guidance has come into the picture only after the initial spur has been supplied by others. Guidance persons often view such efforts with suspicion. Somewhat belatedly, in some instances, guidance personnel and those who have attempted to develop such programs have recognized that the goals of both groups are virtually identical.

CHARACTERISTICS. The major characteristic of this approach to guidance and mental health is the *broad concept of personal development* that stresses self-understanding and maturity. Approaches to this goal may be highly varied. Group work is frequently a major tool of this approach.

The push for an *integrated effort* by persons from all major areas of education often involves cross-disciplinary courses and social action or work study groups. These have had a significant influence upon the entire school.

STRENGTHS AND WEAKNESSES. A mental health approach has many strengths that serve to unite the efforts of all personnel within an institution. The integration of learning within the individual becomes the primary goal. Weaknesses exist when those working for such a goal are not equipped to use many of the tools of guidance. Tests and measurements, counseling, case analysis, and group work may or may not be seen to be related to mental health and human relations objectives.

CURRENT STATUS. Many significant research and action experiments have taken place as mental health and human relations objectives have been integrated into the total educational pattern of specific schools or communities. *The Personnel and Guidance Journal* sponsored a series of seven articles that summarized seven different institutional approaches to human relations and mental health. *Basic Approaches to Mental Health in the Schools* (Samler *et al.*, 1959) is a reprint series available from the American Personnel and Guidance Association that describes these approaches. The American Council on Education also sponsored a series of experiments in a related area that are summarized in the publications of Hilda Taba and others (1950, 1952, 1955).

The success of these and related efforts has helped to insure that the perspectives of mental health and human relations are not lost in most schools. Teachers have been helped to understand the development of children and to cooperate with all efforts designed to reach the common objectives of guidance, mental health, and human relations.

A MODERN GUIDANCE MODEL

It is doubtful that any school or college possesses a perfect model or pattern of guidance. However, guidance has been involved with students and with education for many years, and the features of a modern model can be extracted from present guidance practice.

No attempt to diagram a perfect model for a given community can be offered. However, it may be possible to identify the dimensions of a program that reflects modern practice. The problem of size is frequently faced and handled by school communities banding together into regional schools or employing specialists cooperatively. Financial considerations will always enter into the implementation of desirable practice. Modern goals, practices, and policies need to be examined in order to know the purposes for which money can be raised, appropriated, and spent.

Philosophical Premises

A modern guidance program is based upon the philosophical premises that the individual student is its center, and that guidance is the primary instrument for individualizing education. The free and responsible person who is capable of problem-solving and of independent mature functioning is the single overriding objective of all guidance.

The internecine conflict between the generalist and the specialist has been abolished by a greater synthesis in philosophical thinking, permitting the goals of the generalist to be implemented through the use of specialized services and personnel. No conflict need exist between the specialist and the teacher, or between the generalist and the specialist, when guidance can be seen to be greater than any of these parts. Guidance becomes a unitary concept in all education and recognizes its partnership with teachers, administrators, and all who work for the education of the person and for the greater good of the individual and his society.

Use of Tools

Appropriate guidance tools are available which can be used to help students in all types of programs. Counseling, testing, group work, and casework are recognized to be vital parts of any guidance program, but no one tool is equal to the total guidance program. Differential skills may be possessed by guidance workers in the various tool areas. Some persons may be primarily skilled as counselors, and others may be specialized in other areas. But all tools need to be coordinated in their use and understood to be related to one another, to the goals of the guidance program, and to education.

Services

Guidance or personnel services are extended to many areas of educational practice. Guidance programs that are mature and responsible will not attempt to create "empires" by assuming that only guidance is equipped and skilled to help students in all areas outside of the classroom. Particular school traditions and practices may dictate that other arrangements be employed. Mature guidance workers will be primarily concerned that service or aid is available to students and that it operates in an effective and efficient manner.

Normal services will encompass or be related to such areas as:

(1) Student Attendance
(2) Health Services
(3) Remedial Education
(4) Educational Social Work
(5) Parental Service
(6) Research and Evaluation
(7) Articulation and Orientation
(8) Admissions
(9) Vocational Planning
(10) Educational Planning
(11) Housing
(12) Student Activities
(13) Placement and Follow-up

Organizational Patterns

Modern guidance programs need to be coordinated or headed by skilled and experienced administrators from a broadly defined education and guidance background. These administrators need to be capable in all the major tool areas of guidance and should be able to understand the work of specialists in the guidance or pupil personnel area.

The guidance program should be organized to take advantage of the broad philosophical goals of the generalist view of guidance, but it should also be constructed to build upon the individual efforts of specialized clinics, personnel, and service units. Curricular guidance courses will usually be integrated into the school or college program at appropriate levels. The objectives of mental health and human relations will characterize the entire program.

ADMINISTERING A GUIDANCE PROGRAM

Many problems exist in organizing and administering a guidance program in any school or college. Small school systems may have only a director of guidance, with no other guidance workers or even counselors. Large city systems or urban universities may have hundreds of persons working cooperatively under an administrative head.

Many guidance workers, involved in helping students achieve individual freedom and personal development, may wish to avoid any type of administrative responsibility. Administration somehow seems to be inimical to guidance objectives. Other guidance persons seem to seek administrative positions for their own sake within or outside of guidance. These extreme positions, each representing a false interpretation of administration, can cripple or inhibit the effectiveness of guidance.

Administration is neither simply directing other persons nor assuming unto oneself all power and decision-making authority. Administration is the process through which people of differing talents, skills, and interests are able to focus their efforts and to offer in concert what could not be offered by any single member of the group. Administration, particularly in guidance, must be concerned with appropriate interpretations of authority, responsibility, freedom of action, and respect for the integrity of others.

Authority

Even in children's games there is a recognition of the need for someone to make decisions, to assume the initiative, and to act. The president of a democratic nation is held responsible and is given the authority to serve as chief executive. A guidance program also needs to have a person or a committee vested with the responsibility and the power to reorganize, administer, and implement the objectives and practices of guidance in a school or college.

Vested is an important word with regard to authority. Democratic authority is not derived, as is the God-given right of kings or lords, nor is it the usurped power of a dictator; it is vested, or temporarily given, by those who hold the ultimate authority—the people for whom the government is organized and for whom all institutions in a free society exist. A guidance program draws its institutional authority from the administration of the school or college. The administrative or executive leadership of an educational institution draws its power from a school board or a board of trustees. All such bodies are vested with authority in the public interest.

Authority is thus the privilege to act for the best interests of those who have sanctioned it. The citizens of a community are the "public interest" that permits an independent college or public school system to exist. Authority provides the opportunity to work for meaningful objectives and to implement the goals and wishes of the persons for whom any institution exists. Decisions must be made in accord with this grant. Power may not be held as an end in itself, or denied through the abrogation of responsibility. Authority presents the administrator with the opportunity to complete a task, and demands that the task be done and that the administrator be judged on his effectiveness.

Responsibility

The reverse side of authority is the concept of responsibility. Authority and responsibility must be conceived to exist together; otherwise one or the other is false. A community, a board of trustees, or an educational administrator cannot hold another responsible for the success or failure of a task if no authority has been extended. Responsibility demands that meaning be given to authority.

Guidance programs, personnel, and administrators must face the responsibility to be judged in their assigned tasks. Such tasks are created out of a body of professionally held knowledge, correlated with local needs and preferences. The substance of guidance as a discipline grows out of its stature as a professional body of knowledge and practice.

The guidance administrator and guidance practitioner are thus bound by and responsible to both a local and a professional authority. Neither may be ignored or assumed to be supreme. Conflicts in local and professional authority must be resolved by an ethical code of practice that provides guidelines for the community, for individuals, and for professional practitioners. Guidance codes of ethics which function in this specific area are available from the American Personnel and Guidance Association, the American Psychological Association, and the National Education Association.

Freedom

Authority and responsibility establish the basis for freedom of operation for guidance personnel. A professionally prepared person must be free to function in accord with professional practice. Personal freedom also provides the opportunity to assess circumstances and to act in accord with one's own judgment. When conflicts occur, adjudication may be necessary. An administrative head of a hospital cannot presume to tell a surgeon how to operate upon a tumor. Nor can a guidance or educational administrator prescribe the counseling, group, or case-conference technique to be used. If improper choices are made, or if the results are unprofessional, an administrator has the authority and responsibility to remove, replace, or prohibit further practice by the person involved. But the proscribing of the freedom of operation of a professional guidance worker is not the prerogative of an administrator.

The guidance worker must accept the principle that individual freedom of operation carries with it the responsibility to be judged and evaluated by those in authority. Authority, responsibility, and freedom in administration and in guidance practice are all intimately involved and interrelated.

Respect

Respect for oneself and for one's co-workers is a fourth major factor in the administration of a guidance program. Guidance is primarily concerned with the personal freedom and responsibility of the individual. Such a concern demands that all who touch a guidance program or work with guidance personnel be accorded such privileges.

Administrative needs for scheduling classes may concern guidance workers. Janitor service may provide for conflict in student activities. The cafeteria and food service personnel may have problems that impinge upon guidance activities. All who are affected by guidance must be accorded the privilege of respect for their own freedom and responsibility. Guidance thus must respect itself, all who work in guidance, and all those in an educational pattern. No other practice can permit the integrity of the individual and of guidance as a discipline.

Evaluation and Change

No guidance program can exist in a static state. The need for evaluation and change is constant. The nature of guidance and of individuals is dynamic and demands planned reassessment and restructuring. The normal follow-up of student graduates and of program effectiveness can chart the guidelines for future change.

The role of guidance in education requires that other persons in the educational pattern be included in evaluation and planning. The administrators of the institution or system, the parents, the pupils, the teachers, and the guidance personnel are all involved and affected by possible changes in the program. The complexity of the process of guidance often leads to dismay when change is contemplated. But the breadth of the base upon which guidance operates can be viewed more positively as a strong support rather than as a burden. Necessary developments and changes can permit guidance to serve better all who are affected by it.

PERSONNEL AND STAFF PATTERNS

Guidance programs are constructed out of the efforts of individual guidance workers. A program can only be given life by those who are able to function to help students. A philosophy of guidance may be desirable and may make a difference to the total school operation. But if no teacher or administrator has the time or freedom to work with individuals and small groups of students and no guidance persons are employed, no guidance program can exist.

The persons who serve as guidance workers in a school or college program are active reflections of the basic assumptions of the program. They are the specific means by which objectives can be achieved. There must be leaders or administrators who assume authority and responsibility for the entire program. There must be individuals who can work as specialists in the many tool and service areas of guidance. Moreover, these administrators and specialists must be able to cooperate with the regular educational staff to provide the many services that are a significant part of a guidance or personnel program. Those who function in these professional guidance roles must be prepared through their own education and experience. Guidance workers must be seen as individuals with particular characteristics and personalities. These concepts, each of which will be examined, form the "staff-personnel" side of guidance.

Administrative Leaders

The person or persons who assume the authority and responsibility for an entire guidance program at any level must be philosophically oriented and practically trained to implement guidance objectives. The head of a guidance program in an institution is normally trained through the doctoral level, and usually has had education and experience in most tool areas of guidance.

It may frequently be assumed that the smaller the school the less need there is for a person to have significant advanced training. Actually, since the smaller school requires that a smaller number of persons (sometimes only one) be involved in the program, the need for wide experience and adequate training becomes even more vital than in a large system. The actual possession of a doctoral degree may not be necessary, but it is certainly desirable.

The larger a system or program of guidance may be the more it becomes necessary for the head of the program to be able to function as an administrator. Such problems as the coordination of effort, the relating of specialized services to one another, and the identification of referral resources require that administrative leadership be of appropriate scope and vision.

Staff meetings become a necessity when more than one person is involved in a guidance program. The head of the program must serve as convener, leader, and interpreter of all parts of the program. The staff of guidance workers must relate to other groups within the institution, such as faculty, administrators, and supervisors. Guidance is first judged on the personal merits of the staff. The specifics of the program are next evaluated. Thus guidance as a concept depends upon the persons who serve and on the specifics of a program. The nature of interpersonal relationships demands that ideas and specifics be related by individuals. The head of a guidance program needs to understand that such evaluations are common and expected portions of any guidance position.

Specialized Workers

Individual guidance workers who are skilled and experienced in counseling, group work, testing, and casework are the fundamental blocks in the construction of a guidance program at any educational level. The need for competent professional workers in all of these areas cannot be overstressed. The educational philosophy of an institution must provide a climate for guidance to operate, but guidance cannot exist through fiat or wishing. The individual counseling sessions, small and large group meetings, a testing program, and individual case studies are the elements that can be integrated into the various service areas that comprise a guidance program.

Individual specialists who are able to function in these four areas are highly desirable commodities for a guidance program, but are difficult to obtain. Few if any guidance workers can function in all four areas unless they are educated to the doctoral level. Moreover, not all doctoral level specialists are competent in all four areas. The development of a balanced staff is the task of the administrative head of the program. All guidance workers must understand and accept the importance and operation of persons equipped to work in areas different from their own.

Some guidance workers may prefer and be able to teach several courses within the school curriculum. Such flexible talents can add to the stature and effectiveness of a guidance program. Some specialized guidance workers may wish to teach in subject-matter areas such as history or science. Others may wish to confine their teaching to occupations courses, mental hygiene, or other special courses particularly related to the over-all guidance effort. Flexible arrangements will permit the utilization of persons with many varied talents and skills.

Traditional specialists, such as school social workers, school psychologists, nurses, and physical education teachers are comparable to a trained counselor, a group-work specialist, or a testing specialist. The nature of guidance is such that the efforts of all such personnel need to be integrated. The public school "guidance team," made up of a counselor, a social worker, and a psychologist, which was pioneered in Connecticut (Mahoney 1955, 1961) is an example of such coordinated practice. Although guidance is broader and demands the integrated efforts of more than three such persons, the team system has helped point the way for future patterns of related specialist action.

Training Levels

The levels of training desirable for the personnel who comprise the guidance staff of a school or college have been already mentioned. Guidance persons are often quick to call the attention of school administrators to the ideal ratio of one counselor to three hundred students. This ratio is becoming widely accepted as a pattern for accreditation and professional practice. But guidance persons also need to require adequate training and preparation for themselves as professional workers.

Details of training programs for guidance persons are considered in Chapter Seventeen. But it is necessary to identify briefly the levels of preparation as problems of administering and organizing a guidance program are examined. Professional practice currently demands that any guidance worker be prepared through the master's degree level. Persons below this level can be employed as trainees, but they must be under the supervision of professional guidance workers. There is much evidence to indicate that the one-year master's degree program is now only a part of the preparation of a professional guidance person. Requirements for supervised practice in counseling, group work, and other guidance tool areas demand that educational preparation go beyond a one-year graduate program.

Graduate programs can begin to prepare a person to function as a full-time guidance worker. Frequently it is possible to become prepared in one of the tool areas of guidance in a one-year training program. Counseling is an exception to this general statement, since it is increasingly clear that two years of graduate preparation, with supervised practice, is necessary before a guidance person can function effectively as a counselor.

Doctoral level training is becoming a necessity for a fully professional person in guidance. Such a person can function as a competent counselor and can be equipped to serve as a group leader, helping others to become skilled in group work, supervising and administering all types of group and individual tests, preparing case studies, and leading case-conference sessions. Doctoral level preparation as well as subdoctoral level specialities needs to be grounded in adequate knowledge of the behavioral sciences, the social sciences, and in a broad conceptual knowledge of science and the humanities.

Many faculty members will participate in a guidance program. They may be called "teacher-counselors" or they may serve as sponsors, advisers, or interviewers. The names chosen are not significant; the quality of supervision and the help available from full-time professional guidance persons are the major factors in the success of such cooperative efforts.

Personal Characteristics

Many writers have assumed, and even recommended, that guidance workers be paragons of everything. There is no question that those who would help others need to examine their own lives to determine their adequacy. Yet no guidance person can expect perfection in his own life, any more than he can expect it in a student.

Guidance persons are close to students and are placed in a position of serving as models whether or not they wish to do so. The importance of the values held by teachers, counselors, administrators, and any person who plays a large part in the life of a student is obvious. The values the person holds will be apparent to the student whether or not the guidance person wishes to influence him. The value patterns of guidance persons need not be cast from a single mold, but they must be capable of withstanding the closest scrutiny by any who would examine and evaluate. The problem is that those who evaluate often presume to know what is best for others and to compromise their freedom and responsibility. Standards of behavior are outgrowths of man's understanding of the culture within which he lives and the sociological forces that mould him. Guidance persons must face the mores and customs of the community within which they work. Guidance workers may choose to refocus such patterns. When a guidance person feels that he cannot accept the patterns that a community holds, he must choose to work elsewhere or be evaluated and even judged by those with whom he works.

The life of the guidance person needs to reflect a broad understanding of individual freedom and responsibility. The practical implications of anthropology, sociology, psychology, and all of the disciplines that support and aid guidance can provide the guidance person with an insight into his own functioning as an educator and guidance worker. The whole person chooses, values, lives—the guidance worker, like others, must accept life as a free and responsible person.

SUMMARY

Guidance programs must begin and must be initiated through an identifiable process. The first major section of the chapter has examined the steps that can underlie the establishment of a guidance program. Programs of guidance may assume varying formats. Four major patterns or models have been developed out of the history of guidance within American education. These patterns have been identified and briefly characterized as (1) generalism, (2) specialism, (3) curricular models, and (4) human relations and mental health. A modern model for guidance has been constructed out of the best features of all four historical approaches.

The administration of guidance programs is a companion problem to the organization of a guidance effort. Four of many possible administrative principles have been offered as vital for the success of a guidance program. Authority, responsibility, freedom, and respect are significant factors in administration of any type, but they are fundamental in guidance administration.

The existence of a guidance program depends upon the persons who can give life to a set of philosophical principles. Leadership and participation patterns for guidance personnel have been listed and analyzed. The educational levels of all guidance personnel have been presented in outline form. The personal characteristics of guidance personnel have been examined in light of the interdisciplinary nature of guidance.

REFERENCES AND SUGGESTED READINGS

Anderson, Gordon V., "The Organization and Administration of Guidance Services," *Review of Educational Research,* XXVII (1957), 165–173.

Association for Supervision and Curriculum Development, *Guidance in the Curriculum,* Washington, D.C.: National Education Association, 1955.

Borow, H., "An Appraisal of Courses in Vocational Planning," in H. T. Morse and P. L. Dressel (eds.), *General Education for Personal Maturity,* East Lansing, Mich.: Michigan State University Press, 1959.

Borow, Henry, "College Courses in Vocational Planning," *Vocational Guidance Quarterly,* IX (1960), 75–80.

Borow, Henry, "Curricular Approaches to Personal Development: Some Problems of Research," *Journal of Counseling Psychology,* V (1958), 63–69.

Borow, Henry, "Modern Perspectives in Personnel Work," in National Society for the Study of Education, *Personnel Services in Education,* Fifty-Eighth Yearbook, Chicago: University of Chicago Press, 1959, 210–230.

Borow, Henry, "Vocational Development Research: Some Problems of Logical and Experimental Form," *Personnel and Guidance Journal,* XL (1961), 21–25.

Cantor, Nathaniel, *The Dynamics of Learning* (2nd ed.), Buffalo, N.Y.: Foster & Stewart, 1950.

Cantor, Nathaniel, *The Teaching-Learning Process,* New York: Dryden, 1953.

Carpenter, C. R., "The Pennsylvania State Pyramid Plan: Interdependent Student Work-Study Groupings for Increasing Motivation for Academic Development" (paper read at the 14th National Conference on Higher Education, Chicago), March, 1959.

Chipp, J. D., *et al., Group Guidance Resource Units, Eighth Grade* (rev. ed.), Rochester, N.Y.: Board of Education, 1960.

Christensen, T. E., and M. K. Burns, *Resource Units in Self-Appraisal and Careers,* Worcester, Mass.: Public School, 1954.

Clark, Burton R., *The Open Door College: A Case Study,* New York: McGraw-Hill, 1961.

Coleman, William, "Basic Steps in Developing a Guidance Program," *The Clearing House,* XXVI (1952), 474–479.

Council of Chief State School Officers, *Responsibilities of State Departments of Education for Pupil Personnel Services: A Policy Statement,* Washington, D.C.: The Council, 1960.

Dressel, Paul L., "The Interrelations of Personnel Services and Instruction," in National Association for the Study of Education, *Personnel Services in*

Education, Fifty-Eighth Yearbook, Part II, Chicago: University of Chicago Press, 1959, 246–258.

Dugan, Willis E., "The Organization and Administration of Guidance Services," Review of Educational Research, XXX (1960), 105–114.

Glanz, Edward C., *et al.,* "The Freshman Psychology Course as the Basis for a Student Personnel Program," *Personnel and Guidance Journal,* XXXVIII (1959), 290–295.

Glanz, Edward C., "Patterns and Constructs in Guidance," *Personnel and Guidance Journal,* XL (1961).

Hardee, Melvene D., "A Time for Caring and Coordinating," *Journal of College Student Personnel,* III (1961), 89–92.

Hoppock, Robert, and N. Stevens, "High School Courses in Occupations," *Personnel and Guidance Journal,* XXXII (1954), 540–543.

Ivy, Allan F., *A Study of Two Types of Guidance Staff Organizations and Their Relationships to Student Perception and Use of College Guidance Services,* Cambridge, Mass.: Harvard University (doctoral dissertation), 1959.

Johnson, W. F., *et al., Pupil Personnel and Guidance Services,* New York: McGraw-Hill, 1961.

Katz, Martin R., *You: Today and Tomorrow* (3rd ed.), Princeton, N.J.: Educational Testing Service, 1959; *Teacher's Guide* available.

Katz, Martin R., and Benjamin Shimberg, *The Evaluation of You: Today and Tomorrow–Student Learnings and Teacher Reactions,* Princeton, N.J.: Educational Testing Service, 1960.

Lowe, R. N., *A Rationale and Models for Organizing and Administering Programs of Pupil Personnel Service,* Eugene, Ore.: Bureau of Educational Research, University of Oregon, 1962.

Mahoney, Harold J., "The Team Approach to Pupil Personnel Services," paper presented to Interprofessional Conference on Pupil Personnel Services in the Public Schools, Washington, D.C., Sept., 1961.

Mahoney, Harold J., and R. Engle, *Points for Decision* (rev. ed.), Yonkers, N.Y.: World Book, 1961.

National Educational Association, Commission on the Experimental Study of the Utilization of the Staff in the Secondary School, *Report,* Washington, D.C.: The Association, 1961.

Neugarten, Bernice, *et al., National Forum Guidance Series,* Chicago: National Forum, 1946 (6 Vols. for grades 7–12).

Noall, M. F., and L. Winget, "The Core Curriculum Project," *Bulletin of the National Association of Secondary School Principals,* XLIII (1959), 196–203.

Noall, M. F., and T. H. Bell, "Core Curriculum at Weber County, Utah," *Bulletin of the National Association of Secondary School Principals,* XLIV (1960), 141–147.

Norris, W., *et al., The Information Service in Guidance,* Chicago: Rand McNally, 1960.

Peters, H. J., and G. F. Farwell, *Guidance: A Developmental Approach,* Chicago: Rand McNally, 1959.

Polmantier, P. C., and F. McKinney, "Programs of Personnel Work," *Review of Educational Research,* XVIII (1948), 150–156.

Roburfield, W. A., and R. Hoppock, "Occupations Course Evaluated Eight Years Later," *Vocational Guidance Quarterly,* X (1961), 45–49.

Rothney, John W. M., *Guidance Practices and Results,* New York: Harper, 1958.

Samler, J., *et al., Basic Approaches to Mental Health in the Schools* (reprint series), *Personnel and Guidance Journal,* Washington, D.C.: American Personnel and Guidance Association, 1959.

Scott, T. B., and R. Hoppock, "College Courses in Careers," *Personnel and Guidance Journal,* XXXIX (1961), 373–375.

Sinick, D., and R. Hoppock, "Research on the Teaching of Occupations 1956–1958," *Personnel and Guidance Journal,* XXXVIII (1959), 150–155.

Stoops, Emery, and G. L. Wahlquist, *Principles and Practices in Guidance,* New York: McGraw-Hill, 1958.

Taba, Hilda, *With Perspective on Human Relations,* Washington, D.C.: American Council on Education, 1955.

Taba, Hilda, and D. Elkins, *With Focus on Human Relations,* Washington, D.C.: American Council on Education, 1950.

Taba, Hilda, *et al., Intergroup Education in Public Schools,* Washington, D.C.: American Council on Education, 1952.

Winget, L., *et al.,* "What Are Some Experimental Changes in Class Schedules, Student Groupings, and Team Teaching Being Tried in Junior and Senior High Schools?" National Association of Secondary School Principals, XLIII (1959), 108–112.

Wrenn, C. Gilbert, *The Counselor in a Changing World,* Washington, D.C.: American Personnel and Guidance Association, 1962.

Zeran, F. R., and A. C. Riccio, *Organization and Administration of Guidance Services,* Chicago: Rand McNally, 1962.

THE INTEGRATION OF GUIDANCE

THE INTEGRATION of guidance into a total educational program is basic to even first-level operational success. Any academic discipline has more concrete and more easily defensible objectives than guidance. Guidance presumes the goal of individual growth and development. At the same time guidance must assume the responsibility for implementing the specific and general objectives of the academic institution that surrounds it, and integrating these objectives with the aim of individual growth.

Guidance is not the province of the specialist alone. The teacher, the administrator, the counselor, the tester, and the innumerable persons within a school associated directly or indirectly with the educational process are all involved in guidance.

The teacher is the single most vital element in the integration of guidance in education. Guidance services cannot exist in a vacuum of faculty nonconcern and rejection. The role of the teacher in aiding the integration of guidance into the educational program assumes an importance equal to or greater than that of any other service.

The administration of any school unit provides the leadership

PART FOUR

that creates an educational climate in which guidance may either prosper or die. Vision is required to make education creative and guidance important to educational construction and reconstruction. Such vision is dependent upon the cooperative relationship that is established between administration and guidance as well as between the personnel in both areas.

Parents and the community provide financial support for each student. Guidance bears a heavy responsibility to the individual parents and to the collective sponsors of the children in school. The resources of parental groups and community units are frequently untapped when guidance attempts to aid the individual child. But if parental and communal resources are united with educational and guidance strengths the child can ultimately profit.

A study of the integration of guidance within school and education demands that all of these areas be examined in detail. The four areas of focus in Part Four of this book are (1) the teacher in guidance (two parts), (2) administration and guidance, and (3) parents and the community.

THE TEACHER IN GUIDANCE: I

THE ISSUE. The teacher is a key figure in American education. The teacher is similarly vital to the success of any guidance program. Teachers can contribute to guidance informally as well as formally. Creative teaching helps students learn the meanings of freedom and responsibility and the potential meaning of the self and the world. The teacher's concern for students and the cooperative problem-solving relationships that teachers can develop with students serve actual guidance objectives although teachers are functioning as effective persons in their own educational role.

More formal relationships to guidance are established by teachers who are involved in teacher-counselor programs, sponsorship of student groups, case-conference meetings, and parental contacts. Teacher attitudes and performance in all of these areas serve as informal "thermometers" indicating the acceptance that guidance may have within a school or college.

The effectiveness of the communication pattern that exists between teachers and guidance personnel in any institution is a foundation for successful cooperation between these two groups. The identifications or allegiances of teachers and guidance workers can be studied to uncover actual processes of communication in an institution. Mutual respect for one another must be the basis of a useful pattern of communication.

Student learnings can arise out of experiences with teachers and guidance personnel. The issue is the learning that may take place, not the arena of action for the learning.

❦ ❦

The teacher in America has been frequently attacked as the destroyer of a society, and as frequently defended as its savior. But the

CHAPTER THIRTEEN

teacher is neither as incapable as some critics would have us believe nor as much of a key to the development of an individual as apologists would claim. Individual teachers are often involved in significant experiences with students of all ages. The circumstances of teacher influence depend upon the student, the teacher, and the problems that are encountered. However, the total effect of teachers as a group in our society is very great. Ashley Montagu (1958) has called teachers the ". . . unacknowledged legislators of any land."

Guidance has vacillated between accepting and condemning teachers. During its early days, guidance was inclined to use teachers as "whipping boys" in order to obtain reforms. Mature guidance workers and educators have always defended the proposition that teachers are a vital portion of any guidance program.

This chapter will deal with the philosophical and practical importance of teachers in the guidance program of any school or college. The mutual attitudes and perceptions of guidance personnel and teachers link this recognition of the role of teachers and their involvement in a specific program. The attitude of teachers and the status of teacher-guidance communication are the foundation upon which programs of cooperative action can be established. The next chapter will describe actual methods of seeking faculty and guidance cooperation.

THE TEACHER

The teacher needs to be clearly recognized as a member of the total educational team by the guidance person. Idealized and distorted views of the teacher can only confuse the guidance worker. No single concept of the teacher can symbolize the many teachers in American schools. Yet there is need to see the teacher at his best as well as at his worst. Human failures are common to all occupational groups. The guidance person needs to understand the potential capacity and skill of all teachers.

Harold Taylor has described the teacher at his best in an essay included in the search for the dimensions of the legendary *Two Ends of the Log*. Taylor writes:

> The teacher begins to move toward the enhancement of his talent as an artist in the field when he thinks of himself as an educational planner and not simply a lecturer or vehicle for disseminating knowledge. He must think at many levels about his teaching. He must ask himself questions about the readiness, aptitude, talent, and interest of his students, and about the selection of materials from the variety of things he knows which might be relevant to the student's readiness to receive the knowledge he wishes to impart. He must consider the effect of his own enthusiasm for a given body of knowledge on the receptivity of the students, and he must understand the effects on his students of their own enthusiasm for the studies they have undertaken [1958:150].
>
> I say therefore that the teacher at his best is a person who is enriched by the scholarship of his students, who gains nourishment and spiritual sustenance from the work with students. Creative teaching is an art, and it is an art which infuses one's own learning with the discoveries and contributions of the student. It is teaching which accepts the student as an intellectual colleague and which makes no separation between the intellectual problems of the young and the intellectual interests of the professional academic man. It is the teacher's responsibility to fuse the student's interests with his, or so to teach that the student will come to have the same vision of the possibilities and satisfactions of learning which the serious teacher and the serious thinker both have as their badge of office [p. 163].[1]

Taylor neither distorts nor idealizes the potential of teaching at any level. He sketches the teacher as an artist, whose full dimensions may be attained by teachers who are vitally concerned with the learning process. All teachers are not and cannot be capable of achieving such exciting visions of education. While some teachers can be creative and contributing, some are encapsulated and bound by their roles as teachers. They must fight to maintain their own existence as persons with an identity. The occupational prison of teaching is strengthened almost every week when teachers are censured or released for dancing, drink-

[1] From *The Two Ends of the Log: Learning and Teaching in Today's College*, Russell M. Cooper (ed.), Minneapolis: University of Minnesota Press. Copyright 1958 by the University of Minnesota.

ing, or even thinking. The drab existence of some teachers is relieved only by their almost mystical faith in the importance of their tasks. Willard Waller painted a depressing picture of the pressures that can bind teachers as he wrote in 1932 about "What Teaching Does to Teachers." That psychologists could reprint this article in 1960 among a collection of articles entitled *Identity and Anxiety* is a telling commentary upon the lack of progress in some sections of the country. Fortunately the picture is now at least more uneven, and the developing nature of teaching is attracting new teachers and renewing the faith of older members of the profession.

It is important to note that these descriptions and profiles of the functions of teachers at their best or worst do not include an emotional involvement or even a problem-solving involvement in the blockings and frustrations of students. Some teachers may become concerned with the nonacademic problem-solving of students and may be exceedingly helpful in the resolution of difficulties. Other teachers need to receive aid in this area and should be able to turn to guidance persons for such help.

Guidance workers need to face squarely the fact that they do not have a corner on the market of helping students. Many persons including teachers may be a part of this process. The uncertainty of possible help is often a source of great distress to guidance personnel. Some teachers are constant in their refusal to relate personally to students; others are variable in their rejection and in their aid. The nature of teaching is artistic rather than scientific in its essential nature. The functioning of great teachers and failures may sometimes be surprisingly similar.

Outstanding teachers at all levels have in common a concern for students and can display, in frighteningly different ways, their sincere desire for students to learn, grow, and succeed. Students are quick to perceive this quality in teachers and will accept wide variations of approach, attitude, and behavior. Teachers, guidance workers, and unfortunately even administrators sometimes never learn that the diversity of teaching artistry is something to be studied and cherished. The roughshod methods of creating conformity to a guidance concept or even to an academic climate can often destroy the very attitudes and climate that are desired.

THE TEACHER IN GUIDANCE

Teachers may participate in guidance programs and help fulfill guidance functions in many different fashions. The formal and informal contributions of teachers offer a series of flexible patterns that can promote a higher level of guidance in any school. The overlapping of teaching, learning, and guidance is a complicating factor in considering any separation of guidance and teacher-involved learning. Elements that may be labeled "guidance" may be considered to be dimensions of good teaching, and many guidance activities are easily identifiable as teacher responsibilities. These concerns may be assumed by an individual or shared by individuals from different educational areas. The accomplishment of a task is the important fact for guidance.

Informal Contributions

The quality of guidance in any school is raised by the effective functioning of teachers in several specific roles. Creative teaching depends upon the development of open-ended learning situations for individuals and groups. An enthusiasm for learning and studying a subject can be translated into personal learnings and development. The history of education shows clear dependence upon the assumption that such attitudes will help students plan for their own lives and careers. A concern for the individual as a person and as a learner is a property of both guidance and teachers. Teachers can also participate in cooperative problem-solving with guidance personnel, students, and administrators.

CREATIVE TEACHING. Many teachers rightly assume that they are carrying on guidance with their students by creating learning climates and class situations that contribute to individual growth and development. One method of creating such a climate is described below.

> Mr. Fisher is a bear. We don't dare go into class with him unless we are prepared and willing to have a real discussion about the readings. We were afraid of him in the beginning, and we still are at times, but we know that he is sincerely interested in literature and in our understanding of literature. He seems to be able to get a right answer out of us one way or another. The members of the class have begun to capture some of the enthusiasm that he has for his subject.
>
> You know . . . he gets angry with us when we don't do our work, but he wants us to succeed and to learn . . . he really does. And we know he is pleased when we do.

Some teachers are able to infuse a group with a desire for learning that can rival the excitement of a cheering squad at a football game:

> Mr. Hausmann had us organize ourselves into study groups. We divided the functions of the city government into five major areas and

each of our groups collected data for the report and turned in a final report on our area of study. Our group was charged with a research report on the redistricting plan that has recently been adopted in our town.

> One night we finally got an appointment with one of the city officials and really had him on the spot. He didn't want to take us seriously as ninth-graders but we persuaded him to let us see the work plans of the redistricting committee. It was after nine o'clock when we left the city hall. We spent another hour and a half with Mr. Hausmann after our meeting downtown. He had to call our parents to explain why we would be getting home so late.

There can be excitement and fun in learning. Teachers who can help students participate in the thrill of discovery and knowledge are creating first-level forces in students for self-directed learning, studying, and self-directed lives. Is not guidance also concerned with the development of students oriented in a positive fashion toward learning, knowledge, and career-planning? Education is a unitary process. As students are able to succeed and progress in the curriculum, as they are able to utilize learning to guide themselves in their life decisions, the purposes of guidance are served.

INDIVIDUAL CONCERN. To teach students rather than subject matter is the goal of most teachers. Through a concern for the individual student, teachers are able to fulfill this goal and simultaneously to perform many guidance functions.

> Miss Jonas keeps a loose-leaf notebook on every student. She records grades for all of the quizzes and exams, but she records much more. She keeps a record of all conferences with students. She knows a great deal about each student and his or her background. She makes it a personal rule to invite every student in to see her early in the year. After the first conference it is up to the student to stop in to see her whenever it is desirable. Her room has students in it until late in the afternoon every day.

> Professor Overman and his wife have invited every graduate student in his classes into their home for many years. It is their hobby. They devote one or two nights to students, entertaining almost every week of the school year. Sometimes his classes have over two hundred students in them. Of course not all of his classes are that large, but he extends an invitation to every student, every year.

> Our teachers voted to do away with the "open house" last year. They said that such a general meeting with so many parents for such

> a short time was really quite worthless. They decided to invite *every* parent into school for a short conference. Many parents come every year of course; this program was designed to urge every parent to come for even a short meeting. Some of the teachers were meeting parents before eight o'clock in the morning and late in the afternoon. We had to get the janitors to open the building earlier than usual and to keep it open later than usual.

Teachers are concerned with individuals and with their progress in subjects, in school, and as persons. Good teaching or guidance functions are not the prerogative of any one person or group of persons in an educational institution.

COOPERATIVE PROBLEM-SOLVING. Teachers are in contact with students many hours of the day. The alert teacher is aware of health problems, financial needs, personal defeats and achievements, future plans, educational crises, "Dear John" letters, and a multitude of other problems that students have from kindergarten to graduate school.

The attitude of most teachers toward referral is related to their concern for the individual child. Teachers will work with those persons who can help their students. The danger is that often a teacher is expected to call the attention of the specialist to the problem and to leave the rest to him. Some teachers may want to "dump" the student on the specialist, but most are interested and concerned about student progress and are willing to aid in any fashion that is appropriate. The failure to enlist the support, understanding, and action of the teacher is a critical issue in many guidance programs. The teacher is in a position to observe daily the progress, relapses, and plateaus that students reach in their problem-solving. Skilled teacher-involvement can contribute to the problem-solving of any student.

Guidance personnel need to evaluate accurately the role of the teacher as a partner in the guidance of students. Whether the student is referred to a specialized clinic or to the counselor in the guidance office, it is necessary to keep the teacher involved, informed, and respected as a part of the problem-solving process.

Formal Contributions

The teacher can and is expected to fulfill many functions that are closely related to guidance in all schools and colleges. The important issue is that they be recognized as valued members of the educational process and not as supernumeraries to a guidance program. It is true that a guidance program is charged with the responsibility of providing counseling, student activities, and referral resources within the community, and with the general conduct of parental relations. How many guidance persons would wish to undertake all of these functions without the active contributions that teachers regularly make? Teachers are by their very nature unofficial members of the guidance staff and in many cases receive no pay, no release from teaching duties, and perhaps no recognition for their efforts. Teachers need to be accepted and valued as voluntary partners in the formal as well as the informal guidance program.

Teachers may be said to be participating members of a formal guidance program whenever they fulfill duties as interviewers, group sponsors, members of conference groups on student problems, or representatives of the school in the community. Teachers may function as counselors or advisers, club and group sponsors, members of case-conference problems-solving groups, parental interviewers, and placement conference leaders within a formal guidance program. A brief identification of the functioning of teachers within such areas of guidance follows.

TEACHER-COUNSELORS. The whirlwinds of controversy have surrounded the role of the teacher as counselor. The semanticists have managed to *say* that teachers are not counselors. However, many teachers, unaware of the fact that they are not counselors, have continued to talk with students and to be involved with them in solving problems of all types. Teachers cannot be other than counselors, unless they are able to persuade the administration to install a mythical elevator to lift them into the classroom and drop them out of sight when the lecture is over. Even such a device may fail. A graduate student put it this way: "I am in the front row, nearest the door in his class. I am closer to the door than he is, but I can never beat him out of the door. I don't know how he does it, but he does. We get him though. The students line up outside of his office and he can't get out without seeing them. He spends about as much time as any other professor with students, but he won't talk with them after class." Students have a great deal of perseverance.

Educational advisers to the seventh grade, college advisers, fifth-grade teachers, and even laboratory assistants cannot avoid talking to students. Purists may insist that talking with students is not counseling. However, it seems that guidance persons are ignoring the facts of academic life if they refuse to help teachers, teacher-counselors, and educational sponsors function more effectively, rather than debating about the classification into which such talking may be placed.

Many patterns for aiding teachers as counselors and advisers exist. Guidance persons have a responsibility to know such programs and to adapt them to their own use or to create new ones that will serve the needs of the teachers in their own school.

Group Sponsors. The school newspaper, the yearbook, the senior girls club, the playground kickball team of the third grade, the philosophy reading group, and many political groups are served by teacher-sponsors. The guidance worker could do little testing, counseling, placement, or educational or vocational advising, much less any leadership training, if he alone were charged with serving as the sponsor of all student groups. The task of the guidance worker is to help the sponsors to do a better job. He needs to help with budget problems, scheduling conflicts, record-keeping, recruiting, and publicity and public relations, and to assist when crises occur within and outside of the school. In other words, he must help in any way that is desirable and practical.

A guidance program is concerned with the morale and attitudes toward learning and school present within an institution. The guidance person who has no time for such "silly" student concerns as dances, music recitals, or chess clubs may find that the problems of the school and of its surrounding climate are such that he can do little except work as a remedial therapist in a clinic. Guidance cannot afford the sterile educational climate of the isolated child guidance clinic or the Children's Floating Hospital. Guidance must remain at the scene of education. Sponsors and guidance workers need to work together in all areas of student learning.

Case-Conference Members. Teachers are prime sources for information about students. Data from teachers about students can be used to assess the dimensions of many problems and to develop causal relations. Similarly, teachers can suggest proposed actions and help to evaluate as well as participate in treatments.

Problem-solving conferences may be informal or formal. Casual conversations may be productive, but they are often exceedingly superficial. Such conversations are perhaps questionable as an ethical procedure, since a nonprofessional atmosphere may encourage gossip. It is more desirable for a teacher or a group of teachers to participate in specific, scheduled conferences planned for individual students.

The climate of a discussion with teachers about students is basic to the effective involvement of teachers. Teachers' ideas, observations, and even suggestions for action can be encouraged or discouraged by the atmosphere that is established by guidance workers, administrators, medical personnel, or psychiatrists. The attitude that teachers' contributions are needed and desired can produce meaningful results.

PARENTAL CONTACTS. Parents are closely involved in the progress or problems of students. Guidance workers and teachers often feel that they could do a great deal for a student, were it not for his parents. But parents cannot be removed from the psychological and developmental pattern of their youngsters. Their effect is present even when children are removed from the home.

Parents see teachers as important people in the lives of their children. However, teachers may feel that guidance personnel have a more sophisticated knowledge of the student and his problem. It must be recognized that parents and students can be helped by both teachers and guidance personnel. Occasionally parents feel that the "left hand isn't speaking to the right hand" (as one confused parent observed). Teachers and guidance persons cannot escape their joint responsibility in such cases.

Many programs of teacher-guidance aid to parents are possible. A joint concern is necessary if the problem is to be seen through the eyes of the parent.

"ATTITUDINAL THERMOMETERS"

The importance of teachers in a guidance program may be further understood when they are seen to be "attitudinal thermometers" that can indicate through their emotional acceptance the success level of a guidance program in a school. The attitude of a single teacher can never be used as an accurate reflection of the acceptance or the operation of guidance in a school. However, the attitudes of many teachers can effectively reveal the level of the acceptance of guidance in a school, the involvement of teachers in a guidance program, and the general effect of guidance efforts upon students. The following teacher responses were offered to various queries and situations in different schools; all statements reveal aspects of the emotional attitude toward guidance:

> "No, Miss Forbes has gone home. She doesn't have to waste her time around this place after school is over."
>
> "Yes, we now have a guidance counselor. I've got plenty of kids that he can have, plenty that he can have."

> "Tom is on the Curriculum Committee of the Faculty; he's a guidance guy but we've found him to be of real help."
>
> "The pupils are going to be disappointed next fall. They have been used to talking with the teachers and using their free time to work on projects and discuss things with their teachers. The new plan will not let us do that."

The implications of these comments are clear. There is little question that it would be diagnostic quackery to assume that one could judge an entire school on the basis of one or two of these phrases. Listening to many teachers from one school can, however, rather effectively reflect guidance operations. Experienced observers and evaluation teams often attempt to spend time with teachers as well as pupils to assess the emotional climate that surrounds a particular program. Through conversations, when time allows, it is possible to establish the actual atmosphere dimensions within which guidance must function.

Program Patterns and Teachers

The specific form of a guidance program is variable, and depends on the evaluation of many factors. Teachers are needed at all times to translate any program into actual practice. Specialized programs of clinics, special services, bureaus, or diagnostic study and referral depend upon the teachers' attitude toward referral. The student must return to class after assistance or special programing. Teachers need to be informed of the results and of the recommended procedures that must follow special help.

Teachers are also frequently involved in the creation of treatment procedures and climates for individual students. Decentralized programs frequently depend upon the aid that teachers can offer as faculty advisers, team members, or case-conference participants. Teacher rejection of guidance can spell the ultimate defeat and failure of any program, any specialist, and any school system.

The need to include teachers in the patterning of any new school guidance program is an immediate conclusion that must be drawn from an awareness of the importance of teacher attitude. Established programs of guidance need to include teachers in regular evaluation process. The program that was originally developed with teacher aid may become a vestige of what a group of teachers once believed in and would support. The thermometer must be used to check the temperature of the patient at reasonably regular intervals.

Teachers' Attitudes

Teachers cannot be separated from the operation of guidance. Traditionally they serve such part-time roles as psychological testing program proctors (hopefully they are not forced to be scorers), academic advisers, team members, schedule signers, club sponsors, and teacher-counselors. The attitude of teachers in the performance of these responsibilities can help either to strengthen the operation of a guidance program or to destroy the effectiveness of the group of specialists.

Teachers as guidance staff members are not administratively responsible to a guidance director, and thus they are bound only by an educational concept and a belief to the operation of the guidance program. Narrowness of design or ineffectual programing can drive out a staff that does not have to stay involved.

The quality of guidance-teacher cooperation is often determined by the attitudes of the guidance persons who initiate or implement guidance goals within a school or college system. The guidance person who rejects the teachers as cooperative staff members may have been previously rejected by the faculty as a whole or by significant members of the faculty. Industrial sociologists have determined that the quality of union leadership is often a reflection of that of management. School situations are similar in that the relationships among administration, guidance, and instructional personnel are a reflection and result of the attitudes of the leaders of each of these areas. Communication processes are the means by which attitudes and involvement are combined.

THE COMMUNICATION PROCESS

Counselors and guidance persons of all types often ensconce themselves in strange locations in the school. Some find it comfortable to be isolated in a tiny room closed off from everyone for privacy, while thers find it more desirable to be placed next to the principal, superintendent, dean, or president. Seemingly the guidance worker in the first situation is afraid to be a part of any related process of education; in the latter situation he may wish to be handy in case he is needed to act as "acting principal" or "acting dean." The location may be chosen by the guidance person or it may be dictated by others. The results of either location are significant. The expectations of the faculty, administration, and parents, as well as the communication processes that result, are all intimately related to location and the attitude arising out of or reflected by it.

Communication among guidance workers, teachers, and administrators is based upon more than mere location. Physical location and its cause may often reveal factors related to communication, but they may not explain or characterize the patterns that actually exist. That patterns of communication exist and that attitudes determine them cannot be doubted. Guidance as a process and persons in guidance are a part of the official and open communication processes as well as of the unofficial "grapevine" systems that exist in any organization.

Group Identifications

Teachers, supervisors, coaches, and of course students at every level seek to identify with one another in small informal groups. Larger common identifications can exist when groups are joined, and cross-group identifications may also be found. The fundamental fact that group loyalties exist among departments, schools, and grades must be faced in an examination of communication problems. Simple contiguity can establish a pattern of communication between teachers who share a common wing, classes which border the teachers' room, or departments which are housed on the same floor.

Teachers establish a sense of unity whenever they face those who are outsiders. The administration, counselors, guidance people, parents, and even students are the "others" for teachers. These outsiders are the "they" that are often referred to by teachers discussing their world among themselves. All outside groups function in a similar fashion; to a common in-group all others are "they." This state of affairs is a natural and expected pattern of group life and important for communication-pattern analysis. Guidance workers are seldom numerous enough to become a strongly unified group and often become "outsiders" to all other groups.

The isolation of the guidance worker in a school or college system must be faced and accepted at times. Insecure guidance workers may attempt to gain the acceptance of an established group, but the guidance worker who tries to crash the gates of the faculty is frequently rebuffed. Dressing in white bucks and chino pants cannot make students accept a guidance person as a student. Administrators also may close their "inner circles" to guidance workers. Desperation may lead the counselor to establish his private room or to become the "assistant administrator."

Guidance patterns or programs within a school or college must seek to identify the group units that exist. Communication with teachers and administrators must be established. Meaningful professional relations with teachers and open communication systems are a basic necessity for all guidance programs. Acceptance needs to be built, not demanded.

Communication Problems

That guidance workers and counselors can never be fully accepted as "real" teachers is almost an axiom of the psychological climate that surrounds guidance. Even if guidance workers teach some course and rotate between teaching and guidance assignments, teachers usually feel that the guidance person does not belong to their "group." These facts of psychology and communication are not offered as unhappy commentaries upon teachers or guidance workers. Nurses and physicians are both necessary to the medical care of a person in a hospital; however, physicians and nurses are not the same. The case of the teacher and the guidance worker is similar. Communication channels can be established if care is taken to understand the climate and attitudes that will surround any formal or informal communication network.

Teachers and guidance persons are people. Each must learn to accord the other respect and consideration in joint or related learning processes. The need to share and exchange information cannot be denied. Unofficial teachers' room conversations will often be a pattern, if no better system is available. These conversations will take place, however, only between those who trust one another.

Philip Runkel completed a study of communications between teachers and counselors that clearly showed their desire to communicate with each other, the need to establish lines of communication between identifiable groups, and the extreme "care" that was exercised by both groups as they shared information with each other. Runkel writes: ". . . apparently the counselor typically begins his service in the school at a lower-than-average level of effectiveness and does not reach a maximum for four or five years" (1961:3).

When one examines the turnover of counselors in schools and colleges, one would have to conclude that some counselors never reach an effective level of communication with teachers. Runkel's study does not state whether varying patterns of communication or actions on the part of guidance persons can materially reduce the time needed for effective communication.

Mutual Respect

Effective communication channels depend upon the mutual respect and recognition of teachers and guidance workers. Teachers are often repelled and alienated by guidance persons or counselors who seek to bolster their own egos through the use of an esoteric vocabulary. Measurement terms, Freudian jargon, and knowing nods between guidance workers can be interpreted as saying to teachers, "We know something you don't know." Teaching is seemingly denied as a significant element in the process of helping students when guidance persons consciously or unconsciously reject teachers.

The isolation of the guidance person is frequently recognized by the teaching faculty but ignored by the guidance staff. Respect for the guidance person as an individual must precede the acceptance of a guidance program. Respect can be won when it is offered to others. The teacher is entitled to recognition as a professional person with professional skills. Cooperative problem-solving and aid to students can be obtained from teachers who feel that they are treated as equals in the process rather than as second-class citizens. The attitude and beliefs of the guidance worker may speak louder than any words of entreaty or invitation. As respect of this type is offered, respect is returned.

In-service training is a term that is often insulting to teachers and administrators. Guidance persons come into a school situation and assume that they will help teachers and others help the student. The teacher's reaction may often be: "Well, I see that we are going to have a series of lectures and a discussion of techniques to teach us how to help students. They are going to tell us how to do something that we have been doing for years before we had guidance in the school. . . ."

The defensive reaction that may be aroused in the faculty can cloud or even cover a real desire for help and knowledge about guidance techniques. The student and his need for help can be forgotten as teachers and guidance persons vie for superiority and prestige. The guidance worker must bear the primary responsibility for these developments. The atmosphere of cooperation in a school depends upon the attitudes and approaches of teachers and guidance personnel. The guidance worker must find an approach that will enlist the help and not arouse the resistance of the teaching faculty. Specific methods of providing a base for faculty participation in a guidance program will be presented in the next chapter. The issue of philosophy and attitudes must be faced before any specific program is considered. Faculty members, like students, are attuned to the actual rather than the theoretical attitude or approach of guidance.

TEACHING AND LEARNING

Teaching can facilitate learning, but it cannot produce learning. The role of the teacher in student learning is similar to the role of the counselor in counseling. The counselor cannot solve problems or learn for the student. Learning is the bridge that unites the teacher and the guidance worker in seeking to assist students. The process of learning underlies the behavioral change that takes place both in the classroom and the counseling room.

The attitudes held by earlier teachers and guidance workers often seemed to resemble the behavior of two swains seeking the hand of a fair maiden. Guidance persons seemed to feel that teachers were competitors for the loyalties of students, and teachers often reflected this view. It must be recognized that the development of the student into a free and responsible citizen within a society depends upon both the teacher and the guidance worker. Guidance persons and teachers cannot look upon themselves as rivals; rather they must view themselves as participants in the single process of learning and behavior change.

The "dangling puppet" organizational chart often places the school board and the superintendent at the top and the student at the bottom of the pile. Teachers and guidance workers are often inclined to vie for a higher position on the chart in seeking to determine whom they must obey and who must obey them. The traditional organizational chart is outlined at the top of page 306.

A view of the learning process that is basic to both guidance and teaching is indicated second. Such a view, in which the student becomes the center of the process, enables teachers and guidance persons to re-evaluate their own positions and their relations to students.

An important factor that is often forgotten by both teachers and guidance persons is the element of time and space. Significant learnings may come in class, in the counseling room, on the playground, or even on silent walks home from school. The school is charged with the task of aiding students to learn. The importance of any single person or process within the total learning that takes place is not significant to the learner. He is concerned with what is learned.

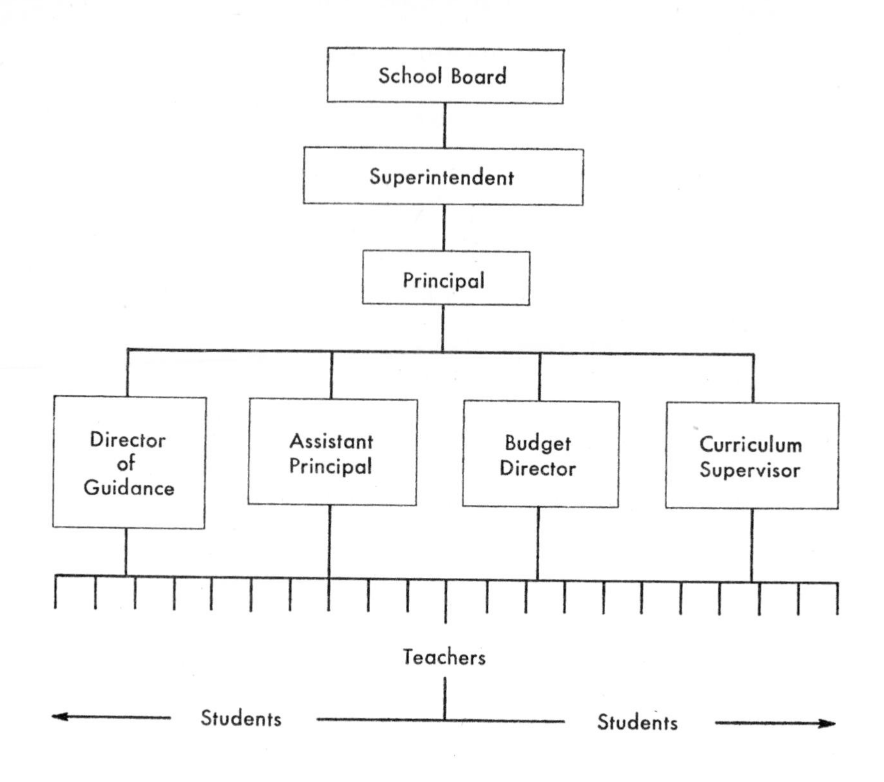
School Board
Superintendent
Principal
Director of Guidance
Assistant Principal
Budget Director
Curriculum Supervisor
Teachers
Students
Students

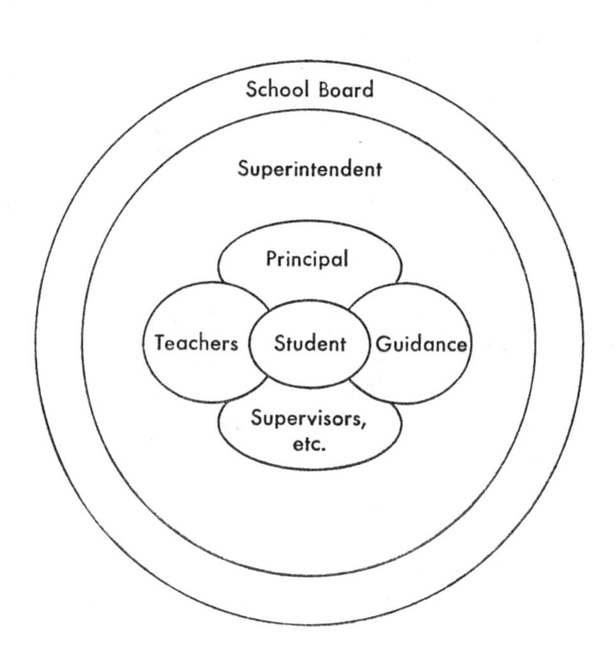
School Board
Superintendent
Principal
Teachers
Student
Guidance
Supervisors, etc.

An incisive commentary upon the learning process from the point of view of the learner was offered by George Pierson in the *Personnel and Guidance Journal* as he investigates the "teacher-counselor" issue:

> It came to pass that a certain student fell among evil companions. They stripped him of his allowance, induced him to forsake his studies, left him outcast by his elders, wounded of pride, and fallen by the wayside.
>
> And by chance there came that way a Keeper of Records who saw that the student had fallen. And, as is the custom of record keepers, he recorded it. And he said unto the student, every student who falls by the wayside should be helped. There should be no partiality. Would that I could help all students, then I could help thee! And so saying, he consulted his book and found that it was so written, and he passed by on the other side.
>
> And there likewise came that way a Test Maker and he looked upon the student and it appeared that he was sorely beaten. He examined his allowance and found that it was 98 percent empty. He consulted his companions and discovered that seven out of ten of them were evil. He talked to the elders and learned that they had all rejected him. He devised an ingenious method of measuring the extent to which the student's pride had been wounded. He at last became convinced that here, indeed, was a student who had fallen by the wayside!
>
> And the Test Maker assembled paper and pencils and wrote a mighty dissertation recommending that help be provided. And he filed his dissertation and passed by on the other side.
>
> And there also came that way an Interviewer. And he looked upon the fallen student and said, "How feelest thou?" And the student answered saying, "My pride is wounded, my companions were false, the elders have forsaken me, there is no hope!" And the Interviewer said, "Thou feelest then, that there is no hope." And the student cried, "Woe is me, my mistakes are grievous, I have been false to my heritage, leave me that I may mourn alone!" And the Interviewer said, "Thou wouldst have me go." And the student answered, "Thou sayest." And the Interviewer made note of it and passed by on the other side.
>
> But there also came that way a certain teacher. And when he saw the fallen student, he had compassion on him. He found linen and oil and helped the student bind up his wounded pride. He directed him to an agent who found work to replenish the misspent allowance. He helped the student rediscover his studies. And he assisted him in convincing his elders that he should no longer be rejected.
>
> Which, now, of these four, sayest thou, was counselor unto him who had fallen? [1955][2]

[2] Reprinted with permission from the *Personnel and Guidance Journal*, XXXIII (April, 1955), p. 443.

Teachers and counselors, guidance workers, administrators, and even custodians and campus police need to recognize that learning, education, and student growth is the concern of all who participate in the educational process. The tasks and responsibilities are different for all, but the goals are similar. Gardner Murphy has attempted to identify the common concern that unites all persons who work in an educational setting:

> . . . what do good teachers, parents, group leaders, clinicians actually do to release the potentialities of those whose development they cherish? First of all, good teachers seem to me to be concerned with more than helping to fit a child into a socially specified pattern; they seem to be on the watch for the reaching out, the sense of exploration, the insatiable curiosity, the urge to new experience, the delight in manipulation and mastery of new media. Those who conceive of education in terms of systematic mastery of all that one's culture has achieved, as for example in the incorporation within oneself of the one hundred great books or the great central ideas of western civilization, seem to be missing something very fundamental; indeed, I fear that the very heart is missing. For the heart, as I see it, is the demand of the person for life, the nourishment and the enrichment of what he already is [1958:316 f.].

It must be recognized that a philosophical view of guidance and of guidance processes are practical items for the guidance person. Man can see no further than his dreams; guidance persons cannot hope to function more effectively than their hopes and visions allow. The teacher, the counselor, the test specialist, the administrator, and all the other persons who work with students are involved in the learning and educative process. The guidance person needs to accept the idea that at best he is only one of the persons who can work with and help students. As the teacher is seen to be the primary point of contact with students, the guidance person can begin to realize the significance of the role of the teacher in guidance. Guidance cannot function without teachers.

SUMMARY

The role of the teacher has been examined as it relates to the operation of guidance. The significant central position of the teacher in fulfilling formal and informal guidance functions has been viewed.

The informal contributions of teachers that have been identified are: (1) creative teaching, (2) individual concern for students, and (3) cooperative problem-solving. The more formal contributions that have been examined are: (1) the teacher-counselor, (2) case-conference participation, and (3) parental contacts.

Teachers have also been shown to be "attitudinal thermometers" that reflect the success level of a guidance program. The attitudes of teachers have been examined as they relate to specific programs.

The communication process between teachers and guidance workers has been shown to be basic to the acceptance of a guidance program in any school. A broad view of the teaching-learning process is important to all guidance functions.

REFERENCES AND SUGGESTED READINGS

See Chapter Fourteen.

THE TEACHER IN GUIDANCE: II

THE ISSUE. The vital importance of the teacher to all education is frequently stressed. That teachers are also primary elements of guidance is proudly claimed by teachers who consider students and subject matter equally important.

A commitment to student growth and development in freedom, responsibility, and maturity is a hallmark of most outstanding teachers. Such teachers have found ways and means to relate themselves to students. Guidance has come into education to help teachers, yet it has helped push the teacher and the student apart. Even the most sensitive performance by counselors and guidance workers can sometimes widen the gulf that teachers may experience in attempting to understand and help students.

Guidance workers need to be aware of the effects of their program on an educational environment. Guidance is responsible for the ways and means to help students and teachers work together. Not blatantly, not with a crass patronizing attitude, but with an awareness of natural student-faculty relationships—guidance must help. Some would suggest that perfect teachers and perfect programing would eliminate the need for guidance personnel. Although guidance has now adopted ways of relating to students that may call this opinion into question, it is still based upon an awareness of the ideal teacher-student relationship. How can guidance fulfill its expected function while aiding teachers in the defense and enhancement of their own traditional educational roles?

Underlying conflict or hostility can exist within schools or colleges where a guidance program has been recently established or even

CHAPTER FOURTEEN

where a program has functioned for a long period. The very nature of counseling and the process of guidance are conceptual extractions out of the traditional faculty-student relationship. Guidance persons need to understand this fact in attempting to involve faculty members in a guidance program. Faculty members are not only vital to student growth and development, but they have preceded guidance persons in working for these goals. Guidance persons may be appropriately considered as "deeper teachers"; however, teachers may legitimately believe that they also fulfill a guidance function in spite of large classes, overextended curriculums, or lack of administrative understanding.

The long-standing dictum that guidance persons and counselors must have prior teaching experience is partially an outgrowth and defense of the unstated belief that all teachers are experienced in "deeper teaching." Expansion of the guidance movement has tended rather legitimately to question the necessity of an apprenticeship in teaching before the completion of guidance education. The process of helping students learn can exist both inside and outside of the classroom. The question of whether previous teaching experience is necessary for all guidance workers may or may not be appropriate; however, all guidance persons need to understand the basis upon which such a requirement has been developed.

Faculty members have continued to reserve certain guidance functions for themselves despite the growth and expansion of guidance as a profession. These areas of faculty interest need to be respected. Areas of cooperative operation can be found in all schools and colleges. New areas and methods of cooperative faculty-guidance action are being created out of the broad educational experience of guidance and faculty. Guidance workers need to understand all methods of faculty-guidance cooperation. Teachers who are interested in their students as persons are always anxious to learn more of the ways and means that can help them achieve the goals that they have established for themselves in becoming teachers. This chapter will explore the traditional guidance roles of teachers and the practical methods for faculty-guidance cooperation.

ACADEMIC ADVISING

Faculty members have long helped students plan their curricular programs and explore the vocational and career implications of their academic choices. The faculty adviser who schedules a tubercular student for eighteen hours of classes, including four to six additional hours of laboratory work, and encourages part-time work outside of school is largely a straw man manufactured by guidance workers. Such advice may have been given, but it cannot be assumed that it is typical, or even countenanced by most faculty members. Although sadistic or insensitive teachers may exist in schools or colleges, no institution can long exist based upon such principles. Guidance programing needs to count upon and enhance the normal faculty-student relationship that can be developed through academic advising.

It is becoming more common for a guidance worker to intercede and block normal faculty-student-parent relationships. One parent complained: "My youngster cannot even get to see the teacher and neither can I. We have to 'clear through' a counselor. What's happened to the schools in the name of progress?" Such incidents are hopefully as uncommon as the faculty adviser who is neither interested in nor cares about the student.

Course Concerns

A faculty member will usually be concerned about the progress of every student in his class. The class may be Humanities 202 or fourth-grade multiplication. Guidance workers need to encourage and defend the privilege of faculty members to aid their own students.

College "warning" procedures or elementary school specialists can inadvertently interfere in faculty-student course-problem-solving. Warning letters may encourage college students to seek aid from counselors or from study-habit programs without first asking for the help of the faculty member who teaches the course. Reading diagnosticians, speech specialists, or other highly trained persons may involve students and parents in discussions about the student's progress without prior consultation with faculty members. Such action can easily cause friction with the faculty.

All academic problem-solving needs to be initiated by student-faculty efforts. The student may not necessarily know of the problem or even wish to face the issue. The faculty member may prefer to examine the problem without the help of a professional guidance worker. If the teacher does not wish to involve the guidance person, such should be his privilege. Widespread difficulty in several course areas may result in automatic referral to the guidance worker or to any specialist within the school. Such procedures should be established with the participation of all faculty members. They must not only accept but also approve of such referral activities; otherwise the students and the guidance worker will be laboring under a handicap.

Follow-up of personal or emotional problem-solving will also involve the academic performance of students. Again, the primacy of the teacher in the academic area needs to be honored. Consultation, adoption of special procedures endorsed by the faculty, and total cooperation by the guidance worker are most desirable.

Educational Patterning

The selection of courses to fulfill an area of specialization in college or graduate school and the courses selected by a student in an advanced sixth-grade team-teaching unit are legitimate concerns of the faculty. Guidance workers may help in selection, counseling, patterning, or even evaluation procedures, but again, the primacy of the faculty member in educational planning needs to be recognized.

The history of counseling and guidance practice may have helped confuse modern practitioners. Frank Parsons' original work in vocational counseling was not directed to the establishment of vocational or educational training requirements. Parsons was concerned with helping the student determine whether he possessed certain qualifications, whether the job or vocational area was appropriate for him, and whether there was an adequate "fit" of all elements. The counselor was not necessarily a specialist in any work area. Further consultation with those persons most familiar with the work or career was necessary. The student needed to determine what the requirements were, and then to decide whether or not he could or wished to fulfill them.

The modern teacher has not changed his role. He is a specialist in his subject matter. Even the first-grade teacher assumes a knowledge of first-grade reading that is greater than that of parents, counselors, or administrators. This specialization is more easily recognized at the secondary school or college level. The faculty member in chemistry is theoretically best able to help a student explore some of the intricacies of chemistry training and required courses. It is possible that such persons may not have the knowledge to advise or explore the issues. Moreover, faculty members may not wish to involve themselves in such student problems. They need to be accorded the privilege of failing or denying the opportunity to examine such issues with students. Guidance persons or specialized counselors need to recognize the teacher's interest and prerogative. Even if fictions may need to be maintained, such as the faculty privilege of turning down a student's request for a conference that may never be granted to any student, the guidance person is not primary within the area of academic specialization.

Positive Programing

Since academic advising procedures are among the prerogatives of faculty members, guidance workers need to coordinate such programs with the consent and cooperation of faculty members. Conferences of guidance persons and faculty committees, full faculty discussions, group study and exploration projects—the appropriate methodology is unimportant, but the involvement and the primacy of the faculty is vital. Revisions of procedures and reinvestigation of privileges are also part of the faculty's prerogative.

The desirable role for guidance persons in establishing academic advisory programs is that of consultant to faculty members, faculty committees, or faculty representatives. The exploration of goals and purposes, the study of other school systems or programs, the integration of advisory programs with total guidance programing, the investigation of student needs and interest, record systems, conference procedures, and data scheduling—these are the raw materials of a faculty advisory program and areas in which guidance persons need to aid faculty members. Principles of operation may be secured from an examination of guidance research or school programs. The keys to successful programs appear to be in the adoption of programs that provide for faculty-student contact, priority of local needs, and the sensitive cooperation of guidance persons.

TOOL AREAS

Faculty members at all school levels are necessary components in the operation of counseling, group work, testing, and case-study procedures. Guidance is an unusual profession in that it does not seek to perform its task in isolation, but depends upon the cooperative support of other members of the educational community. Theoretically it might be possible to staff a school or college with so many guidance persons that faculty cooperation would not be necessary; however, such a scheme would be ludicrous and would fall of its own weight.

The dependence of guidance upon the aid and support of faculty and administration is clearly demonstrable in the tool areas of guidance. Counseling problems will turn up in faculty offices or in the classroom regardless of the attempt to restrict all such problem-solving to the counselor's office. Groups of students will turn to faculty leadership and will seek the resolution of academic issues. Achievement tests are outgrowths of faculty efforts in classes and curriculum-building. Case-study meetings and scheduled conferences about students cannot be complete without the contributions of faculty members.

The recognition of faculty support and initiative in all areas of guidance establishes a foundation upon which guidance or personnel programs can be built. Guidance workers who understand the importance of faculty members are able to ask the question: "How may guidance help teachers help students?" The question of whether or not faculty members belong in such activities is not a legitimate issue.

The four major guidance tools provide areas for faculty cooperation that need to be explored. The creative understanding of these areas of joint operation can promote a higher level of student achievement in any school or college.

Faculty Counseling

Informal counseling is an expected part of any educational relationship between faculty members and students. Academic advising can easily develop into personal problem-solving. Special programs may be established to promote greater success in these areas. Such programs are as important as any specialized program organized around highly trained guidance counselors. Many school systems or colleges have attempted to defend the concept that both approaches to counseling are equally important. The development of guidance has shown that the contributions of both approaches are needed. One concept supplements the other, but neither can replace the other.

The traditional system for establishing a faculty counseling program is to divide the number of students by the number of faculty and assign the students to teachers alphabetically. Administrative fiat may specify the number, content, and even duration of the conferences held in a particular year. Although some programs may offer greater flexibility in some areas, this pattern can be found in many schools and is often defended.

The goals of an educational program will help determine the pattern to be used in a local situation. Academic advising may or may not include personal counseling. Students need to feel free to examine their problems with those whom they trust and with whom they feel comfortable. Faculty members will fall in this category, and rigid adherence to a fiat can only embarrass faculty and professional counselors and lead to student distrust: "You know we can talk only to old Mr. Jones. Well, I just don't want to talk to him, so I guess I won't talk to anyone." Mr. Jones may be the counselor in the school, the director of guidance, or the American History teacher.

Some of the many possible patterns for involving faculty members in a flexible counseling program are: (1) assigned academic advisers, (2) a rotating corps of special counselors, (3) grade counselors, and (4) voluntary choice programs. Each of these will be briefly examined to demonstrate the variability that is possible in faculty counseling programs and the integrative concept upon which professional guidance programing rests.

Assigned Faculty Advisers. Faculty members can be assigned to students on many bases. Similarity of academic interests is used as a criterion in many upper-division college programs. Lower college levels, junior colleges, and public or private schools may find that such a scheme presents many problems. Alphabetical assignment is a method used by administrators to avoid problems. A research study on the college level showed that actual contact with faculty members was the most desirable basis for assignment of lower-division students to faculty counselors (Glanz, 1950). Schools at all levels have also found this principle helpful. Operation entirely on this basis may not be possible, and it can be combined with other systems. Rapport is basic to a counseling relationship. The student who has to seek out a faculty member who is unknown and who may be unrelated to his educational plans may never reach his counselor.

> My faculty adviser was the coach. I suppose he was a nice enough guy, but he was not for me. I had to go to the gym to find him. I

wasn't an athlete and I felt kind of peculiar walking around the locker rooms and seeing so many of the star players for the school. I never did find him that day. I was supposed to see him but I never went back" (alphabetically assigned student).

After a student has established his interests, other patterns may be used to supplement the "contact" basis of assignment.

ROTATING COUNSELORS. Some schools and colleges have helped teachers relate to students by including them as temporary members of a specialized office for a stated period. Faculty members can be relieved of a teaching assignment to work the school placement office for half a year. Other short-term rotating assignments can be made in reading clinics, study-habits programs, career days, housing programs, and even in counseling bureau offices.

The concept of rotation is basic to this pattern. To be sure, it is possible to staff a guidance program with part-time workers. This method may be appropriate; however, such persons, if assigned on a permanent basis, become guidance workers. Part-time guidance persons can become full-time, and many guidance workers have begun their careers in this fashion. Still it is not a pattern for permitting faculty counseling, but is designed to staff a professional program.

Rotation permits regular faculty members to become familiar with many aspects of the guidance program. They may volunteer for whatever area of operation they prefer. The in-service experience is vital and is better than any lecture course to "tell" faculty how to "do guidance." A brief orientation course for specialized service and regular attendance at staff meetings can quickly permit faculty members to make a valuable contribution in many areas of the school.

GRADE COUNSELORS. The use of grade counselors is widespread from junior high school through to college. Freshmen counselors and seventh-grade counselors have the same advantage in common. They have focused their efforts, and frequently their experience, upon one particular level of student experience. They are comfortable and able to relate to students because they can understand the problems that are common to a given age or developmental group. The participation of such a corps of counselors in the orientation and articulation efforts of the school or college is highly desirable. These faculty members become the joint representatives of the faculty as a whole and of the guidance department.

The assignment of several counselors to a grade level is often most desirable. Perhaps the new eighth-grader may prefer a man or a woman.

Perhaps he may not like the assigned counselor (his brother may have told him to watch out for that guy!). Students who are free to choose can better plan their own actions and assume responsibility for them.

VOLUNTARY CHOICE. Voluntary choice programs can sometimes refer to the active "choice" of the faculty to participate in the counseling program. Administrative assignment to other school programs, such as club or group sponsorship, may be equated with service as a counselor to students. *Voluntary choice* sometimes is used to describe the student's privilege to choose his counselor. If such a scheme can be made to work over a long period of time, perhaps it may be most satisfactory, particularly on the upper levels, if the faculty is known to the students. However, students may often be prompted to choose or avoid faculty on the basis of questionable criteria.

All students should be free to seek out and discuss problems of any type with anyone. Guidance persons need to defend this principle within the school, and must be available to aid such persons as they help students. However, semistructured programs are often needed to help those students who may not take the initiative to seek it. Flexibility is the keynote in this area of programing, as it is in so many areas of guidance operation.

Faculty counseling of any type needs to be related to group activities, testing programs, and case-study and case-conference plans. In-service training can best be offered within the framework of actual cases rather than in an atmosphere of "guidance telling the faculty." Each school needs to examine its own structure and to design its program to fill the peculiar needs of its faculty, traditions, student body, administrative plans, and physical facilities.

Group Work

Faculty members can be helped to function as group leaders in orientation programs, clubs, career exploration units, field trip programs, and countless other areas. The ingenuity of guidance programing is the only limiting factor in this area of faculty cooperation. The preference of the faculty member may dictate the assignment. As in counseling activities, there may be an opportunity for the rotation of assignments to provide various learning and service experiences for faculty members and students alike.

Guidance can fulfill a service role to all faculty members who participate in a group effort. Consultation in leadership problems, budget provisions, record-keeping, report-writing, and other burdensome tasks can be kept from the shoulders of faculty members. The role of the faculty needs to be seen not as the work of the guidance department but as a service that may not be available without their participation.

Psychological Testing

Faculty members can provide a valuable resource in the use of psychological test data. Students can be helped to understand the meaning and implications of test data by the understanding aid of teachers.

Faculty members cannot be viewed simply as a ready source of cheap labor for testing programs, although it may be necessary to use teachers as proctors for testing. The day of using faculty members as scoring clerks has hopefully passed. The electronic marvels of today must be used to free teachers and guidance workers from such drudgery. The cost of scoring, profiling, and reporting test scores needs to be considered as a part of the cost of testing.

Faculty members can also be involved in the use of test data. Profiles of elementary classes and local norms developed for all fourth-grade students within the community, the state, the region, or the nation may be of help to the creative teacher. Appropriate data on all children should be made routinely available. Data on individual students should be made available for teachers whenever they feel it desirable. The responsibility of guidance personnel is to help teachers learn about and use such data. Case-study conferences are a primary avenue to create a broad understanding of the meaning and use of test data. Most teachers have been instructed in measurement principles and in the concepts of individual differences. They need to be helped to understand the specific applications of the tests that are used in their own community.

Involvement procedures for teachers can include case conferences, class-profiling, school-profiling, parental conferences, curriculum-planning, homogeneous grouping plans, and literally all areas of guidance and education. Test data are pieces of student behavior that may be compared to other group patterns. Teachers can profit from the use of these data when they can be helped to see that testing is a tool and not an end in itself.

Case-Study Conferences

School records, student problems, and guidance can come to life for the teacher as he becomes involved in an actual case-study process of solving problems. The data that can be offered by faculty members in such meetings are unavailable from other sources. The patterns that may be pieced together by skillful clinicians will help faculty members to relate themselves to the growth of their pupils.

Case conferences may be scheduled and teachers invited. However, many may not appear if they do not understand the purpose and function of such meetings. A high-powered public relations program is not necessary nor desirable to promote faculty involvement. If the conferences are concerned with actual problems and the faculty members are informed of the specific recommendations that may be made, they will soon demand that they be permitted to attend. In such cases the faculty may forget the earlier invitations that they declined. A concern for the problem and a willingness to work together would dictate that such lapses of memory should always be overlooked.

SERVICE AREAS

Faculty members can add meaningful dimensions to many areas of guidance service. Again, the philosophy of the guidance persons who wish to work with teachers is vital to such involvement. Faculty members will participate in many types of activity because of their own interest and desire to help students. Guidance workers must not view them as subordinates who are to be supervised and directed. A consultative relationship between equals is required for meaningful patterns of cooperation. The service areas mentioned in earlier chapters are appropriate for the involvement of faculty members. Four major areas of faculty-guidance cooperation will be analyzed as typical and illustrative of such joint effort. These areas are (1) orientation and articulation, (2) parental conferences, (3) student activities, and (4) housing services.

Orientation and Articulation

The opening days of school are important for both new and returning students. The process of orientation and articulation was earlier examined in order to present the major areas of student concern. Physical, emotional, psychological, and academic elements are present in all programs. Faculty members can contribute to student adjustment in all areas, but they usually prefer to focus their efforts in the academic area. Actually, as faculty members can help students to examine the academic issues that lie ahead in a particular year, success in other areas naturally follows.

Group discussions are productive patterns for orientation and articulation programs. Faculty members are accustomed to meeting with small groups of students and are able to draw upon their normal methods of relating to students. Students can come to recognize that learning is central to their school experience as academic orientation is stressed at all levels.

The Rochester, New York, City School District produced a booklet, cooperatively authored, entitled *More Willingly to School.* The brief paper-bound volume attempts to help teachers understand the basic issues of helping students to capitalize on their natural curiosity for learning. The foreword from the Superintendent of Schools, R. L. Springer, states: "This booklet has been prepared to share selected ideas to stimulate your thinking and planning for a most favorable beginning of the new school year. Motivate and whet the mental appetite of your pupils; then give time and opportunity for them to learn and to react" (1961:1).

The booklet defends the concept that teachers can destroy student-faculty cooperation and communication in the learning process when such statements as these open the school year:

> "Tell me what you did last summer, and then you can write a composition about it." Or,
>
> "Just look at all those cartons of supplies. Now if everyone cooperates, we'll have everything put away by Friday."
>
> . . . TEACHERS make the difference in attitude toward learning. Indifferent teachers invite pupil apathy; unprepared teachers invite classroom confusion. There should be an annual September rendezvous of enthusiasm in which the teacher, the students, and the content of learning are fused to bring genuine desire to learn [p. 3].

The booklet offers suggestions for orientation at all levels. Future revisions, based upon teacher contributions, are planned. The booklet warns against "one-shot showmanship," but helps teachers recognize the importance an atmosphere of interest, capacity, and psychological preparation has for the opening days of school. Can guidance afford not to be interested in this type of activity?

Guidance must face its responsibilities to help in such ventures and to initiate, consult, supervise, or retire from the scene. Guidance as a professional discipline cannot seek the praise, but must work for the results.

Parental Conferences

The expectation that parents and teachers will talk together about the student is time-honored in education. Guidance workers need to realize that their own involvement in such work is complementary and not a replacement for teacher conferences. Parental conferences are in this respect similar to academic advising or course discussions. Faculty members feel both defensive and proprietary about these privileges. Perhaps the distant future may see guidance programs or specialized counselors serving all student and parent needs that are not academic in content or implication. But that day is not here, and hopefully it may never come. The teacher and the guidance person must work together to help students and their parents.

Guidance workers need to seek ways to help teachers become more effective in conferring with parents, just as faculty members need to profit from the tools and techniques of counselors as they meet and talk with students. Teacher conferences can be supplemented by follow-up or referral to guidance specialists. Together, teachers and guidance workers are able to offer to parents an understanding of the classroom learning experience and the generalizations and abstractions that may help them understand more fully the student's behavior and learning (or lack of learning).

Elementary schools are somewhat more active and effective in bringing together teachers and parents than are higher levels of education. "Parents' Night," "Open House," and similar activities are often used to bring parents into the school. Appointments are made for individual conferences. Some schools have experimented with half days or even full days reserved exclusively for conferences with parents. Such programs can utilize the guidance staff as consultants and second-line referral resources.

Some secondary schools and colleges seem to say to parents: "We'll talk to you if you wish, but you'll have to work a little in order to see us." This attitude is easily perceived by parents. Fewer conferences are scheduled, and emergency action is often the only way that some parents can be brought into the educational process of their children. Parents often resist, and teachers may feel that even halfway efforts are sufficient. Educational theory places equal responsibility upon parents and teachers to help youngsters grow, learn, and develop. However, since teachers are more specialized in this process, it seems only reasonable, and parents often defend this position, that the teachers make the major effort.

Guidance can become the mediating and referral resource for such problem areas. Aid to teachers in scheduling the necessary parent-teacher conferences can be a vital guidance service. The goal is not greater control for guidance, but rather the productive meetings of parents and teachers. Guidance programs can work toward this objective through special programing, cooperative efforts with administrative planning, or joint faculty-guidance planning sessions.

Guidance programs can be helpful at all school levels in aiding teachers and parents to profit from the use of school records and the analysis of student behavior in varying environments. Counseling by guidance personnel can help parents and can be scheduled to follow academic discussions with teachers. The guidance worker is in a position to view the student in a broader perspective than any single subject-matter teacher. However, the counselor, although he may be talking about emotional problems or personality conflicts, is no more important in the total process than is the teacher. The student needs education in order to plan and live his life. Teachers and guidance workers are both needed in the total process of education.

Student Activities

Student clubs, newspapers, annuals, creative writing efforts, school, college, or community government, and many other areas of student interest existed before the arrival of guidance. Guidance needs to be concerned and responsible for the over-all organizational structure and pattern of an activity program, but teachers are still at its center.

Faculty counseling or advising assignments may be rotated with sponsorship of student activities. Some schools expect that faculty members will fulfill both roles concurrently. In any case it is desirable, when possible, to provide for faculty choice in the selection of student group sponsorship. Student preferences may also enter into the selection process, and administrative control can provide for equitable assignments.

Guidance personnel can help teachers become more effective with student groups. The training of student leaders with the cooperation of the club or group sponsors is a practical method of aiding student groups. Budget provision and financial control is frequently offered to college groups by guidance. The establishment of a student activities committee or an executive board within the student government can help to strengthen the institution. An informal or semiformal organization of club and group sponsors will also help bring about the discussion of mutual problems and concerns among the faculty. Such informal groups can seek to help themselves through an understanding of group procedures and techniques.

Coordination among the various athletic activities of the school, for example, such as varsity and intramural athletics, major and minor sports, and probation and eligibility requirements can be examined and administered through administrative and guidance cooperation. The competition for funds and preferential treatment in athletics or other activities and the resulting student disillusionment may be precluded by a single faculty or guidance policy-making group establishing common policies for all activities.

Special planning and cyclical programing may be among the most productive elements of a student activity program. The joint efforts of faculty members, guidance personnel, and student committees can provide the foundation for more meaningful activity programing. Some schools and colleges provide a rotation of historical and political conferences. Additional efforts may be directed to art and music festivals. Colleges often provide for religious conferences that are beyond the normal province of public school programs. The strength of these festival programs lies in the cooperative planning that brings together the academic and social concerns of students. Student activities can best serve students as they provide a link between these elements of student life. Similarly, faculty members are most willing to aid students when they feel that their efforts are connected to meaningful learnings.

Many student activities are of a completely "fun" type. When such activities are planned by students, it would seem appropriate that faculty members be asked to serve only on a voluntary basis and, if no faculty member is available, that guidance persons assume the responsibility for chaperoning or planning aid. Student football rallies, pep parades, float parades, and dances are all examples of such activities. Such activities are as important as the more academic type, but guidance persons need to recognize that faculty members may or may not be interested in making their own time available for such plans. Faculty efforts may be necessary in other areas, but all student activities are a part of a guidance responsibility.

Housing Services

Dormitory supervision and dormitory counseling programs are beyond the province of most public school systems, but are everyday elements of colleges and most private schools. The question of responsibility for students within a housing situation is typical of many educational problems. Faculty members may be assigned the entire responsibility for the housing program, or they may be aided by professionally trained guidance persons. Usually guidance, acting through housing deans, is the responsible agent.

The problems of a dormitory are different from but closely related to academic issues. The dormitory cannot be seen as a detention house or as merely a convenient place for students to hang their hats. Dormitories can be an integral part of the educational pattern of the school. As such, dormitories have a significant role to fulfill. Such problems as physical, social, health, discipline, and academic needs can all be focused in school dormitories.

Some schools have assigned particularly interested and specially hired teachers to fulfill such responsibilities. Housemaster duties are a part of a teacher's contract arrangements in many private schools. Many Ivy League schools have appointed housemasters as a specially chosen honor for extra financial renumeration. It seems desirable to fulfill both qualifications in involving faculty or guidance persons in housing assignments; 24-hour duty is a demanding task and should be entered into only through common consent and for extra salary.

The dormitory assumes an academic role as it is properly viewed within an educational scheme. Academic study periods can be interwoven with social activities, student government functions, discipline procedures, athletic programs, and related activities. The principles earlier offered for all of these areas can also apply to a dormitory or house setting. The physical proximity of the participants, the social forces that arise within the restricted setting, and the psychosocial pressures all combine to make dormitory programing vital to the educational and guidance objectives of an institution.

The entire area of student housing, counseling, guidance services within a student housing unit, and the interrelationships of these concepts have received much experimental attention in recent years. Early housing programs were designed simply to permit adequate housing and nutritious food. Today's efforts are original plans created to take advantage of the forces, pressures, and physical proximity that were formerly considered disadvantages. Stevens College in Columbia, Missouri represents a new trend in college housing, and Newton High School in Newton, Massachusetts is a unique development within public education. Each will be examined briefly to demonstrate the principles underlying the programs.

Stevens College established the "House Plan" as a resident system in 1961. Faculty members who form a "team of instructors" are housed in the same building as the students. Special activities are planned by the girls, the faculty, and by joint committees. The advantages of the program far outweigh many of the immediately observable disadvantages.

The Newton Public High School has established a "house plan" for the traditional nonresident student body. The large high school is divided into major units or houses. A common room, classrooms, teachers, counselors, and similar facilities are arranged in contiguous units. Actually, such planning may be viewed as similar to a university plan that provides for a division into colleges. This effort helps to reduce the impersonality found in many large public high schools. Perhaps such a plan is more accurately an administrative rather than a housing program. Regardless of the classification, it seems to be an appropriate step to encourage the individuality of students and a meaningful learning environment. Guidance needs to be concerned with such developments. The Andrew Warde High School in Fairfield, Conn. has an unusual plan which is outlined below.

ANDREW WARDE HIGH SCHOOL[1]
Fairfield, Connecticut

Kenneth R. Petersen, Headmaster
Vincent D. Strout, Assistant Headmaster

GUIDANCE HOUSEMASTERS

Josephine O'Dwyer, Barlow House
Raymond Condren, Smedley House
Grace Carroll, Mason House
Arnold Wile, Wolcott House

HOUSE PLAN

Each house is a cross section of the school, grades 9–12 and has about 400 pupils. The Administrative and Guidance Housemasters work as a team with 22 teachers. The plan provides many advantages of a small school and retains the benefits of a large school.

COMMUNITY

Fairfield County: Population: 46,000. Suburban Community 50 miles from New York City and six miles from Bridgeport, Conn. Primarily a residential community with broad representation of social-economic groups.

SCHOOL

Enrollment: Grades 9–12 .... 1,595 students
Average Class Size: 25 Faculty: 95
Accreditation: NEACSS Median I.Q. 110
based on Holzinger–Crowder Mental Abilities

[1] Reprinted courtesy of Andrew Warde High School.

MARKING POLICY

A+ superior quality work in high ability group
A superior quality work
B very good work
C average work
D lowest passing grade
E failing grade

There are no subdivisions in the curriculum of Andrew Warde High School. We operate a single curriculum and have no breakdown into college prep, general, etc. A pupil's program and group are determined by analysis of his abilities rather than upon election by course. Pupils are marked against their grade range. A pupil in English 12 is compared with all the pupils in English I and not just the Group 2 pupils. A student's mark should reflect how he would do if he were in a heterogeneous group.

GROUPING POLICY

Pupils are grouped in English, Mathematics, Science, and Social Studies according to their ability and performance.

These subjects are coded to indicate the grouping. The first digit signifies the year of the course and the second shows the group. English 22 means 2nd year English in Group 2. Languages are coded to show the year of the course and the elementary language experience of the pupil. French 21 indicates 2nd year French for pupils who started French in Grade 3. French 22 is second year French for pupils who started French in Grade 9.

Group 1 highest ability about 15%
Group 2 about 40% of the class
Group 3 about 35% of the class
Group 4 lowest ability about 10%

TESTING PROGRAM

PSAT–SAT–NMSQT
Holzinger–Crowder Mental Ability Test
STEP–Reading–Writing–Social Studies
Subject Achievement Tests (National norms)

SPECIAL PROGRAMS

APP–English and Mathematics
Elementary School Language Program
Oral–Aural approach in languages

CLASS OF 1961

Students: 356. 169 Students took SAT
Number of colleges attended 95
Started technical training 6%
Started college 56%
Continued schooling 62%

Four-Year Grade Average

QPR – A = 4

4.0 up	A+	2%
3.5–3.9	A	6%
2.5–3.4	B	28%
1.5–2.4	C	50%
.8–1.4	D	15%

1961 SAT

Boys	Verbal	Girls
5%	800 650	2%
9%	649 600	11%
10%	599 550	9%
7%	549 500 M	14%
19%	499 M 450	23%
23%	499 400	20%
18%	399 350	13%
9%	349 200	8%

1961 SAT

Boys	Math	Girls
5%	800 650	2%
12%	649 600	6%
11%	599 550	8%
18%	549 500	17%
16%	499 M 450	15%
19%	449 400 M	20%
10%	399 350	15%
7%	349 200	17%

COOPERATIVE DESIGNS

Many possibilities exist for bringing together the efforts of teachers and guidance personnel in helping students complete their education more effectively. The essential relationships of guidance persons and faculty members are becoming more clearly delineated as educational practice evolves. The student profits as each member of the educational group can create better ways to relate to and function cooperatively with each other. Traditional patterns of cooperation exist within most school programs, but a newer design of team teaching is emerging at all levels of education. The single emphasis pattern will be examined briefly, and the newer concept of team teaching and learning will be explored in greater detail.

The Single Emphasis

Many schools have seized upon a single aspect of a guidance philosophy and have attempted to implement it in great detail. Counseling, group work, casework, or testing has been selected out of a developing concept of education and guidance. The narrowness of the position is seldom seen by the institution or school system. The impact of individuals or groups committed to a particular philosophy have frequently intensified such a development. Some schools have emphasized records and created a magnificent system of data processing. Counseling may suffer because the potential for faculty involvement is drained off in a single direction. Occupational literature, group work, "Career Days," "College Nights," student activities, and even discipline have been the focus for some schools.

> Our school became "obsessed" with our honor system and honor court. Students and faculty members were completely dominated by the philosophy, practice, problems, and advantages of the honor code we had developed. There was no question that the system worked and that it was helpful to students. It provided a dimension to our educational program that many other schools did not have. But . . . we did very little with student counseling except as it related to "honor" problems. We had no testing program of any consequence. Our student activity program was almost nonexistent. Student government was the dog that got wagged by the tail that was the "Honor System" (High School Counselor).

Many persons could describe their own schools in these terms by substituting another emphasis. Many schools have developed counseling to the point that there are counselors in the dormitories, in the grades, in the counseling bureau, in the clinics. There are social counselors, vocational counselors, and counselors for referral. The student is naturally a little confused about what counseling is. Test programs have frequently caught the imagination of a school to the point where similar distortion occurs.

The single emphasis within any program tends to obscure the broader needs of students. The necessity for balanced programing within a school is not primarily the responsibility of the faculty members. The guidance administrators need to design a pattern in conjunction with faculty members and general administrators. Faculty members have their own problems in planning and implementing their courses, in preparing for classes, and in similar academic areas. They are often willing to cooperate, but they need to have help and direction. They are the members of the team and cannot be held responsible if the quarterback is calling only one set of signals.

The Team System

The recently developed team system has helped to provide a design that permits new and effective patterns of cooperation between the teaching faculty and the guidance personnel of a school. No single team system exists, and many variations have developed from the original patterns. The concept has grown with a vigor that is unusual in education. Many communities have constructed new buildings especially designed to implement team concepts. Team-teaching schools therefore exist as an architectural fact as well as a pedagogical system. The unusual fact about this design is its flexibility. Not only has it been used in college and elementary schools, where it originated, but it has also expanded into the junior and senior high school levels.

Probably the earliest educational use of the team system was in 1950 at the College of Basic Studies (formerly The Junior College) of Boston University. Elementary schools soon followed suit, and a rapid growth followed throughout the decade 1950–1960. The Claremont, California, District School System has adopted many aspects of the team system. Special schools have been designed and built in Wayland, Massachusetts and in Norwalk, Connecticut. In 1961 the University of Maine was provided with half a million dollars to explore the uses of the team system in educational practice. Harvard University's School of Education has investigated the many ramifications of the team system while also exerting a necessary brake upon overly rapid acceptance. Stevens College, as earlier mentioned, has applied the team system to their dormitory plan. Southampton College of Long Island University and the University of South Florida are using modifications of the team approach in the first two years. The team system has provided a valuable structure for new developments that have permitted all school personnel to function more effectively.

TEAM DESIGNS. When the word *team* is used, it is possible to infer several uses and several types of programs. The early use of the team system on the college level at Boston University (described by Glanz, 1955, and Anthony *et al.*, 1956) brought together teachers from the humanities, social science, science, and communication courses to cooperate with the guidance worker. These five persons represented the general education program prescribed for all students. Each group of students, approximately 125 to 140, shared the same four instructors and the same guidance counselor. Several such teams made up the college. Schedules and student programs were developed by teams and by sections within teams. Teams (except for the guidance worker) were housed in a single large office.

A type of team that developed rapidly in the elementary schools was the use of three or four subject-matter teachers to serve approximately 100 students. These teachers constructed their own curriculum for a given period and cooperatively planned the year's activities. The involvement of the guidance worker was sometimes provided for, at other times guidance came into the scene only irregularly. A second type of elementary school team program was the pairing of two instructors, one relatively inexperienced and one senior in terms of experience and training. This system of team teaching was really a type of apprenticeship program. The lure of the word *team* was perhaps overwhelming and was probably sometimes used with questionable appropriateness.

Secondary school and junior high school programs helped to extend the concept of the team. Many varieties of teams were constructed. Teams were established in a social studies unit, a science program, and in any area of school programing. Guidance was sometimes included and sometimes not.

Pupil teams (Durrell, 1961; Durrell, Scribner, *et al.*, 1959) are another interesting variation on the theme of teams. Within an elementary school grade groups of students were organized to conduct relatively independent work projects. Teachers served as supervisors and helped the groups focus their efforts and define the dimensions of the project. Evaluations were made and student motivation increased. Although these groups can be called teams, perhaps they can be better subsumed under the category of creative group work.

Guidance teams were developed as counselors or guidance persons were helped to work with school social workers and school psychologists. Early legislative efforts were made in this area in Connecticut in 1950 and 1951. Throughout the 1950s this idea of interdisciplinary cooperation among personnel specialists was developed and improved in many Connecticut school systems. Other school districts and individual school units have also developed this pattern. Mahoney (1961) describes some of the history and the operation of this type of team in Connecticut. This concept of the team was placed within the organizational framework of guidance in Chapter Twelve, "Guidance Programs and Patterns."

THE CONCEPT. Two basic team concepts are identifiable in the literature and the practice of the last 15 years. One concept of team teaching stresses the cross-disciplinary roots of the team members, the second stresses varying experience levels within one subject-matter area. The second concept may have considerable merit in training apprentices, but the first seems to be the most basic design of team effort within a broad educational environment.

Cross-disciplinary efforts are characterized by cooperative and integrated academic planning. Teachers from different subject areas are enabled to plan the yearly curriculum in overlapping and meaningful patterns. The student, who has long been obliged to do his own integrating, has been helped by teachers who recognize that they must be aware of all the elements that make up the student's total educational experience.

The guidance worker can become a natural member of the team. Teachers who coordinate their academic concerns soon begin to ask questions about student motivations, learning skill, problem-solving, counseling needs, life styles, and purposes. The artificial barriers of individual subject-matter areas cannot stand the pressure for common awareness by all faculty members. The next logical step is the recognition that the student is more than a receptacle for information. Guidance becomes a normal and expected element in the development of team planning. The student profits from the new-found cooperation that exists between the faculty, the guidance staff, and the curriculum.

ADVANTAGES. The team system has many advantages. Teachers who participate in a team system are able to understand each other's work more effectively and to see the student as the ultimate consumer of all procedures and subject matters. The guidance person is able to assume a natural teaching relationship with the faculty. Counseling, faculty counseling, testing, case-study work, and even group work that is undertaken by guidance can be related to the education of the student. The student becomes the center of the educative process.

Teachers are able to see the guidance program as a close partner to their work with students. Guidance is seen to be allied with the educative function, rather than being attached as an administrative appendage. The relationships of guidance persons to team members which develop out of problem-centered discussions focus the combined efforts of all members of the school faculty on common goals. Guidance and counseling are placed within the perspective of student service and student learning. The tendency of guidance workers to be separate or to function in therapy-type relationships is dispelled as teachers share in counseling, test interpretation, and case-study work.

Every team meeting that brings the teachers and the guidance worker together to talk about student progress becomes a type of case conference. The common goals of the teachers and the guidance person involve and give meaning to school records, test data, student behavior, and related data.

DISADVANTAGES. Although the team system is extremely valuable, it must be recognized that certain features may create difficulties.

The individual independence of faculty members and the guidance worker is limited by the need to share ideas and to be responsible to group planning. Problems occur that must be solved with a common understanding and with an appreciation of the positions of all members of the team. Individuality must be maintained while team goals are developed. Students who have the same team of instructors and guidance counselor are quick to compare and evaluate the efforts of their team with another. The problems of poor instruction, confused educational goals and practices, and personality clashes between students and faculty are quick to appear. But although such problems occur more quickly with a team system, educational rewards and achievements are also reaped more rapidly.

GUIDANCE PERSONNEL AND TEAMS. Sometimes it is possible to staff each team with a full-time guidance worker. Such practice may become more widespread as guidance assumes a greater role in education. Currently it is usually necessary for one guidance worker to serve two or more teams. The contributions of the guidance person to the team are limited by such an administrative design. But until funds or educational practice can catch up with theory, it is better to have some guidance available rather than none.

The guidance person should serve the team as if it were a small school and faculty. The team is a school in itself for the students, and the guidance person will need to function as counselor, group leader, test interpreter and user (with both faculty and students), and frequently as a case-conference specialist. The additional resources of the guidance department or other guidance personnel can be brought to the attention of the team, but the team will frequently demand that their guidance man do the job.

The guidance person who works with teams should give his allegiance and understandings to the faculty rather than to the administration. Perhaps there is no conflict in these roles; however, directors of guidance have too often been substitute administrators in many schools. Guidance, in serving the team, must examine its relation to learning, problem-solving, and student growth and development. Certainly this is not an undesirable result. Involvement in attendance-taking, study-hall supervision, coaching, and similar tasks will be difficult if guidance persons are full-fledged members of the team.

Orientation courses may be taught by guidance persons who serve as team members. Extended courses in occupations, psychology, or even mental health can be integrated into the program offered by the team. Problems of course integration, testing, written work for students, and academic goals become the natural concerns for team discussions. Guidance persons should become members of the team in these discussions as well as in meetings devoted to student progress. The team becomes a device for integrating the guidance person into the total task of education.

PUPIL-CENTERED TEACHING

Pupil-centered teaching is usually assumed to be concerned with student progress in subject matter, as well as with personal growth and development. Teachers define their roles as pupil-centered as they view their relationship to students and to the curriculum. Guidance persons need to recognize that although they are specialists in helping students examine and plan for their own lives, students can also be helped by teachers who are interested in similar goals.

The need for guidance persons to re-examine the practices of their school or college to determine how they can further the work of teachers is the key to the relationship between teaching and guidance. Teachers may be anxious to improve their home-room programs or their faculty advisory program, or to develop a team system. The guidance person needs to be brought into the process. But the guidance worker cannot assume that he alone can lead the way to truth. The recognition of pupil-centered practices is the responsibility both of the guidance program and of the faculty. Cooperation and joint involvement of equals who are seeking common goals can avoid the type of jurisdictional dispute that is so common in both older and more modern programs.

Pupil-centered teaching can bring teachers close to a guidance program. The name or the particular history of the effort is not important. The interests of the faculty should determine the nature of the guidance response. Guidance is only a partner in the process of education and has no claim to infallibility or omniscience. Mature teachers and guidance persons will find ways to combine their efforts and to help students profit from their joint efforts. Students are the center of both guidance and the educational process.

SUMMARY

This chapter has presented specific methods for involving the faculty member in the total guidance effort of any school or college.

Academic advising has been explained as part of the traditional student-faculty relationship. Guidance persons need to serve in a resource relationship to the faculty but must not attempt to usurp or weaken this relationship. Faculty members can be helped to participate in guidance efforts in each of the major tool areas of guidance. Counseling, testing, group work, and case-study efforts all contain meaningful roles for the faculty. Specific assignments that faculty may assume are available and can be identified with faculty assistance.

Service areas of guidance have also been examined as conceptual units of guidance within which faculty members and guidance personnel can combine their efforts. Orientation and articulation programs, parental conferences, student activities, and housing programs have been explained in detail as representative of the many areas in which faculty can broaden and deepen their relationships with students.

Several types of cooperative designs for faculty and guidance functioning have been described in the latter sections of this chapter. The major applications of the team system in its many forms have been analyzed to show its value for faculty and guidance efforts. A descriptive analysis of the concept of pupil-centered teaching concluded the chapter.

REFERENCES AND SUGGESTED READINGS

Adelson, Joseph, "The Teacher as a Model," in Nevitt Sanford (ed.), *The American College,* New York: Wiley, 1962, 396–417.

Anderson, A. Edwin, and J. H. Banks, "Team Approaches to College Teaching," Research Bulletin No. 5 of the Peabody Public School Cooperative Program, Nashville, Tenn.: George Peabody College for Teachers, 1958.

Anderson, R. H., "Team Teaching," *National Education Association Journal,* L (1961), 52–54.

Anthony, V. A., *et al.*, "The Team Approach to General Education," *Junior College Journal,* XXVI (1956), 319–327, 405–410.

Cantor, Nathaniel, *The Teaching-Learning Process,* New York: Dryden Press, 1953.

Clinchy, Evans, *Profiles of Significant Schools: Rich Township High Schools,* New York: Educational Facilities Laboratories, 1960.

Clinchy, Evans, *Schools for Team Teaching,* New York: Educational Facilities Laboratories, 1960.

Commission of Teacher Education, *Helping Teachers Understand Children,* Washington, D.C.: American Council on Education, 1945.

Connecticut State Department of Education, *Team Approach in Pupil Personnel Services,* Hartford, Conn., 1955.

Creedon, Gertrude C., "A House Plan for Newton High School," *The Educational Forum,* May, 1960.

Dillon, Carl L., "Taylorville, Illinois, Senior High School Uses Tape Recorders, Team Teaching, and Large-Group Instruction to Improve Staff Utilization," *Bulletin of the National Association of Secondary School Principals,* XLV (1961), 179–188.

Durrell, D. D., "Implementing and Evaluating Pupil-Team Learning Plans," *Journal of Educational Sociology,* XXXIV (1961), 360–365.

Durrell, D. D., *et al.*, "Adapting Instruction to the Learning Needs of Children in Intermediate Grades," *Journal of Education,* CXLII (1959), 1–78.

Fleming, C. M., *Teaching: A Psychological Analysis,* New York: Wiley, 1958.

Glanz, Edward C., *Case Studies of Faculty Counseling Programs* (dissertation), Teachers College, Columbia University, 1950.

Glanz, Edward C., "The Faculty Team in General Education," *Journal of Higher Education,* XXVI (1955), 389–392.

Goodlad, J. I., "Experiment in Team Teaching," *Elementary School Journal,* LIX (1958), 11–13.

Gordon, Ira J., *The Teacher as a Guidance Worker,* New York: Harper, 1956.

Guetzkow, H., *et al.*, "An Experimental Comparison of Recitation, Discussion, and Tutorial Methods in College Teaching," *Journal of Educational Psychology,* XLV (1954), 193–209.

Hanvey, R., and M. S. Tenenberg, "University of Chicago Laboratory School, Chicago, Illinois, Evaluates Team Teaching," *Bulletin of the National Association of Secondary School Principals,* XLV (1961), 189–197.

Ivy, Allan F., *A Study of Two Types of Guidance Staff Organization and Their Relationship to Student Perception and Use of College Guidance Services,* Cambridge, Mass.: Harvard University dissertation, 1959.

Jensen, L., *et al.*, "Eighth Grade Team Teaching at the Roosevelt Junior High School," *California Journal of Secondary Education,* XXXV (1960), 236–243.

Johnson, R. H., *et al.*, "Extensive Study of Team Teaching and Schedule Modification in Jefferson County, Colorado, School District R–1," *Bulletin of the National Association of Secondary School Principals,* XLIV (1960), 78–93.

Johnston, Edgar G., *et al.*, *The Role of the Teacher in Guidance*, Englewood Cliffs, N.J.: Prentice-Hall, 1959.

Jones, Mary C., "A Comparison of the Attitudes and Interests of Ninth-Grade Students over Two Decades," *Journal of Educational Psychology*, LI (1960), 175–186.

McCollum, T. E., *et al.*, "Snyder, Texas Continues Team Teaching," *Bulletin of the National Association of Secondary School Principals*, XLIV (1960), 2–7.

McKeachie, W. J., "The Work of the Teacher," in Nevitt Sanford (ed.), *The American College*, New York: Wiley, 1961.

Mahoney, Harold J., "The Team Approach to Pupil Personnel Services," paper presented to the Interprofessional Conference on Pupil Personnel Services in the Public Schools, Washington, D.C., Sept., 1961.

Miller, Frank W., *Guidance Principles and Services*, Columbus, Ohio: Merrill, 1961.

Miller, T., and M. S. Morris, "Critique of the Team Approach," *Education Forum*, XXIV (1960), 207–208.

Montagu, Ashley, *Education and Human Relations*, New York: Grove, 1958.

Murphy, Gardner, *Human Potentialities*, New York: Basic Books, 1958.

National Association of Secondary School Principals, "And No Bells Ring" (2 ½-hour films), 1960.

National Society for the Study of Education, *In-Service Education*, Fifty-Sixth Yearbook, Part I, Chicago: University of Chicago Press, 1957.

Noall, M. F., and G. Rose, "Team Teaching at the Wahlquist Junior High School," *Bulletin of the National Association of Secondary School Principals*, XLIV (1960), 164–171.

Noall, M. F., and L. Jensen, "Team Teaching at Roosevelt Junior High School, Duchesne County, Utah," *National Association of Secondary School Principals Bulletin*, XLIV (1960), 156–163.

Pierson, George, "The Parable of the Teacher-Counselor," *Personnel and Guidance Journal*, XXXI (1952).

Redl, Fritz, and W. W. Wattenberg, *Mental Hygiene in Teaching*, New York: Harcourt Brace, 1959.

Runkel, Philip J., "Communication Between Counselors and Teachers," *Newsletter of the National Council on Measurements in Education*, IV (1961), 1–4.

Sarason, S., *et al.*, *The Preparation of Teachers: An Unstudied Problem in Education*, New York: Wiley, 1962.

Sharp, O. Louise (ed.), *Why Teach?*, New York: Henry Holt, 1957.

Sivon, A., *et al.*, "Experiment in Team Teaching," *Ohio School*, XXXIX (1961), 34–35.

Stetson, G. A., and J. P. Harrison, "Junior High School Designed for Team Teaching," *American School Board Journal*, CXL (1960), 38–42.

Strang, Ruth, *The Role of the Teacher in Personnel Work* (4th ed.), New York: Bureau of Publications, Teachers College, Columbia University, 1953.

Taylor, Harold, "The Teacher at His Best," in R. M. Cooper (ed.), *The Two Ends of the Log*, Minneapolis, Minn.: University of Minnesota Press, 1958, 149–163.

Thelen, Herbert A., "Role-Playing in the Classroom," in R. M. Cooper (ed.), *The Two Ends of the Log*, Minneapolis, Minn.: University of Minnesota Press, 1958, 243–253.

Waller, W., "What Teaching Does to Teachers," in M. Stein *et al.* (eds.), *Identity and Anxiety*, Glencoe, Ill.: Free Press, 1960.

Watson, N. E., "Glenbrook High School, Northbrook, Illinois, Projects on Internship, Large Classes, Team Teaching, Teacher Aides, and Language Laboratory," *Bulletin of the National Association of Secondary School Principals*, XLV (1961), 51–56.

Wise, William M., *They Come for the Best of Reasons: College Students Today*, Washington, D.C.: American Council on Education, 1959.

Wrenn, C. Gilbert, "Student Personnel Services and Teaching," in R. M. Cooper, *The Two Ends of the Log*, Minneapolis, Minn.: University of Minnesota Press, 1958, 273–281.

Wrenn, C. Gilbert, *Student Personnel Work in College, with Emphasis on Counseling and Group Experiences*, New York: Ronald, 1951.

Zirbes, Laura, *Spurs to Creative Teaching*, New York: Putnam, 1959.

SCHOOL ADMINISTRATION AND GUIDANCE

THE ISSUE. The perspectives of both administrators and guidance personnel are affected by the vantage point from which they view one another. The school administrator, whether a superintendent, principal, college dean, or president, often seems to be cast in the role of the villain by guidance workers. School administration in turn may often feel that guidance persons prefer the role of the prima donna. Today's schools cannot afford to defend mutual misunderstandings that preclude the effective functioning of administrators or guidance workers. It is only in period pieces such as *East Lynn* that the villain is constant in his evil intent and the sweet heroine never grows up.

Guidance persons need to recognize their obligations and responsibilities to the educational administration. Turnabout is not only fair play, but is also necessary for a mature organizational structure. Administration has corresponding obligations and responsibilities. Neither guidance nor administration can afford to demand that the other be more gracious and more willing to cooperate. Guidance and administration depend upon more than an equal contribution by each.

The mutual need to understand and the natural misunderstandings that can occur color the relationship between guidance and administration. Guidance workers can grow in perspective as they come to understand the nature of educational administration. Administrators, with the aid of guidance persons, can learn that guidance can help solve many pervasive educational problems.

The educational administrator faces a large task in organizing and administering a school program. Problems of heating and ventilation vie for his attention with problems of selection for a new cur-

CHAPTER FIFTEEN

riculum program or for National Merit Scholars. The administrator cannot afford to focus upon any single aspect of education, for he is given the authority and has accepted the responsibility for the entire educational effort. Guidance, as one of the major units of education, is a responsibility of the administration. Guidance personnel need to recognize that their obligations to education include an awareness of the total process as well as of the contributions that they can make in their own area.

The concept of service needs to be placed ahead of privilege in the relationship of guidance and educational administration. Guidance persons must fully understand their own obligations to the administrative leaders of the school program. After, and only after, guidance fulfills its own responsibilities can it begin to be concerned about whether or not administrative offices have understood and appreciated its needs. Several specific services that guidance can offer administration can be identified. Each of these areas will be examined in detail. What guidance can expect from administration is then a legitimate issue. After each party to the process of implementing guidance is able to face its own responsibilities, a higher level of cooperative service to students and to the community is possible. The integration of effort is the last major unit of the chapter.

GUIDANCE SERVICES TO ADMINISTRATION

Guidance attempts to offer a meaningful point of view about education and students that can be implemented at all levels of education. The acceptance of this offer has made it necessary for guidance persons to clothe their proposals with meaning and specific applications. The pioneers of guidance and the philosophers of education who helped make guidance an accepted portion of modern education did not spell out the details of appropriate guidance practice. These proposals and details of operation are the responsibility of the present-day guidance person as guidance is integrated into the local educational system.

Guidance can and must offer aid to administrators in specific areas of operation. Such areas are programing, budgeting, administrative record-keeping, reports that provide permanent data, and evaluation directed toward program revision.

Programing

A primary responsibility of guidance to educational administration is the offer of a specific program. No guidance textbook can ever anticipate all the specific issues existing in a particular community or school unit. The guidance person must assess the situation and be able to describe the services that guidance can offer. The actual program may be developed in cooperation with faculty and administration, but views of what guidance can be must be available.

The questions asked by the buyer from a mail-order catalog are partially appropriate. What will it do? How will it work? How big is it? How much will it cost? What changes must be made in order to use it?—these are questions that any administrator has not only the right but the responsibility to ask. The administrator, like the mail-order purchaser, must decide for himself whether and in what manner the item can be paid for. Frequently the description of guidance potential must include several levels of cost. It may not be possible to afford the best the first time. The need to provide sound foundations for future development is in the mind of the administrator; the guidance person must similarly consider a developing program.

The following types of questions will be in the mind of an administrator who is assessing guidance for possible use in his school or college:

1. What are the dimensions of the program of guidance?
2. How many persons will be required to staff it?
3. What space will be needed to house the personnel, records, program units, and other elements of the proposed program?

4. How will guidance relate to the present educational program of the school or college?
5. What will be the probable outcomes of such a program?

When the administration can answer these and other questions, it will be possible to measure a potential guidance program against the total educational environment that will surround it. The possible effect upon pupils, parents, and the community can be compared with the cost and availability of guidance. The guidance worker needs to understand that an administrator is not acting or thinking simply from a personal perspective but must fulfill the total responsibilities of his office.

A new guidance program will demand careful and detailed consideration of all possible program combinations. Later changes will reflect earlier discussions and can also be outlined for an administrator.

The questions and issues that administrators must face in examining guidance are no different from any other educational decision. The administrator will hopefully realize the importance of guidance and have a thorough understanding of its nature. He must then place a potential guidance program within a total educational effort. Guidance personnel can help administrative persons serve guidance better as they help them fulfill their own responsibilities.

Budgeting

Guidance personnel must be able to offer administrators a detailed breakdown of the costs of the suggested guidance program. Several approaches are possible and frequently it is desirable to combine several budget proposals. Total cost, cost per pupil, and unit cost figures will permit an administrator to assess the immediate costs of a program as well as long-range or overhead expenses.

Cost figures will be needed for all of the suggested areas of guidance. Any general list cannot be exhaustive but merely suggestive. Local needs and traditions or specially planned emphases may require additional budget data. Cost data need to be supplied on factors such as:

1. Salary total for guidance personnel
2. Materials needed for programing:
   a. Furniture
   b. Telephones
   c. Special items such as files, recorders, etc.
   d. Printing or cost figures for records
   e. Special rooms for special activities (testing, groups, etc.)

3. Program costs:
   a. Testing schedule (including purchase, scoring, profiling)
   b. Routine supplies
   c. Awards or prizes
4. Student services:
   a. Orientation and articulation
   b. Student activities (including athletics)
   c. Placement
   d. Student publications
5. Administrative costs:
   a. Secretaries
   b. General office help

Administrators will be able to supply fixed costs such as heat, light, and other factors that will necessarily be included in a total budget. Again, the guidance person needs to understand the position of the administrator and to help in supplying data that will answer the practical question of "How much?"

Record-Keeping

Student records are a normal part of any guidance program. Frequently guidance records will be separate from those kept by the administration. Whether or not the two types of records are integrated, records of an administrative type should be available and regularly provided for administrators.

An account of the daily, monthly, and annual number of student counseling sessions offers a meaningful statistical picture of one of the major areas of guidance. The student demand for opportunities to talk with counselors is a reflection of many factors. Definite time cycles can be derived from year-to-year records. Counselor activity is also better understood as student appointment loads are analyzed. Such data are typical of the records that administrative persons need to understand guidance.

Group counseling sessions, group meetings, and other types of group activity are also a meaningful dimension of guidance within a school. Data about numbers of students involved in such activity provide important information. Brief statistics about the numbers of students accepted into a college or the number of students placed within a community are also relevant. The guidance administrator who is able to assess his own program accurately will learn much about his program and also supply useful data to educational administrators.

Administrative records are subject to much misuse and abuse.

The two most common problems are those of inaccurate or inappropriate fact-gathering and distorted use of data. The number of times students come into an office, even to inquire the time, may be recorded. It is questionable whether such information is necessary or desirable. Secondly, administrators should be careful in the use of many data. Guidance and educational administrators cannot assume that the counselor who sees the most students is necessarily the most effective. Factual data that are gathered for administrative purposes are similar to psychological test data in that the problem of use is separate from that of the collection of data.

Evaluation and Change

Guidance programs should be dynamic and reflect the needs of current rather than former students. The demands of changing societal patterns need to be reflected by improved practices in the school program. The preparation and placement of stable grooms is an unlikely task for modern public schools. However, adequate preparation to help students live in a space age is equally far in the future in some static school programs. The placement program of a school is one area in which current community practice must be accurately reflected in the daily work of the guidance program. There are other areas, less obvious, that are perhaps even more important. Guidance programs need to assess themselves constantly against current and future objectives. Change that is planned should grow out of an accurate knowledge of present successes and failures. Evaluation and research can supply the data for such knowledge.

Educational administrators need to be involved in the process of evaluation and change. Change in a program is similar to the establishment of a new program. Administrative needs are real and defensible, and evaluation is an appropriate concern for educational administrators. Guidance persons who attempt to hide inadequate areas of operation or to furnish less than complete information to administrative officers ignore their responsibility to the school as the ultimate consumer of the educational program. Static mediocrity can flourish in isolation; however, alert and aware educators can build and change programs to create excellence in policy and procedure.

Reports and Permanent Records

Student records become part of the life of a school or college. To obtain data about students, even years after such data are collected, is an expected right of the community. Administrative record-keeping and report-writing can furnish the institution with a permanent organizational record that can provide a continuing service regardless of personnel change.

Guidance personnel, like all others in education, are subject to organizational and geographical changes of work assignments. However, if guidance is to be a professional area of education, there needs to be a continuous operation and a dependence upon previously developed programs and policy.

The leader of a guidance program needs to supply accurate annual reports. The data that are obtained from evaluations, administrative record-keeping, and other appropriate sources can be summarized each year in systematic reports to administrative officials. Such records provide a continuous record for new personnel. Too frequently guidance workers move into a new situation and assume that they must start afresh, as if no guidance program had ever existed. If the existing guidance program is so faulty that such an assumption is necessary, the school, students, parents, and most of all the guidance profession are hurt.

Systematic records and reports to the administration can provide an effective spur for guidance persons to maintain appropriate records for their own use. Each source can share in the benefits of a systematic operation of a guidance program.

ADMINISTRATIVE CONTRIBUTIONS TO GUIDANCE

Educational administration involves more than signing of diplomas and officiating at graduation ceremonies. The varied tasks of the educational administrator need to be understood by guidance personnel as they work within a school or college. Guidance personnel can share the administrative burden of principals, deans, and other officials as they function as partners in the total educational process.

Aiding administrators involves neither being an assistant administrator nor giving aid and comfort to the "enemy." Both these dangers have marked the practice of guidance personnel who have not understood the mutual dependence of all areas of an educational enterprise. The most meaningful type of aid is provided by an understanding of the problems and issues that everyone on the staff must face. Obsequiousness is not necessary or desirable in understanding administrative tasks. Decisions may need to be made, and the guidance worker can help if he can appreciate the need.

Final responsibility for educational decision-making usually lies with the chief administrator. Whether or not school is to be dismissed because of a bomb threat, whether a major increase in the budget will be requested, whether new counselors will be added to the staff—dozens of such issues must finally be decided by administrators. Guidance persons need to make the most meaningful possible recommendations in their own area. No administrator can have all the facts nor make decisions in a vacuum. The recommendations of professional guidance persons can help an administrator in programing. Perhaps the decision may be to ignore the recommendation; however, the recommendation is still useful and appropriate.

Guidance workers need to know their own program areas, to supply data to administrators, and to offer meaningful recommendations about policy decisions. An understanding of the joint tasks of guidance and education can permit guidance to seek administrative understanding of its program in return.

Guidance as a professional part of education can expect understanding and appreciation from an administrative unit in many areas. The basic philosophy of an educational program can provide the basis for a functioning guidance program. Proper facilities, an adequate budget, clerical and administrative assistance, and a demand for excellence of service are additional contributions that guidance can expect from educational administration.

Educational Philosophy

The educational philosophy of the administrators of a school has practical implications. Actual program development and practice are outgrowths of philosophical belief. Educational administrators are thus among the prime users of educational philosophy. Whether or not every act may appear to be determined by the philosophical principles of the school or college is not the issue; long-range plans and perspective on day-to-day decisions can reveal the dimensions of a philosophy. Even a confused and contradictory philosophy will be revealed by the practices of administrators.

Guidance workers should assume that the role of guidance within a system will be related to the philosophical beliefs of the administrators who permit, encourage, or retard its development. When the establishment or change of a guidance program is contemplated within a school, a detailed examination of the primary philosophical principles of administrators and guidance persons is necessary.

Guidance workers may defend the concept that counseling should be carried on only by highly trained psychologists. Administrators may not share such a view. It is important to recognize that many of the conceptual patterns of guidance are still controversial. When guidance persons are unable to agree among themselves, it is questionable whether administrators should be expected to adopt a particular philosophical view without question. Perhaps the administrator will agree with the view of the guidance director, but such agreement is coincidental rather than theoretically necessary.

Guidance personnel can assume that the administrative leaders of a school or college will understand the nature of guidance and that the relationships of guidance and education will be accepted. The techniques and specific practices that may be adopted to achieve the objectives agreed upon may differ from school to school and from administrator to administrator. When support and understanding do not exist, the guidance person must attempt to create it. However, a guidance person alone cannot remake a school or a community.

The necessity for the support, understanding, and leadership of administrative officers cannot be overstressed. "An institution is affected by the long shadow cast by its leader," is the way one university board of trustees member phrased this belief. The importance of administrative leadership in helping guidance fulfill its position within an educational scheme is the major reason for recommending that the guidance worker spend considerable time discussing the dimensions and practices of a possible program with the administrators with whom he will work. When administrators and guidance persons have diametrically opposed views of what guidance is and what it can do, the guidance program and the student will be the losers. Earlier chapters stressed the unique relationship that guidance seeks with faculty members. The relationship that exists with teachers extends into guidance-administration cooperation. Guidance cannot exist in itself and go its own way. A guidance effort will affect the entire school program as well as all of the persons within that school. If guidance seeks to go its way alone with no concern for its relations with the other component parts of the school, guidance is handicapped from the beginning.

Facilities

The physical facilities needed for guidance may be of many types, sizes, and shapes. Zeran and Riccio (1962) outline many of the pressing problems that face guidance in assessing physical facilities. The administrative responsibility in this area is clear.

Guidance persons need to recommend physical appointments in accord with over-all program plans. The effect of environment should be seen in all such decisions. The physical arrangements of a guidance program can determine many of the influences of guidance. The guidance office that is next door to the principal's office will connote something different from the guidance office that is placed in the newly painted basement.

The location and concomitant atmosphere that is established for the guidance office are elements that the guidance worker must understand from his knowledge of sociology and psychology. An administrator will permit as much latitude as possible in most situations if he is fully apprised of the reasons underlying the recommendations of a guidance committee or director. Much has been written about the "image" that modern corporations present to the public. Guidance persons have long been aware of such concerns in establishing a central guidance office, counseling rooms, testing areas, and group meeting rooms. Administrators have to be helped to understand the rationale for any recommendation.

Counseling programs present many special physical problems. Privacy is highly desirable when possible. Early guidance programs were often forced to settle for superficially private settings provided by room dividers and screens. However, student issues become public concerns when privacy is denied counselors. Such supplies as office files and telephones can also be included in administrative budgets when their importance is clearly understood.

Clerical and Administrative Aid

"Our Kuder Profiles are all colored with a distinctive color for each vocational interest area." Statements such as this frighten administrators about the clerical needs of guidance. Administrators may not know what the Kuder Profile is, but he can recognize that clerical help is being misused.

The other extreme is also common in some schools. Both teachers and guidance workers have been forced to spend literally hundreds of hours in scoring intelligence and achievement tests. Guidance workers must usually labor alone in such schools to score other tests, which are considered to be "just for the guidance department." Guidance workers need to help administrators understand that test scoring, profiling, and the development of norms are regular parts of test expense. Many test publication houses are beginning to offer package plans for all types of tests. To consider that the price of testing is only the price of a reusable test booket and answer sheets is to deny the meaning of such tests.

Guidance persons need to outline clearly their clerical and administrative needs. Typing of recommendation letters is as necessary as the coloring of Kuder profiles is unnecessary. Each guidance activity will need to be ranked within the over-all program to determine the amount of clerical and administrative assistance that is appropriate. This task is one for guidance, not for administration. The recommendations of the entire guidance program need to be examined, rather than presenting each problem as a separate issue for administrative decision.

An estimate of the total budget for secretarial and clerical help is a service that guidance persons must supply to administrators. How much of the recommended budget can be implemented is a decision that the principal or dean must make. However, the apportionment of the established budget within a guidance program is the province of the guidance administrator.

"Great Expectations"

One of the most significant services that educational administrators can render to guidance persons is to hold "great expectations" for the guidance program.

> Our Dean always stressed that he wanted our program to be the best that could be developed. He was constantly raising questions about how the program could develop next year and in the years ahead. We were not always blessed with all of the budget support that we needed. Our achievement was not always what we all wanted. However, within what we had money-wise, he always expected the best.
>
> Probably in his heart he wasn't sure that our program was the best possible one. Still, he always wanted the best for us and would do all within his power to get it. His attitude pervaded all of our program and helped us to seek better ways of doing things. His expectations helped us to have a better program every year [College counselor].

The climate and atmosphere that administrative officers create for their colleagues and institutions is a practical advantage or handicap that pervades all guidance as well as all education.

Decisions

Guidance programs can prosper when decisions are made by administrators who view the entire school program in perspective. One of the most difficult environments within which guidance may have to operate is the vacuum of lack of decision. Program development and future effectiveness may be stymied by inactivity. The indecisive or vacillating administrator can act as a brake, not only on guidance, but on an entire situation.

Guidance administrators and workers need to help administrators in this area of operation. Too frequently guidance workers are prone to bring problems rather than planned solutions to administrators. The administrator has his share of problems and does not appreciate the "dumping" of issues. Guidance workers, most familiar with their own problems, need to assess the total situation and be prepared to offer alternative solutions to difficult problems. The administrator can then consult with the guidance person to seek the preferable solution.

The privilege of seeking decisions from an administrator is often overlooked by a new guidance worker. The student who is planning to run away from home and has left a note for the counselor is a case in point. Should the parents be notified immediately? Should the police be first to know, or should they be notified at all? Is the student seeking attention through his actions? What is the responsibility of the guidance counselor, and of the principal? The questions multiply. The guidance director may be best equipped to assess all of the various dimensions of the problem. The guidance person may decide that Plan A is best, but the principal needs to know and to approve. The guidance person can bring his assessments and planned actions to the principal and discuss the entire situation with him. The school is represented by the principal; the counselor may represent the pupil. Guidance persons need to share not only problems but also the possible solutions with administrators.

INTEGRATION OF EFFORT

The ideal level of cooperation between administrators and guidance personnel may not exist within a particular school. How may this issue be faced and resolved? How may specific problems be solved to provide for the development of a positive atmosphere for integrated effort? What are the responsibilities of the guidance person when he has determined that professional integrity has been compromised? What can a guidance worker expect from an administrative leader when he has failed or indulged in unethical practice? These issues are practical and at the same time reflections of the philosophy of all participants in an educational effort.

Problem-Solving

When professional persons disagree upon policies, practices, or planned actions, decisions must be made. Within a guidance staff or program such issues can often be resolved through discussion and fact-finding; when such processes are inadequate it is usual for the senior administrative officer of the guidance group to make the decision. Similar steps are appropriate when problems between guidance and administration are encountered. The educational administration of a school must keep the entire effort of the school or college in perspective and must have the authority to render a final decision.

Decision-making authority arises out of the concept of office. When Mr. Jones, the Assistant Principal, offers the opinion that there will not be enough space for another counselor's office without restricting the space needed for classrooms, he may be speaking as Mr. Jones or as the Assistant Principal in charge of space allocation. His opinion as Mr. Jones may be no better than that of the Director of Guidance. As the Assistant Principal in charge of space problems, his opinion is presumably based upon a detailed study of the problem. The guidance person does not have the right to question the integrity of the decision. It may be possible to find another solution to provide a new counselor's office. The search for a solution will hopefully involve both Mr. Jones and the guidance worker. But the concept of authority must always govern such problem-solving.

Someone may suggest that perhaps Mr. Jones is making his decision on a personal basis. If such is the case—and to be certain of such a fact is not easy—the guidance person is still required to accept the professional opinion of the educational officer. If the decision is based upon personal bias, the facts will need to be uncovered and the problem solved by the principal or superintendent. The guidance person cannot be the keeper of the moral seal of the school.

Such extreme situations can only reveal principles. They cannot be assumed to be expected practice. Acceptance of the good will and professional conduct of another person is the only basis upon which mature problem-solving can exist. Foundations of professional ethics and practice permit the more positive problem-solving tactics of (1) voting, (2) compromise, (3) consensus, and (4) block-and-gap consensus.

VOTING. The tradition of voting is well established in the fabric of our culture. The positive values of voting are well known, but its negative features for specialized professional practice are not clearly understood. Voting in a democracy is based upon the belief that all persons qualified to vote have an equal right and responsibility to share in the determination of the actions of their government.

Professional practice is based upon detailed accumulation of specialized knowledge and fact. The budget director in a college is not usually equipped to vote upon action recommended for a pre-psychotic student. Even a well-prepared coach who is a member of a personnel staff may be equally unprepared to vote on such a question. Experience within a school program is a factor in the granting of a franchise for faculty members. Schools and colleges have varying requirements for new faculty before they can become voting members of a group. Both education and experience are factors in solving professional problems. A vote is often a poor way to express these two elements.

Voting on an issue may or may not be appropriate. The question of the qualification of the voters is only one problem. It is sometimes not realized that a vote tends to divide the group into parts. The vote may solidify the positions of the parties to the discussion before any decision should be reached. The vote within a professional group on issues of professional practice is not as simple as it appears. The group and its leaders need to be fully aware of the issues in using voting techniques to solve problems.

COMPROMISE. The process of compromise is an ancient and honorable problem-solving technique in the American tradition. Some problem-solving specialists have pointed out the dangers of compromise. Some participants may remain "unreconstructed." Their opinions can be altered only through education and experience rather than any by decision-making device.

The necessary components of compromise are the good will of participants and the desire to solve a problem within professional policies and practices. Compromise can be useful when used carefully.

CONSENSUS. The opportunity to discuss issues long enough to arrive at a complete consensus is desirable but seldom possible. The members of a group frequently agree to disagree and tend to resist the attempt to force agreement at any cost. Whenever consensus is possible, it is desirable. However, leaders and group members need to recognize when other types of decisions and problem-solving actions are more appropriate. A drive for consensus at any price can increase the division it was trying to overcome.

Block-and-Gap Consensus. Perhaps the most useful process of problem-solving for professional practice is the attempt to define specific areas of agreement and to build upon them. Frequently groups and individuals focus upon the areas of disagreement, and differences become magnified as personal status, prestige, and power are involved to defend a point of view. Avoiding the areas of disagreement, even temporarily, can provide the opportunity to concentrate upon areas where agreement and positive action is possible. When all areas of agreement have been utilized, methods may be evolved to deal with disputed problems.

The Crisis

No school or college guidance program can long exist without being involved in an administrative crisis. A guidance program will seldom even be able to come into existence without resolving various critical situations. An administrative crisis may be as simple as the disagreement between the director of guidance and the principal over the need for a telephone or as complex as the "discipline crisis" referred to in Chapter Eleven. *Disagreement* may be a better word than *crisis,* depending on the degree of conflict. An examination of true crisis may reveal principles that can be useful in resolving simple disagreements.

Professional practice is the basis of mutual respect among school personnel. If one assumes that policy, practice, or recommendations are based on other than professional ethics, it is impossible to work. To be sure, it is also necessary to recognize that a professional person is also an individual with human frailties. The issue is the premise and emphasis upon which one operates. The trust that can arise out of assumptions of integrity can bind professional persons to one another. To assume that personal avarice, bigotry, or family aggrandizement is the foundation for educational practice is to anticipate defeat before one starts.

Whenever it appears that professional ethics are not being observed in interpersonal and program problem-solving to the degree that work cannot proceed, the professional person has no alternative but to resign. Normally such a resignation will take effect at the end of an academic year. Students are the primary consumers of an educator's effort and they should not be made to suffer for education's weaknesses. The lack of professional ethics in another can never excuse the failure of a guidance worker to function in a professional manner. The guidance person who may resign as an outcome of a crisis still has an obligation to perform as a professional until he leaves the institution.

The resolution of such an extreme situation offers a guide for the solving of more common difficulties. The standard of professional performance is the assumption that must guide practice. Partial excursions down the "primrose path" of nonprofessional behavior by guidance persons, administrators, and teachers are not only possible but, if one recognizes the nature of human beings and understands some of the principles of psychology, they are inevitable. Such problems must be solved as they occur and yet must not color the entire decision-making process. However, an accumulation of such incidents can lead to the decision to seek other locales for one's efforts.

The possibility of resignation should not be used as a weapon to bludgeon others. A professional person neither offers a resignation as a threat nor refuses to honor the resignation of another. A resignation is the most severe step possible and can be offered only as a last resort.

Cooperative Effort

The administrative leaders of a school or college theoretically should have no basic disagreements with guidance persons that cannot be worked out to the satisfaction of all parties. Guidance and education are related processes that depend upon the effort and maturity of those who seek their common goals. However, philosophical differences of opinion may lead to varied actions and plans. To admit that there is no single common philosophy that can guide and direct the entire educational effort of a free society is not to admit any failure, but to recognize that the essential nature of a free educational system is dynamic rather than static. A democratic pattern of problem-solving demands the most mature type of professional practice and personal security. Educators are charged by their supporting society to lead in the process of showing the younger members of the society that democratic patterns of life are worthwhile and effective. Administration, guidance, and faculty must serve as models of democratic action within the school.

THE FUTURE

What the future may hold for guidance and education is unknown. The dimensions of the future will reflect some of the efforts of the past. However, no practice can be entirely rooted in the past. The traditions of a free society have shown the vitality of an open-ended educational philosophy and practice. Guidance workers face the challenge of the future as they attempt to show that guidance can be a full-fledged partner in the educational process. The newcomer is always more "under the gun" than the more traditional members of a group. The newcomer of education, guidance, has shown amazing vitality in its growth during the last half-century. The future of guidance will hopefully reflect the best of the past while adapting to the developments that still lie ahead.

SUMMARY

School administration and guidance have many areas of practice that overlap. The need for both parties to recognize their mutual dependence and the profit that can occur from integrated effort are the underlying principles that have been offered in this chapter.

Guidance has obligations to all educational administration as it attempts to fulfill a professional role in education. The dimensions of this responsibility have been examined in detail. Programing, budgeting, administrative record-keeping, reports and permanent records, and constant evaluation and change are the major dimensions of the guidance responsibility to educational administration.

The mutual relationship of guidance and educational administration has been further delineated as administrative services to guidance have been presented. A broadly conceived educational philosophy, physical facilities, clerical and administrative aid, "great expectations," and decisions are positive factors that guidance persons and programs can expect from educational administration.

The integration of effort of both administrators and guidance personnel depends upon the ability to resolve disagreements and crises. Methods of problem-solving have been presented to make possible the integration of effort that education demands from both parties. Voting, compromise, consensus, and block-and-gap consensus were the four major methods of problem-solving offered. The future relations of administrators and guidance workers have been briefly viewed.

REFERENCES AND SUGGESTED READINGS

Allen, Richard D., *Organization and Supervision of Guidance in Public Education,* New York: Inor, 1937.

Block, Virginia L., "The Secondary School Administrator Views the Counselor," *California Journal of Secondary Education,* XXX (1955), 335–342.

DuPont, Henry J., "The Principal and the Guidance Program," *Educational Administration and Supervision*, XLIII (1957), 359–363.
Furry, R. D., "Better Staff Utilization in the Guidance Program in Springfield," *Bulletin of the National Association of Secondary School Principals*, XLIII (1959), 266–269.
Kitano, Harry H. L., "Perceptual Changes in School Administrators Following Consultation About Problem Children," *Journal of Counseling Psychology*, VIII (1961), 129–235.
Parker, Kenneth, "Location of Guidance Facilities Within the School Plant," *Personnel and Guidance Journal*, XXXIV (1957), 251–254.
Rosecrance, Francis C., and Velma Hayden, *School Guidance and Personnel Services*, Boston: Allyn & Bacon, 1960.
Shear, Bruce, "Physical Facilities for Pupil Personnel Services," *The American School Board Journal*, CXX (1950), 24–27.
Stripling, R. O., "How About Physical Facilities—Are We Selling Student Personnel Services Short on Space?" *Personnel and Guidance Journal*, XXXIII (1954), 170–171.
Zeran, F. R., and A. C. Riccio, *Organization and Administration of Guidance Services*, Chicago: Rand McNally, 1962.

PARENTS, THE COMMUNITY, AND GUIDANCE

THE ISSUE. Counselors and teachers alike are often inclined to believe that student problems would be much less intense if the youngsters did not have problem parents. "Oh, if it weren't for the parents!" sometimes seems to be a cry to create orphans.

A plea for different background forces is second only to the hope that parental influence could be lessened. The child who must overcome a tragic or debilitating community environment is often viewed as a pawn of his society and culture. Teachers and counselors who focus upon the individual often decry the burden that family and community may impose upon the unwitting child. The classic elements of the Greek tragedy seem to fall, unwanted, upon the child-hero.

Can a child truly ever leave his family behind? Is it possible for a child to seek brighter horizons and cross the bridge into another world with never a look behind? Is it a victory for a child to leave behind his family and community as he exploits his own full potential for a new life? Or are there roots and interlacing connections among family, community, and the individual that can never be really removed or even masked? Should a person be encouraged to leave one world to enter another? What loyalties are beyond all change? How can the community help?

Guidance enters into the mysterious world of personality and culture as an individual is helped to explore the meaning of his own freedom and responsibility. Who will direct the guidance person who must seek to guide others?

Guidance personnel of all types are close to the student as he attempts to establish connections between his family, his school, his

CHAPTER SIXTEEN

community, and his future life. The individual himself is the only link between all of the primary groups that influence his life. The family, the church, the community, peer groups, and all similar forces are vital factors in the development of a life and in the individual's evaluation of that life. Guidance persons are not all-knowing and all-wise. How issues can and should be resolved is not easily known. Yet the student who is seeking to find answers for himself will turn to the counselors, teachers, and guidance workers who are available. Guidance has offered to help the person as problems of life are solved. The influence of family and community is present in all problem-solving. Guidance workers need to understand the dynamic nature of these forces and the dimensions of their influence.

THE MEANING OF THE FAMILY

The family is the primary unit within which the development of personality takes place. The family also serves to pass on to the new member of a society the accumulated culture of that society. Family patterns may differ from society to society, with matriarchal lineage or with sibling relationships that differ from our own western civilization. But most cultures in the world recognize the primacy of the family unit. The essential facts of the family structure in our Western civilization are biological, psychological, and cultural. Economic and historical features are added in other cultures of the world. The nature of the relationship between the family and the guidance person is one of the most confusing questions in guidance. Each of the elements of the family will be examined in turn. Guidance persons need to understand and appreciate the biological, psychological, and cultural dimensions of the family.

The Family "Facts of Life"

A child may have biological parents and psychological parents. Birth may be an accident or a result of planned and desired family life. The actual biological fact of parenthood cannot be changed or renounced by the child or the parents. Psychological parentage is often, but not necessarily, identical with biological parenthood. The psychological parents of the child are those who function as parents. Adopted parents, substitute parents, or even institutional parents can serve in such a role. The child will come to know as psychological parents those persons or institutions who serve as his parents.

The adopted child who, late in childhood or adolescence, first learns he is adopted can experience a cruel conflict. His biological parents exist, or did exist. His psychological parents have little or no biological relationship to him. Many children have expressed this feeling by saying, "I know that she is my mother—but she really isn't my mother." Confusion about both the real and the adopted parent can be expressed by this phrase. The child may feel loyal to his biological or his psychological parent. The biological parent may even be idealized. The facts of two types of parenthood cannot be legislated, loved, or otherwise driven out of existence.

The effects of parents of both types upon children are omnipresent. The child who marries an idealized image of a parent reflects such influence. The child who denies the image and marries one who varies from it is similarly affected. Even the child who runs away from home to avoid his parents' influence affirms their effect. There is no escape from the psychological effects of parents upon children. The cycle is carried on from generation to generation. Therapists tell us in theory and research that only through acceptance and understanding is it possible to free oneself from parental influence.

The "results" of family life are encountered in all life situations. More significant is the reaction of the person to the facts as they exist. Sally, a high school senior, revealed the "secondary reaction" described by psychologists as she talked of her father: "My father has been an alcoholic as long as I can remember. He is a heavy weight hung around the necks of all of us. Mother has learned to live with it and has helped all of us children to do the same. I don't hate him; I don't love him. He is my father and there is little that I can do about that."

Sally had learned to accept the facts of her life. She was neither bitter nor did she pity her father. She accepted him and perhaps understood more of his life than she told. She was an excellent student with no obvious personal problems. She achieved honor grades and after graduation from college married and has begun to build a meaningful life of her own. A psychiatrist could doubtless find many levels of understanding and meaning in Sally's relation to her father and her family.

Other children who have had to deal with alcoholic parents may turn to membership in the WCTU. Some may, through complex learning processes, hate the facts of alcoholism but follow the same trail themselves. The facts are not necessarily determining forces; the way a person learns to live with and deal with the facts is the vital consideration. The same gas flame can harden water into ice cubes and melt butter in a frying pan.

The Lifelong Family

One lives with one's family throughout life. Only the beachcomber who buries himself in the anonymous South Pacific islands hopes to cut himself off from all family ties. These ties may be masked and denied, but they cannot be destroyed. It is more realistic and desirable to examine the more common situation in which the person makes his own way in life and yet continues to carry his family with him.

The family which we all have with us is not simply the hereditary line as illustrated in the famous Jukes and Kallikaks of genetic research. The lifelong family ties that are common to all arise out of the child's potent learnings. Wordsworth's statement "the child is father of the man" is a psychological fact. The family is the arena for the learning of customs, mores, ideals, values, and religious beliefs. These elements of personality are more a part of the individual than his hair color. One need not reflect the exact beliefs of the family to acknowledge their effect. The influences may be reversed, distorted, or repressed, but they are always present in some form. The person grows and develops within the family environment; learned patterns of problem-solving and behavior become just as much a part of the person as the family "inheritance" passed on through genes and chromosomes.

Parental Surrogate?

The kindly dean of women or counselor who offers to be a mother to each child takes unto herself the privilege and honor that the legal structure of our society permits only rarely. Parents are legally and morally responsible for their children until these privileges are suspended by death or legal action. Guidance persons, deans, principals, even relatives cannot usurp this responsibility even if they judge it to be desirable.

The law has upheld the privilege of a school or college to act whenever parental permission or consultation is impossible. Legal issues or emergency problems of illness or accident may require the action of a representative of the educational institution "*in loco parentis.*" The principle has been established that educators, if they have acted in their best judgment, and only when parental consultation was impossible, have acted properly. That such a principle applies only to emergency action is important to note. The philosophical and moral issue is clear; guidance workers, administrators, friends, relatives—no one can replace the parent.

Guidance workers may be placed in the position of ethical responsibility for another person as parental deputy or surrogate. Clearly, the privilege and responsibility must not be assumed without careful thought. The issue is seldom clearly drawn, and guidance persons need to examine the facts from various perspectives before acting.

The Role of Guidance

The guidance person must tread carefully as counselor or as administrator whenever parents are involved. The need to help students learn to be free and responsible may create problems in student-parent relationships that are not easily resolved. The line between improper freedom and the opportunity to learn for oneself is variable and dependent upon particular circumstance. The student who wishes to withdraw from college without his parent's consent or knowledge, the high school junior who skips school and does not want his parents to know that he has been caught, the junior high school student who wants to drop or elect a new course without consulting his parents, and the elementary pupil who hides examination grades all illustrate the problem of the counselor. What are the obligations of guidance persons to parents and to students?

The dignity and integrity of the individual are not values that come into being at any special age. The development of these concepts is cumulative and constant from the earliest years of life. Adults who compromise these essential elements of personality at any age do the child, themselves, and the parents a disservice. Children are under the moral and legal guidance of their parents until they either leave the home or attain a specified certain age, which varies in different states.

However, the recognition of this principle may hurt the child when parents are themselves petty, vain, or childish. Guidance workers can attempt to help parents understand their children, but they cannot substitute for parents.

A positive view of the relation of guidance to students and to parents is reflected in the policy of the guidance program described below:

> Our policy is to treat the person as a mature individual.
>
> We recognize the rights and privileges of parents but attempt never to compromise the integrity of the student. Parents are requested to establish appointments through their children's efforts and in any case with the knowledge of their children.
>
> Parents often want to talk over their children's progress or problems, but often say "Please don't tell Johnny that I have been here" (or "called you on the phone," or "written you"). We do not refuse to talk with parents, but encourage them to talk over the conference, of their own accord, with their child. We seek to have the same privilege—that is, to inform the pupil that a parent conference was held. Exact details do not need to be revealed; the student, we believe, has the right to know that the conference has taken place and, in general, what was discussed [Director of Pupil Personnel Services].

The child becomes the person. Dignity and integrity are not attributes of age and experience.

Extreme problems can also reveal the nature of the relationship necessary for parent-guidance problem-solving. A typical college problem is the student withdrawal:

> Jane had been talking with me for several weeks. She was fed up with college and wanted to withdraw. Her parents had given her the "option" of leaving home, living on her own, supporting herself, and no longer being a member of the family, or going to college. She had wanted to marry a high school boyfriend. She endured college for six weeks.
>
> "Mike is picking me up in front of the college in an hour. I came in to tell you that I was leaving. Thanks for everything; I know what I want to do."
>
> Her home was several hundred miles away and she had not told her parents anything about her plans. I asked her if she planned to notify her parents. She said "No."
>
> I explained to her that the college would have to notify her parents if she didn't. I asked her to call her mother from my office. She didn't want to do it, fearing her mother's reaction and influence, even over the phone. I offered to call and requested that she stay in the office while I did so. She finally decided that she would call her mother and conveyed my offer to talk with her parents if they wished to meet with me. She left and waved from the front door [College Dean].

A public affairs pamphlet on mental illness once recommended that if a parent must be removed to a public or private mental hospital his dignity and integrity must not be compromised. The words and actions at such a critical moment may have much to do with the ultimate return of the parent to the family circle. Nothing that is said or done should reflect a spirit that denies family membership or love. The British definition of a gentleman as one "who never knowingly inflicts pain or hurt upon another if it can be avoided" is also appropriate to the handling of extreme problems by guidance.

Guidance bears the responsibility to develop positive programs of cooperation between the school and the home. "Parents' Night" and visitor's days are not enough. Positive programs for seeking out the aid and assistance of parents in the education of their children are necessary. Some schools provide for special group discussions between parents and students before the opening of school. Planned periods of parent-teacher conferences, followed by scheduled conferences with counselors or other guidance persons when needed may also be established. Colleges often provide parents' manuals, special letters about college activities, and regular patterns for parental meetings and conferences.

A remarkable story of parent-school cooperation was told in New Haven, Connecticut several years ago:

> We wanted a school for our end of town. The local school authorities and the town officials all agreed with us that it was needed. Finances always prevented the realization of our dream. Our neighborhood started a campaign to get the school. We had meetings, wrote letters to the newspapers, visited school officials, established committees and developed a "post card plan." We wrote post cards to the mayor and he got them by the bagful. (He later admitted that he hated to see the morning mail because of the deluge he knew would be there.)
>
> The school was built, but the parents did not relax their efforts. Every teacher had several "room mothers." A teacher could call upon more parents than she needed for any field trip. Mothers were available for supervision of the class whenever the teacher had to meet with the principal and in every way the parents were involved in their school [School Counselor].

Guidance workers need not institute "post card plans," but they should not fear the meaningful involvement of parents in the school. Guidance programs can seek methods to make education a cooperative effort of the professional educator and the parents. The student gains from the combined contributions of all.

THE ENVIRONS OF LIFE

Each individual lives within a personal community bounded by his own perceptions of himself and his world. Each person is also bounded by a subculture made up of his immediate environment and the larger community or society. The many communities that encapsulate the person are not only determining forces in his life but also resources that can be tapped as guidance and education attempt to aid him in his growth and development. Each of the many elements that affect the person and any efforts of guidance to help him must be understood both as determining and as rehabilitative forces.

A Personal Culture

Each person exists within an encapsulated world made up of personal and environmental forces that are only partially understood. Each individual develops a concept of self that is the core of his personality. The adjustments, attitudes, and values that are acquired through life are the raw materials out of which this concept of self are created. Each action of the individual is partially determined both by his opportunity to act and by his concept of himself.

Each child in a family experiences a different family life. An oldest son has an experience different from that of a youngest daughter. The effects of environment are transmitted and interpreted by those who are close to the individual. In turn the person interprets his own experience and incorporates it into his concept of himself through his values, attitudes, and adjustments.

Although clear-cut answers are still not available, it is evident that the heredity, temperament, and environment that each person possesses are unique and particular in their effect upon his development. No single factor exists in isolation, nor can it produce effects that are not colored by related forces. Each person's culture is a private dimension of life. The examples of Tom and Clara demonstrate this fact in strikingly different but theoretically identical ways.

> Tom told his story at a meeting of guidance workers. He was among a group of four "classical underachievers" who had changed their school standing from the bottom of the class to the top. He described a return visit to his home community over a Christmas vacation:
>
> ". . . and then I decided I would visit the old hang-out. During

high school we had always been able to find a crowd at 'Mike's.' They were there. I sat down with the bunch that I had hung around with for so long. After a few pleasantries they kind of ignored me. They were at the usual topics—girls, dates, money, living it up.

"As I listened, I wondered why I had yearned so hard to belong to this group when I was in high school. Some of them had been athletes but others were just 'big operators.' I had been on the fringe of the group last year and was always impressed with this talk. Now it just seemed to be small talk. I tried once or twice to raise another issue; they didn't want to talk about anything else.

"I didn't stay too long. I slipped away and walked home. I wondered why it had meant so much to me to belong to this group last year. I wondered why I didn't care now."

Tom went on to explain why he believed he had changed. He recognized that his environment at home had not changed, but that he had.

Tom had been caught in a web of forces that had helped to determine his values, attitudes, and adjustments. He had established new values and patterns in college and was startled to return to his old world and to find himself as an observer. All college students experience such events to some degree; Tom had isolated his own experience and related it to his changed attitudes toward learning and study.

Clara was the "new girl" in school. Her family had moved to the town during the summer and she became a member of the seventh grade. Her problems had come to the attention of the counselor:

"Clara had lived in a community where everybody was different from what she found in our town. Her father had done very well in business. The family bought a new home in our town and was living in a world almost unrelated to her past existence. She was very confused and hurt by what had happened.

"Clara had been popular and well accepted by her peers in her previous school. But she found that her language, dress, attitudes, and ideas were so very different from those of her new peers that she didn't know what to do. She knew and used every four-letter word in the book. She was much more interested in boys than were the other girls. The girls in her new school simply didn't understand much of what she was talking about. The parents in the town soon recognized what was involved and discouraged their daughters from associating with Clara.

"Clara soon began to understand what was going on, and to change her behavior. She was quick, bright, and a likable youngster. She made the grade with the girls before the year was over. The problem of her family, as a total unit within the community, was not as simple."

Clara had not changed; her environment and personal world had been changed by the family move. She found that her previous methods of solving problems and establishing interpersonal relations were no longer adequate. Her personal world had changed, and she found that to be accepted she had to change also.

The issues and influences of personal or environmental change or conflict are innumerable. The forces that arise out of the individual culture within which one lives are intermingled in psychological, sociological, and cultural areas. The changes which impinge upon the individual vary; the personal reaction to such forces is a product of the force and of the person's previous reactions to that force. Kvaraceous (1959) sees these changes and the resultant conflicts between social class, environmental force, and cultural determinants as primary causes of juvenile delinquency. Guidance workers, if they are to understand and help young persons, need to be able to assess and evaluate the effects of all such factors and of the person's possible responses.

The Community

Each person "comes from" somewhere. Our common speech reflects this fact as we describe our friends, family, or ourselves. Where are we from?

Environmental forces are not simple. The community of the person is made up of his personal culture as well as of the more usual dimensions that sociology describes as a subunit of society. The young Chinese student who comes from the Chinatown section of the large city demonstrates the problems involved. At any age, he carries with him his physical characteristics that arise out of his heredity. He is a product of a particular environment that has provided him with his languages, his accent, his food preferences, and his attitudes toward family, school, and adults. His environment has colored all of his previous life and will help to determine his future. He faces possible discrimination because of his community affiliations. He himself may be a "bridge" between two worlds. He may undergo a constant conflict that arises out of his connections between two worlds, or he may have no problems.

Every student brings to school similar community affiliations. The physical characteristics, cultural mores, and customs may not be as identifiable or as noticeable as those of the young Chinese student, but the stamp of the community is written upon the life of every child who is its product. Pat, earlier described in his relations to Maia in Chapter Three, particularized his own community to a counselor: ". . . and I never want to cross that bridge when I get through college. Every morning I come across it and enter into a world that is different from the world in which I live. I like this new world and I don't want ever to return to the old. That bridge is symbolic for me. As soon as it is possible for me I am going to stay on this side of the bridge and never go back across." Counseling with Pat involved many discussions about the bridge and its meaning. Although his family lived on the other side of the bridge, he was unable to think of them when he visualized himself in the future. He loved his family and wanted them to share his possible success, but he knew in his own mind that he did not want to share his future with his family or community. He gradually faced his problems as he began to understand his family, his community, his future goals, and the interrelationships of all of these very real elements in his life. Only slowly was he able to recognize that he would always have to cross that symbolic bridge, even if he could remove its actual existence.

The personal culture and the private community of each person are very real forces in his life. The individual may deny, or wish to ignore, the significance of the forces that have helped to mold and partially determine his existence. But when the individual begins to understand and to appreciate these elements, he begins to create his own concept of freedom and responsibility. Each person becomes free when he is able to choose alternatives from among the possibilities that are present in his life. Man begins to be free as he is able to recognize the forces that have determined him.

Guidance in the Community

Guidance personnel need to be aware of the forces and influences that help to create the students who seek help within the school. A creative guidance program must be aware that the individual exists 24 hours a day, not merely the few hours that are spent at the school or college. A good many colleges have recognized this problem and have begun to explore the educational potential of the dormitory. High schools have also attempted to structure their facilities in accord with the nonacademic influences isolated in the lives of students. The Newton and Andrew Warde High School House Plans (see Chapter Eleven) are examples of such efforts.

Guidance workers have often tended to restrict their areas of operation and concern to the "in-school" life of the student. The school social worker may be more equipped to assess and to explore the problems that arise outside of the institution. Guidance persons who are blinded to the significance of community forces will be unable to appreciate fully the lives of their students.

Guidance workers may be able to learn more of the students in a school as they learn more about the personal cultures and the communities from which their students come. Statistical reports can provide the skeleton of the problem, but the actual understanding necessary for effective relations with students may need to arise out of case conferences that accurately portray the lives of the students who are attending the school. Actual counseling experience with individuals or groups of students with similar and different backgrounds can also bring out the full flavor and meaning of student lives. By abstracting out of student lives the essence of personal growth and development, the guidance worker can appreciate the variable forces that play upon the particular students that compose the total student body of any school at any level.

THE RESOURCES OF LIFE

Each individual's personal culture and private community is also a part of a wider concept of societal life. The Chinese second-grade pupil or the high school student who belongs to the Church of Christ of Latter-Day Saints (Mormon) may have specific advantages and resources which can be discerned from a study of the community.

Our Western civilization has developed the concept of a "public community" through governmental and private service agencies that supplement and may substitute for traditional family, clan, or communal sources of aid. The local hospital, mental health clinic, the Visiting Nurse Association, the Family Service Association, and many similar agencies are supportive of individuals and groups who may need assistance.

Guidance persons have seldom been as well prepared as social workers to help individuals learn from and share in the resources of their community. The local social service agencies may offer more sources of aid than are normally within the known referral techniques of guidance workers. If young members of a subsociety may be partially determined, molded, or handicapped by their membership within a group, they have every right to expect that their membership may in turn be of possible aid to them. The key in such issues is the recognition of the appropriateness of aid and assistance in accord with need and with the design of a community service.

Students, parents, and guidance persons recognize the opportunity to attend state-sponsored universities, technical institutes, junior colleges, and technical high schools as one of the privileges of group membership. However, many specialized schools are unknown to parents and students. Medical resources are less well recognized and in turn less utilized. Business, cultural, social, and many miscellaneous services are also available to members of individual communities. Guidance persons, as they learn more of the surrounding environment that supports and colors the lives of individual students, need to learn also about the advantages and resources that can be used to help each person in patterning his own life. The major types of community resources that are usually available to individual students, as well as to particular groups, will be briefly analyzed. Educational, medical, business, cultural, and miscellaneous social service agencies can all aid individuals.

Educational Resources

American public schools are among the best examples of community provision for individual growth and development. Education and guidance have arisen out of a public concern for aid to individual members of a society. The sponsoring society provides such help, not only as a matter of long-range survival, but out of a belief in the importance of the individual.

Public education has grown to include 12 years of opportunity, culminating with the completion of high school. Many states and communities have provided further general, technical, and business education through two-year and sometimes four-year college programs. Such provisions have become common knowledge through mass communication systems and family experience. However, students and their families frequently may not be aware of available specialized or technical education below the college level. The "trade school" has largely gone out of fashion. Many newer technical high schools and regional programs now offer up-to-date curriculums to serve students talented in areas other than the college preparatory curriculum.

Almost every state and many communities are now experimenting with various types of institutions for post-secondary-school training. Some grant general degrees, while others are organized to offer specialized training programs in specific job areas. Guidance persons and programs may be virtually accused of malpractice if such resources are available and they are unable to offer up-to-date and appropriate information for students who seek, or may be able to profit from, such factual knowledge.

Special programs beyond the regular school system are normal concerns of guidance persons. It is also necessary to be aware fully of all resources within the school itself. Large city school systems may develop unusual services of which members of the staff may not be aware. Guidance persons need to be clearing-houses for such internal services.

Medical Resources

Physical and mental health problems are everyday items in the guidance program. The child who slips on the ice and breaks a leg, the convalescent pupil who must restrict his activity, the retarded child—the list could be expanded to include hundreds or even thousands of problems. The guidance program needs to serve as a referral resource for the stricken child and as an articulation service for returning pupils.

The school program may provide for home visits by teachers, state aid for tutoring, and counseling assistance for the family, the pupil, and the faculty. Other schools or colleges may place the entire responsibility upon the guidance program. Regardless of the local custom or the legal requirements of the town or state, there is need for guidance personnel to be thoroughly knowledgeable about all available resources.

Many communities will have an adequate number of physicians, surgeons, and various medical specialists. Area hospitals may provide a method of coordinating the resources of the communities served. School programs for physical examinations, immunization schedules, special community service programs such as polio prevention, and individual immunizations are traditional public health measures. The guidance program can not only cooperate in making such community projects more efficient, but can also use such activities to become familiar with the local resources. Personal knowledge of the medical personnel and the clinic units within a community can provide for integrated action when the need demands.

Regional effort in mental hygiene has permitted the establishment of child guidance clinics, mental health projects, and related programs. The school guidance worker will become an important referral and articulation resource for such units. Elementary guidance personnel in particular are frequently specialized in social work techniques.

An Eastern community with a population of hundreds of thousands attempted to create favorable relations among all community resource persons:

> We had a meeting about every two months. There was no formal organization with officers or by-laws. Our programs were designed to inform and to permit all members of the group to learn how to co-operate with others. Psychiatrists, physicians, social workers, psychologists, general practitioners, hospital personnel, and school guidance persons took turns presenting information about their own specialities.
>
> We tried to know one another on a first-name basis and kept the focus upon our services and not our status and prestige. Some persons would come only once or twice and others were regulars. Our referral procedures depended upon picking up the telephone and calling someone that we knew [YMCA Counselor].

The size of the community can permit variations on such activities. Local guidance organizations such as the American Personnel and Guidance Association also serve such purposes by planning programs to inform their membership and help them promote integrated services.

Social Services

The variety of community service agencies that are available to offer aid to individuals in large urban centers is almost beyond belief. The guidance person is again in a key position to help pupils and their parents receive assistance whenever community resources are available. Each community has a particular pattern of social service agencies that can be understood with experience and effort. Resources in the following areas are usually available in every community: (1) Service Clubs and Fraternal Organizations, (2) Mental Health Agencies, (3) State and Federal Organizations, (4) Occupational Agencies, (5) Private agencies and schools, (6) Religious groups, (7) State Departments of Education, (8) Children and Youth Agencies, (9) Aid to Dependent Children, and (10) Universities and Colleges. Rural areas may have them on a regional basis; large urban centers may duplicate services on a city, state, and national level. Each of these service agencies may offer special help for retarded or legally blind pupils, the gifted student, or the juvenile delinquent. All are entitled to aid. Frequently these agencies may be unable to aid in a particular problem, but will know of other sources of assistance.

The guidance worker will seldom know all such sources from personal experience. But he must know how to find the necessary aid. Directories of social agencies are available in all public libraries. Handbooks developed by the community are often available. Each community poses a special problem that must be faced as a guidance program is developed and keyed to meet local needs. A city directory and even the Yellow Pages of a local telephone directory can be helpful. The Boston Yellow Pages lists almost 200 agencies that can be of help to a guidance person in the greater Boston community. The scope and depth of such community services can be glimpsed from a small section of the Boston listing:

Big Brother Association
Big Sister Association
Boston Aid to the Blind, Inc.
Boston Baptist City Missions Society
Boston Children's Friend Society
Boston Children's Service Association
Boston Guild for the Hard of Hearing
Boston Legal Aid Society
Boston Nursery for Blind Babies

SUMMARY

The integration of guidance into the family and community is a responsibility that is as important as the coordination of guidance services within a school. The nature of the family and the community will determine the appropriate philosophy that guidance persons can utilize in helping individual pupils.

The psychological, sociological, and anthropological meaning of the family has been assessed to provide perspective for guidance workers. The family is a lifelong possession of the person. Guidance persons who are faced with responsibility, both legal and moral, for action with students need to understand the role of guidance with the family. These issues have been presented for study.

The environment within which each person lives is made up of varying levels and dimensions. These environments have been viewed first as a personal culture, then as an immediate community, and further as larger social units that guide and determine major portions of each person's life.

The chapter closed with a review of the resources that exist within every community. These resources are different aspects of the same environment that was previously examined as a determining force in the life of the person. Help can be provided by the family, the town, the region, the state, and the nation. Guidance programs and guidance persons must integrate their service and understanding of the pupil with the surrounding and supporting climate of his life.

REFERENCES AND SUGGESTED READINGS

Brownell, Baker, "The Community in College Teaching," in R. M. Cooper (ed.), *The Two Ends of the Log,* Minneapolis, Minn.: University of Minnesota Press, 1958, 282–292.

Conant, James B., *The American High School Today,* New York: McGraw-Hill, 1958.

Conant, James B., *Slums and Suburbs,* New York: McGraw-Hill, 1961.

Cunningham, E. C., "My Child's Teacher and I," *Phi Delta Kappan,* March, 1956, 254–258.

Cuony, E. R., "Helping Parents Understand Adolescence," *Bulletin of the National Association of Secondary School Principals,* May, 1961, 27–31.

de Huszar, George B., *Practical Applications of Democracy,* New York: Harper, 1945.

Essex, Martin W., "Bring Community Resources to the Guidance Program," *The Nation's Schools,* XLIX (1952), 48–49.

Gibson, Robert L., "Pupil Opinion of High School Guidance Program," *Personnel and Guidance Journal,* XLI (1962), 453–457.

Gillin, John, *The Ways of Men,* New York: Appleton-Century-Crofts, 1948.

Gordon, Ira J., "Guidance in the Small Community: The Role of the Teacher," *Understanding the Child,* XXIII (1954), 10–15.

Gordon, Ira J., "The Teacher as a Guidance Worker: Understanding the Child's Community," *Understanding the Child,* XXIV (1955), 15–19.

Hays, Donald G., and John W. M. Rothney, "Educational Decision-Making by Superior Secondary School Students and Their Parents," *Personnel and Guidance Journal,* XL (1961), 26–30.

Hoyt, Kenneth B., and J. W. Loughary, "Acquaintance with the Use of Referral Sources by Iowa Secondary School Counselors," *Personnel and Guidance Journal,* XXXVI (1958), 388–391.

Jacobs, P., *Changing Values in College,* New York: Harper, 1957.

Kammerer, Gladys M., "The Organization of Child Welfare Services," *Public Administration Review,* XVIII (1958), 28–36.

Kvaraceus, W. C., *et al., Delinquent Behavior: Culture and the Individual,* Washington, D.C.: National Education Association, 1959.

Kvaraceus, W. C., *et al., Delinquent Behavior: Principles and Practices,* Washington, D.C.: National Education Association, 1959.

Lynd, R. S., and H. M. Lynd, *Middletown,* New York: Harcourt, Brace & World, 1929.

Malinowski, B., *A Scientific Theory of Culture,* Chapel Hill, N.C.: University of North Carolina Press, 1944.

Mariner, A. S., *et al.,* "Group Psychiatric Consultation with Public School Personnel: A Two-Year Study," *Personnel and Guidance Journal,* XL (1961), 254–258.

Mueller, W. J., and J. W. M. Rothney, "Comparison of Selected Descriptive and Predictive Statements of Superior Students, Their Parents, and Their Teachers," *Personnel and Guidance Journal,* XXXVIII (1960), 621–625.

National Society for the Study of Education, *Community Education,* Fifty-Eighth Yearbook, Part I, Chicago: University of Chicago Press, 1959.

National Society for the Study of Education, *Mental Health in Modern Education*, Fifty-Fourth Yearbook, Part II, Chicago: University of Chicago Press, 1955.

Ojemann, R. H., "The Role of the Community in the Mental-Health Program of the School," in National Society for the Study of Education, *Mental Health in Modern Education*, Fifty-Fourth Yearbook, Part II, Chicago: University of Chicago Press, 1955, 125–144.

Warner, W. L., and P. S. Lunt, *The Social Life of a Modern Community*, New Haven: Yale University Press, 1941.

Wrenn, C. Gilbert, "The Culturally Encapsulated Counselor," *Harvard Educational Review*, 1962.

GUIDANCE AS A PROFESSION

Guidance has only recently begun to come of age as a professional discipline. Many would still dispute whether guidance has achieved maturity as a profession within education. Yet guidance must examine its professional ethics, its structure as a group of practicing specialists, and its relationship to the entire concept of American education. The issues of professional versus nonprofessional practice must be faced in viewing guidance as a distinctive process.

The methods by which individuals may become professional guidance workers are being more strictly controlled. This development has aided guidance and at the same time has accelerated the creation of a small, tightly knit, professional in-group. The issues and unsolved prob-

PART FIVE

lems raised by these developments must be faced as guidance is viewed within the over-all educational structure of any community. The prospective professional guidance worker can legitimately ask about the educational experiences and skills that he must develop if he selects guidance as his vocational goal.

The education of guidance persons is an important issue to the consideration of professional stature and practice. As the basic problems within one of these areas are solved, the basic issues within the other area may be clarified and organized for solution.

Part Five presents the issues inherent within education for guidance and within guidance as a profession.

EDUCATION FOR GUIDANCE*

THE ISSUE. A central need in guidance, as has been made clear in the preceding chapters, is the necessity for a philosophy that will directly relate the functioning of the school counselor to his education. That such a universally accepted philosophy does not now exist is a primary reason for the failure of the general public and of educational leaders to accord a truly professional status to the guidance worker. Two vociferous critics of the present situation, state the problem in these words: "Thanks to the lack of focus within the guidance area as a whole and the many possible focuses within the specialized area of vocational guidance, the program within any particular school is usually centered upon whatever the counselor in charge considers to be his area of strength. . . . Only in the guidance programs which emphasize counseling is there a beginning of truly active concentration upon the individual student. Even within some counseling programs, however, the focus upon the individual gets lost in a morass of other emphases" (Barry and Wolf, 1962: 218–219).

Perhaps the most surprising aspect of the present situation is the fact that, despite the uncertainties implied by the lack of an overriding guidance philosophy, the public (i.e., parents, the press, the Congress) has been willing, possibly even too anxious, to place extraordinary confidence in guidance. The needs of an increasingly complex world of work have dictated that guidance counselors carry out certain functions in every school. School administrations have responded to the demand by supplying ostensible guidance programs. But they have seen the functions of the counselors in such programs in various ways. By and large, the tendency has been to emphasize the immediate needs as

* This chapter is written by James F. Penney, Associate Professor of Education, School of Education, Boston University.

CHAPTER SEVENTEEN

expressed by parents and employers of high school students: "guidance" is to get students into college and to place graduates in jobs that need filling.

Personnel to fulfill the expectations of such narrowly conceived guidance programs have usually been recruited from classroom teachers, subadministrators, and peripheral educational persons. In meeting the immediate needs of college admission and job placement, such persons have in many cases been able to function adequately and occasionally even splendidly. But such short-run success has obscured the fundamental issue of the place of guidance in education and the needed preparation of guidance personnel for the long future of guidance.

Until very recently there has been a surprisingly limited consideration by leaders in the guidance field of the function and philosophy that should dictate the education of guidance workers. Training programs have too often been dominated by considerations of how long the training should take, the techniques to be used, and the proliferation and elaboration of visual aids designed to provide students with information about fields of work and occupational training programs. Certification requirements have also often served to inhibit the development of creative training programs rather than to provide flexible regulations to be changed to accord with the new and developing concepts of professional guidance. Even those programs that emphasize the counseling aspect of the guidance process have tended to concentrate on the details of technique and the establishment of satisfactory client-counselor relationships, and they have paid relatively little attention to the more fundamental issues of the long-range objectives for counseling and guidance in general and of the role of the counselor in the school. Whether the guidance counselor is "guide," psychologist, test administrator, therapist, assistant principal, or part-time teacher has not been settled, as evidenced by school practices. Until it is, the most appropriate educational preparation for the position cannot be readily determined.

FUNCTIONS OF GUIDANCE IN THE SCHOOLS

Although this book has centered on the role that guidance and guidance counselors should play in American education, a review and summary of the basic postulates presented earlier is in order, so that what will be said concerning the education and preparation of the counselor may be seen in immediate and clear perspective.

Guidance programs exist in schools to aid students in the positive development of attitudes, value systems, adjustment skills, and decision-making competencies; in short, to help to develop free and responsible citizens. Such aspects of learning can only be partially handled as subject matter in classrooms. Guidance must therefore be seen not merely as facilitating the work of the teacher, but as providing an additional educational dimension that is essential to the development of individual potentialities.

A functioning guidance program has three basic characteristics that differentiate it from any other aspect of education: (1) it is dedicated to aiding students to individualize and to make personally meaningful the academic, social, and ethical aspirations of the institution; (2) it takes a holistic approach to the individuals it serves, in contrast to the tendency of other phases of school experience to pay attention to the intellectual, athletic, or social-stimulus characteristics of students; and (3) it is differential and flexible, in that it has available a variety of approaches and facilities which may be drawn upon as needed in individual cases, with the result that what is done for a particular student is not likely to be needed for all students. The "program," then, cannot be one that has been formulated in a distant ivory tower or in the superintendent's office or even in a committee meeting; it is a combination of services that may be used as needed to eliminate blocks to self-understanding and self-direction and to provide resources for prevention of personal, mental, or social imbalances.

The objectives of guidance can be summarized as being (1) to increase the accuracy of the individual's self-perceptions, (2) to increase the accuracy of his environmental perceptions, (3) to integrate his self-perceptions with perceived environmental realities, (4) to present relevant information when needed, and (5) to improve the individual's ability to make and execute plans. This is not to say that guidance attempts to reinforce the social pressure toward conformity. On the contrary, guidance is interested in aiding the student to broaden his interests, aspirations, and knowledge so as to enable him to move ever closer to the psychological functioning that Abraham Maslow has called "self-actualizing." In short, the student is aided to change, and to change in ways that will be personally rewarding, socially productive, and morally satisfying. Such a view of guidance and the functions of the counselor implies that counselor education must be centrally concerned with developing both the personal characteristics and the professional competencies of guidance practitioners.

PERSONAL CHARACTERISTICS OF GUIDANCE WORKERS

Guidance has long recognized that the kind of person the guidance worker is determines in large measure the kind of relationships he is able to establish with students. Without effective relationships at the intimate personal level, guidance techniques, no matter how skillfully applied, will be of very limited value. Williamson has entitled a provocative discussion on this point "The Counselor as Technique" (1962:108–111). In examining personal characteristics, the essential elements would seem to be the guidance worker's concept of himself, his value structure, and his concept of the nature of man.

What the counselor[1] does during the counseling process is not only a measure of his techniques and methods but is also a measure of the self-concept which determines his goals and objectives as a counselor. By virtue of his acceptance of position of counselor, he implies that he holds certain attitudes toward himself. Among these attitudes might be (1) that he has certain knowledge and skill that he can make available to others, (2) that young people in the course of development are likely to profit from the formation of a close relationship with one possessing

[1] *Counselor* and *guidance worker* are used interchangeably by many writers. *Counselor* is used most frequently in this chapter from this point on to simplify the issues under consideration.

his abilities, (3) that he is secure enough himself to deal objectively with the concerns of others, (4) that he has the acuity to perceive the needs and feelings as well as the words and actions of others, (5) that he has (at least implicitly) formulated theoretical constructs that adequately explain his own and others' behaviors, (6) that he accepts responsibility for his own actions and is willing to share the burden of responsibilty for the actions of others, (7) that he himself is psychologically healthy enough to recognize and control the effects of his own needs as they influence his behavior as a counselor, (8) that he is able to accept thoughts and behaviors of others that he himself finds illogical, unrewarding, or erroneous, and (9) that he has enough confidence in his ability and nature to proceed with his professional tasks in the face of criticism from teachers, school officials, parents of clients, and clients themselves. In short, he is pleasant, competent, strong, and secure.

Values

Values are implicit in every human action. A counselor cannot escape his own value system in counseling and in other relationships with students, teachers, and parents. Even though his moral and ethical standards may not be explicitly clear to clients, or even to himself, they influence his reactions to what he is told by others, his emphases, his choice of objectives, and his counseling techniques.

Other nonindividual value systems also help determine the counselor's methods and objectives. The beliefs which prevail within the school concerning the aims of education, the nature of children, and the purpose of guidance will to some degree determine the objectives toward which the counselor is expected to direct his efforts.

The mere recognition that values determine behavior fails to meet the issue unless the values, assumptions, and goals underlying specific actions are also investigated and as clearly understood as possible. Smith makes the point explicit:

> . . . a person acts responsibly to the extent that his behavior meets at least three conditions: First, he is aware of the value context in which he is acting. His goals have been subjected to conscious scrutiny, and his behavior is explicitly related to his values. Second, his choices are made in the light of as adequate an understanding of their probable consequences as he can achieve. The relations that he assumes between means and ends are examined critically, not taken for granted. Third, he is ready to be judged in terms of his choices of both ends and means, and has the flexibility to reconsider both. In a word, he assumes responsibility for his decisions and actions [1954:513].

Such a definition of responsibility implies that counselors need to understand their objectives clearly and to examine their professional and personal behavior in terms of its relevance to those objectives. It also implies that, since values cannot be divorced from the guidance relationship, it becomes part of the counselor's function to assume some responsibility for the value formation and education of his students. This function in turn reinforces the necessity for the counselor to understand implicitly and to be prepared to handle explicitly the values he espouses in his behavior.

Conceptions of the Nature of Man

Historical views of the nature of man may be reduced essentially to two fundamental positions: that of Augustine, in which man is seen as basically hostile, antisocial, and carnal; and that of Rousseau, in which man is viewed as originally perfect and unsullied, but corrupted through the influence of an imperfect society. For purposes of discussion, Freud can be simplified to exemplify the first view, and Carl Rogers can stand for the second. In this century a third position has been identified—the "neutralist" or "behavioristic." It sees man as a "blank page" to be filled, shaped, and directed by experience and by the controls exerted by men and the social order. J. J. B. Watson and B. F. Skinner can exemplify this position.

What approximation of these fundamental views the counselor takes will be crucial in determining his approach to his work and to his student clients. The Augustinian-Freudian view would appear to suggest that students need controlling, supervision, and strong direction, since their task is to compromise their natures so as to make a satisfactory adjustment to the demands of civilization. The Rousseau-Rogers position suggests a very different counselor role: nondirection is not only justified, but is mandatory as well. Aims and goals become only problems of identification, and counseling becomes a process of enabling natural virtue to emerge from beneath the repressions of a restrictive society. A neutralist view of the nature of man implies that counseling as a phase of education is reducible to the provision of positive reinforcements for "good" decisions and actions and negative or nonreinforcements for "wrong" decisions or actions. In this view, the counselor is a manipulator and controller of destinies.

Values and conceptions of the nature of man are, then, crucial issues for the counselor. They cannot be neglected in his education, for they determine the kind of person he is, and this in turn determines the kind of influence he will exert on students and others with whom he works.

Education for Personal Character Traits

It is a simple matter to list desirable qualities and characteristics which the counselor should possess. It is quite another matter to specify the educational program that will contribute to the development of the sorts of persons described. Human beings have been at the business of education for thousands of years, and America in the twentieth century has an almost blind faith in the power of education to produce "good" individuals. Yet there is still little direct evidence of the effects of education—as opposed to training—on the personality. To talk of the specifics of education is often to be reduced to espousing generalities and occasionally banalities.

The counselor's education needs both breadth and depth—breadth in the sense that he is aware of the varieties and diversities of human experience that are involved in the formation of cultures and personalities, depth in the understanding of his own nature. A comprehensive grounding in the social sciences—psychology, anthropology, sociology, comparative cultures, history (particularly cultural and ethnic group history), and government—is essential. The formulation of a self-concept that enables the counselor to place himself in the stream of culture and history is a primary need. It seems probable that an examination of the major philosophical points of view concerning the nature of man would aid in self-concept formation.

But the self-concept, ideas about the nature of man, cultural objectivity, and relativism do not come only from the social sciences. Many of man's greatest insights concerning himself and his fellows have come from the pens of poets and novelists and from the brushes of painters. Music has tremendous powers to affect man's deepest thoughts and to move him to heights of creativity and to depths of despair out of which have come new understandings. The "compleat counselor" should have had experiences in these areas of human endeavor too.

It has become a truism that one must know himself if he is truly to be able to help and understand others. Indeed, there are those among mental health educators who are convinced that no man can be an effective therapist or counselor unless he has himself experienced intensive therapy by which he plumbs the depths of his own being. This may put the case too strongly for the school counselor, but there remains the very real need for counselors to examine their own motivations, limitations, and capacities with great care before beginning their work with young people. This stipulation is probably met most successfully through the study of the psychology of personality, with additional opportunities for personalizing the objective data of formal classroom work in this and related subjects. The possibility that the objective of self-understanding may come through other avenues, however, cannot be ignored and a rigid requirement that counselors be "majors" in psychology (or any other academic discipline) is unrealistic as far as assuring that self-examination will occur. Unfortunately, neither undergraduate nor graduate education as presently constituted makes adequate provisions for such examination as a routine matter.

Stipulations concerning educational programs for counselors would be incomplete without consideration of the selection process. The individual to be chosen for specialized training in guidance and counseling is the crucial element, and only if potentially strong candidates are chosen will strong counselors emerge from the educational experience. Many of the points given above concerning the desirable characteristics of counselors will not result from the graduate education program, but will be products of earlier—perhaps much earlier—educational experiences. Thus it is necessary for the selectors of counselor trainees to join other emerging professional groups in the search for improved techniques and approaches to the assessment and utilization of data about prospective trainees, so that the field may steadily upgrade the caliber of entrants. In addition, the guidance field must undertake improved methods of professional reward and recognition, so that greater numbers of highly qualified candidates will be available.

PROFESSIONAL COMPETENCIES OF GUIDANCE PERSONNEL

Wrenn's study, *The Counselor in a Changing World,* in a section concerned with "What Counselors Will Be Expected to Do in the Future" (pp. 123–126) has postulated the major areas of competence for guidance workers. These include:

1. Becoming well informed on student developmental needs and on the decisions to be made by students in their school programs.
2. Acquiring a thorough knowledge of the culture in which the student lives, since self-understanding cannot be in isolation from the culture.
3. Becoming more effective in providing psychologically meaningful assistance in the making of educational-vocational plans.

4. Acquiring competence in the processes of psychological appraisal as it is affected by the use of tests.
5. Studying cultural and occupational changes as these may affect the general development of the student as well as his educational and vocational planning.
6. Enhancing his contribution to the teaching staff, administrators, and parents, to serve as a major resource person in the community on human development.
7. Participating actively in the development of school curricula.

Wrenn concludes the particular section: ". . . the activities upon which the identity of the counselor will be validated are, in order of importance, (1) his counseling; (2) his advising of teachers; (3) his revision of programs of education; (4) his programing and use of machines that convey the information that he seeks" (1962:126).

It would seem reasonable to conclude that the counselor's professional competencies must minimally include comprehensive knowledge of the social and economic world in which his students live, skill in personal and group counseling (including all the ancillary functions that may be seen as contributing to counseling, such as assessment, information, and interpretation), an effective and communicable philosophy of education in general and of some level of school organization in particular, thorough knowledge of the operations of the community's schools and other human and social resources, and a high level of ability to communicate ideas and concepts to children, adolescents, and adults.

Professional Education of the Guidance Worker

Such a view of the counselor's or guidance worker's education demands and implies that he will indeed be a professionally trained and recognized member of the school and community. In using the term *professional* in discussing education, it must be noted that the concept is of preparation beyond the general, liberal background that is considered basic to any truly high-level undertaking in American society. In the present context, it is meant to imply that the breadth of education stipulated in the foregoing section *must* precede the depth of education of the graduate program, and that the graduate program in guidance and counseling should not include preparation in the more general cultural background materials. Too many graduate programs in the past have attempted to include both the breadth and depth aspects, with the result that only a minimal level of professional competence has been attained.

The ancient professions (law and medicine) as well as the newly emerging ones (social work, teaching, the mental health occupations) require internship or practicum work as a major portion of the preparation of workers. Such work must be done under the close supervision of fully accredited members of the professional group. There can be no true guidance profession until this sort of control is insisted upon. If such a requirement is not written into legal stipulations for entry into the field, then the professional organizations themselves must insist upon the requirement.

The internship needs to be served in the type of institution in which the trainee will work rather than, as has too often happened in the past, in a peripherally related enterprise. School counselors must intern in school situations, not in such locations as university counseling bureaus, hospitals, or community guidance centers. This is not to say that experience in such enterprises is unimportant; it is to say that the *basic* internship should not occur there.

Closer control and observation of neophytes need to be instituted by training institutions. A true profession that is to take responsibility for its members' competencies must be able to assess and certify those competencies before job entry. Under systems prevailing in many places today one might be certified by, say, the education department of a state government but not by one's professional group. Such a situation would be ludicrous, but unless the professional groups in the guidance and counseling area broaden their perspectives to the point at which they and the training institutions see themselves as leaders in developing certification standards for governments (as does the medical profession) the possibility given could happen. It will, hopefully, become more and more unlikely if governments and professional leaders continue their efforts to bring about a situation wherein the awarding of a degree or certificate by a graduate school automatically attests to the competence of the recipient and will lead to certification. Then the "credit-counting" and "course-title juggling" activities of state education departments will be properly relegated to the past.

If it is assumed that a large bloc, perhaps up to a half, of the professional training of the guidance worker should be in supervised practice, then it is reasonable to suppose that some course work would be taken concurrently with the practicum, and that other course work should follow completion of the practicum. The opportunity to reflect upon and to view objectively the work done in supervised practicum would seem essential if the experience is to be maximally helpful to the trainee. Too often on-the-job workers have too little time or incentive to be able to organize experiences into clear perspective that will lead to changes in operation and to improvement in ability.

The necessity for guidance workers to have prior experience in teaching or in formal course work in "education" has yet to be demonstrated. However, it seems highly desirable that as a result of appropriate practicum and internship experiences, the prospective school counselor will be "at home" in school situations. Indeed, there is probably no better way for a new counselor to ruin his prospects for acceptance and effectiveness in a school than to show by behavior or words a lack of understanding and appreciation of the problems, needs, and concerns of the classroom teachers with whom he must work and upon whose good will his success with students will depend.

EDUCATION FOR FUNCTIONAL ROLES IN GUIDANCE

One of the difficulties inherent in specifying training programs and requirements for school guidance personnel results from the varying views of the roles and functions of guidance. There sometimes seem to be almost as many concepts of the job of the counselor as there are counselors and school administrators. At one extreme guidance counselors function as school lackeys or sweep-up boys, doing all the odd jobs about which neither the administrators, the teachers, nor the janitors wish to be concerned. One task of the Association for Counselor Education and Supervision (a division of the American Personnel and Guidance Association) has been to work out a formula concerning the concept of the function of the counselor. The "counselor" who chooses, whether for reasons of ignorance, weakness, or insecurity, to function as corridor policeman, school disciplinarian, or detective is doing a serious disservice to guidance and to the school and children whom he "serves." As education standards are raised, such people hopefully will become obsolete, and guidance counselors will recognize that their function is neither that of school administrators, social workers, psychotherapists, psychometricians, nor clerks.

The guidance worker will often see himself as primarily concerned with counseling, but also responsible for identifying critical adjustment problems, making proper referrals in serious cases, and providing informational services for assistance to the staff, the community, and the parents. At the same time he is likely to be coordinator of the testing program and the record system, and operator or coordinator of a group program.

RECENT HISTORY AND THE FUTURE

It has sometimes been said that a counselor works with an undefined technique which is applied to unspecified problems with nonpredictable outcomes. Although in the past decade there has been some progress toward agreement regarding the general areas that should be included in counselor education, there remains much diversity in the content, techniques, and organization of programs. The task of improving counselor preparation is vastly complicated by the multiplicity of tasks the counselor performs, by lack of understanding of the counseling process, by confused interprofessional relationships, and by problems of semantics. For several years the American Personnel and Guidance Association, the American Psychological Association, the United States Office of Education, and various regional groups have been attempting to formulate standards for the preparation of counselors.

Two events that had a major impact on the field of guidance and counseling in the schools were only to a very slight degree the products of the school or of professional guidance and counseling personnel. These were the publication in 1959 of *The American High School Today* by Dr. James Bryant Conant, and the passage by Congress in 1958 of the National Defense Education Act, which was sparked by the Russian adventure into outer space. Both Conant's book and the legislative act stressed the need for guidance and counseling services in the schools, though for reasons that would be only partially valid in the thinking of most guidance professionals. Nevertheless, these events were more effective than the long struggle of guidance workers to impress the American people with the great need for more and better services.

During this same period the Ford Foundation made a grant to the American Personnel and Guidance Association to be used for the appointment of a commission to look ahead at the role of the counselor in the American school of the next decade. The resulting document, *The Counselor in a Changing World,* has produced much discussion and argument since its publication in 1962.

Under provisions of the National Defense Education Act, the United States Office of Education was designated as the agency to disburse millions of dollars for the professional education of school counselors. It soon became embarrassingly evident that there was little or no information available as to what constituted a professionally sound counselor education program and which graduate institutions could offer such programs. It was also painfullv evident that there was little agreement among institutions as to just what they were educating the school counselor or guidance worker to do. The availability of millions of dollars for "counselor education" was most inviting and encouraged many institutions and ostensible counselor educators suddenly to feel a need to increase their interest in counselor preparation. Thus the immediate result of the National Defense Education Act was increased confusion.

In 1962 the American Personnel and Guidance Association published *A Progress Report on Standards* summarizing the work of committees of the Association for Counselor Education and Supervision and of the American School Counselors Association, which had been working since 1960 on a five-year effort to develop standards and guidelines for the preparation of school counselors. The proposals contained therein were further refined and presented in a pamphlet entitled *Working Paper on Standards for Counselor Education in the Preparation of Secondary School Counselors,* which formed the basis for considerable discussion during the American Personnel and Guidance Association convention in April, 1963. Further recommendations and refinements are to be made at the 1964 convention in San Francisco, and implementation of final minimal standards is hoped for by 1968. These proposals, embodying the concerted experience and aspirations of both counselor educators and practicing school counselors, provide the most significant and potentially far-reaching consideration of counselor education ever undertaken, and will influence the guidance movement for many years to come. Therefore a summary of their recommendations is in order.

Six major areas of counselor education are considered: (1) philosophy and objectives of the training institution; (2) curriculum; (3) supervised experience; (4) selection, retention, endorsement, and placement; (5) research; and (6) support for the counselor education program, administrative relationships, and institutional resources. The section headings under each of these titles provide a guide which indicates the direction educational programs are and will be taken.

I. Philosophy and Objectives
   A. The institution has a stated philosophy and has developed a set of objectives for counselor education.
   B. The philosophy and objectives are accepted and implemented by staff members.
   C. The philosophy and objectives of the counselor education program are in harmony with generally accepted school guidance programs, aims, needs, and trends.

D. The staff continues to review the philosophy and objectives of the program.

E. There is a continuous study of the extent to which the stated philosophy is transmitted and the objectives are accomplished.

II. Curriculum

A. The competencies needed by the school counselor require a minimum of two years of graduate preparation, a substantial portion of which is taken in full-time study.

B. There is evidence of quality instruction in all aspects of the counselor education program.

C. Planned sequences of educational experiences, spiraling toward progressively more advanced work are provided.

D. The curriculum is in general agreement with currently accepted areas of preparation for school counselors.

E. There is close inter-disciplinary cooperation between staff members directly responsible for the professional education of counselors and representatives of departments or schools offering courses in cognate fields.

F. Within the framework of the total counselor education program, there are available curriculum resources as well as procedures that make it possible for the counselor candidate to develop understandings and skills in an area of special interest beyond the minimum requirements of the program.

III. Supervised Experience

A. Supervised experience in counseling and other related guidance activities is provided as an integral part of the total counselor education program.

B. Three aspects of supervised experience are provided in the counselor education program: (1) laboratory experience, (2) practicum, (3) internship.

C. A well-qualified staff with adequate time allocated to supervision is provided.

D. Facilities, equipment, and materials are provided for supervised experiences.

IV. Selection, Retention, Endorsement, and Placement

A. The institution has a procedure for identifying and selecting candidates for counselor education.

B. The institution follows a defined procedure for the selective admission of candidates to the program of counselor education.

C. The institution administers a well-defined program of selective retention.

D. The institution endorses successful candidates for certification and employment upon completion of the program.

E. The institution provides a placement service.

F. The institution has a well-defined plan and adequate procedures for follow-up of former students.

V. Research
   A. The counselor education program encourages among staff and students the spirit of inquiry and the production and utilization of research data.
   B. The program provides for the development of research competencies.
   C. The members of the staff demonstrate the importance of research through professional activities.

VI. Support for the counselor education program, administrative relationships, and institutional resources
   A. Administrative organization and procedures include a recognition of and designated responsibilities for a counselor education program.
   B. The institution provides an atmosphere of professional development which is conducive to the professionalization of the staff as well as students in the counselor education program.
   C. The institution provides adequate faculty and staff for all aspects of the counselor education program.
   D. The institution provides for the counselor education program facilities and a budget which are adequate to insure a continuous operation of all aspects of the program.
   E. The institution recognizes the individual needs of graduate students and provides services to encourage maximum opportunities for personal as well as professional development.

Critical self-study of graduate programs for the preparation of school counselors is being undertaken by a number of colleges and universities as a result of the appearance of these preliminary standards. Counselor educators and state supervisors of guidance have led these efforts in self-examination because of a growing national concern about the quality and quantity of counselor preparation. Nearly all established programs of counselor education in graduate schools have greatly expanded both in numbers of students and in staff size during the past five years. Practically all colleges with some graduate offerings in guidance and counseling areas have tended to emphasize their programs and to attract more students to counselor preparation. In addition, many new programs of counselor preparation have appeared in colleges not previously engaged in such work.

It is natural that institutions offering graduate programs in counselor preparation should be concerned about the quality of their programs and should support cooperative effort in the development of standards. Criteria to be used as guidelines in the development of a new graduate program or in the expansion of an existing program have been almost totally lacking. Eager participation in the national study of standards has resulted.

Counselor education is expanding at a rate which raises justifiable concerns among professional educators and practicing counselors about standards and the quality of the graduate. High expectations and support now favor counseling services and school counselors to an ever increasing degree. An immense amount of base data and descriptive information is needed to clarify the level and characteristics of counselors and counselor education programs. All professional persons engaged in school counseling, counselor supervision, or counselor education have a stake in the clarification and development of standards for preparation, certification, and performance which will continue to assure high quality within the guidance profession.

The answer for a "best" program of "counselor" or "guidance worker" training is not yet available. As American education and as the guidance profession can clarify their related and independent roles in our society, so educational programs can be better organized to prepare guidance personnel.

SUMMARY

The education of guidance workers has been examined in light of the present confusion that exists in the preparation of counselors and guidance personnel.

The functions of guidance in the school and the personal characteristics of the guidance worker have been highlighted. Values, conceptions of the nature of man, and the process of educating for personal character traits were the major subjects presented.

The needed competencies of guidance personnel, taken from recent professional publications concerned with educational programing, have been briefly examined. The areas summarized were: (1) philosophy and objectives, (2) curriculum, (3) supervised experience, (4) selection, retention, and endorsement, (5) research, and (6) institutional support.

REFERENCES AND SUGGESTED READINGS

American Personnel and Guidance Association, *Counselor Education—A Progress Report on Standards,* Washington, D.C.: The Association, 1962.

American Personnel and Guidance Association, "Standards for the Preparation of School Counselors," *Personnel and Guidance Journal,* XL (1961), 402–407.

American Psychological Association, Division 17, *The Scope and Standards of Preparation in Psychology for School Counselors,* Washington, D.C.: The Association (mimeographed), 1961.

Barry, Ruth, and Beverly Wolf, *An Epitaph for Vocational Guidance,* New York: Bureau of Publications, Teachers College, Columbia University, 1962.

Conant, James B., *The American High School Today,* New York: Harper, 1959.

Crow, L. D., and A. Crow, *Readings in Guidance,* New York: David McKay, 1962.

Farwell, G. F., and H. J. Peters, *Guidance Readings for Counselors,* Chicago: Rand McNally, 1960.

Landy, Edward, "Counselor Education—Research," in *A Progress Report on Standards,* Washington, D.C.: American Personnel and Guidance Association, 1962, 49–55.

Lehner, G. F. J., "Comments," *American Psychologist,* VII, No. 9 (Sept., 1952), 547.

Penney, James F., "Counseling: Its Causes and Cost," *Journal of Higher Education,* XXXII (1963), 402–404.

Pierson, George A., and C. W. Grant, "The Road Ahead for the School Counselor," *Personnel and Guidance Journal,* XXXVIII (1959), 207–210.

Rogers, Carl R., *On Becoming a Person,* Boston: Houghton Mifflin, 1961.

Smith, N. Brewster, "Toward Scientific and Professional Responsibility," *American Psychologist,* IX, No. 9 (Sept., 1954), 513.

Tooker, E. D., "Counselor Role: Counselor Training," *Personnel and Guidance Journal,* XXXVI (1957), 263–267.

Viteles, M. S., *et al., Vocational Counseling* (*A Reappraisal in Honor of Donald G. Paterson*), Minneapolis, Minn.: University of Minnesota Press, 1961.

Williamson, E. G., "The Counselor as Technique," *Personnel and Guidance Journal,* XLI, No. 2 (Oct., 1962), 108–111.

Williamson, E. G., *Student Personnel Services in Colleges and Universities,* New York: McGraw-Hill, 1961.

Wrenn, C. Gilbert, *The Counselor in a Changing World,* Washington: American Personnel and Guidance Association, 1962, pp. 123–126.

Wrenn, C. Gilbert, "Selection and Education of Student Personnel Workers," *Personnel and Guidance Journal,* XXXI (1952), 9–14.

Wrenn, C. Gilbert, "Status and Role of the School Counselor," *Personnel and Guidance Journal,* XXXVI (1957), 175–183.

PROFESSIONAL GUIDANCE WORK

THE ISSUE. Whether or not guidance is a professional discipline has been a question inherent in many public evaluations of guidance programs. That guidance can operate at a level less than what could be termed "professional" has not been denied, but that guidance can operate at less than a professional level and still fulfill its inherent nature has been emphatically denied in every chapter of this book.

What are the roles that must be fulfilled by responsible guidance persons who have been properly and effectively prepared for their work? Definition of these roles is necessary, for preparation in guidance does not automatically guarantee that a professional stature will be secured and maintained by the individual.

Professional guidance work demands that guidance exert an independent influence for good in the development of education and educational practices. What are the dimensions of the force that guidance can be? Is guidance mature enough to live up to such an obligation and privilege?

Local needs and traditions need to be balanced with professional criteria or, more broadly, a systematic body of knowledge that determines the operation of guidance. Ethical codes to direct individual practice can also help the professional worker. Professional guidance organizations are exploring the meaning of professionalism in guidance. Their influence has been variable, and the future may cast such organizations into a new role within guidance. What are the possible dimensions of this new role?

Finally, guidance as a profession and guidance workers as individuals have obligations to themselves and to their society to act freely

CHAPTER EIGHTEEN

and responsibly. What guideposts are possible for guidance and guidance workers in this area?

Throughout the long debate about the professional stature of guidance there has been an increase of professional practice and professional knowledge. While debating whether or not the horses could or should be permitted to escape from the barn, guidance personnel have continued to work for educational objectives and individual student goals. A systematic body of knowledge has been developed in several major areas that now permits a school or college to explore the meaning of guidance as a profession and to adopt guidance within its educational structure.

Counseling is not the same as guidance; testing cannot substitute for counseling. Such issues have been resolved quietly in many schools where guidance has been seen in its broadest perspective. Counseling, testing, group work, casework, and the many related services that arise out of these tool concepts of guidance have been undertaken, and the divisive controversies that have occupied the attention of many specialists within education have been ignored. The issues of "either-or," "which," and even "how" have been resolved. Although the trees have at times obscured the growth of the forest, the forest has now grown tall and straight for all to see.

Several major issues should be faced as guidance is viewed as a profession within education. The dimensions and effects of the force which guidance can exert on education can help describe guidance as a profession. Additional professional issues are those of leadership through research and evaluation, ethical standards and practice, mature and responsible national organizational patterns, and the meaningful aid to persons and society through programs that can help produce free and responsible persons.

AN INDEPENDENT FORCE

Guidance as a professional force within education can exert a beneficial force on education, particularly for the more meaningful development of individual students and citizens. Participation in curriculum planning and construction, leadership in parent-school relations, and service in helping to reveal the true meaning of education are major areas in which guidance can serve education.

Education has traditionally been concerned with *what* a student learns and only secondarily with the effective *use* to which a student puts his learning. Guidance, in centering its effort on the individual student, has been unable to ignore what a student may do with his learning. Static learning is of little value to a student; the integration of learning into life and into life's activities is the significant test for all learning. Sarason, Davidson, and Blatt (1962) describe the problem as too much concern with what is *put into* a student and virtually no concern for what *comes out*. Guidance focuses upon what comes out of the student as the student lives his life.

The Curriculum

Guidance workers can help other educators construct and implement the curriculum of the school. Programs of study are made up of the subject matter that is deemed significant enough to require students to learn or at least be exposed to it. Guidance persons functioning as professional members of an educational team should be prepared to assess the student's ability to understand, appreciate, and utilize a potential curriculum.

Guidance persons have often been not only excluded from the faculty curriculum committee, but also viewed as "other than faculty," not even accorded membership in the regular faculty group. Professional stature demands performance as well as privilege. As guidance persons are able to demonstrate the contributions that they can make to a school, the right to full faculty membership becomes virtually automatic.

Ideally, the broad preparation of professional guidance workers permits them to understand the potential contributions of all areas of education, although they themselves may not be specialists in any of the major disciplines. The entire history of the general education movement shows a concern for meaningful learnings by students. Guidance workers have only recently begun to recognize the relationship of guidance to general education. The goals and objectives of both guidance and education are similar and build upon common understandings of human behavior and the function of education in a democracy.

The emphasis on the integration of general education and on the meaningfulness of learning for students are both parts of the conceptual design of guidance. Learning that is meaningful for students can lead to the development and adoption of value patterns that can guide an individual life. Life objectives must arise out of an integration of subject matter with personal planning. What a person does with his life is an outgrowth of his own personality and learning experiences. Education may not be directly involved in the determination of a single life objective, but no life objective can be established without the influence of learning. Learning of all types is a concern both of the guidance worker and of the curriculum specialist.

Not all schools or colleges place guidance in a central position. The following quotation, while emphasizing the role of guidance, also indicates other possibilities:

> THE PIVOT OF INSTRUCTION
>
> Each unit of activity and each course of instruction . . . is viewed as an essential element in an evolving pattern of instruction. The aim throughout is to promote the growth and development of the student's total personality; to enlarge his interest and engage his drive; to utilize to the greatest possible degree his potential for successful, rewarding, and useful achievement in response to the challenge of life in our time and place. The subjects covered, the extensive assignments, the demonstrations, laboratory exercises, discussions, counseling, and other individual phases of instruction, are all part of a carefully calculated plan, an expression of maximum concern for the welfare of the individual and the full employment of human resources.
>
> This emphasis upon the individual in his development and adjustment as a total personality places the Division of Psychology and Guidance at the very center of the educational picture. Just as another type of integrative program might establish either the social sciences, the natural sciences, or the humanities as the key area of instruction to which major units of instruction are orientated and related, so in this sense the . . . college regards every phase of instruction as an extension of the work carried on by the psychology and guidance counselor and teacher. The common concern of all instruction is the intellectual, social, and personal development of the individual [Butler, 1956:15].

Parent-School Integration

Although Admiral Hyman Rickover may believe that the PTA is an "infernal nuisance and should be done away with," it is doubtful that parents will or should ever resign from their interest and involvement with the schools of their children. That PTA groups can and ought to be more effective than they frequently are is undeniable. But the solution to the problem is not to abolish such groups but to find more meaningful patterns of relationship that can help parents, students, teachers, and education as a whole.

Teacher-parent conferences involve the most emotionally important area of a parent's life—children. Teachers are often unprepared and unequal to the tasks involved in parental conferences (Sarason, Davidson, and Blatt, 1962). A teacher may believe that a conference with a parent is simply an exchange of information that is important to both persons and to the child under discussion. Rather, parent-teacher conferences must be understood as counseling problems which need to be approached with an understanding of human behavior that can permit true communication.

Guidance workers can provide counseling techniques which can help teachers, administrators, and parents to communicate more effectively. Such leadership may take many avenues. There is no single pattern of help that is appropriate. Each guidance program will need to explore local traditions and expectations. As guidance workers begin to understand and appreciate the situation, they may be able to assume a useful consultant role within a specific program.

The role of guidance and of specially trained counselors in parent-teacher communication cannot be that of a condescending specialist. Experience which divides is worse than none. Guidance persons and a guidance program must be able to demonstrate the maturity and responsibility to be concerned with the professional solution of problems, not with the accretion of status, prestige, and power. Such assumptions are a part of professional practice for guidance personnel and guidance programs.

Learning and Meaning

Perhaps the most significant independent force that guidance can exert within education is toward the accomplishment of meaningful learning by all students. Such a force may take many pathways. Curriculum, parental relations, community service, and all of the usual school and guidance services can operate to this end.

A force for meaningful learning is not merely a force for useful or practical learning. Many things may be useful and still be meaningless to students. True education is concerned with learning how to live rather than with learning how to make a living. Many so-called "pragmatic" or experimentally oriented educational programs at all school levels mistake that which is useful for that which is significant. It is significant for a child to learn about the beauty of a picture, a sculpture, or a poem. Such learnings may be only aesthetically useful, but they are certainly significant. Life can be barren and sterile if it lacks appreciation of beauty.

Guidance workers as professional educators need to be interested and concerned in all that takes place within the school and in the lives of students in or out of school. Such a broad concern does not necessarily mean that guidance workers are effective in problem-solving in all areas or even possess the ability or skill to understand all problems. But they must be concerned with the total experience of the learner. The student at all levels is the ultimate concern of the educational institution. Guidance has no choice but to be concerned about the meaningfulness and significance of all types of student learnings.

Concern for students can never allow guidance persons the right to "play god." True interest and concern breeds a humility that is exactly the reverse of "playing god" or assuming that one's own profession is the "chosen group."

RESEARCH AND EVALUATION

Research and evaluation are traditional parts of all educational enterprises. The previous discussion of these topics examined the role that guidance needs to play as a member of an educational community. More basic to education is the development of meaningful research within local situations. Active research designs can help provide new and appropriate means of educational problem-solving. Experimental approaches to specific local problems may be described in nonprofessional terms to help community members understand the efforts of their schools to help students. Guidance workers can help bridge the gap between traditional research and the public served by school units, can provide meaningful data on student growth and achievement, and can support open-ended projects that seek better and more effective methods of education.

Traditional Research Data

Traditional research sometimes seems to be written and published to protect university faculty members from the "publish or perish" dictum. Some research and writing seems to serve no other purpose. Personnel within the public and private schools whose tasks are to teach, to counsel with students, and to populate the frontier of educational practice are often dismayed and confused by the piles of data that accumulate in educational circles. Guidance workers, although often no better prepared than other educators in research, need to be concerned with the translation of valuable research data into a form which will be useful to teachers, parents, and themselves.

Guidance persons need to be concerned about research developments because of their concern for the growth of students and of school programs for students. Administrators share this concern. Administrators and guidance workers together can help others apply new practices and ideas in their own schools. The actual methodology for each school or college cannot be prescribed but must be developed out of local traditions and needs. The sharing of research and theory articles that affect the total school or major segments of the school may be one way of translating research developments into local practice. College research and evaluation can call upon guidance persons to help in the screening and evaluation of materials to be distributed to other members of the staff.

The guidance worker's responsibility to be aware of total school growth and progress can breed a dangerous "know-it-all" attitude if he is not professional and helpful in his attempts to aid others in using new data to build better programs of their own. However, the contributions of an aware guidance worker can be great. The following description of the operation of a guidance worker illuminates such activities:

> Our guidance man is tremendously helpful in all areas of the school. He tries to stay up on new research in his own field and in many related areas. He shares articles from professional journals that relate to the program in all sections of the school. He has been most instrumental in developing an awareness of professional research on the part of the entire staff. We now exchange materials that previously we might have even ignored ourselves.
>
> Even more important in our school is the belief that the guidance group (our staff) will support and help another area in a new project. If students need to be interviewed to determine the advisability of something new, or, if students need to evaluate something that has been tried in the school, the guidance department will help in the job. The

fact that the guidance personnel will be sympathetic or at least interested in a new task or project has helped to develop a spirit of inquiry and experiment within our school. [High School Principal]

Student Growth and Development

Student growth and development are natural outcomes of educational programs. But how frequently are parents, the community, or even students themselves adequately informed about the results of their growth? Group specialists refer to the availability of data about oneself as *feedback*. Feedback can be a useful concept in education and is a legitimate obligation of guidance workers.

The feedback of student growth and development data can begin with a guidance worker exploring the tremendous amount of test data stored in student records. How frequently are students brought up to date on changes in their own achievement? Group statistics on such data as the results of achievement tests, reading rates and comprehension, and writing skills, can be made much more meaningful. Additional screening of such data can provide raw material for special mailings to parents, to local newspapers, and to school board committees. Local newspapers print word-by-word minutes of community planning board meetings, selectman's notes, and similar information that affect townspeople. Educational experimentation in communication can be undertaken with leadership from guidance workers who are naturally concerned with all who are affected by such data. Special guidance research studies of student graduates, college entrance, and work positions can form the basis of a communication program that can ultimately extend into all areas of educational practice within a community.

ETHICS AND STANDARDS

Ethical practice is the mark of a professional group. Some authorities have claimed that to be a profession a group need only require "relatively long and specialized preparation" and be "governed by a code of ethics" (Good, 1939:18). Some guidance writers have seized upon this statement as adequate evidence that counseling and guidance are professional and should have "privileged communication." The issues of ethics and "privileged communication" are important items for guidance as a profession to examine. Simple answers cannot be offered to such complicated problems.

Ethical Practice

The writings of C. Gilbert Wrenn are important whenever professional issues and ethics are considered in the counseling and guidance field. His long concern with these areas has been one of the most important reasons for his present leadership in the profession. He has always placed ethics, professional practice, and legal issues within a value orientation that provides a systematic framework for issue analysis. An early paper presented by Wrenn (1952) as a "Presidential Address to the Division of Counseling and Guidance" (now known as the Division of Counseling Psychologists) of the American Psychological Association helps to provide perspective and insight into the ethics and values which are necessary for guidance persons. Wrenn's later writings (1957; 1959), culminating in his major contribution to the field, *The Counselor in a Changing World* (1962), should be required reading for any professional guidance worker. A further up-to-date treatment of the ethical and legal problems of counseling and guidance is available in Chapter 15 of McGowan and Schmidt (1962).

The efforts of Wrenn and many others helped to provide two major sets of ethical practice codes for guidance workers. The American Psychological Association, after a three-year study of ethical issues undertaken by a committee headed by Dr. Nicholas Hobbs, published in 1953 *Ethical Standards of Psychologists* (available from the Association Headquarters, 1333 Sixteenth Street, Washington 6, D.C.). The American Personnel and Guidance Association published in 1961, in the Association journal, a *Code of Ethics* (available from this group's national headquarters, 1605 New Hampshire Avenue, N.W., Washington 9, D.C.). These publications provide the dimensions of professional practice for all types of guidance workers and counselors.

Conflicts of interest cannot be avoided in the specific problem-solving of guidance. The important issue is the resolution of such conflicts in accord with a mature and professional value system. The examples and problem areas referred to in the APA *Ethical Standards of Psychologists* can illuminate many guidance problems. The APGA code provides a pattern of belief and a guide for action in more typical guidance situations. Both publications can be of help to the guidance worker.

Privileged Communication

The right to hold confidential any communication from another person is reserved in our legal codes for only three classifications of professional workers—physicians, lawyers, and officially ordained ministers, rabbis, and priests. Because of the personal nature of counseling, psychologists and counselors have long been agitating for the legal recognition of privileged communication in their field.

It often seems as if many counselors approach the problem backwards. Dewey's statement that report cards should be eliminated when a proper educational experience has been established has often been misinterpreted to make the first step doing away with report cards. Counselors seem to start with the demand for privileged communication rather than earning the privilege by demonstrating professional practice that shows a need for such action. That psychologists may need such protection in private practice may soon be legally recognized; school counselors may never need or wish to have such a moral and ethical responsibility. The issue is by no means clear-cut at the moment. Further evidence is needed prior to the wholesale granting of this privilege to every person who is called a school counselor. The problem of defining what constitutes a licensed or legally qualified school counselor has not yet been solved. When this problem is clarified, it may be desirable to examine the issue of privileged communication for such persons.

PROFESSIONAL ORGANIZATIONS

A profession that is marked by a systematic body of knowledge and by ethical practice is usually represented by an organizational structure that can order the affairs of the group. Guidance organizations are numerous and have often "organized" conventions, meetings, and committees to promote professional stature for all areas of guidance and counseling. Major organizational structures within guidance at the present time include (1) The American Personnel and Guidance Association, (2) The National Association of Student Personnel Administrators, and (3) The National Association of Deans and Counselors of Women.

Many regional, state, and local groups also bring together guidance persons from all levels of school operation. These organizations and their constituent units serve large numbers of guidance workers. Many broad education groups, such as the National Educational Association and the American Council on Education, have subgroups that concern themselves with guidance, counseling, and personnel work.

More and more guidance workers are recognizing that the broad basis of guidance demands that professional affiliations go beyond narrow professional group membership. Organizations such as the American Psychological Association, sociological and anthropological associations, and The Society for the Psychological Study of Social Issues relate to guidance. Individual guidance organizations function on a national level to encourage professional practice through publications, conventions, research projects, and regulatory efforts. Associations that cooperatively support guidance may serve in all but the regulatory area. An anthropology association would not attempt to define the functions of psychological testing within an elementary school. However, attempts to pattern guidance relationships and operations by nonguidance groups are not unknown. The American Psychological Association has attempted to influence the tasks, training, and functioning of the school counselor. However, this national group is perhaps the closest of the listed groups to guidance and many guidance persons maintain joint membership.

Publication, sponsorship of meetings, research project development, and service to members are growing and developing aspects of the professional affiliation of guidance workers. Certainly it seems desirable for every guidance worker to recognize his professional connections to other workers and to a growing field through professional organization membership.

The regulatory function of most national organizations has been slow to develop. The increased effort to redefine and clarify the preparation and education of counselors (and hopefully of guidance workers) is a step in the direction of professional development. The need to be aware of and avoid unprofessional practice and to help school and community officials select, promote, and reward professional activity has been slow to develop. National guidance organizations are on the threshold of new and creative functioning. As guidance itself becomes mature and professionally oriented, guidance organizations will reflect such growth.

REFERENCES AND SUGGESTED READINGS

Adelson, Joseph, "The Teacher as a Model," in Nevitt Sanford (ed.), *The American College,* New York: Wiley, 1962, 396–417.

Benezet, L. T., "The Trouble with Excellence," *Saturday Review,* Oct. 21, 1961, 44–45, 63–64.

Bond, Horace B., *The Search for Talent,* Cambridge, Mass.: Graduate School of Education, Harvard University, 1959.

Brameld, Theodore, *Education for the Emerging Age,* New York: Harper, 1961.
Butler, J. R., *A Program in General and Developmental Studies for Freshmen and Sophomores,* Boston: Boston University Press, 1956.
Gallagher, Buell G., *The Not-So-Silent Generation,* New York: The City College (presidential address), 1960.
Goldberg, Maxwell H., "General Education and the Explosion of Knowledge," *College and University Bulletin,* XIV, February 15, 1962.
Good, Carter (ed.), *Dictionary of Education,* New York: McGraw-Hill, 1939.
Kagan, Jerome, "The Choice of Models: A Developmental Analysis of Conflict and Continuity in Human Behavior," speech to American Personnel and Guidance Association Convention, April 18, 1962.
McGowan, J. F., and L. D. Schmidt, *Counseling: Readings in Theory and Practice,* New York: Holt, Rinehart & Winston, 1962.
Morse, Arthur D., *Schools of Tomorrow–Today!,* New York: Doubleday, 1960.
Morse, Horace T., and Paul L. Dressel (eds.), *General Education for Personal Maturity,* Dubuque, Iowa: William C. Brown, 1960.
Parnes, S. J., and H. F. Harding (eds.), *A Sourcebook for Creative Thinking,* New York: Scribner's, 1962.
Phenix, Philip H., *Education and the Common Good,* New York: Harper, 1961.
Sarason, Seymour B., *et al., The Preparation of Teachers (An Unstudied Problem in Education),* New York: Wiley, 1962.
Shoben, E. J., Jr., "Some Thoughts on Interprofessional Relationships," *Journal of Counseling Psychology,* II (1955), 196–201.
Thomas, Russell, *The Search for a Common Learning: General Education, 1800–1960,* New York: McGraw-Hill, 1962.
Trump, J. Lloyd, *New Directions to Quality Education,* Washington, D.C.: National Education Association, 1960.
Trump, J. Lloyd, and D. Baynham, *Focus on Change Guide to Better Schools,* Chicago: Rand McNally, 1961.
Trump, J. Lloyd, and D. Baynham, *Guide to Better Schools,* Chicago: Rand McNally, 1962.
Wrenn, C. Gilbert, *The Counselor in a Changing World,* Washington, D.C.: American Personnel and Guidance Association, 1962.
Wrenn, C. Gilbert, "The Fault, Dear Brutus–", *Educational and Psychological Measurements,* IX (1949), 360–378.
Wrenn, C. Gilbert, "Philosophical and Psychological Bases of Personnel Services in Education," in National Society for the Study of Education, *Personnel Services in Education,* Fifty-Eighth Yearbook, Part II, Chicago: University of Chicago Press, 1959, 41–81.
Wrenn, C. Gilbert, "Professors and Professional Membership," *Occupations,* XXX (1951), 24–29.
Wrenn, C. Gilbert, "Status and Role of the School Counselor," *Personnel and Guidance Journal,* XXXVI (1957), 175–183.

FREEDOM AND RESPONSIBILITY: AN OVERVIEW

GUIDANCE IS concerned with the development of the free and responsible person. To say that guidance workers themselves, as professional members of an educational group, need to be free and responsible persons is perhaps to state the obvious. Still, it needs to be said that those who would guide others need to be aware of their own ability to function as effective persons within a society. The dimensions of freedom and responsibility in the professional practice of guidance within the school have been described throughout this book.

The consideration of the guidance worker as a person must always come first whenever guidance is examined within a professional framework. A person is a person first and all else afterwards. He needs to be aware of his own freedom and of his own responsibilities to himself and to his society. When this dimension of individual existence is seen clearly, it is possible to establish additional relationships such as professional functioning and educational programing.

The guidance worker reveals his own values and his own life objectives in becoming a guidance person. To help others examine their own lives and values and establish life objectives and life purposes demonstrates the guidance worker's active faith and belief in what Archibald MacLeish calls the "American Proposition." Guidance believes in the ability of a free people to create the future for themselves. Guidance believes in "not the Truth but the man." The faith of guidance is, in MacLeish's words, ". . . in the human being, the human spirit, the hungers and the longings that lead it to its images of truth its perceptions of the beauty of the world" [1951].

ANNOTATED GUIDANCE BIBLIOGRAPHY

THE ANNOTATED bibliography which follows is designed to assist guidance workers to become familiar with some of the major sources that influence the operation of guidance. Four major areas are included in the list: General Sources, Philosophy of Education, Anthropology and Sociology, and Psychology.

The books included in each section are not the only books that can provide valuable information to guidance persons. The bibliography is not offered as definitive, but merely as suggestive and selective. Each of the listed sources have been helpful in the preparation of this textbook and contain additional information about many areas that are discussed. Each guidance worker will want to add his own special sources that help him in understanding and aiding individual students.

GENERAL SOURCES

Bryson, Lyman, *Science and Freedom*, New York: Columbia University Press, 1947.

Freedom and science are defined and related to social change. Education is explained as cultural and social engineering within the framework of our society. The philosophical base of individual freedom is seen to be an outgrowth of the good society. Man is described as his own "toughest problem." Bryson presents the need for understanding man and his society together. He concludes with an examination of the "good society."

Compton, Arthur H., *The Freedom of Man*, New Haven: Yale University Press, 1935.

Compton discusses freedom as it arises out of man as a natural being and social animal. Science is seen, not as exact, but as following the laws of probability. He places man and man's freedom within a framework of science, philosophy, and religion. These three disciplines all support man and permit him to be free, not determined.

Conklin, Edwin G., *Freedom and Responsibility,* Boston: Houghton Mifflin, 1935.

This book is the text of a speech delivered in Boston in 1934. The author, a Princeton University biologist, examines the issues of freedom and responsibility within the schools and the society as a whole and wrestles with the natural and cultural concepts of freedom. He anticipates some of the concepts later developed in psychology, anthropology, and education. He sees the need for "training to be free." He describes the basic purpose of government as education for freedom.

Grinker, Roy R. (ed.), *Toward a Unified Theory of Human Behavior,* New York: Basic Books, 1956.

Specialists from several disciplines attempt to examine the common concepts of human behavior. The volume is an outgrowth of a series of conferences devoted to this problem, and includes discussions which give the flavor of immediacy. The content and approach are not elementary; the goal of the group is beyond the conception of some specialists. The book is stimulating and occasionally depressing. The task is immense and the progress slow.

Lerner, Max, *America as a Civilization,* New York: Simon and Schuster, 1957.

Lerner characterizes himself as a "tough-minded liberal and a radical humanist." This volume is a massive treatment of the many sides of American life. It is readable and provides perspective on the sociology and culture of our own civilization. It can provide background for uninformed readers and fill in many blank spaces for the more sophisticated.

MacLeish, Archibald, *Freedom Is the Right to Choose,* Boston: The Beacon Press, 1951.

MacLeish offers in this volume twelve of his essays covering the period from just before World War II until the date of publication. He focuses upon what he calls the "American Proposition"; he defines, illustrates, and applies it in national and international affairs. His prose reads like poetry. His premise illuminates the basic task assumed by guidance in American education.

Malinowski, Bronislaw, *Freedom and Civilization,* New York: Roy Publishers, 1944.

A monumental book by one of the most important figures in anthropology. Malinowski builds upon his wide knowledge of primitive and modern societies to examine the intimate relationships that exist between the individual and his surrounding and supporting culture.

Freedom is described as an outgrowth of the interaction of the individual and his culture. Malinowski's work is fresh and vital to any social scientist and particularly to anyone concerned with the nurture and development of individual freedom.

Mason, A. T., and R. H. Leach, *In Quest of Freedom,* Englewood Cliffs, N.J.: Prentice-Hall, 1959.
The book presents an analysis of the political concept of freedom from its beginnings to present-day issues. The relation of the individual to his government is explored throughout American History. Man, majority and minority rights, constitutional powers, and judicial restraints are all examined as they affect the freedom of the person. Freedom is seen as a concept that can only be understood as the individual and his government are interrelated.

National Society for the Study of Education yearbooks, sponsored by the Society and written by specialists in the subject matter areas. Distributed by the University of Chicago Press, published annually.
This organization has tackled the major tasks of education for over 50 years. At least one volume has been published every year and often more than one. The yearbook usually provides a timely and comprehensive review of all significant issues within the chosen topic. Guidance workers will find of particular interest the following recent yearbooks: *General Education,* 1952; *Modern Philosophies and Education,* 1955; *Mental Health in Modern Education,* 1955; *In-Service Education for Teachers, Supervisors, and Administrators,* 1957; *Education for the Gifted,* 1958; *Integration of Educational Experiences,* 1958; *Personnel Services in Education,* 1959; *The Dynamics of Instructional Groups,* 1960.

Palmer, George H., *The Problem of Freedom,* Boston: Houghton Mifflin, 1911.
A Harvard Professor of Philosophy, Palmer summarizes the issues facing the person who would be free. The determinants and limitations of freedom are explored in detail. Palmer also summarizes the major philosophical positions of his day about freedom, free will, and determinism. Although more than half a century old, this book provides a broad perspective on many present-day issues.

Sanford, Nevitt (ed.), *The American College,* New York: Wiley, 1962.
This volume is large both in contribution and in size. The contributing authors have examined portions of American college education in great detail. The volume was sponsored by the Society for the Psychological Study of Social Issues, but it offers much more than a psychological view of the topics. Each issue is placed in a cultural, sociological, and philosophical framework. The volume as a whole possesses a unity that is frequently lacking in such major works. This volume should be required reading for any college personnel person. Other guidance persons who deal regularly with college issues will also find it rewarding.

Standen, Anthony, *Science Is a Sacred Cow,* New York: Dutton, 1950.
This is a readable and clever attack on the unusual status accorded to science by those who do not understand science. It is written by a chemist who often tends to infuriate his fellow scientists. The nature of science is closely related to freedom and thoughtful scientists as well as those in other fields will find the volume entertaining, revealing, and helpful.

Thomas, Russell, *The Search for a Common Learning: General Education, 1800–1960,* New York: McGraw-Hill, 1962.
Thomas provides the first comprehensive history of action and thought in the "general education" movement. Issues are examined and practical solutions found by individual schools and colleges are described. The nature of guidance is closely related to general education by their common concern for the individuals' integration of learning. The concept of a common learning for all citizens in a democracy which Thomas presents is challenging. The style is readable and the many detailed case studies will appeal to college-level guidance persons.

PHILOSOPHY OF EDUCATION

Brameld, Theodore, *Cultural Foundations of Education,* New York: Harper, 1957.
This book is a major statement of Brameld's broad view of American education. He places education in the center of culture and believes that education is a primary tool of all cultures. Reconstruction of the world as a better place is offered as the goal of education.

Brameld, Theodore, *Philosophies of Education in Cultural Perspective,* New York: Dryden, 1955.
Brameld characterizes himself as a "reconstructionist" in the tradition of Dewey. This treatment of educational philosophy covers the major streams of educational thought and places them within a broad perspective of American culture and life.

Bruner, Jerome S., *The Process of Education,* Cambridge, Mass.: Harvard University Press, 1960.
The book is the report of the cross-disciplinary Woods Hole Conference of 1959 devoted to curriculum development in science education. Issues, principles, and values that transcend all levels of education are stressed. The "spiral curriculum" is used to examine these concepts at all levels of education.

Dewey, John, *Democracy and Education,* New York: Macmillan, 1916 (paperback, 1961).
This book provides an introduction to Dewey's philosophy of educa-

tion. There are treatments of many topics and all chapters reflect Dewey's pervasive belief in education as a force for democracy. The role of the individual in education is clearly outlined in Chapter 22. All chapters are appropriate for guidance workers.

General Education in a Free Society, Cambridge, Mass.: Harvard University Press, 1946.
The well-known "Harvard" report on the importance of common learnings for all in our society has helped steer American education in the early post-war years.

Hodgkinson, Harold L., *Education in Social and Cultural Perspectives,* Englewood Cliffs, N.J.: Prentice-Hall, 1962.
The broad perspective available from this small paperback volume can help any person in education to put greater value in the essential nature of education. The final chapter tersely puts the case for education as an effective force in a democracy.

Hullfish, H. G., and P. G. Smith, *Reflective Thinking: The Method of Education,* New York: Dodd, Mead, 1961.
This practical and very readable treatise presents thinking as the central issue in all of education. It was written by a well-known and respected educational philosopher and a co-author who is aware of current practices. Reflective thinking is problem-solving and is closely related to any phase of guidance.

Kilpatrick, William Heard, *Philosophy of Education,* New York: Macmillan, 1951.
Kilpatrick, one of the major followers of James and Dewey, gives a summary statement on the philosophy of education. This book helps to place Dewey in a more nearly contemporary role. All sections are appropriate for guidance persons, particularly Chapter VI, *The Culture: Builder of Men and of Civilization,* and Chapter VII, *The Individual and Society.*

Morris, Van Cleve, *Philosophy and the American School,* Boston: Houghton Mifflin, 1961.
The role of philosophy in American education is poorly understood by many who practice education. Morris directly tackles the issues of "what is real, what is true, and what is good." This introduction to many philosophical issues is clearly written and can be useful in the examination of more complex approaches.

Thayer, V. T., *The Role of the School in American Society,* New York: Dodd, Mead, 1961.
Thayer provides a relatively recent view of a problem that is always current and vital. Historical roots are treated along with pressing issues arising out of the political conflicts that impinge more and more upon the public schools. Many topics are covered in a relatively brief fashion that can provide a quick perspective for further detailed study.

ANTHROPOLOGY AND SOCIOLOGY

Barron, Milton L. (ed.), *American Minorities: A Textbook of Readings in Intergroup Relations,* New York: Knopf, 1957.

This source book provides information about the many minorities that form a part of our American civilization. The guidance worker can obtain valuable data on subcultures and sociological forces that characterize many minority groups.

Benedict, Ruth, *Patterns of Culture,* Boston: Houghton Mifflin, 1934 (also a Mentor Book, paperbound).

The book is a classic examination of the effect of culture on individual behavior. The different ways of life in the Zuni, Dobu, and Kwakiutl societies clearly help to determine the development of the individual member of that society.

Berger, Morroe, T. Abel, and C. H. Page (eds.), *Freedom and Control in Modern Society,* New York: Van Nostrand, 1954.

This anthology contains essays written by fifteen contributors to honor Robert M. MacIver. Sociological issues of control through the group and the individual are exposed for study. Freedom as it relates to the state and society as a whole is the subject of the second section of the book. Each essay stands alone as well as in relation to the others.

Caplow, Theodore, *The Sociology of Work,* Minneapolis: University of Minnesota Press, 1954.

Work and the job are viewed in their sociological structure. The role that work fulfills in our society and the effects of the work situation are analyzed. The book rests upon, and reviews, much of the research done in this field up to its publication.

Commager, Henry Steele, *The American Mind: An Interpretation of American Thought and Character Since the 1880's,* New Haven: Yale University Press, 1950.

The title offers a precis of this readable survey of American thought, particularly as it applies to social development and social value structure. An historian, Commager shows the interrelationships of sociology, culture, and historical event as all of these forces shape the individual and the society.

Hinkle, R. C., and G. J. Hinkle, *The Development of Modern Sociology,* Garden City, N.Y.: Doubleday, 1954.

One of the Doubleday "Short Studies in Sociology," this book briefly treats the nature and growth of sociology into a discipline in brief fashion. Major views of sociology and the contributions of major writers are reviewed.

Hollingshead, August B., *Elmtown's Youth,* New York: Wiley, 1949.
Hollingshead examines the social class structure in a small midwestern town in detailed fashion. The lines of social control on individual behavior are vividly drawn to show life in contemporary America. The book is particularly useful when compared to anthropological studies of primitive cultures such as those by Benedict or Mead.

Kluckhohn, Clyde, *Mirror for Man,* New York: McGraw-Hill, 1949.
This is a good introduction to anthropology and its relation to modern life. Anthropology is distinguished from archeology and from what Hollywood shows. This book is enjoyable and stimulating.

LaPiere, Richard T., *A Theory of Social Control,* New York: McGraw-Hill, 1954.
This advanced treatment of the meaning and significance of the concept of "social control" describes and analyzes specific techniques. The cultural basis of social control is outlined.

Lazarsfeld, Paul F., and Morris Rosenberg (eds.), *The Language of Social Research,* Glencoe, Ill.: The Free Press, 1955.
Various articles show the methodology and techniques that are used in social science research. A familiarity with research methods can permit a guidance worker to utilize present and future research.

Linton, Ralph, *The Cultural Background of Personality,* New York: Appleton-Century, 1945 (paperback, 1962).
Written before many of the currently used sources on personality formation, this book influenced many subsequent treatments of personality as a learned pattern. The various relationships among culture, society, and personality are explored as individual development is analyzed.

Linton, Ralph, *The Study of Man,* New York: Appleton-Century, 1936.
Most textbooks have not been included in this bibliography. However, Linton's book is a classic in the field of anthropology and deserves review and study if it is available.

Luszki, Margaret B., *Interdisciplinary Team Research Methods and Problems,* New York: New York University Press, 1958.
Whenever specialists from different disciplines attempt to design and carry out research projects there are issues which transcend any single discipline. This volume helps workers face though not always solve these issues. The book is not overly technical and is appropriate for guidance workers involved in a program that includes specialists from other disciplines.

Lynd, Robert S., and Helen M. Lynd, *Middletown in Transition: A Study in Cultural Conflicts,* New York: Harcourt, Brace, 1937.
The days of depression, unemployment, and constant conflict in "Middletown, U.S.A." provide the raw material for an examination of value and belief systems in transition. The analysis shows the structure of change in society.

Malinowski, Bronislaw, *A Scientific Theory of Culture and Other Essays,* Chapel Hill, N.C.: University of North Carolina Press, 1944.

The book summarizes the functional view of a theory of culture. Malinowski represents the broad view of the science of man, grounded in research and personal experience. Along with *Freedom and Civilization,* referred to in the first section of this bibliography, this shorter treatment can help the nonspecialist in anthropology to understand the significance of the field.

Mayer, Kurt, *Class and Society,* Garden City, N.Y.: Doubleday, 1955.

One of the "Short Studies in Sociology," the book presents the concepts of class and social stratification, particularly as they apply to the United States, with historical perspective and an analysis of current effects.

Mead, Margaret, *Coming of Age in Samoa,* New York: Morrow, 1928.

The book is a classic study of how individuals develop in a culture very different from our own.

Mead, Margaret, *Growing Up in New Guinea,* New York: Morrow, 1930.

Another of the original studies of a primitive culture by an anthropologist who studied the group first-hand, this treatise covers the Manus tribe and focuses upon child-rearing practices and on socialization as a process that helps to determine individual behavior.

Nottingham, Elizabeth K., *Religion and Society,* Garden City, N.Y.: Doubleday, 1954.

This is one of the longer of the Doubleday "Short Studies." It places religion within a social and cultural framework. Religion is seldom treated as an objective item in a social or cultural setting. This book attempts to do so.

Reuter, Edward B., *A Handbook of Sociology,* New York: Dryden, 1941.

Reuter provides summaries and definitions of most major terms and concepts used in sociology. Useful to help the nonspecialist cope with special terminology in other readings.

Riesman, David, *Individualism Reconsidered,* Glencoe, Ill.: The Free Press, 1954.

Riesman offers 30 essays on many varied topics. America as a culture is reflected in the many commentaries on social, individual, and psychological issues. Values, ethics, minorities, popular music, bookworms, and football players all receive notice. The material is uneven, but stimulating for any person working in education.

Riesman, David, *et al., The Lonely Crowd: A Study of the Changing American Character,* New Haven: Yale University Press, 1950.

What is the nature of man as a social and individual animal? The forces of our society produce varying reactions in different individuals. These roles and their formation are the concerns of this incisive book.

Sherif, M., and C. W. Sherif, *Groups in Harmony and Tension,* New York: Harper, 1953.

The book describes large-scale experimental work with children's gangs and groups. A campsite is used to induce conflict and harmony between groups and to provide raw data for research. Individual and group data show the importance of psychosocial analysis.

Timasheff, Nicholas S., *Sociological Theory,* New York: Random House, 1957.

A review of the major theoretical positions in sociology is presented along with a history of the individual sociologists who created them. The pioneer writers such as Come, Spencer, Cooley, and Durkheim as well as more contemporary persons such as MacIver and Homans are included. A valuable resource for nonsociologists as well as a reference for more sophisticated educators.

Waller, Willard, *The Sociology of Teaching,* New York: Wiley, 1932.

Waller's is an early study of the teacher and the school as a social system, and the effects of social processes upon pupils, teachers, and the community. The open and private controls that the community exerts are clearly identified. This book is historical, but also revealing of the strength and endurance of social processes and controls.

Whyte, W. F., *Street Corner Society,* enlarged ed., Chicago: University of Chicago Press, 1955.

This is a classic report on life in the street corner gang. The structure and patterns of the gang are analyzed by an observer who lived with the group. The gang is viewed from the inside and from the perspectives of the gang members.

PSYCHOLOGY

Allport, Gordon W., and Leo Postman, *The Psychology of Rumor,* New York: Holt, 1947.

Allport gives a thorough but interesting account of what rumor is. Many variations of the rumor are presented along with detailed analysis of the social and psychological forces that support rumors. The treatment of the impact on the "hearer" is particularly valuable.

Bion, W. R., *Experiences in Groups,* New York: Basic Books, 1961.

The experience of a practicing English psychoanalyst in group therapy makes for excellent exploratory reading. Few if any guidance persons will deal with such problems, but anyone concerned with groups and group counseling will be rewarded for an involvement with these data.

Edwards, Allen L., *Statistical Methods for the Behavioral Sciences,* New York: Rinehart, 1954.

This widely used textbook offers an analysis of all major statistical methods in the behavioral sciences. The overlapping contents of the behavioral sciences can be better understood as common methodologies are examined. This is not for the beginner, but is appropriate whenever detailed research data must be analyzed.

Fleming, C. M., *Teaching: A Psychological Analysis,* New York: Wiley, 1958.

Fleming, writing from the University of London Institute of Education, surveys psychological literature as it applies to teaching. Motivation, learning, and individual development receive detailed analysis. The more traditional areas of "craftmanship," administrator, and "therapist" also are included. Fleming gives a thorough view, from a different perspective, of a common task.

Fromm, Erich, *The Sane Society,* New York: Rinehart, 1955.

Fromm serves as a commentator on and analyst of society. He also offers his methods for the development of a more meaningful way of life. His comments are both psychological and political. He applies Freud to modern problems and recommends psycho-political answers.

Jones, Marshall R. (ed.), *Nebraska Symposium on Motivation, 1961,* Lincoln, Neb.: University of Nebraska Press, 1961.

This is the ninth volume in a series that began in 1952. The series provides up-to-date research data and commentary on varied problems of motivation. Papers are drawn from animal experimentation as well as human learning and school situations.

Koch, Sigmund, *Psychology: A Study of a Science,* vols. I–V, New York: McGraw-Hill, 1959–1963.

This series covers all areas of psychology as a science. Seven volumes are planned. Each volume is a series of papers relating to conceptual and systematic studies and empirical substructure and relations with other sciences. Much of the material is beyond a beginning student in psychology. However, the papers can supply significant data in many specific areas of guidance. Definitive articles by Carl Rogers, Herbert Thelen, Dorwin Cartwright, and others can fill many gaps in tool and service areas of guidance.

Maslow, A. H., *Motivation and Personality,* New York: Harper, 1954.

Maslow presents his holistic theory of motivation. He is readable and appropriate for psychologists and guidance workers. He is often ignored by the "scientific" writers in motivation, but gives a sense of comprehension that is so often lacking in psychological treatments of motivation. His work relates well to Rogers, Combs and Syngg, and other field theory writers.

Murphy, Gardner, *Human Potentialities,* New York: Basic Books, 1958.

The author, noted for his broad view of psychology and personal development, explores the meanings of what "human potentiality" is. The perspective is sweeping, optimistic, and grounded in the author's knowledge of individual personality development. Every guidance person can profit from this view of what the individual is capable of doing.

Mussen, Paul H. (ed.), *Child Development: Handbook in Research Methods,* New York: Wiley, 1960.

This anthology examines all areas of study in child development. Specialists from every discipline offer articles that provide a very meaningful picture of what it means to study the individual child. It is an appropriate sourcebook for anyone who deals with individuals.

Redl, Fritz, and W. W. Wattenberg, *Mental Hygiene in Teaching,* 2nd ed., New York: Harcourt, Brace, 1959.

A treatment of problems of adjustment that students may have in school environments that presents a sound theoretical basis and very practical suggestions for all teachers. Guidance persons can use this volume to help teachers help students of all ages. This volume is typical of some of the excellent source material that can bring teachers into case conferences, counseling programs, and group efforts.

Sarason, Seymour B., K. S. Davidson, and B. Blatt, *The Preparation of Teachers (An Unstudied Problem in Education),* New York: Wiley, 1962.

The authors view the teacher as a kind of "psychological diagnostician and tactician." Their premise is that the contents and procedures of teacher education have little relevance to the actual teaching tasks. They analyze the duties of teachers and their training and find little congruence. The book is readable and stimulating. Guidance persons will know more of teachers and their problems through this volume.

Shaffer, L., and E. J. Shoben Jr., *The Psychology of Adjustment,* rev. ed., Boston: Houghton Mifflin, 1956.

This is a most widely used and respected book on adjustment. Basic theory and practical understanding are woven together in an interesting style. The concepts and material in this book are "musts" for any person working in a guidance program.

Spence, Kenneth W., *Behavior Theory and Learning,* Englewood Cliffs, N.J.: Prentice-Hall, 1960.

The book presents a series of papers on the behavior theory of learning. The research testing of the position is carried through with animals and in human experimentation in laboratory programs. The material is advanced and appropriate only for students with a considerable background in psychology and learning theory.

Stephenson, William, *The Study of Behavior,* Chicago: University of Chicago Press, 1953.

Stephenson describes the "Q-Technique" and its use in studying human behavior. Personality change and the accompanying concerns that arise in psychology and in guidance make it necessary for guidance persons to be able to assess research results and to design new research. Stephenson's book will be important in all such activities.

Symonds, Percival M., *From Adolescent to Adult,* New York: Columbia University Press, 1961.

This is the last volume written by the brilliant psychologist who combined his scientific training with a true interest in education. It is a follow-up of 28 adolescents into adulthood. Fantasy, as measured through projective techniques, is related to personality organization and its stability into adulthood.

Wylie, Ruth C., *The Self Concept,* Lincoln, Neb.: University of Nebraska Press, 1961.

The author attempts to summarize the explosive research literature dealing with the "self concept." No other single area in psychology has had so much attention in the last 10 to 15 years. Wylie attempts to order the empirical data and to relate present thinking back to early theory-building. All counselors or guidance persons who concern themselves with the self need to be familiar with this work.

INDEXES

INDEX OF NAMES

INDEX OF SUBJECTS